Rebel Leadership

COMMITMENT
AND CHARISMA
IN THE REVOLUTIONARY
PROCESS

James V. Downton, Jr.

The Free Press   New York
Collier-Macmillan Publishers   London

Acknowledgments

Malcolm X, The *Autobiography of Malcolm X* (New York: Grove Press, 1966). Reprinted by permission of Grove Press, Inc., copyright © 1964 by Alex Haley and Malcolm X, and copyright © 1965 by Alex Haley and Betty Shabazz; and by permission of Hutchinson & Company (Publishers) Limited, London.

Theodore Abel, *Why Hitler Came Into Power: An Answer Based on the Original Life Stories of Six Hundred of His Followers,* © 1938, Renewed 1966. Reprinted by permission of Prentice-Hall, Inc., Englewood Cliffs, New Jersey.

The Free Press

A Division of Macmillan Publishing Co., Inc.

866 Third Avenue, New York, New York 10022

Collier-Macmillan Canada Ltd., Toronto, Ontario

Library of Congress Catalog Card Number: 72-77283

printing number

1 2 3 4 5 6 7 8 9 10

For Mary

Contents

Preface

The objective of this book is to develop an understanding of the nature and function of rebel leadership in the context of more general theories of leader-follower relations, commitment, and revolutionary change. Thus, while the book focuses on rebel leadership, its theoretical reach encompasses much more. I have tried both to synthesize and to expand our knowledge of the leadership field. In the first instance, a vast body of theoretical and empirical analyses of leadership is either discussed or identified. At the same time, I have borrowed important theoretical perspectives from others in related fields when I thought they would help to illuminate our thinking about leadership or revolutionary change. In following this course, my objective was to connect various lines of thinking that heretofore had not merged. But, while synthesis is important in developing some sense of what we know about leadership, it is not enough. In the process of bringing things together it is necessary to add new conceptualizations and theoretical insights beyond what others have done. This is part of what I have tried to do in this work.

Several people have contributed in important ways to the development of this study and I would like to acknowledge their assistance with my sincere thanks. First, I am deeply indebted to my wife, Mary, whose critical assessments of all stages of the project added significantly to the formulation of various theoretical perspectives. In addition, her insistence on clarity of expression prevented me from falling into the obscurities of jargon more than once, thus improving the sharpness of my own thinking and writing, which I feel greatly enhanced the value of the book. I am also personally indebted to James C. Davies for the helpful suggestions he offered for strengthening the book in its earlier stages and for his words of encouragement along the way. Neil J. Smelser also contributed significantly to the theoretical formulation of the study, for I learned a great deal from his critique of an early draft and from his suggestions for enriching it. Chalmers A. Johnson, who is responsible for sparking my interest in rebel leadership, gave me wise council in the beginning, criticized the manuscript in its early form, and contributed to the development of my thinking in more subtle ways. Finally, I would like to acknowledge the contribution of my former Research Assistant, James C. Hobart, whose work added great depth to the chapters dealing with charisma. My thanks are also conveyed to those who contributed to the book in somewhat smaller but nonetheless important ways.

J.V.D.J.

Rebel Leadership

1 □ LEADERSHIP IN SOCIAL SYSTEMS

□ Only a few rebel leaders succeed in making revolutions.[1] These are the men and women who, by the very nature of their successes beyond the pattern of everyday life, assume a mythical stature and join history's collection of heroic figures. Such persons as these are enshrined by nations and loved by the masses because they seemed able to change the course of history by the power of their social vision, through their cunning, and by the force of their will. "In all epochs of the world's history," Thomas Carlyle informs us, "we shall find the Great Man to have been the indispensable saviour of his epoch;—the lightning, without which the fuel never would have burnt."[2] Following in the footsteps of Carlyle, Max Weber used the term "charisma" to explain the development of authority around the heroic personality. From Weber's perspective, the follower perceives the leader to be one invested with God-like qualities and identifies with his special mission, relinquishing the right to criticize while happily accepting the obligation to follow orders. Thus, it is the leader's "charisma" that is the basis for his success in mobilizing support for his cause.

To locate the sources of a rebel leader's success by reference to personality, will, or fate is apt to convey a narrow and incomplete view of the determinants of mass mobilization. Can we speak of a rebel leader's success in building and maintaining a mass following without some understanding of the way in which the political environment was prepared for collective action? In addition to the force of the leader's personality, there must be some appreciation of the way the ruling leadership and events played into his hands.

This work is a response to the romantic view of leadership conveyed by Carlyle and Weber, a perspective that has permeated the social sciences and the discussion of laymen. One need only observe the popularity today of the adjective "charismatic" as it is applied to one leader and then another with careless abandon. There is a sense in which the layman falsifies the

facts pertaining to followers who join mass movements. By assuming that
a leader has created some mysterious hold over his followers, the casual
observer can avoid the troubling feeling that something is wrong with the
arrangements of political life. Why social scientists persist in using "charisma" in this general manner is puzzling, unless we assume that Carlyle's
romantic view of leadership is still very much alive in academic thinking.

Revisiting the concept of charisma is only one limited concern of this
study, although an important one. In the broadest sense, "charisma" can
be given the precise meaning it deserves only by raising questions pertaining
to the nature of leadership and the basis of leader-follower relations. It is
within a broader perspective of leadership that I propose to do this, a
perspective that encompasses both psychological and sociological modes of
analysis. For an empirical base I have chosen to examine four different types
of collective movements, hoping to discover the extent of similarity in
leader-follower relations between one context and another. This chapter lays
down the foundation from which later chapters are derived; consequently
it is quite general in the issues it treats, covering a number of concerns from
the problem of defining leadership to the utility of tension theory in ap-
praising individual motives as they converge into a single line of action.

The Scope of Leadership Analysis

With a few exceptions,[3] social scientists have neglected to develop
comprehensive perspectives of leadership that, among other things, would
explain the basis of leader-follower relations. A cursory review of the vast
literature on leadership discloses a preference for the limited focus wherein attention narrows to specific approaches and concerns. Thus, one does
not have to search very long to find studies that examine opinion leadership,
small-group leaders, leadership in decision-making processes, and the like.[4]
In addition, structural-functionalists and systems theorists have discussed
leadership in only the broadest sense, owing to their preference for higher
levels of abstraction and to their lower level of interest in power relationships.[5] Lewis Edinger has discussed this tendency toward the narrow
focus in his introduction to *Political Leadership in Industrialized Societies.*

> The variety in scope, theory, method and data presented here and in other
> studies of political leadership may cause one to wonder whether a comprehen-
> sive approach can ever be achieved. The answer, as one social psychologist
> recently suggested, depends largely upon one's aspirations. The editor of this
> symposium shares the belief that the task of integration may be difficult but
> not impossible, provided one's approach is broad enough to encompass research
> by all the social sciences on many societies and political systems.[6]

This search for the all-encompassing perspective of leadership is desirable. But, if Edinger has in mind a single analytic framework that would

integrate the diverse approaches in the field, then the search should be abandoned. For a perspective with such general applicability, even if it could be developed, would probably be so abstract and general that it would have little value. In this respect, Abraham Kaplan has warned "that great generality is achieved at the cost of trivializing the generalization."[7]

One of the basic problems with so many social scientific analyses today is the tendency to shape a description of the world to fit some analytic framework. Often the fit is bad and the entire framework may fall into disrepute as a consequence, even though it may remain a valuable tool for some purposes. I am thinking especially of the occasionally over-extended use of structural-functional models and the overly harsh criticisms of the approach that have arisen in some circles. Like all analytic approaches, structural-functionalism has limited utility. For example, it may provide keen insights into the complex network of structural arrangements in society, but be a burden in analyzing power and political strategies.

Instead of modifying the world to fit our favorite analytic model, we should change frameworks to fit the occasion. Thus, in developing a comprehensive perspective, be it of revolution or leadership, several different analytic tools may have to be used. Each framework should provide organization and special insight into some particular part of the full spectrum of concerns. Following this general idea, I will introduce and utilize several analytic modes of analysis to examine different aspects of leadership. If a meaningful comprehensive perspective of leadership is to be found, I am convinced it must come through the more specialized use of the tools at our disposal. It will be left to the reader to decide whether I have chosen the correct tools and combined them in a way that contributes to the development of this comprehensive view.

Three goals come to mind as tentative guidelines in constructing a comprehensive perspective of leadership. It should be *comparative*, providing for the analysis of factors associated with different leader-follower contexts and across national boundaries. It should be *interdisciplinary,* allowing for the inclusion of social and psychological approaches. Finally, as a deductive approach it should *stimulate the development of testable theories,* generating hypotheses about such things as changes in leader-follower patterns, leadership styles, and the like.

Defining "Leadership"

"As social scientists have learned to probe beneath the manifest aspects of leadership and have become correspondingly more sensitive to the relevance of numerous and complex latent facts, they have found it more difficult to agree on what leadership is and does."[8] This statement by Edinger points up one of the recurring difficulties in the study of leadership; namely, the problem of coming to some general agreement about the precise meaning of the term. This point is especially troublesome when one's objective is to construct a view of leadership that encompasses many different types of leaders and varying leader-follower situations.

The difficulty of defining leadership in a strict sense, which means establishing the *exact* meaning of the term, is similar to the problem of defining "ideology." Actually, both these terms are analytic constructs that were developed to identify sets of variables that seemed to cluster together. As constructs, neither term would be amenable to strict definition, for "theoretical terms—and in practice, most constructs—are not capable of definition in the strict sense."[9] From this perspective, constructs like leadership or ideology should be specified in terms of their "implicit definition" in which meaning is indicated in more general language. Thus the implicit definition of leadership might be derived from a specific theory, from which general meaning could be inferred.[10] But from what body of theory or from what analytic model do we infer meaning? Our answer must be given with respect to the level of abstraction from which the analysis of leadership is begun.

Since it is logical to begin at a fairly high level of abstraction in constructing a comprehensive perspective of leadership, the structural-functional mode of analysis seems to be an appropriate starting point, keeping in mind that the approach has limits and explanatory weaknesses. Still, its higher level of abstraction and broader generalizations do provide a good general framework within which other analytic approaches and more concrete factors can be integrated. The attention of the functionalist shifts from the question of what leadership is to what it does as a structure in social systems and what functions it performs. Thus, the approximate meaning of leadership is derived from its general contributions as a structure within the social process and from a careful enumeration of its functions with respect to the preservation of both social and personality systems. While it is true that there may be as many implicit definitions of leadership as there are theoretical approaches, the choice of the functionalist position has definite advantages. It will provide an implicit definition of leadership that is inclusive enough to be useful for comparing leadership in different nations, or different leadership types within a single state. Furthermore, a functional definition is sufficiently general to allow an interdisciplinary approach, for the analyst can feel equally at ease studying the contributions leaders make to organizations or the contributions that are made for restoring balance to a follower's personality.

An Overview of the Functionalist Orientation

Before a functional definition of leadership can be specified, we have to know something about the nature of the conceptual universe from which it is derived. A brief description and interpretation of the main conceptual units of structural-functional theory should be sufficient as a preliminary step for developing a functional definition of leadership. The general definition will be sharpened considerably in Chapter II when I attempt to distinguish and discuss the possible functions leadership performs. For a more thorough treatment of structural-functional theory, the reader is advised to seek out the numerous excellent analyses specifically devoted to its study.[11]

The Organic Analogy

The functionalist's debt to the biological sciences is well known. Attracted to the study of the internal structures and processes of living organisms as systems, earlier thinkers such as Pareto and Durkheim sought comparable counterparts in the social context. The questions were simple, but thought-provoking. If organisms can be conceived as systems of interdependent structures performing functions (exclusively or in harmony) to preserve homeostasis, then could a similar conceptualization be developed pertaining to social organization? Could societies and organizations in general be profitably analyzed as organic systems with similar problems and varying capacities for survival?

These questions have produced repeated efforts to draw analogies between the living organism and persistent patterns of social interaction, commonly called "social systems." This use of analogical reasoning, although it may lead to absurdities if carried to extremes,[12] has produced two separate analytic approaches—general systems theory and structural-functionalism.[13] As we know, both these orientations use the concept of "system" as a theoretical starting point. Consequently, any description of structural-functional theory has to start by first describing the characteristics attributed to "social systems" as analytic abstractions.

William Mitchell has offered what is perhaps the best description of the properties of a "social system." It includes

> . . . *two* or *more persons* who are engaged in a *patterned* or structured form of *relationship* or *interaction,* and who are guided by sets of *values and norms* generally called roles. It must also be noted that the interaction is *relatively persistent;* a chance meeting of strangers on a street cannot be considered as a social system. From these properties it is also easily seen that a social system has certain *boundaries,* that is, it is possible to determine who is or is not a member of the system. The last property of a system—all systems—is implied in other properties of "patterned-interaction," "boundaries," and persistence; that is, the system tends to establish an *equilibrium* or balance of the forces that tend to integrate and disintegrate.[14]

Given these properties, the next step is to consider which of the many persistent patterns of social interaction qualify as social systems. As we would expect, the list is extensive, ranging from the most complex pattern found in the world system to the least complicated two-member family. Of course, revolutionary organizations would easily qualify since they too meet the requirements of the definition.

Properties of Social Systems

Structural-functionalists have taken five basic elements from the organic metaphor by way of analogy. These are the notions of purpose, function, structure, interdependence, and equilibrium. A careful review of the literature reveals a surprisingly high level of ambiguity and little consensus about the precise meaning of these terms. Consequently, each of these elements and the approach as a whole must be open to critical and interpretative reappraisal.

The "Purpose" of Social Systems—Diverging from the political-philosophical emphasis on normatively ascribed ends for society, such as Justice or Equality, functionalists have used a modified form of teleological reasoning that emphasizes the organic nature of system ends. If the living organism has no other purpose than self-preservation, the reasoning goes, then a social system's *purpose* might be conceived analogously as *survival.* This view allows us to "talk about the 'purpose' of a part within a system even when we do not know, or doubt, that it has a conscious purpose."[15]

The assumption that survival is the purpose of social systems has some utility, since it does eliminate the problem of specifying goals for each system or structure one may want to examine. But I wonder if there is not another "purpose" that could be ascribed to social systems that would take into account the basic problem of fit in the organism-social system analogy. For the analogical deduction that social systems are like organisms with respect to ends is quite tenuous and should be accepted only with caution. It is quite important in this case, as in all uses of analogical explanation, to recognize in what specific ways the analogy is weak. One basic difference between these systems is especially obvious, but important. The human organism is made up of organs, tissues, and cells that have neither desires nor interests; whereas, social systems are patterns of individuals in roles that operate from private goals and interests that are related to need gratification. It is possible to argue that individual goals and interests will simply affect the social system's capacity to survive, but this argument suggests that there may be another end that is unique to the social system and that affects its ability to persist.

That social systems are oriented to survival problems is fairly clear and is consequently not at issue here. What is open to question, however, is the assumption that the structures of a system are automatically and exclusively geared to survival. Is it not equally plausible to suggest that a system's "purpose" is to serve those individuals who feel they are entitled to benefits? Thus, the survival of a social system is dependent on agreement by members of the system that it is able to contribute to the gratification of their needs. Among those with status in a declining social system, we should expect a defensive posture to develop, owing to the rewards they receive from that system. So even when a large part of the public loses confidence in the ability of a social system to perform services, there will be forces working to preserve it. This is not an organic operation, but is the consequence of purposeful choice on the part of those in the system who have the most to lose by its demise.

When a social system is no longer necessary for need gratification or is unable to provide expected services, it may lose public support to the point where even its defense by stalwart supporters will not save it. The decay of political party machines in the United States is a good illustration of this point. Urban machines developed to perform definite services for immigrants that were not being offered elsewhere in the political system. Bosses found jobs, distributed food, bailed people out of trouble, and performed other favors. Each of these services contributed to individual need gratification in some way, with the clear understanding that votes would be given in exchange. But as the federal government began to restrict the flow of immigrants and to expand its own services under the New Deal, the demand for machine services declined. This development reduced the machine's capability to get votes, which, in turn, reduced its ability to gain access to the resources that were the basis for its service potential. As the number of its service operations declined, so did the machine as a system.[16]

Considering the *purpose* of a social system to be *service* diverges quite sharply from the accepted way of looking at system ends. However, I think there is some value in this perspective, since it does not force us to assume, as the other interpretation does, that individuals, structures, and subsystems in society are necessarily contributing to the preservation of the larger system of which they are a part. Furthermore, service becomes an important criterion in our effort to understand why social systems persist or decline.

The Notion of "Function"—The second element of the structural-functional model has been an especially bothersome one. For definitions of "function" have been imprecise and often misleading. On this point, Oran Young has concluded:

> There is a good deal of terminological confusion surrounding this concept [function] in the literature; difficulties are often raised by efforts to pin down the nature of a function alternatively as an objective, a process, or a result. In a general sense, however, a function may be defined as the objective conse-quence(s) of a pattern of action for the system . . . in which it occurs. . . . Functions deal ultimately with objective consequences, but they may be per-ceived as objectives, processes, or results from various points of view and for various purposes.[17]

This perspective is in harmony with the general disposition to view functions as the effects of structures, or, what structures have done over time.[18] Yet, this does not provide us with a very clear or useful meaning of "function."

If we assume that the purpose of a social system is service to its members, then the work of the system must be assigned and tasks carried out in order to perform the services that perpetuate it. In this sense, I would prefer to consider a "function" a *task* that is relevant to the system's performance of services. When functions are ascribed to specific structures within a social system, we are simply specifying the tasks that are allocated to or assumed by those structures. It is the work of each structure in performing its tasks that enables the social system to increase its capacity to serve and, consequently, to persist.

The Meaning of "Structure"—"Structures" may be conceived as the working parts of a social system, converting resources into services or enhancing the system's service potential. In this context, the tasks of the social system are distributed among structures as a way of increasing productive capacity. However, the distribution of tasks within structures is a somewhat different analytic consideration, directly related to the recruitment process and more generally to the socialization of members into roles, or "the tasks which are divided up and assigned in the division of labor. . . ."[19]

If a *structure* can be conceived as the *working unit* of social systems, then roles can be seen as more specialized assignments, for structures are simply clusters of roles. The role concept is a more precise and convenient way of locating: (1) the assigned work (focusing on role requirements); (2) the level of work efficiency (analyzing role performance); and (3) structural efforts to increase work efficiency (considering the socialization to roles, enforcements, and incentives like monetary and social rewards).

In summary, functions describe *what* work needs to be done, structures describe *how* work is done, and purpose (service) describes *why* it is done.

"Interdependence" and "Equilibrium" as Elements—"Interdependence" is a consequence of the insufficiency of single structures to do all the work of social systems. As work assignments become specialized, a degree of mutual dependence among structures is created. Thus, when we speak of interdependence, "we mean that when the properties of one component in a system change, all the other components and the system as a whole is affected."[20] Organisms and social systems are considered to be analogous in this respect. For example, the human organism will automatically concentrate its energies when confronted with a virus, marshaling defenses in order to destroy the foreign bodies. Through the operation of self-adjusting mechanisms, the body is returned to a homeostatic state, which can be described as "health." Like the human organism, social systems are thought to have self-adjusting mechanisms that automatically respond to threatening forces, enhancing the balance of integrative and disintegrative tendencies.

Sherman R. Krupp has stated this position more precisely:

> Functionalist theories usually describe some of the relations within the system as self-regulating mechanisms. The "self" that is regulated is the system as a whole; the mechanism describes the way in which the dysfunctional movement of one variable stimulates a compensatory movement in another variable . . . . These mechanisms constrain and secure a chain of mutual adjustment among the variables, so that the system moves toward a given state of equilibrium and restores this state when it is disturbed.[21]

The notion of "equilibrium" is used by structural-functionalists in a fashion similar to the use of the word "homeostasis" in medicine. While it is extremely difficult to define or measure the extent of systemic "equilibrium," the tendency has been to assume that social systems may be viewed as having "healthful" and "sick" states, just as the human body. Consequently, there is much talk about the stability of social systems, where efforts have been undertaken to find indices that may be used to discover when they are out of equilibrium.[22]

Organisms and social systems may appear to be similar in this context, since both seem to possess structures permanently sharing work and capable in some ways of temporarily assuming the work of disequilibrated structures. Yet, there is an obvious divergence. In only a superficial way can we assume that their self-regulating capacities are similar. Quite unlike human organisms, in which adjustive mechanisms are automatically set into operation, social system responses must be initiated in a cultural and political environment that may inhibit or even prevent adjustive efforts. While it may be reasonable to argue that there is a tendency within social systems toward adjustment, in a single instance the employment of appropriate mechanisms can neither be predicted nor assured. Five factors that would affect the system's self-regulating capacity come immediately to mind: existing values, beliefs, and customs; the influence of interest groups on decision-making structures responsible for adjustment; the purposive judgments of leadership (the trustee role); enforcement capabilities; and, productive capabilities.

The Universal Problems of Social Systems

A world system, family system, or revolutionary system must solve essentially the same problems if it is to survive. These problems have been described in terms of "functional prerequisites" and have been discussed by Gabriel Almond and G. Bingham Powell, Jr., with respect to system "capabilities." However, these two orientations can actually be integrated, since the emphasis is different in each case. "Functional prerequisites" focus attention on the problems that must be solved, while the notion of "capabilities" refers to the capacity of the system to solve them.

All social systems, be they revolutionary organizations or political systems, must attempt to solve the problems of *adaptation*. In the broadest sense, this attempt requires constant adjustment to pressures that develop within the system, as well as to pressures on a system's boundary that may arise from threats of external attack or control. But adjustment cannot simply be willed in either case. Rather, it is accomplished by mobilizing the necessary resources to reduce pressure. Almond and Powell discuss this adaptive problem in terms of the extractive capability of political systems, which refers to the system's performance in drawing material and human resources from the domestic and international environments.[23]

Extractive capability has to be measured in relation to the system's success in maintaining public support. For example, a political system may successfully collect taxes from its citizens but lose their support if these taxes are considered excessive. In turn, this loss of support may increase the problems of extraction in other areas, reducing adaptation and inviting serious disorders. Consider the extractive capability of czarism in the eighteenth century as a case in which effectiveness in collecting taxes created a serious political crisis. After the serfs were freed by Czar Alexander II in 1860, the burden of taxation fell heavily on their shoulders. Redemption payments for the land that was placed under their control and the introduction of poll taxes kept peasants in debt and at marginal levels of subsistence. Support for the czarist political system fell sharply, affecting rural incentive to produce and to improve the methods of production. In addition, peasant outbursts of violence against the aristocratic manors forced the czar to mobilize additional resources for purposes of social control. In both instances, the political system's extractive capability was reduced, for later the shortage of agricultural goods, the unwillingness of the peasant to fight in the trenches in World War I, and the continued violence in peasant sectors were factors, produced by extractive abuses, that ensured the collapse of czarism.

The second functional prerequisite for maintaining equilibrium is effective *integration and social control.* The adaptive problems of a social system necessitate a considerable degree of regulation both with respect to the allocation and integration of roles and the control of behavior that transcends normatively specified limits. It is in the context of control that Almond and Powell speak of the regulative capability of political systems, but they are not exclusively concerned with the capacity to control deviation. In a broader sense, regulative capability may also be measured in terms of the effectiveness of performance in controlling the behavior of individuals and groups who are known to be loyal.[24] Actually, what is at issue here is the ability of the political system to effectively penetrate other systems for purposes of control and adaptation. For example, in totalitarian states little autonomy may exist for the military, economic system, church, and family. Through a political party apparatus, the ruling leadership can consistently penetrate these systems to extract resources and support. In democratic societies, on the other hand, the penetration of systems by political authorities is often quite restricted and may be initiated only on the heels of an abrupt crisis. It took a severe depression in the United States, for instance, before Congress could enlarge its regulative capability with respect to the economy.

The regulative capability of political systems is an especially significant factor in the analysis of revolutionary movements, for it is common for revolutionary leaders to test the regulative potential of the political system they aspire to overthrow. They initiate demonstrations and may even make direct assaults on the ruling government in order to gauge its regulative performance and potential. They may be attempting to measure the ability of the political system to control military behavior or to control the economic conditions that make military preparedness possible. For example, the Nazi *putsch* in 1923 can be considered a test to determine the strength of the Weimar Republic. Hitler found its regulative capability stronger than he anticipated, thereby leading him to develop an entirely different strategy. Faced with a similar decision, contemporary revolutionary leaders might choose guerrilla warfare as a way of reducing a political system's regulative capability. But Hitler decided to use the electoral machinery of democracy, thinking that this would be more economical and effective than further assaults against the system.

The *setting and attainment of goals* is the third functional prerequisite that, according to Talcott Parsons, is the primary (although not exclusive) function of leadership.[25] Development of decision-making structures is the system's organic effort to allocate rewards and respond to the constant shifting of environmental pressures. It is in this context that Almond and Powell discuss a political system's distributive capability, meaning its performance in allocating goods, services, honors, statuses, and opportunities to the various sectors of society.[26] Here, communication structures play a key role, for leaders must have information concerning what their different publics want and need if the appropriate goals are to be set and realized. A more equitable distribution of rewards may be attempted by giving disadvantaged sectors opportunities for making their demands known within a political party, but this approach may not ensure that they will actually get what they want. For ruling leaders may not respond to demands for various reasons, including ideological or religious differences with those making appeals for change.

The resistance of the ruling leaders to change may reduce what Almond and Powell describe as the responsive capability of the political system, even under conditions in which some channels of access are available for communicating demands. "Responsive capability" refers to the relationship between structures that collect demands, such as associations, political parties, bureaucracies, and governmental structures, for example, legislative bodies, bureaucracies, and courts.[27] If the responsive capability is low, riots and political demonstrations may become new forms of communication, announcing impending crises if the ruling leadership persists in following its course of action. Look, for example, at the collapse of the Provisional

Government in Russia during October, 1917, and you will see that it was precipitated by the unwillingness of the ruling leaders to change goals to correspond to the public mood. Opportunities to organize and participate within the government were expanded, which should have increased the political system's responsive capability. But the leadership would not respond positively to the rising demands for "land, bread, and peace," the issues that would eventually send Lenin into power.

Finally, all social systems must minimize cleavages as much as possible by socializing members to a common set of values and beliefs. The *development and maintenance of common values* is thus the fourth prerequisite of systemic balance and, if achieved, can reduce adaptive and integrative strains. "With regard to the organization of the division of labor," we are told, "values obviate the need to rest the inescapable discriminations among the supply of talents and the demands of environmental adaptation primarily upon coercion."[28]

General adherence to a set of values is relevant to the survival of a system in still another way: Values are the source from which leaders draw symbols to integrate roles and recruit followers. Leadership enhances the symbolic capability of a political system by reference to historical heroes, to the outstanding achievements that have resulted from the value system, to religious principles and ceremonies that sustain the accepted values, to the powerful spirits that may be working to preserve the value arrangement. This symbolic capability does not refer to the frequency of symbol use, according to Almond and Powell, but rather to the capacity to use symbols effectively.[29] In some cases, there may be an inverse relationship between the frequency and effectiveness of symbol use. At other times, frequency of use may increase as a necessary step in making radical changes that might normally create integrative strains on the system. Here, the greater use of symbols may be viewed as a compensating device. For example, the Nazi political system tapped popular beliefs and attitudes by frequently utilizing symbols from *volk* culture, especially the notions of Blood and Soil, as a way of reducing the problems of extraction, regulation, and distribution.

Leadership as the Coordinating Structure of Social Systems

Typically, insufficient emphasis is placed on the role of leadership as the chief coordinating structure of social systems. By assuming that social systems are self-regulating, structural-functionalists have been led generally to overlook the contributions that leadership makes in the adjustment process. Even more significant has been their failure to examine in depth the ways in which leadership behavior may undermine effective adjustment. Since leadership is responsible for setting goals that affect the level of capabilities within a social system, there is every reason to assume that the purposive behavior of leaders will be a primary factor in system maintenance. In this respect, it is not very illuminating to assert that revolutions are the result of inadequately operating adjustive mechanisms unless we specify how leadership has failed to maintain the capabilities that make effective adjustment possible.

Through the goals leaders set, a political system's capabilities may become so low that it can neither regulate behavior nor defend itself from attack. Unable to perform its services for the polity, the ruling leadership loses public support, which aggravates the problem of extracting the resources that would enhance its ability to serve. By their own choices, ruling leaders either diminish or increase the extractive, regulative, distributive, symbolic, and responsive capabilities of a political system. Consequently, by their action social problems may be ripened for revolution.

During revolutionary troubles, when values and the requirements of adaptation diverge, "truly creative action by the leaders of a system is required. They must maintain some degree of integration, even if only through the existence of physical force; at the same time, they must mobilize and inspire innovations in all roles in order to resynchronize the values and the environment."[30] Actually, there are a number of creative alternatives within the range of capabilities that are related to the coordination of a social system. Ruling leaders attempting to restore political equilibrium may increase their efforts to arouse support by developing new symbols, responding to latent nationalistic sentiments, prejudices, or fears within the polity. Attempts to increase the system's extractive capability for the purpose of offering a more equitable distribution of goods is another possible source of action. In this context, leaders may choose to create an artificial foreign threat, as in George Orwell's *1984,* encouraging individuals to give financial and moral support as a defense against invasion. On a somewhat different point, the pressures of distribution may be relieved somewhat if the ruling leadership can persuade loyal forces, such as the military and labor unions, to reduce their demand for goods so that scarce resources can be concentrated in the sectors most clearly on the brink of revolutionary commitment.

While creative leadership is possible during such periods, history shows that ignorance, ideological intransigence, and dissension are the common features of ruling leadership prior to successful revolutions. Czar Nicholas II was more ignorant of facts than he was ideologically intransigent, while Rasputin's leadership in the Czar's absence was ideologically reactionary, resisting any change whatsoever and harking back to the old ways. In a different revolutionary setting, leadership within the Weimar Republic was weakened in part by ideological dissension, which made integration within the national legislature difficult and, as a result, made adaptation inadequate. Unable to resolve their ideological differences, leaders were unable to set goals that might have increased the extractive and distributive capabilities of the political system. Dissension within the ruling leadership made the democratic processes seem cumbersome and Hitler's alternative an attractive escape.

But the coordinating capacities of ruling leadership may be affected in still another way, for it can capitulate to revolutionary demands by deciding not to fight. If exile is made attractive by the legitimacy of graft, for instance, the political environment will be made more fertile for such capitulation. Ruling leaders are especially vulnerable to the enticements of exile in some Latin American countries, owing to the possibility of accumulating state finances in Swiss banks. For example, Castro's revolution succeeded partly because Batista decided that the pleasures guaranteed in Switzerland were considerably greater than the risks and uncertainties of continued struggle. If a ruling leader simply chooses not to fight, a revolutionary movement, like the 26th of July Movement in Cuba, may overthrow the old regime, even when its own capabilities are quite limited.

It should be clear by now that leadership can be given general meaning within the structural-functional framework. As I have interpreted the approach, leadership can be broadly defined as the coordinating structure of social systems. Through goal-setting and attainment, leadership coordinates the activities of other structures in order to increase the capabilities of the system. By increasing capabilities, leadership contributes in a positive way to the service capacity of the system, which enhances its ability to persist. This implicit definition of leadership will become more concrete when I enumerate the more precise functions of leadership in the next chapter.

Leader-Follower Relations: Motivation and Mobilization

My main concern up to this point has been to understand leadership's place as a coordinating structure within social systems. Now, the follower must be elevated to his rightful place in the discussion, for the social system's ability to serve is obviously affected by leader-follower relations. While some may like to think of social systems in organic terms, actually they are patterns of human interaction that may be charged with all the feelings that we associate with mankind.

Indeed, the task of coordinating social systems is complicated by the effect of private passions, interests, and capacities on role performance. In order to reach the goals set by leadership, persons with the appropriate skills must be mobilized and they must be motivated to perform their roles efficiently. By manipulating rewards and punishments leadership attempts to achieve effective role performance and the appropriate integration of roles within structures. In studying rebel leadership, it is especially important to consider how coordination is achieved within the rebel organization, how followers are mobilized and motivated to contribute to task performance.

But mobilization and motivation are crucial factors no matter what type of leadership is under examination, for they direct our attention to the social and psychological forces bearing on the follower's willingness to accept the initiatives of leadership. In the analysis of rebel leader-follower relations, it is especially important to take into account both the social and psychological factors that determine the mobilization and motivation of followers.

For rebel leaders may be able to mobilize and motivate followers because they promise to reconstitute the political system, or, at the latent level, they can mobilize followers who have been unable to cope with the anxieties created by increasing structural stress. In this latter case, leadership may actually help to coordinate the personality systems of some followers.

Both the social and psychological explanations of why followers accept the initiatives of leadership have their place in the analysis of rebel leader-follower relations. Especially during revolutionary periods, some consideration must be given to the psychological factors that lead followers to impute special qualities to leaders, which becomes the basis for a strong emotional attachment. But to focus on psychological factors is not enough. It is also necessary to consider how the environment is prepared for the growth of these emotional ties.[31]

The relationship between personality and social systems analysis has been clearly discussed by Neil J. Smelser and William T. Smelser in their introduction to *Personality and Social Systems*.[32] From their perspective, personality and social systems analyses focus on essentially different, but interrelated, units of analysis. In studying personality, the observer's attention is centered on the individual as an organized system of needs, feelings, attitudes, skills, and defenses: the conceptual unit is the person. The social systems approach, on the other hand, considers the relational aspects of two or more persons interacting with one another: The authors argue that the units of analysis are not persons per se, but roles and social organization. How an event is interpreted is contingent on one's choice between these conceptual approaches, for no occurrence is inherently psychological or social. "An outburst of anger, for instance, may be 'psychological' in the sense that it gives rise to recriminations of conscience and subsequent adaptations to these recriminations by the individual. The same outburst may also be 'social' in the sense that it strains family relations."[33] Since any social situation involves both psychological and social variables, claims for both approaches are possible. Thus, a decision must be made about how useful each is for a particular focus. At times it may be desirable to combine both sets of variables in a single explanation. In predicting the occurrence of delinquency, for example, a study may combine psychological factors, such as ego control of the id, with social ones, the position in the community class structure for instance. At other times, psychological and social factors may be considered independently, each bearing on different aspects of behavior. However, the normal pattern has been to use one or the other of these approaches exclusively. If only one of these approaches is applied, the danger is that explanations may become over-simplified or they may unnecessarily distort our picture of the facts. This criticism has been advanced by George Devereux against those who choose to examine follower motives from the social perspective only.

According to Devereux, preference for the social explanation tends to correspond to the breadth of a particular focus. When the "number of bodies to be studied become unmanageably large, it becomes more efficient, economical and accurate to ignore the individual particles and to study instead the system, or aggregate itself, in terms of statistical mechanics."[34] Accepting this social frame of reference may have the negative consequence of obscuring individual differences, as when a sociologist develops a "modal" man (from the social variables assumed to be salient) in order to explain the action of many individuals. Devereux's discussion of the social and psychological explanations for the Hungarian revolt of 1956 is worth extensive comment, because it is quite germane for understanding current efforts to explain the motivations of followers in accepting the initiatives of rebel leadership.

The sociological explanation for the Hungarian freedom fighter's motivation placed primary emphasis on his desire to overcome "cynical exploitation and brute oppression." Given this underlying explanation for revolt generally, sociologists imputed characteristics, patriotic and freedom-loving attributes, for example, to persons in general when they might have concentrated on differences. Interpreting the motivation of Hungarians in terms of these characteristics, sociologists were attempting to account for mass participation utilizing a very narrowly defined motivational stimulus. Uneasy with the social explanation, Devereux offers a number of criticisms that help to highlight the difficulties of generalizing about political behavior in collective movements. It is hoped that these criticisms will help us to understand the ambiguities surrounding the use of charisma as an explanatory tool.

From a tabulation of the conscious motivations of the Hungarian freedom fighters, Devereux found that many who were involved had "no genuinely personal experiences" with the exploitative and oppressive Communist regime. Many also failed to explain their action in terms of the expected patriotic motive. These responses lead the author to wonder "whether it has not become customary to cite sociologistically conceived motives *only* where *no information* about the individual's subjective motivation is available."[35] Devereux offers a somewhat different perspective, combining the social and psychological dimensions in an important way.

He openly rejects the notion that motives imputed to individuals engaged in a mass movement can accurately reflect real motives. From his vantage point, there can be many disparate individual motives for action:

> Where one man revolts because he has been exploited, another because, twelve years earlier, the Russians had raped his wife, another because he hates all authority, still another may revolt because he wishes to impress his girl friend with his patriotism and valor. All these men may fight with equal ardor, kill an equal number of secret police and Russians, therefore achieve *militarily and socially identical results. Psychologically, however, the results may not be the same.*[36]

What is significant is the converging of these many different motives into a generally uniform action. Instead of imputing a narrow range of motives (even, at times, a single motive), Devereux recommends that social scientists begin a more careful examination of the way structural conditions may create opportunities for the convergence of many different motives. During a certain historical moment, structural conditions may be perfect for gratifying various subjective drives. For instance, the Hungarian situation, with its weakened normative structure and widespread collective protest, created opportunities for the expression of private grievances, which had been suppressed in the pre-revolt period due to the more effective operation of social sanctions that created guilt and anxiety among those tempted to deviate.

Structural strain increases tension within the personality system, which may be released by normal energy attrition or, where opportunities are available, through action. To the extent that structural strain becomes intense and generally widespread, many people may be unable to satisfy basic needs. Such need frustrations create collective tensions that become the motive for action to punish those who are thought to be responsible for the miserable state of things.[37] It should be clear with respect to the Hungarian revolt that a variety of needs had been frustrated that were traced to the Communist regime as the responsible agent. As the normative restrictions of the system were relaxed, the political environment became more fertile for a collective outburst, which provided opportunities for reducing various kinds of personal tensions.

Devereux's position is not one to be taken lightly by those of us who are interested in rebel leader-follower relations, especially if we are to avoid imputing motives to followers in the commitment process that are so narrowly conceived that the real complexity of the relation is not understood. It is necessary to order this complexity, not erase it. Yet, in many analyses of rebel leader-follower relations implicit modal personality constructs are used to categorize both leader and follower in a narrow sense. For example, a modal follower personality—the "true believer"—was popular for a time, which attributed motives to followers that were irrationally grounded. The same may be said about the careless use of the "charismatic" adjective to describe rebel leaders in a variety of situations. It, too, is an effort to impute motives, reducing the explanatory possibilities to a point where it limits our ability to develop useful classifications or to generate new knowledge, since any fact associated with the follower's commitment to the leader is explained in terms of the leader's charisma.

The ambiguities and complexities of social change may of course make a precise sampling of follower motives in accepting a particular rebel leader impossible. Two efforts can be made under these circumstances: First, the possible motives for commitment to leaders must be conceived in the broadest terms and, second, the structural conditions that tend to produce a convergence of different motives into a uniform pattern of follower behavior should be noted and discussed. Actually, each of the manifest motives alluded to by followers can be traced to the five basic needs described by A. H. Maslow: biological (the need for air, food, sex, etc.), safety (the need for security), social (the need for love and belongingness), self-esteem (the need to feel important), and self-realization (the need for meaning). Followers may explain their commitment to rebel leaders in terms of different reasons, each of which can be included in one of the five need categories. Some may say they follow rebel leaders because they are out of work and need jobs the leaders promise (biological need). Some may be tired of police harassment and join rebel leaders in their assault on the state (safety need). Other followers may say they follow rebel leaders because of family or occupational pressures (social need) or because their status is being threatened by an upwardly mobile group (self-esteem need). There may even be followers who are holding down good jobs but are bored with them because they have little meaning (the self-realization need).

How conditions become ripe for the convergence of these different motives should be the chief concern of those choosing the social approach as their organizing preference. In addition, it will be advisable at times to consider the psychological factors bearing on follower commitment. Thus, a comprehensive view of leadership should include both the social and psychological approaches. For there may be times when the psychological approach has greater explanatory significance than the social perspective. For instance, I suspect this is generally true with respect to the concept of charisma. But, at other times, the social factors may be primary. As I will attempt to show in the next chapter, these two approaches can be nicely integrated into the structural-functional framework developed earlier.

Notes

1. Throughout this book I will refer to "ruling" and "rebel" leadership. "Ruling" leadership as an analytic category includes the incumbents of political office within the political system. On the other hand, "rebel" leadership describes those who initiate attacks against the political system, utilizing means that are contrary to generally accepted norms for sharply altering the distribution of resources or, intoxicated by the promises of revolution, for assuming political control in order to fundamentally alter patterns of human behavior.

2. Thomas Carlyle, *Heroes, Hero-Worship, and the Heroic in History* (Boston: Heath, 1913), p. 83.

3. A notable exception to the current trend can be found in the theoretical work of Bernard M. Bass, who has persuasively argued for a perspective of leadership that stresses its relationship with group preferences and situational conditions. "if we can determine some of the functional demands and limitations placed on a potential leader in different designated situations, and then determine the personal characteristics associated with persons best able to meet those demands and work within the limitations, we will be in a position to forecast the likelihood of success and effectiveness of each candidate for the leadership of a specified situation, knowing the specific characteristics of the situation and each candidate." Bernard

M. Bass, *Leadership, Psychology, and Organizational Behavior* (New York: Harper & Row, 1960), p. 21.

4. The extensiveness of leadership studies in the United States can be seen in Wendell Bell, Richard Hill, and Charles Wright, *Public Leadership* (San Francisco: Chandler Press, 1961). For a summary of the approaches in leadership analysis, cf. Lewis J. Edinger (ed.), *Political Leadership in Industrialized Societies* (New York: John Wiley & Sons, 1967), p. 12.

5. For example, the separate works of Gabriel Almond and David Easton, which have generated a number of important insights into authority and the problems of legitimacy, have not provided comparable insights into the leadership phenomenon. Cf. Gabriel Almond and James Coleman, *The Politics of Developing Areas* (Princeton: Princeton University Press, 1960), Almond and G. Bingham Powell, Jr., *Comparative Politics: A Developmental Approach* (Boston: Little, Brown, 1966), and David Easton, *A Systems Analysis of Political Life* (New York: John Wiley & Sons, 1965).

6. Edinger, *op. cit.*, p. 25.

7. Abraham Kaplan, *The Conduct of Inquiry: Methodology for Behavioral Science* (San Francisco: Chandler Press, 1964), p. 108.

8. Edinger, *op. cit.*, p. 5.

9. Kaplan, *op. cit.*, pp. 72–73.

10. *Ibid.*, p. 73.

11. For instance, cf. the following: Talcott Parsons, *The Social System* (New York: Free Press, 1951), Marion J. Levy, *The Structure of Society* (Princeton: Princeton University Press, 1952), William C. Mitchell, *The American Polity* (New York: Free Press, 1962), Almond and Powell, *op. cit.*, Oran Young, *Systems of Political Science* (Englewood Cliffs: Prentice-Hall, 1968), and Don Martindale (ed.), *Functionalism in the Social Sciences* (Philadelphia: American Academy of Political and Social Science, 1965).

12. This is a criticism advanced by A. James Gregor in his "Political Science and the Uses of Functional Analysis," *American Political Science Review*, LXII (June, 1968), pp. 427–41. An attack on the functional approach as viewed from the logical positivist perspective, this essay is one every student of comparative analysis should read with care. Similarly, Chalmers Johnson has noted the profusion of misplaced organic analogies including: "the belief that social systems have life cycles (birth, adolescence, maturity, old age, and death) and the belief that social systems cannot freely change their structures because individual organisms cannot freely change theirs . . . . None of these ideas," he continues, "is basic to systems theory; and functionalism, as a method for analyzing how systems operate, is not in any way dependent on the organic analogy for its intellectual rationale." Chalmers Johnson, *Revolutionary Change* (Boston: Little, Brown, 1966), p. 49. Other criticisms advanced against functionalism can be found in Eugene J. Meehan, *Contemporary Political Thought: A Critical Study* (Homewood, Ill.: Dorsey Press, 1967), pp. 161–164; Oran Young, *op. cit.*, pp. 34–37; and William Flanigan and Edwin Fogelman, "Functionalism in Political Science," in Martindale (ed.), *op. cit.*, p. 21.

13. Oran Young distinguishes these analytic approaches in terms of levels of generality: General systems theory, whose objective is to develop "a set of basic principles applicable to a wide range of empirical systems," is formulated at a higher level of generalization than structural-functional theory, which has a more specific bearing on the problem of "system maintenance and regulation." Young, *op. cit.*, pp. 20–28.

14. Mitchell, *op. cit.*, p. 4.

15. Johnson, *op. cit.*, p. 46.

16. For an analysis of the functions of political party machines, cf. Robert Merton, *Social Theory and Social Structure* (Glencoe, Ill., Free Press, 1957), pp. 72–82.

17. Young, *op. cit.*, p. 29.

18. Robert Merton has used the term "function" to refer to "observed consequences," *op. cit.*, p. 74; A. R. Radcliffe-Brown refers to "functions as any recurrent activity" in *Structure and Function in Primitive Society* (Glencoe, Ill.: Free Press), p. 180; Levy considers a "function" to be "a condition, or state of affairs resultant through time," *op. cit.*, p. 56; and Robert Holt defines functions as "system relevant effects of structures" in Martindale (ed.), *op. cit.*, pp. 86–87.

19. Johnson, *op. cit.*, p. 41.

20. Almond and Powell, *op. cit.*, p. 19.

21. "Equilibrium Theory in Economics and in Functional Analysis as Types of Explanation," in Martindale (ed.), *op. cit.*, p. 70.

22. Cf. Chalmer Johnson's chapter, "Measuring Disequilibrium," *Revolutionary Change,* pp. 119–134.

23. Almond and Powell, *op. cit.*, p. 195.

24. *Ibid.*, p. 196.

25. Talcott Parsons, *Structure and Process in Modern Societies* (Glencoe, Ill.: Free Press, 1960), pp. 149–150.

26. Almond and Powell, *op. cit.*, p. 198.

27. *Ibid.*, pp. 201–202.

28. Johnson, *op. cit.*, p. 26.

29. Almond and Powell, *op. cit.*, pp. 199–200.

30. Johnson, *op. cit.*, p. 53.

31. Neil Smelser refers to this as "structural conduciveness" in his book, *Theory of Collective Behavior* (New York: Free Press, 1963), p. 15.

32. Neil J. Smelser and William T. Smelser (eds.), *Personality and Social Systems* (New York: John Wiley & Sons, 1963), pp. 1–18.

33. *Ibid.*, p. 2.

34. George Devereux, "Two Types of Modal Personality Models," in Smelser and Smelser (eds.), *Personality and Social Systems,* p. 25.

35. *Ibid.*, p. 27.

36. *Ibid.*, p. 28.

37. Ralph Turner and Lewis Killian, *Collective Behavior* (Englewood Cliffs: Prentice-Hall, 1957), pp. 17–19.

2 ☐ FUNCTIONS OF LEADERSHIP

☐ Enumerating the functions of leadership is as old as the western political tradition, although, until recently, the list of functions lacked conceptual clarity and was associated with a normative teleology. Plato's delineation of the tasks of rulers and administrators in *The Republic* illustrates the earlier effort to mark off areas of functional responsibility for different sectors of leadership. More recently, specifying a leader's functions has been largely confined to executive leadership in formal organizations or small groups in which the tasks of leadership have been considered in relation to the maintenance of equilibrium.

I would now like to turn my attention to the specific functions that leaders perform for both social and personality systems. Here, the behavior of leaders will be analyzed in terms of its effect on the level of capabilities in both systems, although I am primarily concerned with its impact on the social system's potential to serve and survive.

In this effort to develop a specific framework, we should not lose sight of the fact that any member of a group assumes leadership when he successfully initiates action for the group. In this sense, several members of a system, including those who might be specified arbitrarily as "followers," can share in the performance of leadership tasks. Consequently, leaders must be identified in terms of the relative volume of successful initiatives achieved by each member. Also, it should be clear that a single leadership function can be performed through many different behaviors and that some forms of behavior may not increase systemic capabilities at all. In enumerating leadership's functions, then, we should know what ends are being served by those who successfully initiate action and the different behaviors and styles that can contribute to effective performance. One way of beginning this type of analysis is to consider how the roles of leadership are clustered, which should give us some criteria for specifying types of leadership.

Leadership roles can be clustered into two general categories, which have been labeled the "instrumental" and "expressive" modes of leadership.

These categories were first developed by Robert Bales and Talcott Parsons for the purposes of small-group research but are now applied frequently by others to larger collectivities. "Instrumental" refers to the task-oriented roles of leadership that contribute to organizational effectiveness, such as setting goals, allocating labor, enforcing sanctions, and the like. On the other hand, the "expressive" mode of leadership refers to roles that establish social and emotional ties between leaders and followers, for example, friend, orator, counselor. Amitai Etzioni describes these categories somewhat more broadly: ". . . *instrumental* refers to the need to acquire resources, or means, and to allocate them among the various role-clusters in the system, and *expressive,* to the need to maintain the integration of various parts of the system with each other as well as with its normative system."[1]

This distinction between instrumental and expressive leadership has been used quite effectively by Etzioni to analyze leadership patterns in complex organizations. This categorization can also be used as a general conceptual framework within which the specific functions of leadership can be located, carrying the analysis beyond the small-group and formal organizational settings to encompass revolutionary situations. Here, I will want to discuss the instrumental and expressive functions of leadership as they relate especially to ruling and rebel leadership, since it is important to recognize the similarities between these seemingly disparate sectors of leadership.

Instrumental and Expressive Leadership

A leadership structure is an aggregate of roles played by those who successfully initiate action affecting the coordination of group behavior. In military systems these structures assume a highly formal and differentiated character, with precise statuses that must be gained before initiation of action is likely, and a division of responsibility that is achieved through the specialization of leadership functions. On the other hand, leadership in informal groups, such as gangs, is usually much less differentiated, the leader assuming responsibility in a number of functional areas. Whether a structure of leadership becomes formal and highly differentiated is a function of environmental necessities to a great extent, although we should not lose sight of the influence of power arrangements on the character of leadership. Power can be both a blessing to leadership in its effort to transform society and a confining condition when further differentiation, which is necessary to cope with increased social complexity, is resisted by a powerful leader. Joseph Stalin's resistance to increasing pressures for differentiation and autonomy in the Soviet system is one case in point.

Roles are the most concrete manifestations of the leader's functional contributions to the coordination of social systems. Thus, the particular functional emphasis of a leader can be roughly determined by examining the roles he plays most frequently. And the leader's style, how he plays roles, is an indicator of his organizational mode, be it instrumental or expressive.

In addition, situational variations must be taken into account, since roles will be chosen primarily in response to the environmental problems of the group, including significant shifts in the followers' preferences as they bear directly on the roles and styles of leadership.

There is a tendency for the instrumental and expressive modes of leadership to be assumed by individuals with basically different personal temperaments. Instrumental leaders are usually more aggressive, more able to tolerate hostility, and more anxious to be respected; whereas, expressive leaders appear more accommodating, less able to tolerate hostility, and more anxious to be loved. While these two types of leadership may be provided by a single individual, notably a "great man" such as Napoleon, Hitler, or Castro, the tendency under normal conditions, argues Etzioni, is for these orientations to be adopted by different types. Thus, in order to maximize organizational effectiveness, cooperation between instrumental and expressive leaders is essential. "All other things equal," Etzioni continues, "collaboration is more likely when both of the leaders hold organizational positions, or when neither does, than it is when only one of them does."[2]

When cooperation between these types of leadership is secured, the effectiveness of the organization will be enhanced by making expressive modes of leadership serve the instrumental leader's organizational needs. Justification for this relationship hinges on the instrumental leader's greater contribution to the solution of system maintenance problems. Expressive role activities assume only secondary importance as integrative contributions to insure effective organizational control. "If expressive considerations were to prevail," Etzioni points out with reference to a factory organization, "production considerations would have to be significantly and regularly neglected to assure 'good' social relations between the workers and the foreman."[3]

It is interesting that the shop foreman, like the "great man" in history, must assume both instrumental and expressive roles. Management expects him to bear down on the instrumental needs of the organization, including setting work loads and assignments, supervising production, and maintaining machinery. And, at the same time, "he is encouraged to become the workers' expressive leader as well, to be not only respected, but also liked, popular, loved; to be concerned with workers' personal problems, participate in their social life, be a 'father' and a 'friend.'"[4] When these role orientations come into conflict, as they must in a factory setting, the foreman must decide at times whether to follow the instrumental preferences of management in order to preserve his position as foreman or to side with his men to preserve the expressive leadership he has attained.

That the instrumental and expressive orientations of leadership can also be found in social movements is argued by Joseph Gusfield. The task leader in a social movement, associated with the instrumental orientation, "sets the conditions of work performance and goal orientation," while the social leader, associated with the expressive type, "maintains the morale of the followers and the harmony of the social group."[5] From this perspective, the rebel leader must contribute to the solution of organizational problems by assuming both orientations:

> . . . as an articulator of the movement in the total society, he must learn the limits and possibility of actions in light of the power and ideologies of influential persons and organizations outside of the movement [the instrumental mode]. . . . However, as the mobilizer of commitments to the movement, he is expected to express the sharp disjuncture between the values of the society and those of the movement [the expressive mode].[6]

While Etzioni considers the instrumental mode of leadership as primary in complex organizations, the expressive orientation should assume increasing importance during periods of rapid political change. For disintegrative tendencies in the society necessitate an expressive leader capable of creating and sustaining emotional bonds with followers in order to restore integration where instrumental responses failed to maintain order through social control. In this sense, revolutionary situations should be fertile environments for individuals with definite talents for expressive leadership.

Enumerating functions and designating types of leadership follows, for analytic convenience, in the tradition of Max Weber's use of "ideal types." The functions and types of leadership specified in this chapter are consequently only approximations of real leadership, and we should thus be aware of the many variations from the ideal in actual fact. It is quite clear, for example, that a single leader may behave in a way that is task-oriented at times (instrumental) and social-emotional on other occasions (expressive). A single leader may shift behavior between the two modes of leadership, acting in an instrumental capacity in relation to one set of followers, while he maintains the loyalty of others through expressive behaviors, for example, emotional speeches, providing security, and so on. Adolf Hitler demonstrated this ability in a striking way, moving from one mode of leadership to another to suit his audiences and his own purposes.

An expressive leader also may often make significant contributions to organizational task performance, since the creation of strong social ties can enhance the overall performance of an organization.[7] Changes in the nature of environmental pressures can also force a leader to alter the mode of his behavior in order to create a new emphasis, as Franklin D. Roosevelt did when he confronted the disintegrative tendencies of the Great Depression by placing greater importance on expressive behavior, most clearly represented in his "fireside chats." By shifting to a stronger social-emotional emphasis, he was attempting to maintain the public's trust in the political system. Some leaders are capable of making the transition to a new mode of leadership, but this is by no means assured, since the leader's personal qualities will play a large part. Look, for instance, at former President Lyndon Johnson's personal incapacities for effective social-emotional leadership during the public outcry against U.S. military involvement in South Viet Nam.

The functions of leadership can be usefully discussed within the broad boundaries of the instrumental and expressive modes of leadership. Using these categories, distinctions can be made between functions that are primarily oriented to organizational effectiveness and others that are socially integrative. In the latter context especially, we can begin to understand how a leader's behavior can contribute in a latent way to the maintenance of psychic balance within a follower's personality. Even the purely instrumental leader, whose chief aim is to build an effective organization, may contribute directly to the solution of personality problems. As we shall see, the instrumental leader who builds an aura of power around himself may attract followers who are experiencing the anxieties produced by structural strain and who need the security that his leadership promises. This extension of the meaning of the expressive mode to include the psychological relations between leaders and followers is not completely divorced from Etzioni's usage. For it is possible to show how the development of strong psychological dependencies between leaders and followers affects the integration of a social system and leadership's over-all effectiveness in advancing the system's capabilities.

The Functions of Leadership

Categories of functions performed by leadership should be general enough to apply to all possible contexts of leadership, even though in selected instances some functions may not be performed adequately or may be insignificant due to variations in environmental pressure, structural capacities, and personal temperament. In developing a functional framework for the analysis of leadership, both a descriptive and prescriptive point of reference influence the outcome to some extent. For functions may be derived from hard data bearing on leadership behavior in a variety of situations or, as abstractions, they may provide the analyst with a model that suggests what functions must be performed by leadership to ensure efficient organizational coordination. Even when structured on a solid empirical base, however, any framework ordering the possible functions of leadership can offer little more than organizational guidance that hopefully will produce new insights. As a practical tool, it provides a means for locating and relating important aspects of leadership and leader-follower relations.

Three instrumental functions can be specified that appear applicable to leadership in various situations. Each function will be specified and discussed briefly in relation to two leadership levels—ruling and rebel leadership—highlighting the similar functional emphases of these seemingly divergent leadership sectors. Two expressive functions will also be considered, which provides an opportunity to include the psychological perspective. Since, in the latter case, the unit of analysis is the individual rather than roles and social organization, it is unnecessary to belabor the use of structural examples when speaking of expressive functions of leadership. By considering both structural and personal aspects of leadership functioning, a broader view of leader-follower relations will be developed, which may avoid the pitfalls of reductionism pointed out by Smelser and Smelser and may also take account of Devereux's appeal for a more inclusive perspective of follower motives.

Instrumental Functions of Leadership

Goal-setting Function—Probably the most obvious instrumental task of leadership is the formation of goals. To enhance the capabilities of the system, leaders must persistently alter the goal hierarchy to correspond to changes occurring within and outside the system. It is in this context that Chester Barnard has emphasized the importance of goal-setting for executive leaders: In order to increase efficiency of operations, executives must first define the purposes of the organization, then remain sensitive to the need for constant redefinitions of purpose. A successful pattern of goal change is accomplished through "sensitive systems of communication, experience in interpretation, imagination, and the delegation of responsibility."[8] This advice can be taken as general for, even in the unstructured, informal group, primitive procedures for setting and changing goals are necessary if the pattern of interaction is to remain stable.

There are numerous decision-making procedures for specifying goals, from the simple elite structures of gangs, military organizations, and dictatorships to the legislative, bureaucratic, and executive intricacies of pluralist political systems. In addition, there are varying degrees of concreteness that goals can assume, from written decrees, military orders, and laws to the sometimes vague spoken pronouncements of revolutionary leaders during the genesis of organization. And some goals are so general and latent in systems that they frequently remain unexamined and unchanged.

In the broadest sense, leadership must make adjustments in two essentially distinct goal hierarchies. Preferences must be selected among a number of *general* goals, which are the distant objectives of the social system. Then, more immediate and short-range goals have to be ordered as a means of reaching the generalized ends. These short-range goals make up the *particular* goal hierarchy. In this context, the preferred general goals of leadership will directly influence the organization of the particular goal hierarchy, as, for example, in the relative importance assigned to bills in ordering legislative business. In response to environmental pressures, leadership may be required to alter both goal hierarchies in order to increase the extractive, regulative, and distributive capabilities of the system. In this sense, the general and particular goal preferences of leadership must be brought into harmony with environmental conditions and follower expectations (which may be conflicting). As well, the two hierarchies of goals should be synchronized with each other in order to maximize the performance of structures.

Ruling leadership may place a high value on a general goal and persistently reject devaluation of it, even against severe intrasystem pressures. In the United States, for example, ruling leaders have tended to give a high ranking to foreign policy preferences, emphasizing the development of democratic states throughout the world and defense against Communist aggression—both general goals associated with the boundary problems of the system. With domestic goals placed at a lower level in the preferential hierarchy, products of the political system gravitate to defense activities and war preparations through a national legislative process that sorts out and orders the particular goal responses to synchronize with foreign policy aspirations. While the goal hierarchies appear to be synchronized, domestic problems can be aggravated, producing an environmental crisis within the system and shifting public attention to the debate over generalized ends. The specific policy to go to war in Southeast Asia, a particular goal formulated to reach the distant objectives of the system, has had the effect of alienating sectors of the society, not simply from the war, but from the most preferred goals in the general hierarchy. Criticisms of war involvement have, for some groups, become secondary to the larger and more serious attack on the generalized ends of the political system, most recently demonstrated in the activist attack against "American imperialism." Thus, where the focus of attention centers on the preferential ordering of general goals, withdrawal from a single war may be insufficient to meet the criticisms advanced against ruling leaders. Nothing short of a new ranking among the general goals would be acceptable to those who believe that the political system is moving in the wrong direction.

Reordering the general goal hierarchy is often difficult, largely because it is closely interwoven with aspects of the political culture. Consequently, leaders who are spokesmen for traditional views may resist changing the general goal hierarchy even when increasing pressures for change are building to a dangerous level. It is quite possible to conceive of the United States withdrawing from a single war because of domestic pressures, but, given the values held by leadership and the nature of the international environment, altering the generalized ends of the system must be considered infinitely more difficult. To end "American imperialism," for instance, would require a major reevaluation of the competitive values that are the substructure of the American political culture. Thus, if the attack is centered on general goal preferences, leadership is apt to demonstrate greater resistance to change than if it is directed against particular goals, which are more easily altered. Ruling leaders may actually believe that they are making changes in society when they choose to shift the priority of particular goals, but truly radical departures from the status quo come when there is a shift in the general goal hierarchy. It is, in fact, the general goal hierarchy that becomes the main target of revolutionary leaders, since ultimately revolution attempts to revise the belief structure that underlies the general goal system. In this sense, revolutions are efforts to change the basic values that regulate behavior within social structures.

The goal-setting function is no less important for the rebel leader, who must be able to formulate the goals that specify the grand purposes of the movement and, also, the specific, strategic goals that would bring the movement ever closer to its general aspirations. Discussing the functions that must be performed for successful revitalization, Anthony Wallace considers the formulation of a code to be the first stage in the revitalization process:

> An individual, or a group of individuals, constructs a new, utopian image of socio-cultural organization. This model is a blueprint of an ideal society or "goal culture" [general goals]. Contrasted with the goal culture is the existing culture, which is represented as inadequate or evil in certain respects. Connecting the existing culture and the goal culture is a transfer culture: a system of operations which, if faithfully carried out, will transform the existing culture into the goal culture [particular goals].[9]

If the transfer culture is unsuccessfully instituted, the miserable conditions may persist or the society may atrophy. Under these conditions, rebel leaders turn toward revolutionary options, setting particular goals whose most immediate purpose is to hasten the "death" of the society. Within a revolutionary movement, even when there is consensus about general ends, rebel leaders are likely to openly debate the means to be utilized. Such a debate was clearly manifested in the Russian revolution and can be found elaborated in Lenin's major tract *What Is to Be Done?* Attacking tendencies in the movement that assumed that cooperation with bourgeois elements and encouragement of spontaneity among the masses would be the most effective avenues to communism, Lenin moved in a different direction, providing a set of particular goals that he felt would ensure the success of the revolutionary effort. At the top of the hierarchy was the recommended formation of a vanguard of professional revolutionaries, derived from his belief that "it is far more difficult to catch ten wise men than it is to catch a hundred fools."[10]

Whether we are speaking of a political system, revolutionary organization, military establishment, or street-corner gang, the goal-setting function of leadership is apparent as a crucial facet of organizational control. But leaders cannot arbitrarily impose a mission on their followers, for a leader's options for setting goals are confined by the nature of the organization he leads. Neither can leaders neglect to make a careful appraisal of the environmental limitations that restrict the organization's field of operations. Consequently, the preferential ordering of goals must take into account not only what leaders want from their organizations, but what their organizations can and want to give. "The setting of goals is a creative task," says Philip Selznick. "It entails a self-assessment to discover the true commitments of the organization, as set by effective internal and external demands. The failure to set aims in the light of these commitments is a major source of irresponsibility in leadership."[11]

Communication Function—According to Alfred Kuhn, the purpose of communication is two-fold: to inform and to motivate. "Communication will thus be seen as having two possible major functions," he says, "the one to alter a receiver's concepts, which we will construe as the information function, the other to change his preferences or feelings, which we will construe as the motivation function."[12] Because information and motivation are essential for clarifying the system's goals and encouraging efficient performance of roles, leaders must assume the responsibility for developing communication networks appropriate for the environment and in harmony with the nature of the goals to be attained.

In fact, Herbert Simon considers the development of communication channels essential for the creation of organizations. For it is by the transmission of orders through channels of communication that the group influences individual behavior. This is a two-way process, which includes transmitting orders, information, and advice up and down vertical channels of communication. But there is also a heavy flow of communications horizontally, among various structures of the organization.[13] Of course the character of the pattern of communication varies with environmental conditions and, most directly, with the political culture underlying the organization.

Richard Fagen has discussed the efforts of authoritarian regimes in setting communication patterns and has pointed out common justifications for them in his book *Politics and Communication*. He argues that "authoritarian stabilizations do not simply imply increased insulation of elites from citizens. Rather they suggest that a decrease in certain types of communication up the hierarchy is coupled with an increase in total communication down the hierarchy."[14] Two justifications are often advanced to legitimize this basically unidirectional communication flow. The first, or the tutelary, argument, places the blame on the citizenry, claiming that members of the polity are not yet prepared for participant roles. The second argument claims justifiable expediency as a legitimate grounding, blaming weak institutions that necessitate emergency measures, including some tampering with communication patterns.[15]

While new communication patterns may develop that essentially exclude the masses from the effective communication of preferences, even the most autocratic leadership needs some information about follower opinions and demands in order to set suitable goals for the system. "Although elections may be suspended and critics of the ruling elite may be silenced," says Fagen, "feedback from the masses in some form remains necessary if official action programs are to be related to social reality."[16] Even leaders like Stalin, who prefer to play the trustee role, must be conscious of follower dispositions for no other reason than to develop appropriate counter-strategies of social control or to build acceptable rationalizations for trustee action. Thus leadership in general must develop or utilize existing lines of communication to justify the hierarchical arrangement of goals, whether arrived at through a democratic process, by trustee decree, or a variant like "democratic centralism." Each of the capabilities of organization, from the extractive to the symbolic, depends in an important way on leadership's use of communication channels. For it is through communication that leaders specify what investments followers must make to the organization, how they will be punished for noncompliance, and what they should expect to receive by way of honors, statuses, and other tangible rewards. Also, there may be times when leaders will transmit symbolic messages in order to explain to followers why they are getting less than they expected.

Actually, there are many different channels of communication that can develop within organizations, depending on their size and the freedom to communicate. Simon has identified five formal channels: oral communication (which varies with physical proximity); memoranda and letters; paper-flow (files on membership, for instance); records and reports; and manuals (which communicate organization practices that are relatively permanent). In addition, there are numerous informal possibilities, ranging from communication on the basis of personal connection to gossip.[17] This list is by no means complete when applied to revolutionary organizations, however. For mass demonstrations, violence, and the underground press assume an important communication function outside normal organizational channels. Furthermore, if the operations of the ruling leadership create severe pressures on revolutionary systems, rebel leaders may be forced to divide their organizational apparatus between the underground and a revolutionary cadre in exile. Under such circumstances, the development of good lines of communication will undoubtedly be a precondition for successful revolutionary activity. Rebel leaders in exile or prison are also faced with the possibility of losing control over their organizations when they are unable to dominate the communication network. Hitler's response to this possibility after his imprisonment in 1923 was a creative one: He simply refused to appoint a temporary successor, thereby preventing other aspiring leaders from gaining control over the communication channels of the party and taking hold of the Nazi movement.

The existence of a well-developed communication system that provides for a two-way transmission of messages does not ensure responsiveness from ruling leadership. There are intervening factors that must be taken into account. First, there is a decided tendency for the responsive capability of an organization to decrease when the disposition of leaders is ideological rather then pragmatic. Furthermore, the inadequate rotation of the incumbents in authority can effectively reduce organizational responsiveness. Where this has happened in Latin America the *coup d'état* has been an extra-legal mechanism for rotating elite structures when other procedures were unavailable.

There is an assumption within the pluralist argument that suggests that ruling leaders in the American political system are basically a pragmatic lot, persistently yielding to the sources of communication and political pressure. This assumption can be questioned of course. For, both individual leaders and leadership structures have ideological biases that directly affect the flow and impact of communications from followers.

When I speak of "ideological bias" I am referring to the disposition toward innovation, whether the tendency is to want to make changes or resist them. In the traditional lexicon of politics, these are essentially the differences between the liberal and conservative orientations to social change. The ideological biases of leadership structures result from the procedures that place individuals in authority. For example, as one examines the national political system in the United States it is fairly clear that some structures of government tend to be liberally biased, while others have definite conservative tendencies. The presidency appears to possess a liberal bias because the electoral college system favors the populated states, which have positive orientations to innovation. On the other hand, reapportionment studies have shown that Congress is usually biased in a conservative direction, owing to the fact that rural areas in the country have a disproportionate influence over the electoral outcomes in congressional districts. In addition, the seniority system in Congress, which distributes statuses on the basis of length of tenure, definitely favors the rural and conservative areas of the country, which tend to be heavily marked with "safe districts," those districts in which a political party is without effective competition and can easily reelect its candidate. Leaders coming from such districts are able to build seniority and become entrenched in power as committee chairmen or, if they are not members of the majority party, as leaders of the opposition. The ideological bias of the U.S. Supreme Court tends to reflect that of the presidency, owing to the fact that Justices are appointed by the President (with Senate confirmation). Robert Dahl's analysis of changes in the composition of the court shows that its ideological bias does in fact shift, after a time lag, with the bias of the presidency. The ideology of a single President may even affect the ideological orientation of the court, if his tenure in office is long or there is a rapid turnover in the membership of the court due to the death or retirement of Justices.[18] When the Congress, presidency, and court move simultaneously toward a conservative position the responsive capability of the political system may very well diminish, adding further to the strains that are the causes of public unrest.

Elections are, of course, one of the revered institutions in the American political arena, along with the two-party system. In principle, elections and two-party competitive systems should produce a periodic and thorough rotation of leaders and, consequently, a greater responsive capability. But these two mechanisms operate inadequately in the United States, leaving members of the ruling class more immune from political pressure than may be healthy for the society. Where elected leaders must face the public periodically, Robert Dahl argues, followers are able to indirectly influence the resolution of major policy conflicts that the members of the ruling structure cannot resolve in the private atmosphere of the legislative chamber.[19] Elected leaders supposedly pay attention to the mass of voters because they know that failure to benefit groups and individuals means decreasing political opportunities and rewards for themselves.[20] But what leaders promise in the public arena is not necessarily what they deliver in the privacy of the legislature. Their public and private faces often diverge quite sharply. This is especially true when a leader represents a political party that has less than a majority of the total registrations and consequently needs votes from the opposition party to win public office. Under these circumstances, the public face of the minority party leader comes to be very similar to the private faces of those from the opposition party that he must convince to switch affiliations. For example, Republican presidential nominees must win Democratic party affiliates over to their side to win, often leading them to develop a public face that communicates support for the welfare state concept when their private views run in a contrary direction.[21]

We also discover on close examination that the competitive two-party system, which we persistently hold over the heads of the leaders of developing countries, is the exception in the United States rather than the rule. Except for the competition between the two major political parties for the presidency, the number of congressional and state contests in which the two parties both have a chance to win is surprisingly low. And these competitive contests tend to occur, Fred Greenstein concludes, in the large industrial states where innovative tendencies are strong.[22]

Ironically, if rotation of incumbents in authority is effective, it tends to work against the interests of those seeking innovative politics. The more frequent rotation of office holders in the large, liberal states makes it close to impossible for innovative individuals to build sufficient seniority to affect the congressional power structure. So, even if electoral mechanisms exist to force periodic rotations of leadership, these work in only selected cases, creating political disadvantages for those who live in areas where the electoral system is really effective in producing responsive politics. Thus, before jumping to any unwarranted conclusions about the greater flexibility of democratic political systems because communication is easy, it is wise to examine first the configuration of ideological biases and the extent and effectiveness of elite rotation. For democratic societies also have sectors of structurally entrenched leadership with definite ideological biases that create intransigence toward change.

The willingness to listen to and act on the demands of followers is also variable from one leadership context to another, depending on the nature of the political culture, the personality of leaders, and the particular contribution leadership is making to the solution of environmental problems. In some undifferentiated tribal systems, for example, highly sophisticated communication patterns exist with very responsive leadership. This appears to have been the case in the Ashanti tribes in Ghana, for the tribal chief was very sensitive to follower expectations and was open to the advice of the village elders. "In reality every move and command which appeared to emanate from his mouth," argues R. S. Rattray, "had been discussed in private and had been previously agreed upon by his councillors, to whom every one in the tribe had access and to whom popular opinion on any subject was thus made known."[23] Contrast this pattern with military organizations in differentiated societies, where rules govern what is communicated up the hierarchy as well as when, where, and how the communication must be made. It is because of this control over communication networks that military systems traditionally have had low responsive capabilities, forcing military leaders to increase their regulative efforts as an alternative way of controlling behavior.

In addition to the positive contribution of leader-follower communication patterns in harmonizing follower preferences with leader-initiated goals, communication channels are necessary to bring about the actualization of particular goals. From Simon's perspective:

> The crucial point is whether the recipient of an order, or any other kind of communication, is influenced by the communication in his actions or decisions, or whether he is not. The problem of securing employees' compliance with a safety rule is not very different from the problem of securing a customer's acceptance of a particular brand of soap. In some cases formal authority may be sufficient inducement for the subordinate to comply; but usually the communication must reason, plead, and persuade, as well as order, if it is to be effective.[24]

For instance, Richard Neustadt has argued with respect to presidential leadership that one of the problems a President must confront in actualizing his policies is the difficulty of selecting the appropriate channels for communication, then making his messages sufficiently clear so that the receiver will know exactly what he wants and will thus be unable to balk at requests or commands, later alluding to misunderstanding.[25]

For rebel leaders, who are apt to be faced with a scarcity of resources against a strong ruling leadership structure, the work of communication becomes especially vital. "The formulators of the code," Wallace explains, "preach the code to other people in an evangelistic spirit. The aim of the communication is to make converts."[26] These leaders appear before the uncommitted masses on radio, television, and in the press as champions of the movement, often personifying it in cartoon, picture, story, and legend.[27]

Rebel leaders may differ in their choice of channels of communication, but the purpose is the same—to give information to potential converts and to motivate existing members to higher levels of action and sacrifice as a way of expanding and consolidating the revolutionary organization's base of strength. For this purpose, Lenin placed primary emphasis on the written word, arguing in support of an organization newspaper because it was the best medium for building strong political organizations.[28] Hitler, on the other hand, preferred the spoken word: "The force which ever set in motion the great historical avalanches of religious and political movements," he had said, "is the magic power of the spoken word."[29]

Prison may quiet the rebel leader's voice for a time, but history is full of examples—Lenin and Hitler are two—where the prison cell has become a sanctuary for producing written works that later assumed monumental importance for political movements. It is often in prison that rebel leaders form a new stock of ideas and new goal preferences, which are smuggled to an underground press. And later, when the leader is freed, they are incorporated into a new set of arguments and become the basis for a new organizational strategy.

A significant role performed by leadership in relation to other systems is associated with the communication function, but in a different sense from the intrasystem communication patterns described above. To avoid confusion between these two sectors of communication functioning and to clarify the conceptual distinctiveness between them, I will use Kurt Lewin's term— "gatekeeper"—to identify leadership behavior in intersystem communication networks. Lewin uses the term "gatekeeper" to describe an individual who links intrasystem communication patterns with the external environment. More precisely, gatekeeping refers to strategic control over a channel of communication to determine what information coming through the channel will be allowed to reach the group.[30] A second dimension may be added to this pattern: Leaders may also control the information originating within the system as it is distributed and communicated to external systems.

If leaders are able to perform the gatekeeper role effectively, they may enhance their hold over the follower's attitudinal dispositions and role performances. In terms of concrete action, the leader's relative monopoly of information in selected cases may narrow the options available to followers and, at times, may be sufficiently compelling in argumentative form to insure that the option preferred by leadership is adopted. This occurrence is both natural and necessary for effective goal attainment. Those in possession of the most accurate information must be in positions to exercise a disproportionate influence over decisions for which their information is most relevant. For instance, Thornton Roby has stated, in one of the few functional analyses of leadership, that

> . . . an effective leader should provide a structure that incorporates all major relationships between information and action. . . . At the very least, a leader should prevent situations in which suggestions for action are based on utterly inadequate information. It is almost as important for morale, to avoid putting

people with relevant information in position without commensurate authority.[31]

Followers, on the other hand, tend to be more profoundly influenced by those perceived to have the most appropriate and accurate information, a proposition clearly confirmed by Daniel Katz and Paul Lazarsfeld in their study of opinion leadership, *Personal Influence.*[32] But it is apparent that on most issues followers may have access to many different leaders and numerous other sources of information. Thus, it is necessary to specify more precisely the conditions that may affect a particular leader's ability to perform the gatekeeper role.

Three conditions appear to affect the capacity of a leader to perform as gatekeeper. First, the structure of the communication process itself can be a determining factor. If there are limited opportunities for receiving information from other sources, say in an isolated military unit, followers may become more dependent on gatekeepers for structuring orientations with respect to external systems. On the other hand, if the individual follower interacts in multiple communication patterns, where his loyalty is distributed among several groups, competing interpretations of the environment are possible, thereby expanding the follower's range of choice. This multiplication of informational opportunities reduces the probability that a single leader will monopolize the communication gate.

Trust is the second ingredient that is crucial, a factor that strongly affects the follower's choice among available options for information. Trust is the evaluational component of the follower's orientation to the source of information and is related to the follower's judgment concerning the reliability of information received and the basic integrity of the sender, be it a leader or some aspect of the news media. Evaluating the integrity of the source is especially important, for, implicitly, the follower makes a future projection about the ability of the sender to continue transmitting reliable information. To the extent that the follower attributes a high level of integrity to the sender, he may be willing to accept information with little doubt of its accuracy.

Finally, a third variable is the rise in the demand for information, which often accompanies situations of crisis. Under conditions of environmental ambiguity, followers become susceptible to leaders they trust, but if access to those leaders is made impossible by the structure of the situation, these same followers may be willing to accept information from anyone willing to perform the gatekeeper function. Also, during such crises, followers tend to be less cautious in choosing their sources of information, a fact confirmed by the salience of rumor during crisis situations. That the gatekeeper role is assumed by both ruling and rebel leadership will be shown in the following examples.

One of the better illustrations of how ruling leadership can play the gatekeeper role is the U.S. President's unique position in a communication pattern that excludes many domestic systems from firsthand information about foreign affairs. Clinton Rossiter has said of the President's ascendency in foreign relations: "Secrecy, dispatch, unity, continuity, and access to information—the ingredients of successful diplomacy—are properties of his office, and Congress . . . possesses none of them."[33] Structural conditions appear to encourage an active gatekeeper role for the President: Lines of responsibility—ambassadorial, military, foreign intelligence—run to the President as chief diplomat and commander-in-chief. As a result, the largest body of information about foreign situations comes first to the President. Then, acting as gatekeeper, he determines what information shall be passed on to his different publics, the White House staff, congressmen, the press corps, and the electorate. However, rising suspicion concerning the reliability of information and the President's integrity (the basis of the "credibility gap") can reduce followers' feelings of trust, diminishing a President's capacity to influence followers' attitudes toward his preferred goals. As feelings of trust decline, efforts may be undertaken to find new and more reliable sources of information.

As I suggested a moment ago, during periods of political turmoil the demand for information sometimes reaches hysterical proportions. If lines of communication to the enemy or to generally inaccessible allies are held by a small cadre of rebel leaders, followers may be required by the structure of the communication pattern to rely on information originating with those leaders. The visits of black militant leaders from the U.S. to the Third World nations can in fact be partly explained as an effort to increase their capacities to play the gatekeeper role. In other situations, where followers are desperate for information and normal sources are inoperative, new leaders can rise to the occasion. N. N. Sukhanov describes this sense of urgency for information and his effort to assume the gatekeeper role in the following way Standing in the Tauride Palace in the midst of chaos after the czarist regime had fallen, Sukhanov recalled:

> I decided that if I couldn't find anybody or anything I would start my own activities and try to conduct an agitation among a detachment of soldiers right there in the street, with their help occupy some printing-plant, and there together with the workers compose and distribute some kind of bulletin explaining what was happening. There was nothing whatever found in print. The need and thirst for it were colossal, and the minds of the inhabitants must have been chaos for want of it.[34]

Whether in stable or unstable situations—performed by ruling or rebel leadership—the performance of the communication function appears to be essential to ensure organizational effectiveness. The development of channels of communication, both formal and informal, are the vehicles leaders utilize to gather information about the state of their organization as well as to communicate preferred goals to subordinates who must assume the correct orientation to work priorities. When leaders can gain tight control over the communication network, there is the additional possibility that the flow of information can be regulated. Information screening becomes one of the main sources of a leader's authority and, if used effectively, it can produce an appearance of unanimity in an organization, which diminishes the likelihood that the leader's goal preferences will be challenged. And it may also increase the leader's ability to mobilize support for those goals.

Mobilization Function—Even when they are articulated through appropriate communication channels, the goals of leadership are never embraced with equal enthusiasm by all members of a social system. In discussing the communication function I mentioned in passing how channels can be utilized for exerting influence over subordinates in an organizational hierarchy and also how information received by autocratic leadership serves to improve the operation of social control mechanisms. This situation suggests that communication is essential if leadership is to perform the third instrumental function, which is to accumulate and maintain internal support for goal initiatives and mobilize support from external systems. The mobilization function of leadership is integrally related to the concept of power—how leadership creates conformity to initiatives for which there is little ardor or outright hostility. Robert Dahl's formulation of power is very noteworthy in this respect because it establishes the basic elements of a power relation, elements that can usefully be applied as standards in determining the level of a leader's success in performing the mobilization function.

Dahl speaks of power as a relation between persons in which one person attempts to alter the behavior of another through the application of relevant political resources. "The base of an actor's power consists of all the resources—opportunities, acts, objects, etc.—that he can exploit in order to effect the behavior of another."[35] If actor *A* wants *B* to act in a way contrary to his initial disposition, there are essentially two lines of action open to him. These are the persuasive and coercive aspects of power.[36] First, *A* may attempt to persuade *B* that his initiative is clearly in *B's* interest. If this effort fails, *A* might offer *B* positive inducements, including such things as money and position. If these persuasive efforts fail and *A* continues to place a high priority on *B's* support, then the second line of action may be undertaken: *A* may threaten to harm *B* in some way, by applying sanctions, inflicting pain, or withholding rewards.

A threat is a promise of punishment that, if taken seriously by *B*, can produce conformity without an expenditure of resources on *A's* part. Once *A* makes a threat, *B* must decide whether he really means to actualize it, whether he has the resources to do so, and what specific losses will result if the threat is carried out. For example, the threat of a presidential veto has real bearing on the composition of bills in the legislative process to the extent that the President communicates his intention to veto a bill in clear and forceful language. Knowing that he means to veto a bill and has the authority to do so, congressmen are fast to rewrite legislation to reflect the President's preferences.

In principle, the threat of violence is no different from a threat of a presidential veto, except in the nature of the punishments that are promised for noncompliance. In fact, Dahl's formulation of power is weakened somewhat by his reluctance to consider violence as an extension of power. According to Dahl's operational definition of power, if *A* shoots and kills *B* for noncompliance, then there would be no power relation because *B's* behavior would not have been changed. That makes considerable sense. But what if *A* kills *B* in order to influence the behavior of *C*? This act would clearly involve a power relationship to the extent that killing *B* would indeed alter *C's* behavior.

In revolutionary settings violence is often used in a power-relevant sense.[37] The assassination of a member of the government or of a traitor within the organization is meant to change the behavioral patterns or dispositions of others. Even random terror can neutralize a sizable number of citizens who might have resisted change under normal circumstances. The use of violence as a resource of power should help to explain why so few persons actually become involved in revolutionary incidents and so many go into hiding. The threats of violence from both sides in a revolutionary conflict often depoliticize the masses while they politicize the members of the contesting organizations.

Leadership must contend with pockets of resistance, using persuasion and threats of punishment, as mentioned above, in order to reach what it sees as absolutely essential goals. Whether persuasion or coercion are emphasized must vary with the size of the system under examination, the extent of the adaptive crisis, the salience of the goal toward which the action is directed, the nature of the cultural and legal norms (do the norms prevent the arbitrary use of coercion?), the ability of leadership to persuade, and the relative resource capability to reward or to punish.[38] Given these factors, it is probably not possible to predict exactly how leadership will perform the mobilization function. However, it is feasible to suggest that the mobilization task must be a major responsibility of leadership and that specific strategies employed in the mobilization process will fall within the persuasion and coercion categories developed by Dahl.

As we know, nations differ significantly in the distribution of their political resources, which is the basis of power relationships. For example, the distribution of politically relevant resources in the United States has produced rather extensive areas of conflict among sectors of the ruling leadership structure, which makes the persuasive aspects of power crucial. Presidential power, if we accept the validity of Neustadt's analysis, is more modest than aggressive. Presidents must continually guard their "power stakes," conceived as the total number of politically relevant resources at their disposal, by mobilizing the resources of others through persuasion.

Because of countervailing centers of power, a President will use coercion sparingly, for once applied he may be forced to retreat and lose face, a position in which President Truman found himself when he ordered federal troops to occupy the steel mills during the Korean War, then was forced to retreat under pressure from the U.S. Supreme Court.[39] A careful analysis of the presidential environment leads Neustadt to the conclusion that "presidential power is the power to persuade."[40] In the final analysis, Presidents may threaten sanctions for deviation, but they will make and actualize those threats only after persuasion has failed.

In other circumstances, ruling leaders can rely more heavily on threats and actual punishments, preventing the follower from deviating from the norm by cultivating fear. The history of oppression of black citizens in the United States is the clearest case in which ruling leaders have relied on the instruments of coercion to maintain conformity. And in undifferentiated tribal systems, such as the Ashanti, leadership sometimes ensured support for an initiative by resorting to the coercive potential of the tribal ancestors. As K. A. Busia has shown, the chief's primary means of dissuading dissidents was to play on their fear of ancestral displeasure.[41] Hitler used a somewhat different strategy of coercion for maintaining support: By applying terror openly against "enemies of the state," he demonstrated both his ability and willingness to use force, ultimately making the threat of coercion sufficient to maintain conformity to his initiatives among those predisposed toward rebellion against him. In an important way, the concentration camps became an extension, in macabre form, of the coercive underpinnings of Nazi totalitarianism. Both the Jewish prisoner and the German skeptic became conformists in their own way as politics and social life were reduced to the problems of survival.[42]

The mobilization capacities of rebel leadership will vary, as with ruling leadership, in accordance with persuasive skills and resource capacity. In cases where rebel forces actually occupy territory, as in guerrilla warfare campaigns, coercive capacity can be quite extensive. At other times, coercive potential may be minimal if the resources necessary to threaten and execute punishments are in short supply or are dispersed over a wide geographical area. Furthermore, if target individuals are protected by established authority, rebel leaders are often unable to effectively control those within the system who are noncompliant or to mobilize those standing on the sidelines who might ordinarily be convinced by threats.

Rebel leaders face a dilemma during the mobilization process. In order to counterbalance the resources of the ruling leadership, they may be forced to enlarge the number of their followers, which can produce conflicts within the organization to the extent that it introduces greater heterogeneity of beliefs and new philosophies of action. It is important to recognize that an increase in the size of a revolutionary organization does not come about without components of weakness. The choice to mobilize all who aspire to join creates increasing strain on the organizational apparatus. And to deal with this strain revolutionary leaders must expend greater numbers of their own resources running the organization and maintaining the cohesiveness of the group, resources that might be better spent in more offensive efforts against the political regime.

How much mobilization is required to produce a successful revolutionary attempt of course varies with the strength of the ruling leadership. If the ruling leaders have failed to preserve their capabilities, then they might possess insufficient resources to stop even a small revolutionary cadre. Conversely, the existence of relatively strong ruling leadership may force revolutionary bands to coalesce for strategic reasons even while they disagree to some extent on ends and means. In the Russian revolution, for example, the numerous revolutionary groups were forced into a tenuous alliance during February in order to overthrow what was perceived to be a strong regime. The sharply reduced capabilities of the Provisional Government during the months following the overthrow of czarism, however, created a situation in which Lenin could insist that the Bolshevik faction make no alliances, but instead assault the government singlehandedly. Because of the weakness of the Provisional Government, this strategy proved to be success-ful. Power was taken by the Bolsheviks with scarcely a shot being fired.

The utilization of resources by revolutionary leaders is thus contingent on the ruling leadership's capabilities to extract, regulate, and distribute its own resources. To argue that revolutions are violent by definition is much less interesting than to consider what factors influence the level of violence. The Chinese, Mexican, and Algerian revolutions manifested much higher levels of violence than the French, Russian, and Nazi revolutions during the mobilization stage. How can this difference be explained? The foregoing discussion of power and mobilization leads one to suspect that the level of violence would be a function of the balance of power between the revolu-tionary and ruling leadership structures. Theoretically, I would postulate that the actualization of threats of violence will tend to occur and increase on both sides as each *perceives* the respective "power stakes" approaching equality. For the revolutionaries, it is the belief that the ruling leadership can no longer effectively regulate deviant political behavior. But this per-ception of weakness on the part of the regime is coupled with a recognition that there are still remnants of strength. Revolutionary violence is directed against those remaining capabilities of the ruling leadership structure that, if reduced, would decidedly shift the balance of power in favor of revolu-tionary control. Once this shift occurs, the revolutionary process enters the period of acceleration. In the broadest sense, revolution can be conceptual-ized as conflict between antagonistic social systems whose leaders use re-sources to reduce the capabilities of the opposing organization in order to preserve or gain control over the political system.

Accepting this view of revolution, it is important to consider the relative skills of revolutionary and ruling leadership as they respond organizationally to the crises and ambiguities of the environment. For a revolutionary environment creates numerous surprise moves, planned by the opposition or accidental, that demand quick and creative responses. This fact alone should lead us to wonder whether revolutionary leaders are not better equipped to act more quickly and decisively than ruling leaders, owing to the institutional restrictions, from customs to red tape, that inhibit the freedom of ruling leaders to act. In this sense, creative political action could be a much greater possibility for the revolutionary leader, although he or she, too, will be bound by limitations inherent in organization.

Rebel leaders may share a hope with executives in bureaucratic structures: that subordinates accept commands simply because they are directives from a superior in a hierarchy of authority.[43] How leaders instill respect and obedience to their authority must differ of course. For example, American Presidents have historically supported Supreme Court decisions because a challenge to the authority of the court would tend to encourage challenges to presidential authority. By obeying the court without question, the President sets an example for his own subordinates, whom he hopes will accept his commands with bureaucratic obedience.[44] On the other hand, rebel leaders can attempt to solidify the obligations of followers in more formal ways. The pledge of loyalty to a rebel leader, found in both the German and American Nazi parties, is one tactic utilized to ensure the bureaucratic relation. Other rebel leaders may try to clothe themselves in mystery, developing a prophetic relation with followers which secures obedience by cultivating respect and deference. The creation of the bureaucratic or prophetic relation can be an economic move designed to conserve scarce resources. When possible, the mobilization function should be performed so as to increase one's "power stake," if indeed the revolutionary organization is to survive in a hostile environment, let alone succeed in its assault on the political order.

Expressive Functions of Leadership

Leader-follower relations based on expressive modes of behavior can be psychologically gratifying for the leader as well as the follower. When Etzioni refers to the expressive leader as one who needs to be loved, we are given an insight into the origin of expressive relations. The expressive leader is seen as one who experiences many of the same psychological problems as his followers. One might even argue that these psychological problems are so sharply accentuated in the expressive leader's behavior that followers are able to recognize them as representations of their own anxieties. It is in this context that Erik Erikson speaks of Hitler's leadership: "On the stage of German history, Hitler sensed to what extent it was safe to let his own personality represent with hysterical abandon what was alive in every German listener and reader."[45]

It is ironic that the extremes of behavior that are socially ridiculed during periods of stability should become such useful attributes during protracted crises. Expressive leaders appear to exhibit deviations of character that become real strengths for creating emotionalized political relations. It might even be suggested that the expressive leader who needs to be loved becomes more sensitive to his surroundings and recognizes the latent problems of society. At the same time, his need for approval leads him to found a new community, increasing integration and cohesiveness as one approach to solving the problems he identifies.[46]

In order to understand the expressive functions that leaders can perform for followers, we should probably review the basic outlines of the psycho-analytic theory of personality. In psychoanalytic theory, there are three agencies of the psychic apparatus—the ego, superego, and id. In the most basic sense, the ego is that part of the personality each of us experiences as "me." Together with the superego, it regulates the instinctual drives that originate in the unconscious self, or id. The id is the amoral seeker of pleasure, while the ego and superego are the repositories of civilization that repress the id and channel drives into socially acceptable patterns.[47] The id says "yes"; the ego says "maybe"; and the superego says "no." Here, the ego's task is to mediate between the opposing tendencies of the id and superego.

The superego develops out of the ego in the maturation process, as societal values and socially sanctioned goals develop an independent power to influence the ego. Functional differentiation within the superego creates two fairly autonomous units of direction—the conscience and the ego-ideal. As we are well aware, the conscience is the internalized moral structure of society or, at least, that part of society that we experience in the develop-mental process. On the other hand, the ego-ideal is a behavior model that encompasses a set of goals that the ego must attempt to reach. Both the conscience and ego-ideal guide the ego in its choice of alternative forms of action.

When the conscience is well developed, when it incorporates a large number of rules and severe accompanying penalties, it can actually dominate the ego, producing a Puritan conformist, much like the authoritarian per-sonality. Most often, however, the ego maintains a degree of autonomy and rebelliousness. In fact, the source of guilt is the ego's failure to follow the orders of the conscience. The sense of guilt one feels is based, says Sigmund Freud, on the tension that develops when the ego is criticized by the con-science.[48] But when the ego falls short of goals residing in the ego-ideal the feeling one experiences may not be guilt but rather ego-deflation, the feeling of personal failure.

From Freud's perspective, the "healthy" personality is one in which the ego is the governing agency. Neither the id nor the superego incessantly dominates it. If the ego is weak, however, it can be constantly harangued by one of the other agencies. When the id dominates, anti-social patterns of behavior can emerge, leading to the free expression of aggressive drives, for example. In cases in which the superego is the governing agency, rigid ideologies can develop that essentially tyrannize the ego into submission.

At times, the conscience can even undergo changes that provide moral justification for aggressive behavior, a condition I will examine later. It is important to point out that the increasing strains on the personality that accompany rapid social change alter the equilibrium among the three agencies of the psychic apparatus. These changes can make the personality of the follower receptive to expressive overtures from leadership, if indeed it had not already been prepared by social strains in the family that exist in relatively stable times. The first of the expressive functions of leadership that I will discuss is related to different states of balance achieved within the follower's personality, while the second function solves an existential crisis for the follower.

Ego-support Function—The basic sources of ego weakness have to be explored before it is possible to understand how expressive leaders provide support for the follower's ego. In this context, Hadley Cantril has enumerated four sources of ego discontent, each of which diminishes the individual's feeling of self-regard.[19] (I have reduced the number of categories to three.) These categories can be used to examine the ego weaknesses of both leader and follower, although extreme ego discontent within the leader's personality is not a necessary condition for the development of the expressive relationship. A follower suffering from ego discontent can receive ego support from a leader whose personality would be judged "healthy" in psychoanalytic terms. The most interesting cases, however, are those in which both leader and follower possess weak egos, dominated in large measure by one or both of the other agencies of the psychic structure. In such a relationship, the expressive bond often becomes quite strong and both leader and follower can become dependent on its persistence. The expressive relationship between Hitler and Goebbels was of this kind, as I will try to show within Cantril's classification scheme.

According to Cantril, *the first type of ego discontent arises from the discrepancy between an individual's performance and his aspirations.* To put it another way, ego discontent is partially a function of the distance between the capabilities of the ego and the goals of the ego-ideal. If the distance is slight, the individual experiences periodic moods, but if the distance is great there can be prolonged periods of depression bordering on thoughts of self-destruction. Under these circumstances, expressive leaders can provide support for the follower's ego by improving his performance capabilities, by leading him to believe that he has come closer to his goals than he had thought, or by encouraging him to reappraise his goals in a way that would make them more realistic. A follower suffering from feelings of inadequacy of this type is especially apt to be seduced by praise and flattery, just as the expressive leader who feels personally inadequate can thrive on the follower's deferential statements and behaviors. It is in this context that we can begin to analyze the strong expressive relationship that emerged between Goebbels and Hitler.

Goebbels' life history shows considerable discrepancy between his goals and actual achievements, especially before his rise to prominence within the Nazi hierarchy. The signs of discrepancy appear quite early in his life. At the age of seven he underwent surgery for a bone disease that left him badly crippled in one leg. This deformity, in combination with his frail, stoop-shouldered frame, made it impossible for him to enter into games that required physical prowess. Instead, he withdrew from contact with his playmates into a life of isolation, where books assumed central importance as reliefs from boredom. He developed a quarrelsome disposition in the process and consequently found it increasingly difficult to develop positive relations with anyone but his immediate family. His inability to develop close friendships stemmed from his contempt for people and the human race. This attitude is reflected in his statement: "How horrible: no sooner do I spend three whole days with someone than I no longer like him, and if it is a whole week I loathe him like the plague."[50] Apparently, these were feelings that others felt toward him as well, for he was never very well liked.

The goals incorporated into Goebbels' ego-ideal seemed quite divorced from the reality of his physical and personal limitations. The behavior model that he hoped to reach included heroic, intellectual, and romantic components. He dreamed of making his mark on history in the tradition of Carlyle's "hero" or Nietzsche's "superman." First he aspired to make his impact on history through a military career, then as a man of letters. In his private life, one of his goals was to succeed with women, which he did to some extent. But none of these goals were reached as Goebbels envisioned them, except possibly the literary fame that he was able to manufacture in his position as Nazi Minister of Propaganda.

A military career was impossible, given his physical handicap. Yet, at the age of seventeen he went for his induction examination, hoping that his physical problems would make no difference to the army. The doctor took one look at him and rejected him without even bothering with the examination. This experience had a traumatic impact on him. Humiliated, he went home and locked himself in his room. "For a whole day and night," we are told, "he sobbed like a small child. His mother could do nothing with him. For two days he would speak to no one."[51] His failure to fulfill his military aspirations led Goebbels to concentrate more and more of his time on studying and writing.

His new goal was to achieve fame as a literary figure. He wrote articles, plays, novels, and poems with the hope that some would be published and his genius recognized. But his work was not well received; everything he sent to the publishers was rejected. Later, when his anti-Semitic feelings emerged, he rationalized this failure using the Jew as a scapegoat. "As manuscript after manuscript came back from the publishing houses Goebbels became convinced that unless you were a Jew . . . you could get nowhere in literature, the theatre, films or journalism."[52] Many of these works, which were considered mediocre by the literary critics, would be published when Goebbels achieved political power. However, the fact that his works are literary curiosities rather than enduring masterpieces demonstrates that he fell short of his goal in an objective sense. But it appears that he believed he had achieved his goal when his work went into print during his tenure as Minister. This may help to explain why his later diaries are more descriptions of events rather than introspections on the self: He may have achieved sufficient ego strength to allow him to concentrate on other things besides his own problems.

Goebbel's romantic ventures also fell short of his ideal. Although affairs developed, he was an impossible lover, owing to the extremes of his temperament. "At one moment he was carefree and exuberant, a charming and witty companion. Then as suddenly he would change and become possessed by his suicidal depression."[53] Consequently, even his romantic aspirations did not work out as planned. In a letter to one of his female companions Goebbels raised three questions that provide some insight into the source of discontent in his life: "Is there no solace in this world of chaos and madness? Why then do I suffer so? Because I expected too much of this world?"[54] Or, could we ask, did he expect too much from himself?

Three excesses that became the chief marks of his character developed in Goebbel's ego. He grew intensely mistrustful of others, preferred isolation to interaction, and was driven by a strong need to be loved as well as recognized as a genius. In order to compensate for his feelings of rejection, he developed an exterior that exuded confidence, arrogance, and pride. In private, however, his feelings of inadequacy produced deep depressions and thoughts of suicide. He was an incurable hypochondriac, partly because he found solace in statements by others that he would live a long life. And he was overly sensitive to the public jokes that developed about him.[55] It is understandable why he was so deeply influenced by those who praised his work and flattered him in other ways. In fact, his relationship to Hitler was influenced quite strongly by flattery, for the Füehrer constantly lent support to Goebbels' ego, gratifying the Minister's compulsive need to be loved and to feel important. "The secret of Goebbels is always that he only loved those who openly and emphatically loved him. Hitler was astute enough to discover and exploit this weakness. . . ."[56]

Goebbels' strong emotional attachment to Hitler is well known. His early diaries are marked by references to his love for Hitler and to his belief in Hitler's god-like qualities. On one occasion he could say: "I so look forward to Hitler's visit. I venerate and love him."[57] And a few days later, after one of the Füehrer's speeches, he wrote: "He is a genius. The natural, creative instrument of a fate determined by God."[58] But even for Goebbels there were periods of doubt in Hitler's ability. In fact, these doubts seemed to increase in direct relation to the period of time that elapsed between their meetings. Goebbels' Press Officer in the Ministry of Propaganda noted in his own diary:

Whenever Goebbels goes to headquarters he starts off full of distrust of the
Füehrer's genius, full of irritation, criticism and hard words. Each time he is
determined to tell Hitler just what he thinks. What happens in their talks I don't
know, but every time that Goebbels returns from these visits he is full of
admiration for the Füehrer and exudes an optimism which infects us all.[59]

What did Hitler say in those meetings that purged Goebbels of his doubts
and criticisms? We can infer from Goebbels' diaries that Hitler infected him
with renewed faith by flattery, praise, and affection. A sample of Goebbels'
diary entries after face-to-face contacts with Hitler illustrates this point very
well. "Hitler sees and embraces me," he reports on one occasion. "He gives
me much praise. I believe he has taken me to his heart like no one else."[60]
On another day he says: "He [Hitler] can't find enough words of praise for
me in front of all the others. . . . He cares for me."[61] After a period of doubt
and a meeting with Hitler, Goebbels' enthusiasm is conveyed in his words:
"A star shines leading me from deep misery! I am his to the end. My last
doubts have disappeared." Why? In the same entry he gives us the answer:
"He spoils me like a child."[62]

There is a sense in which the expressive relationship between Goebbels
and Hitler became symbiotic. Both men suffered from strong feelings of
inadequacy. And both undoubtedly received ego support from the exchange
of praise, flattery, and affection that permeated their face-to-face contacts.
Hitler himself seems to have suffered from the discrepancy between goals
and achievements before his rise to power. As a young man, "he was not
only desperately anxious to impress people but was full of ideas for making
his fortune and fame . . . but he was incapable of the application and hard
work needed to carry out his projects."[63] Early failures in life, such as his
inability to gain admission into the Vienna Academy of Arts, created personal problems strikingly similar to those of Goebbels. Hitler is described
as intensely ambitious, resentful of those who disagreed with him, aggressive
against minorities, and egotistical. "His vanity was inappeasable, and the
most fulsome flattery was received as no more than his due."[64]

Goebbels' adulation of Hitler must have had the same ego-supportive
effect for Hitler's personality as Goebbels himself received from the Füehrer's attention. In this context, Hitler's expressive style of leadership should
be viewed not solely as a calculated effort to play on the weaknesses of
others. But rather it should be seen as a form of communication that gave
followers clues about how they should relate to him in expressive ways. For
example, his praise of Goebbels became a communication that demanded
reciprocal responses. In a symbiotic way, the two leaders exchanged the
appropriate statements of praise, flattery, and affection that strengthened
their egos and renewed their self-confidence.

The second source of ego discontent, according to Cantril, *arises from the
improper recognition of one's status.* The feeling is that society has not shown
proper deference to one's position. For example, displaced intellectuals or

striving artists who have failed to gain public favor are likely to experience this feeling in varying degrees. Here, the expressive leader performs the ego-support function by explaining the structural reasons for one's failure to gain proper recognition. Or, if the expressive leader is in power, he can redefine standards in such a way that the work of the unrecognized gains ascendency. By extending honors to those writers with the correct political philosophies, for example, Hitler was able to give Goebbels the recognition that he had been denied as a struggling intellectual.

In a broader context, Hitler also attempted to redefine the respective statuses of different social classes. The most obvious effort in this direction was the development of the Aryan myth. In Cantril's view, "the racial myth served its purpose. It restored the self-esteem, the status of the people."[65] Once in power, he sought to raise the level of esteem of two important social sectors—farmers and workers, whose status had declined with the rise of industrialization. He tried to overcome this status discrepancy by emphasizing the equality of all those who could be classified as members of the German race. A campaign for equalitarianism was begun that was

> . . . intended not so much to change existing class relations, a function of profession and education, as to change status, the self-image, the state of mind. The employer was to remain an employer, and the worker a worker. But these were intended to be occupational designations and nothing more. Under National Socialism the basic determinant of status was common membership in the German people or variously the German "race," not class, education, or occupation.[66]

Tension between one's drives and value orientation is the third source of ego discontent. Theoretically, this is the conflict between the id and the conscience, in which the ego is threatened when it fails to successfully mediate the conflict between these opposing tendencies. For example, these threats to the ego, which become apparent as anxieties, can occur when an individual is angry at another person but is restrained by a conscience that forbids aggressive behavior. If tensions of this type exist in the follower's personality, the expressive leader can reduce the resulting ego discontent in three basic ways: (1) he can reestablish the supremacy of the conscience by reaffirming a follower's commitment to the existing moral code, (2) he can attempt to strengthen the follower's ego so it can more successfully mediate conflict among the other agencies, or, (3) he can change the moral structure of the follower's conscience in a way that allows for the freer reign of the id. Hitler's expressive style emphasized the latter course of action, for he sought to unleash the repressed antagonisms of his followers by arguing that it was morally right for the strongest to dominate. He offered a new moral code (although it was fused with traditional aspects of German political culture) that legitimized aggression against the Jews and against neighboring nations.

The new Hitlerian ethic, which respected the expression of hatred as much as it did obedience to leadership, diminished the tension within Goebbels' personality by providing concrete objects toward which he could vent his general hostilities. Initially, Goebbels was not anti-Semitic. On the contrary, as a youth his favorite professor had been a Jew, as was his family lawyer. However, as his anxieties over failure increased, the anti-Semitic themes in Hitler's arguments began to penetrate and change Goebbels' moral structure. Ultimately, he found the Jew to be a convenient scapegoat and his hatred grew in intensity through the years as he watched Nazi fortunes fade. Once his id gained dominance over his religious training, it took command with a passion. "Goebbels' hatred of the Jews is fanatical," his Press Officer wrote on August 16, 1943. "Everything Jewish is to him like a red rag to a bull. The hatred is so strong that he becomes incapable of even recognizing facts when he has to deal with them."[67] But his wrath was directed toward other groups besides Jews, as he sought to locate other agents that could be blamed for problems. One such group was the Catholic Church, which had fought against the nazification of German society. And he appeared to have a solution for dealing with the Church that seemed to conform to the final solution to the Jewish question:

> It's a dirty, low thing for the Catholic Church to continue its subversive activity in every way possible and now even to extend its propaganda to Protestant children evacuated from regions threatened by air raids. Next to the Jews these politico-divines are about the most loathsome riffraff that we are still sheltering in the Reich. The time will come after the war for an over-all solution of this problem.[68]

Much like Hitler, Goebbels was quite willing to blame failures on those who opposed the state and his leadership. Because this hostility was socially sanctioned and the new moral code had been incorporated into his conscience, he could hate openly without feelings of guilt. He could talk about killing Jews with the same detachment as one would discuss the extermination of lice: "You must either stigmatize them with a yellow star, or put them in concentration camps, or shoot them, or else let them saturate all public life with corruption, especially during a war. There is no halfway measure."[69]

There are two ways of looking at Hitler's efforts to solve similar tensions in his personality through the expressive relationship. One could argue that the positive response of followers to Hitler's legitimization of aggression against the Jews provided him with a rationalization for acting out his own aggressive drives. "If my followers approve," the expressive leader thinks, "then it must be right." But the expressive leader can also be deluded by followers, who know that their status and authority in an organization is dependent on their willingness to praise the leader and to conform to his initiatives, however aggressive they might be. In such circumstances, it is the structure of the situation that contributes to the reduction of the expressive leader's ego discontent. Hans Gerth's analysis of the Nazi party organization illuminates this point very well.

Within the Nazi party, says Gerth, party members who were commissioned by Hitler became part of an "inner circle." Because Hitler's favor was the sole determining factor for placement in this "circle," the way to gain entrance was to conform righteously to his position and flatter him. Once included in the "circle," each lieutenant had to guard persistently against the loss of Hitler's favor and confidence. To preserve their status they were "compelled continually to demonstrate their unswerving belief in the leader's charisma. Even though they might not actually believe in Hitler's abilities, this necessity makes for the exuberant praise and eulogy of the leader's actual or imputed virtues and qualities."[70] And the weaker a member's position becomes, "the more ardently will he emphasize his belief in the righteousness of the leader."[71]

This is an interesting case since the nature of the social structure legitimizes a wide range of behavior for the expressive leader. In the Nazi party, it encouraged Hitler's personality to achieve its greatest excesses. And because they were approved by those around him, he could recommend aggressive behavior without feeling guilty. It was only in the latter months of his rule that Hitler had to face his leadership failures, since even those around him could not entirely overlook the setbacks in the war effort. Then Hitler did try to insulate himself from his followers (who were becoming increasingly critical of his leadership) and he avoided reading depressing news of the war. "Hitler has a pathetic fear of being seen in public and avoids meeting everybody," Goebbels' aide wrote in his diary. "He is suffering acutely from persecution mania. He never goes for a walk, and for days at a time hardly leaves the concrete shelter in the headquarters at Rastenburg."[72] He would not visit the towns devastated by allied bombing attacks, even at Goebbels' suggestion. Furthermore, he did not read the reports of the destruction.[73] It is ironic that both Hitler and Goebbels failed in the war for the same reasons that they had failed throughout their lives. Both had persistently set goals for themselves that neither could reach.

In summary, the effective performance of the ego-support function by leadership reduces the tension within the personality of the follower by helping him resolve the conflicts between the three psychic agencies. Expressive leaders may be able to provide effective rationalizations for failure or change the follower's goals, satisfying the demands of the follower's conscience and leading to a heightened feeling of self-esteem. In addition, the moral structure of the follower's superego may be changed by the leader, such that drives originating in the id can be expressed openly without the ego's suffering reprisals from the conscience. In the latter case, the expressive leader reduces the level of guilt experienced by the follower. By raising the follower's level of self-esteem and by reducing his sense of guilt, the expressive leader is better able to shape his pattern of behavior.

Inspirational Function—Some leaders are able to speak of human problems (the basic problems of existence) in a way that produces integrative consequences for their social groups. Instead of concentrating entirely on short-range goals that can create divisiveness, these leaders focus the follower's attention on general goals that are sometimes projections into a utopian future. By drawing attention to the future, the leader hopes to develop bonds between followers that are sufficiently strong to overcome divergent interests and to effect a broad consensus on a wide range of issues. Actually, utopian thought provides two positive integrative consequences: It (1) identifies areas of common interest by encouraging agreement about a desirable future state and (2) offers followers a degree of creative involvement by allowing them the opportunity to structure the shape of the future in their minds and to act on that mental picture in concrete circumstances. Creative leaders often transmit utopian images of the future that are not only attractive to many of their followers but are sufficiently compelling to overcome the meaninglessness of their existence by instilling new purpose to life and to political action. Leaders who (1) provide meaning to life and (2) impart purpose to action and suffering produce an inspirational relationship with their followers, a relationship I will distinguish analytically from charisma in a later chapter.

That followers can be activated by inspirational leaders who give meaning to life is tentatively substantiated in Viktor E. Frankl's pioneering work in existential psychology, *Man's Search for Meaning: An Introduction to Logotherapy*. Frankl's logotherapeutic method emphasizes man's need for meaning as the primary motivational force within the personality, in contrast to the Freudian school's emphasis on man's will to pleasure or the Adlerian school's concern with man's will to power. Unlike Freud and Adler, Frankl rejects the notion that man's behavior is fully conditioned and determined. Rather, it is his view that man is able to choose and shape what he is to become. "In other words," Frankl argues, "man is ultimately self-determining. Man does not simply exist, but always decides what his existence will be, what he will become in the next moment."[74] Unlike psychoanalysis, which attempts to understand behavior in terms of drives and instincts or as an adjustment to a societal milieu, logotherapy considers man as a being attempting to find meaning in life. In Frankl's terms:

> Logotherapy regards its assignment as that of assisting the patient to find meaning in his life. Inasmuch as logotherapy makes him aware of the hidden *logos* [meaning] of his existence, it is an analytical process. To this extent, logotherapy resembles psychoanalysis. However, in logotherapy's attempt to make something conscious again it does not restrict its activity to *instinctual* facts within the individual's unconscious, but also cares for *spiritual* realities such as the potential meaning of his existence to be fulfilled, as well as his will to meaning.[75]

Many conflicts within the personality are not necessarily neurotic, the author continues. In fact, some degree of conflict within the personality is not only normal but healthy. Normal personalities, in which the ego is the governing agency of the psychic apparatus, experience what he calls "existential frustration," a condition produced by the loss of meaning in life. In this sense, "a man's concern, even his despair, over the worthwhileness of life is a *spiritual distress* but by no means a *mental disease.*"[76] The loss of meaning, termed the "existential vacuum," is manifest in fits of boredom, which are most clearly seen in "Sunday neurosis," a "depression which afflicts people who become aware of the lack of content in their lives when the rush of the busy week is over. . . ."[77] In Frankl's view prolonged consciousness of this existential void can lead to suicide.

According to Frankl, there are three ways to find meaning in life: (1) "by doing a deed"; (2) by experiencing something, for example, an aesthetic appreciation of nature, culture, or art and by experiencing someone in love; and (3) through suffering. Finding meaning through deed and suffering are important to this study because both fall within the range of follower motives in accepting the initiatives of leaders, especially rebel leaders.

Action in behalf of some cause relieves existential boredom and renews the actor's sense of direction and purpose. The leader who constructs and communicates utopian appeals might very well be offering "normal" personalities new options for meaningful action. At the same time, social movements tend to emphasize the necessity and meaning of suffering. This is especially true in religious or quasi-religious movements wherein suffering is given purpose by its close association with purification of the soul. Suffering for a cause tests the human spirit and brings it to a high state of spiritual development. It is one of the expressive tasks of leadership to demonstrate that suffering is meaningful in some way; that it has purpose for an individual. "In accepting this challenge to suffer bravely," Frankl suggests, "life has a meaning up to the last moment, and it retains this meaning literally to the end."[78]

Leadership can mobilize support for its initiatives by imparting meaning to action or suffering, if we assume Frankl's point of view. To endow action or suffering with meaning requires an ability to transmit messages that convey meanings about life that followers can understand and share with the leader. A leader who is able to uplift a following does so not simply by what he says but by what he communicates nonverbally about himself. Erving Goffman would say that the leader "gives off" an expression of himself through the many activities he undertakes. It is not simply what the leader says but what he is in the mind of the follower.[79] Through his example, as much as his word, the inspirational leader shows others how to relate to the problems of life that are the sources of anxiety. In recent American history, John F. Kennedy, Martin Luther King, Jr., and Malcolm X were apparently able to "give off" a set of expressions that inspired followers to act as they acted. Through the impression left by the full range of their activities, these leaders became examples that followers emulated. Lenin seemed to have had a similar impact on his followers, owing to the impression he conveyed as one who was courageous, intelligent, and modest. Gandhi is still another leader who inspired others to follow the path of nonviolence by his personal example.

When a single leader assumes the inspirational role, disintegrative tendencies can result when he dies. In order to cope with these tendencies, new leadership can attempt to transform the deceased inspirational leader into an integrative symbol, using his person, life, and struggle as a reminder of the future goals of a society or political movement. His life will become an example to others that suffering, including death for a cause, is not without purpose. The use of Lenin as an integrative symbol in the Soviet system appears to be a clear effort to remind followers of the utopian goals of the October revolution and the positive value of suffering in achieving those goals. In the American civil rights struggle, a similar role was bestowed upon Martin Luther King, Jr., after his death. The same could be said for Malcolm X, who has been used by various Black nationalist groups as a symbol of protest. It appears that leaders who performed the inspirational function in life can continue to do so after death, thus providing expressive support for new leaders who must carry on the instrumental tasks of a political system or movement.

In addition to developing an analytic framework for studying leadership, I have tried to convey to the reader the importance of leadership structures in social change processes. In the latter case, it is especially necessary to recognize that rebel leaders are not produced miraculously from heaven, as Thomas Carlyle would have us believe, but emerge when ruling leaders perform their functions inadequately. Failing to perform the tasks that make effective coordination possible paves the way for a decline in the general capabilities of the political system. The responsive capability is especially crucial, since the loss of sensitivity to the causes of protest can lead ruling leaders to put their faith in the regulation of dissent as a substitute for problem-solving.

Notes

1. Amitai Etzioni, "Dual Leadership in Complex Organizations," *American Sociological Review,* 30 (October, 1965), p. 689.

2. *Ibid.,* p. 692.

3. *Ibid.,* p. 695.

4. *Ibid.,* p. 696.

5. Joseph R. Gusfield, "Functional Areas of Leadership in Social Movements," *Sociological Quarterly,* 7 (Spring, 1966), pp. 138–139.

6. *Ibid.,* pp. 140–141.

7. The importance of social bonds in creating a strong fighting unit is one example of what I mean. Cf. Edward Shils and Morris Janowitz, "Cohesion and Disintegration in the Wehrmacht in World War II," *Public Opinion Quarterly,* 12 (1948), pp. 280–315.

8. Chester Barnard, *The Functions of the Executive* (Cambridge, Mass.: Harvard University Press, 1962), p. 233. William C. Schutz has assumed a somewhat narrower base for this function: "The establishment and clarification of the hierarchy of group goals and values" is considered a leadership function in conflict-free group spheres. Cf. "The Ego, FIRO Theory and the Leader as Completer," in Luigi Petrullo and Bernard Bass (eds.), *Leadership and Interpersonal Behavior* (New York: Holt, Rinehart and Winston, 1961), p. 60.

9. Anthony Wallace, *Culture and Personality* (New York: Random House, 1961), p. 148.

10. N. Lenin, *What Is To Be Done?* (New York: International Publishers, 1929), p. 116.

11. Philip Selznick, *Leadership in Administration* (Evanston, Ill.: Row, Peterson, and Co., 1957), p. 62.

12. Alfred Kuhn, *The Study of Society: A Unified Approach* (Homewood, Ill.: Dorscy Press, 1963), p. 181.

13. Herbert A. Simon, *Administrative Behavior* (New York: Macmillan, 1961), pp. 154–155.

14. Richard Fagen, *Politics and Communication* (Boston: Little, Brown, 1966), p. 116.

15. *Ibid.,* p. 115.

16. *Ibid.,* p. 116.

17. Simon, *op. cit.,* pp. 157–162.

18. Robert A. Dahl, "Decision Making in a Democracy: The Role of the Supreme Court as a National Policy-Maker," *Journal of Public Law,* 6 (1958), pp. 279–295.

19. Robert A. Dahl, *Who Governs?* (New Haven: Yale University Press, 1961).

20. Gabriel Almond and Sidney Verba, *The Civic Culture* (Princeton: Princeton University Press, 1963), p. 180.

21. For some interesting insights bearing on this point, cf. Herbert McClosky, Paul J. Hoffman, and Rosemary O'Hara, "Issue Conflict and Consensus among Party Leaders and Followers," *American Political Science Review,* 54 (June, 1960), pp. 426–427.

22. Fred I. Greenstein, *The American Party System and the American People* (Englewood Cliffs: Prentice-Hall, 1963), p. 55.

23. R. S. Rattray, *Ashanti Law and the Constitution* (London: Oxford University Press, 1929), p. 82.

24. Simon, *op. cit.,* p. 164.

25. Richard Neustadt, *Presidential Power* (New York: John Wiley & Sons, 1962), p. 21.

26. Wallace, *op. cit.,* p. 149.

27. Gusfield, *op. cit.,* p. 141.

28. Lenin, *op. cit.,* p. 149.

29. Quoted in Allan Bullock, *Hitler: A Study in Tyranny* (New York: Bantam Books, 1958), p. 31.

30. Kurt Lewin, "Group Decision and Social Change," in Guy E. Swanson, Theodore Newcomb, and Eugene L. Hartley (eds.), *Readings in Social Psychology* (New York: Henry Holt, 1952).

31. Thornton B. Roby, "The Executive Function in Small Groups," in Petrullo and Bass (eds.), *op. cit.,* p. 131.

32. Daniel Katz and Paul F. Lazarsfeld, *Personal Influence* (New York: Free Press, 1955).

33. Clinton Rossiter, *The American Presidency* (New York: New American Library, 1956), p. 24.

34. N. N. Sukhanov, *The Russian Revolution 1917,* Vol. 1 (New York: Harper, 1962), pp. 41–42.

35. Robert A. Dahl, "The Concept of Power," *Behavioral Scientist,* 2 (1957), p. 203.

36. Robert A. Dahl, *Modern Political Analysis* (Englewood Cliffs: Prentice-Hall, 1963), p. 50.

37. Robert Thornton makes the power-relevant aspects of violence very clear in his illuminating essay, "Terror as a Weapon of Political Agitation," in Harry Eckstein (ed.), *Internal War* (New York: Free Press, 1964), pp. 71–99.

38. The subjective probability of achieving the goal, that is, the belief that the objective will be easily reached, will undoubtedly make coercion less likely. Coercion may also be sanctioned by followers who see force as a legitimate response to an organizational problem. On the latter point, cf. John R. P. French, Jr., and Bertham Raven, "The Bases of Social Power," in Dorwin Cartwright (ed.), *Studies in Social Power* (Ann Arbor: Research Center for Group Dynamics, 1959), pp. 150–162.

39. Neustadt, *op. cit.,* pp. 28–29.

40. *Ibid.,* p. 10.

41. K. A. Busia, *The Position of the Chief in the Modern Political System of Ashanti* (London: Oxford University Press, 1958), pp. 23–39.

42. In this respect, it is illuminating to compare Hannah Arendt's discussion of totalitarianism with Elie Cohen's account of behavioral patterns in the concentration camp. Cf., respectively, *Origins of Totalitarianism* (New York: Harcourt, Brace, 1951) and *Human Behavior in the Concentration Camp* (New York: Grosset and Dunlap, 1953).

43. Chester Barnard has in fact suggested that "every organization to survive must deliberately attend to the maintenance and growth of its authority to do things necessary for coordination, effectiveness, and efficiency." This includes "the maintenance of morale, the maintenance of the scheme of inducements, the maintenance of schemes of deterrents, supervision and control, inspection, education and training." *Op. cit.,* pp. 230–231.

44. This is an argument made by Samuel Krislov in his *The Supreme Court in the Political Process* (New York: Macmillan, 1965).

45. Erik Erikson, *Childhood and Society* (New York: W. W. Norton, 1963), p. 330.

46. I do not want to leave the impression that followers in mass movements are basically weak personalities who are restabilized by their commitments to leadership and the movement. Nor do I want the reader to conclude that all rebel

leaders operate on the fringes of madness, for Hitler was the exception rather than the rule. Where a leader and follower relate to each other persistently in expressive ways, that is on a strong emotional basis, we should suspect that an important reason for the relation is that psychological needs are being satisfied for both leader and follower. But, at the same time, we should be careful not to assume that these are the only motives for committing oneself to leadership or that they are equally powerful motives for all who follow.

47. Sigmund Freud, *Civilization and Its Discontents* (New York: W. W. Norton, 1961).

48. Sigmund Freud, *The Ego and the Id* (New York: W. W. Norton, 1960), pp. 40–41.

49. Hadley Cantril, *The Psychology of Social Movements* (New York: John Wiley & Sons, 1963), pp. 48–50. The need for self-esteem, it should be recalled, is one of the basic human needs within Maslow's hierarchy of needs. In terms of tension theory, the expressive leader who gives support to the follower's ego reduces tension within the follower's personality, which is experienced as a reduction of anxiety.

50. Paul Joseph Goebbels, *The Early Goebbels Diaries: 1925–1926,* Helmut Heiber (ed.) (New York: Praeger, 1962), p. 27 (August 25, 1925).

51. Roger Manvell and Heinrich Fraenkel, *Doctor Goebbels: His Life and Death* (London: Heinemann, 1960), p. 5.

52. *Ibid.,* p. 34.

53. *Ibid.,* p. 36.

54. *Ibid.,* p. 35.

55. Rudolf Semmler, *Goebbels: The Man Next to Hitler* (London: Westhouse, 1947), pp. 85, 151. Semmler was Goebbels' chief Press Officer and was in a position to observe the private and public life of the Minister of Propaganda.

56. Manvell and Fraenkel, *op. cit.,* p. 54.

57. Goebbels, *op. cit.,* p. 90 (June 12, 1925),

58. *Ibid.,* p. 100 (July 24, 1925).

59. Semmler, *op. cit.,* p. 128.

60. Goebbels, *op. cit.,* p. 80 (April 19, 1926).

61. *Ibid.,* p. 87 (May 24, 1926).

62. *Ibid.,* p. 101 (July 25, 1926).

63. Bullock, *op. cit.,* p. 9.

64. *Ibid.,* p. 168.

65. Cantril, *op. cit.,* p. 240.

66. David Schoenbaum, *Hitler's Social Revolution* (Garden City, New York: Doubleday, 1967), p. 55.

67. Semmler, *op. cit.,* p. 98.

68. Paul Joseph Goebbels, *The Goebbels Diaries, 1942–1943,* Louis P. Lochner (ed.) (Garden City, New York: Doubleday, 1948), p. 146 (March 26, 1942).

69. *Ibid.,* p. 113 (March 6, 1942).

70. Hans Gerth, "The Nazi Party: Its Leadership and Composition," *American Journal of Sociology,* 45 (January, 1940), p. 521.

71. *Ibid.,* p. 522.

72. Semmler, *op. cit.,* p. 150 (September 24, 1944).

73. *Ibid.,* p. 177.

74. Viktor E. Frankl, *Man's Search for Meaning: An Introduction to Logotherapy* (New York: Washington Square Press, 1959), p. 206.

75. *Ibid.*, p. 163.

76. *Ibid.* Frankl cites the case of an American diplomat who had come to him for treatment after being told for five years by a psychoanalyst that his anxiety stemmed from an unconscious hatred of his father that was expressed in hostile feelings against the U.S. government and his superiors on the job. After logotherapeutic sessions, Frankl concluded that this man's will to meaning had been impaired by a vocation that had no purpose for him. Upon Frankl's recommendation, the diplomat began a new professional career. Logotherapy succeeded in confronting him with and reorienting him toward the meaning of his life. As soon as the patient changed occupations, he found instant relief from his persistent anxiety.

77. *Ibid.*, p. 169.

78. *Ibid.*, p. 181. The following case history is an excellent example of the way logotherapy may redirect an individual's life by giving meaning to suffering: "Once, an elderly general practitioner consulted me because of his severe depression. He could not overcome the loss of his wife who had died two years before and whom he had loved above all else. Now how could I help him? What should I tell him? Well, I refrained from telling him anything, but instead confronted him with the question, 'What would have happened, Doctor, if you had died first, and your wife would have had to survive you?' 'Oh,' he said, 'for her this would have been terrible; how she would have suffered.' Whereupon I replied, 'You see, Doctor, such a suffering has been spared her, and it is you who have spared her this suffering; but now, you have to pay for it by surviving and mourning her.' He said no word but shook my hand and calmly left my office."

79. Erving Goffman, *The Presentation of Self in Everyday Life* (Garden City, New York: Doubleday, 1959), p. 2.

3 □ DETERMINANTS OF COMMITMENT

□   When ruling leaders fail in their efforts to relieve structural strain, the fortunes of rebel leaders often improve. It is during such periods that ruling and rebel leaders begin to compete openly for the support of the uncommitted and ambivalent masses. In this respect, Peter Amann has argued quite simply that rebel leaders succeed in making revolutions when the public's habit of obedience to the old regime is broken and the resulting shift in the balance of power makes it impossible for the ruling elite to defend itself from attack.[1] To put it another way: Ruling leaders are unable to maintain the commitment of formerly dependable allies and cannot prevent the rebel leader from mobilizing new converts. As the number of resources available to ruling leaders declines, there is a corresponding reduction in the political system's ability to serve. In such circumstances, only those benefiting from the persistence of the regime can be depended on to defend it in an open struggle. These were essentially the conditions under which the French monarchy collapsed. For, according to Alexis de Tocqueville, by diminishing the number of goods and services allocated to the aristocracy, the monarchy lost the support of a sizable part of the aristocratic class. Without the ability to mobilize goods from this sector of society, the regime's capacity to distribute goods and regulate behavior was impaired.[2] Why do ruling leaders fail to maintain the commitments of important groups and individuals? Equally important, how do rebel organizations and leaders encourage disaffection from the regime and how do they mobilize those affected by structural strain for participation in a revolutionary organization? These are questions I would like to consider in this chapter. First, however, it is important to offer an operational definition of "commitment," which will become the basis for developing a theory of commitment formation and retention.

The Concept of Commitment

Only recently has the concept of commitment received systematic examination. One explanation for the lack of interest in the concept is that scholars have tended to assume that commitments, especially to mass movements, were, on the whole, products of psychological forces. What was needed was a conception of commitment that was more sociological and more operational. Howard Becker has developed just such a conception in his essay, "Notes on the Concept of Commitment." Instead of viewing a commitment as an affective attachment, such as "devotion" or "love," Becker defines a commitment simply as a "consistent line of activity."[3] Here the notion of consistency is the crucial factor, for it forces one's attention to the social and psychological conditions that encourage the follower to accept and act on a rebel leader's initiatives in a consistent way. But, while the notion of consistency is useful, it alone cannot illuminate the differences in the relative strength or intensity of commitments.

Rosabeth Kanter has developed a procedure for gauging the relative intensity of a commitment in her work on utopian communities. She distinguishes three social system axes of commitment: continuance (orientation toward membership in an organization), cohesion (orientation to the social group), and control (orientation to norms and authority). These categories are combined with the cognitive (knowledge), cathectic (feeling), and evaluative (judgment) sectors of the personality as developed by Talcott Parsons and Edward Shils in their work, *Toward A General Theory of Action.* Three types of commitment result: cognitive-continuance (in which a person complies with the requirements of his roles, aside from his feeling or judgment about them), cathectic-cohesion (wherein the member develops a feeling of attachment to the social group), and evaluative-control (wherein the norms and authority arrangement are judged to be good by the member). To determine the extent of an individual's commitment to an organization, be it a utopian community or revolutionary cadre, one need only determine how many of the three types of commitment have formed. This approach leads Kanter to the following conceptualization of a "total" commitment.

> Groups in which members have formed cognitive-continuance commitments should manage to hold their members. Groups in which members have formed cathectic-cohesion commitments should be able to withstand threats to their existence, should have more "stick-together-ness." Groups in which members have formed evaluative-control commitments should have less deviance, challenge to authority, or ideological controversy—of course ignoring for the moment all the other diverse sources of influence on group life. Systems with all three kinds of commitment, *with total commitment,* should be more successful in their maintenance than those without.[4] (Emphasis added.)

Considering a "total" commitment in this way is useful because it locates the sectors of an organization where one could usefully look for the committed. But it is also incomplete, because the author has minimized the importance of consistency as it pertains to the identification of the committed. To argue that one develops a cognitive-continuance commitment because he accepts the requirements of his roles is to overlook the fact that role-playing normally creates infractions of the rules, partly because roles are conflicting in varying degrees. It is important to consider the consistency with which a member of an organization meets the requirements of the many roles he must play. Then, we should wonder what importance different role patterns assume in the creation of consistent behavior.

To suggest that a cathectic-cohesion commitment exists when a member shows strong feelings of support for the social group begs the same question: How consistently does he support the social group and in what circumstances does he do so? Statements of public support for an organization are not necessarily related to one's feeling of attachment. As Gerth has shown in his analysis of the Nazi party, public adoration of Hitler was often the only means of gaining entrance into the "inner circle." Consequently, public displays of affection were not reliable predictors of the real sentiments Hitler's lieutenants held about him. In this case, a more careful analysis of a lieutenant's private opinions and behavior would be necessary to determine whether his public pronouncements were the same as his private opinions. It is also clear that the strength of an individual's feeling for a leader or social group is determined by the specific actions recommended to the individual and whether or not he perceives those initiatives to be in conflict with his private interest. It is in fact one of the persuasive efforts of leaders in their mobilization capacity to convince members that what is in the interest of the group is also in their private interest. If this effort succeeds, the member who initially had a negative disposition toward the group may change his mind and end by supporting it. It has been shown, for instance, that individuals who were initially opposed to the integration of blacks into their communities changed their positions from opposition to support when they were shown by leaders that integration would benefit them materially.[5]

It is also important to consider the factor of consistency when determining the strength of the evaluative-control commitment. To avow the sanctity of the normative system is not necessarily a sound indicator of the sincerity of the advocate. The "con man" is a good case in point, for his pretended support of the norms of society is part of the game he must play in order to successfully break them. Even within a social movement, an individual's public pronouncement of loyalty to an ideology may be viewed with skepticism by core members. For instance, John Lofland and Rodney Stark discovered, in their study of a Northwest religious cult, that verbal claims of commitment to the governing ideology were considered insufficient proof of dedication. Several members of the cult who professed a strong belief in the doctrine were considered insincere by the core members. The strength of an individual's commitment tended to be gauged by how much he had invested in the organization. Those who gave their time, energy, and money were invariably seen as truly converted to the cause.[6]

While both have offered illuminating accounts of commitment, neither Becker nor Kanter offer a completely satisfactory theory of commitment because neither comes to terms with the problem of assessing the process through which commitments form and how to gauge the strength of commitments. In my view, a theory of commitment should attempt to incorporate three basic dimensions: (1) It should identify the factors that create consistency in human behavior, (2) it should explain the logical relationships between stages in a commitment process, and (3) it should take into account the reasons for differences in the intensity of commitments. An attempt will be made to meet these conditions in the following pages, even though I recognize that a theory cannot be proven at this time, owing to the scant data.

A Theory of Commitment

Organizations cannot long survive without members who are committed, who perform their tasks in a consistent fashion. As I suggested earlier, leaders utilize resources in their mobilization capacity in order to create power relationships with others who were noncompliant. When these relationships become persistent, a commitment has been formed. However, while the application of resources by leaders can create consistent lines of action for others, these are not the only influences that bear on the formation of commitments. For instance, a person can pursue an activity quite consistently because his limited experience has closed him off from other alternatives that would tempt him to try a new and conflicting course of action. Or, as Anthony Wallace argues, even when better courses of action are perceived, individuals may persist in their old ways because the prospect of a change in routine causes anxiety.[7] Therefore, a theory of commitment must be general enough to take into account numerous factors, besides power, that influence the extent of consistency.

To come to an understanding of how commitments form, it is necessary to consider first the basis on which an individual chooses one course of action over another. For the consistency with which people pursue their endeavors is largely determined by the choices they make. Sometimes even trivial, day-to-day choices can contribute to the development of an enduring commitment. Often, these are made without any conscious understanding of the criteria that are the ultimate basis for choosing in a variety of situations. Trying simply to make it through the day, most of us are conscious only that a particular activity is desirable while others are less so. Yet, although we might choose to go on a trip to the mountains, practical reasons often restrain us from doing so, just as the individual who dreams of the adventure of revolutionary life decides instead to remain at his civil servant post because such a commitment would disrupt the balance of a happy home. In these two examples, the choice for the practical option, rather than the ideal, is determined by a rather rough calculation of the costs and rewards that each perceived alternative is capable of producing. In drawing up a mental balance sheet of the reward opportunities and cost factors of all his known choices, a person seeks to maximize his profits as much as possible without incurring heavy costs.

If individual choices can be conceived as products of a cost-reward calculation, then commitments (which develop through decision-making) must be understood as behavior that has become consistent because it promises to be more gratifying than costly. Such commitments form through the operation of an additive process in which early choices require investments and sacrifices. In this additive sequence of decisions, a commitment can be partially formed by default, wherein many lower-level choices are made whose consequences are not immediately or fully recognized. "Each step tends to limit the alternatives available at the next step," Becker argues in a companion work, "until the individual finds himself at a decision point with only one 'alternative' to choose from."[8]

If investments and sacrifices have been heavy, an individual could retain his commitment because terminating it would incur too many costs, against the probable profits of an alternative course of action. The extent of an individual's "side bets" can actually lock him into a part of the social fabric from which escape is impossible or undesirable. Even those who are able to escape may choose not to do so on economic grounds. This was apparently the case for many members of utopian communities. For, according to Kanter, "When profits and costs are considered, participants find that the cost of leaving the system would be greater than the cost of remaining: 'profit' compels continued participation."[9]

Determinants of Commitment Formation and Retention

Viewing commitments as products of an additive process, an analyst should not only identify the determinants of commitment, but look for their logical sequence. In this sense, we simply want to know how one factor is added on to another.[10] Such a theory would possess two important features: (1) It would provide a conceptual framework for identifying where particular individuals are in the commitment process and (2) it would help us to understand what other conditions must be added before an individual who possesses the potential for a new commitment actually develops one.

Four determinants appear to influence the formation and retention of commitments. None of these is considered a sufficient condition for producing a commitment. And the presence of each determinant is a precondition for the next stage, although at times the individual may actually enter two stages simultaneously. The four determinants in their logical sequence are: (1) tension, (2) availability, (3) opportunity to act, and (4) high profit potential accompanied by rising investments and sacrifices.

Stage I: Tension—The existence of personal tension is the first condition necessary for the formation of a commitment. In this regard, commitments should be understood as developing from individual efforts to satisfy basic needs. In an earlier chapter, you will recall, these needs were identified as: (1) biological, (2) safety, (3) affection and belongingness, (4) self-esteem, and (5) self-realization. The whole constellation of commitments that an individual forms in a lifetime represents his attempt to find solutions to these personal problems. For example, an occupational commitment develops initially because it provides the resources with which one secures food and shelter. This commitment may be strengthened to the extent that one's career satisfies other needs, such as the longing for social acceptance, the desire for recognition, and the need for autonomy.

Commitments arising in the form of deviant patterns of behavior should be viewed in the same light. Edwin Lemert suggests, for example, that deviants remain in the delinquent subculture because they manage to find better solutions to their problems through deviant activities than non-deviant ones.[11] An inference can be drawn that political deviants, such as self-avowed revolutionaries, find revolutionary life more meaningful for solving their problems than more legitimate options. Certainly, it is true that the revolutionary life may actually increase the tension in some areas of need while it satisfies others. Sacrifices of physical necessities and increasing insecurity in social relations can be compensated for by increases in comradeship, pride, and purpose. This spirit is partially conveyed in the words of a member of the Nazi party: "It was unbelievably exciting to keep firm in spite of bloody sacrifices in our ranks, and to follow the command of the leader to wait. This waiting and these sacrifices were rewarded. . . . We were proud of doing our part quietly and modestly."[12]

Personal tension often varies with strains in social structure. For instance, demographic changes can intensify strain on organizational and role structures in a way that causes direct personal misfortune. An individual moving from a rural to an urban environment with expectations of improved conditions fails to find adequate employment in a deflated economy and exclusionist organizations, which was true for many blacks who moved from the American South into the northern industrial cities during the 1950's and 1960's. Or, personal tension can mount when a chosen occupation is closed, such as the inability of educated politicos, like Fidel Castro, to gain admission into elite structures because of the scarcity of political roles. At other times, entrance into an occupational status is easy but occupational investments go unrewarded, as we see in the case of German farmers who migrated to the cities in the 1920's and were subsequently forced into bankruptcy by the over-proliferation of small shops in a severely depressed economy.

When political leaders fail to set goals and distribute goods, statuses, and honors to relieve tension, the individual experiencing anxiety may seek new ways to satisfy his basic needs. These ways can be legitimate, to the extent that they are available. For example, lawyers preparing for a political career in Latin America could channel their efforts into business or education when political positions were withheld from them. The German farmers could have returned to the countryside to eke out a living from the land. There are many legitimate ways, then, in which individuals can find enduring relief from tension and, of course, this is the normal pattern. But there are also numerous deviant alternatives. The unemployed might turn to crime, alcohol, or drugs instead of preparing for a new occupation. Others find results in peaceful demonstrations and political organization. Some discover solace in rioting and looting. Yet only a small segment of society ever chooses revolutionary life as a response to tension.

Usually, one who develops a commitment through revolutionary activity does so after first pursuing more legitimate options. The attractiveness of revolutionary life is apparently a result of the scarcity of other rewarding courses of action. Lenin did not choose the revolutionary course, for example, until he had experienced the harassment of university officials in his effort to attain a law degree. Decreasing opportunities for upward mobility is only one facet of this issue. More broadly, it is the increase of personal tension followed by decreasing opportunities for the gratification of needs that lead some, like Lenin, to consider revolution seriously. In this sense, a revolutionary organization should be understood as the member experiences it: as an opportunity to solve personal problems that cannot be solved elsewhere, even though these problems are connected ideologically with a set of larger social issues that depersonalize his claim on society.

Tension, by itself, does not necessarily lead the individual to terminate one course of action for a more rewarding one. The fear of change or the inability to move to areas of opportunity are only two of many intervening factors. Neither is a high degree of personal tension a sufficient condition for conversion to a revolutionary perspective.[13] Before a new commitment is possible at all, the individual with a disposition to act must be free to do so. Eric Hoffer's claim that the poor tend not to revolt because they are preoccupied with physical necessities suggests that an individual who might like to act can be restrained by forces that are part of his human situation.[14] In this respect, availability for a new activity, that is, the freedom to take up a new course of action, must be a necessary condition for the formation of a new commitment.

Stage II: Availability—It is not enough for an individual to have a predisposition to act; he must also be free to act. Some free themselves for revolution only after a long and slow process of ending restraints and starting activity that is compatible with the revolutionary life. Others can be shaken so hard by circumstances that the transition to revolutionary action is greatly accelerated. These circumstances can affect individuals, as in Lenin's case, where his father's death reduced the possibility of external restraints interfering with his revolutionary work. Or public disasters, such as wars and depressions, can affect multitudes, releasing individuals from routine and freeing them for new commitments. Consider, for example, the case of the young Russian soldiers who fled the German front during World War I. Without plans and no longer bound by military authority and routine, they were free to begin new activities. They were available for conversion to the revolutionary life. That availability is a crucial stage in the commitment process is clearly supported by the conclusion of Lofland and Stark: All of those converted to the Northwest religious cult "had reached or were about to reach what they perceived as a 'turning point' in their lives. That is, each had come to a moment when old lines of action were complete, had failed or been disrupted, or were about to be so, and when they faced the opportunity (or necessity), and possibly the burden, of doing something different with their lives."[15] With this fact in mind, it should not be surprising that Gabriel Almond could show in *The Appeals of Communism* that most of his respondents had joined the Communist party immediately after World War I, during the Great Depression, during the period of the Fascist advance, and during the enemy occupation of their home countries.[16] These historical periods were ones in which personal availability for new commitments was high.

The state of being in transition between an outmoded activity and a new one is certainly an important determinant of availability, but there are also several impinging factors that will influence the choice of a new preoccupation. The first of these factors is of an ethical nature.

The conscience is the first impinging factor that can affect an individual's choice among numerous possible courses of action. Prohibitions against types of activity that encompass the use of violent means can restrain a person from overt aggression even when pressures are working to produce violence. For example, the Southern Christian Leadership Conference had an important impact on the style of action undertaken by many southern blacks during the height of the American civil rights movement in the 1950's. This impact was due largely to its reinforcement of religious ethics. According to James Vander Zanden, most black people in the South had been socialized in a tradition that encouraged the suppression of hostility and aggression against whites. A good part of this restraint stemmed from a strong religious training that stressed Christian love while it placed taboos on hatred.[17] The influence of the conscience in shaping action is nowhere clearer than in the case of Martin Luther King, Jr. After a series of confrontations with bus and city officials, King wrote: "I was weighted down by a terrible sense of guilt, remembering that on two or three occasions I had allowed myself to become angry and indignant. I had spoken hastily and resentfully, yet I knew that this was no way to solve a problem. 'You must not harbor anger,' I admonished myself. 'You must be willing to suffer the anger of the opponent, and yet not return anger. You must not become bitter. . . .'"[18]

Resource capacity is the second impinging factor. The extent of one's resources limits the number of options for action that can be considered seriously. An individual who is between activities and possesses no ethical restraints against a particular course of action might still be unavailable because of insufficient resources to act. Take, for example, the promise that "any one can be President of the United States." A person may be under so much strain that he could wish to be President to make the changes in policy that he feels are necessary. The chances are that he would have no ethical scruples against being President. But, unless he has numerous resources, such as previous political offices, political party support, experience in national politics, financial backing, he is not apt to consider the course of action seriously. He is not available for that course of action. This is an extreme case, I grant you, but resource considerations actually affect most decisions about action. Not only do we consider what we can invest in an activity, but we also want to know how many resources we will be required to invest and how an investment will affect the allocation of resources to other activities in progress. "Spreading oneself too thin" is a phrase we commonly use to describe a situation in which an individual becomes involved in many activities without resources to cover them adequately.

Countervailing forces can also affect the individual's freedom to pursue a new activity. Thus, a person who has sufficient resources to begin an action can fail to do so if a group or individual, toward which he is attracted, is opposed. Conversely, reinforcing the action increases the likelihood that the individual will initiate it. These countervailing forces seemed to be crucial for those predisposed to membership in the Northwest religious cult. For those with strong attachments to an outside and opposing group or individual, a good possibility existed that a strong commitment would not form or that activity would be terminated completely.

> Pulled about by competing emotional loyalties and discordant versions of reality, such persons were subjected to intense emotional strain. A particularly poignant instance of this involved a newly-wed senior at the local state university. He began tentatively to espouse the D.P. [Divine Precepts, i.e., the ideology of the cult] as he developed strong ties with Lester and Miss Lee. His young wife struggled to accept, but she did not meet a number of conditions leading to conversion, and in the end, seemed nervous, embarrassed, and even ashamed to be at D.P. gatherings. One night, just before the group began a prayer meeting, he rushed in and tearfully announced that he would have nothing further to do with the D.P., though he still thought the message was probably true. Torn between affective bonds, he opted for his young bride, but it was only months later that he finally lost all belief in the D.P.[19]

Even though extra-cult pressures led to the rejection of the governing ideology for this person, such pressures did not exist for many who joined. Most of those who became converts had not developed strong ties with external groups, or were active in groups that were compatible with conversion. For all members of the cult, it was discovered, the development of social ties with others in the movement reinforced their tendency to join.[20] In a similar vein, Almond found that conversion to membership in the Communist party was preceded by political pressure from trusted age-mates or occupational peers.[21] In addition, for many of the newly converted, entry into the Communist apparatus was reinforced by family tendencies, for 34 per cent had come from families with Communist, Socialist, Syndicalist, or Anarchist leanings. This fact led Almond to conclude ". . . that the membership of the party in the West consists to a considerable extent of persons whose backgrounds and upbringings would lead them to be receptive to Marxist and revolutionary ideology. For them, joining the party would be a matter of conforming to the past rather than deviating from it."[22]

It should be clear by now that availability for new activity is not the result of one causal factor but of several in combination. To the extent that these factors are present, there is an increased likelihood that new activity could begin and become consistent over time. Theoretically speaking, availability for a revolutionary conversion should increase when the person who is predisposed to act: (1) is between activities and anticipating a major change in his life, (2) is not restrained from revolutionary activity by strong ethical standards that would create feelings of guilt, (3) is in possession of the resources appropriate for taking on the responsibilities of the revolutionary life, and (4) is reinforced in his revolutionary propensities by peer-group ties or by external groups and individuals (or that, at least, he is able to keep his revolutionary activity a secret, thereby preventing the intervention of external forces that would encourage him to terminate his activity).

Stage III: Opportunity to Act—To examine the development of new activity within an organization, we have to consider whether the roles and statuses for which a person is available are open to him. Scarcity of roles and statuses can be one factor that will prevent the continuing formation of a commitment. Ascriptive criteria for allocating roles and statuses is another factor. A college graduate may experience the first type of closure when he finds that there are fewer teacher positions than there are applicants. In the second case, blacks and chicanos have been victims of ascriptive standards imposed by whites that effectively prevented them from access to roles and statuses traditionally allocated to whites. If opportunities are limited and restricted in this way, the disadvantaged can turn to new organizations or can develop their own organizational base. Collective outbursts, such as riots, can also become escape valves for many persons who either have no interest in long-range organizational activity, meaning that they are not available for the development of a commitment, or have no immediate access to organizations they would gladly join, that is, they are available but have no opportunity to act within an organized context. This latter case is especially important for understanding how revolutionary commitments fail to form among those persons with the proper dispositions.

In societies under heavy structural strains, numerous individuals available for organized revolutionary activity are not presented with adequate opportunities to act. Some find other ways to tolerate their misery; others become part of collective episodes that sporadically and not very successfully challenge the status quo.

There are two conditions that can inhibit the further development of a revolutionary commitment: distance and ascriptive organizational practices. Both these factors worked against the development of revolutionary commitments in the Russian peasant class from 1905 through 1917, for example. Sheer distance from the centers of revolutionary organization, coupled with costly and inadequate transportation, left most peasants outside the organized and on-going revolution. In addition, Lenin's decision to create a small organization of professional revolutionaries further limited the peasants' access. He made little attempt to diffuse the Bolshevik organizational apparatus into outlying areas of the country, which would have increased the opportunities for organized action. Guerrilla warfare, on the other hand is predicated on a different organizational principle. Depending on mass support for its success, the guerrilla organization attempts to create as many opportunities as possible for citizen participation. Through organizational activity, the individual is assumed to develop closer and more enduring ties with the revolution, thereby benefiting a regime that takes the reigns of power during the period in which it must consolidate its power. In practice, this activity has included the use of force against those who fail to take advantage of the opportunities that abound in the revolutionary organization's territory.[23]

Stage IV: High Profit Potential Accompanied by Rising Investments and Sacrifices—The existence of opportunity for action does not ensure that a person will take advantage of it. At this point in the additive process, the individual must make a rough calculation of the short- and long-range rewards that can accrue if he pursues the course of action. The potential rewards must be weighed against expected costs, such as investing resources, sacrificing other rewarding activities, as well as the prospects of costs arising from the opposition of external groups and individuals. Limited involvement can be chosen initially if the individual has developed other obligations, and is consequently unavailable. Or, there are many cases in which conversion to an organization occurred almost instantaneously. Instantaneous conversion is most likely when availability is high, as was the case for Goebbels, who was free to make a rapid conversion to the Nazi organization.

A sequence of earlier decisions is often antecedent to heavy involvement in organizational activity. These decisions include investments and sacrifices that, if sufficiently great, can produce commitments that are neither easily reduced nor terminated. Kanter has provided us with the most incisive description of the influence of investment and sacrifice in the commitment process. "The process of investment," she argues, "provides the individual with a stake in the fate of the organization; he commits his 'profit' to the organization, so that leaving it would be costly. Investment allows a person future gain from present involvement."[24] Sacrifice, on the other hand, operates on the principle that ". . . the more it 'costs' a person to do something, the more 'valuable' he will have to consider it, in order to justify the psychic 'expense' and remain internally consistent."[25] A third factor also governs the operation of this process: The more an individual invests in an organization, the more he will expect and receive in the way of profits. This is George Homans' conception of "distributive justice" in social relationships: "A man in an exchange relation with another will expect that the rewards of each man be proportional to his costs—the greater the rewards the greater the costs—and that the net rewards, or profits of each man be proportional to his investments—the greater the investment the greater the profit."[26] The operation of this standard of justice is quite obvious in William F. Whyte's *Street Corner Society:* Those members of the gang who made the greatest investments and sacrifices expected and received greater profits than those with lower levels of participation.[27]

At each step in the commitment process a person increases his investments, providing a base for making choices involving even heavier sacrifices. For example, an individual may begin the formation of a commitment by attending a single demonstration, unmindful of the way he is preparing himself for other investments. This single act, to demonstrate, is a sign to leadership that he is ready to assume new activities: He may be encouraged to attend a meeting just to "see what's going on," then be asked to distribute leaflets. Each of these choices requires little investment or sacrifice, but once the person has chosen to attend meetings and pass out leaflets, the escalation of investments to a much higher level becomes possible. Minor responsibilities for organizational tasks within the protest group leads to the heavier investments of leadership. So it goes that at each turn the individual's choices prepare him for more costly options until, even before he may be fully conscious of the fact, he has begun to form a strong commitment.

By the time a person has become firmly committed to a protest organization, when his activity consistently adheres to the norms of the movement, he has usually invested considerable time, energy, and money. The chances are that corresponding sacrifices have been made also, for instance, loss of leisure, possibly failing health, the termination of social ties, and diminished economic solvency. Ignazio Silone's testimony concerning his Community party activity is interesting in this respect: "One had to change one's name, abandon every former link with family and friends, and live a false life to remove any suspicion of conspiratorial activity."[28] Confronted with a new opportunity that would require terminating his commitment to the movement, such as being coopted into the ruling circle, a member's decision will not only be related to political ideology, but will hinge as well on the breadth and depth of his investments and sacrifices in the movement. Here the balance of costs and rewards appears to be a crucial standard of judgment in the commitment process, a factor confirmed by Silone's experience: "It should be emphasized," he says, "that the links which bound us to the Party grew steadily firmer, not in spite of the dangers and sacrifices involved, but *because of them.*"[29] (Emphasis added.) It is in this sense that E. Abramson suggests that "committed lines . . . are sequences of action with penalties and costs so arranged as to guarantee their selection."[30]

Commitments become stronger, behavior becomes more consistent, as investments and sacrifices increase, while at the same time goals maintain their attraction for the individual. For example, in comparing successful and unsuccessful utopian communities, Kanter found that successful communities were more prone than unsuccessful ones to extract heavy investments and sacrifices from their members. In all successful communities the new convert was required to sign his property over to the community, whereas in only 45 per cent of the unsuccessful communities was this the case. Eighty-nine per cent of the successful communities enforced celibacy for members versus 9 per cent of the unsuccessful ones.[31] Hence, some organizational initiatives require very small investments and sacrifices, such as presence at meetings, while others demand large ones, like editorial responsibility for a daily publication. Still, the extent of an investment or sacrifice is relative to the individual's perception of cost; that is, the level of investments and sacrifices has to be determined by discovering what a person considers costly.

The strength of a commitment—whether weak, moderate, or strong—can be determined by considering an individual's resistance to new opportunities that would force him to terminate his pattern of behavior. We should expect that (1) resistance to new opportunities will be greatest for those who have assumed the most costly investments and sacrifices and (2) resistance should be overcome when a specific, new opportunity allows the individual to pursue his goals with a greater likelihood of success, adding immediate compensations for investments lost in the former activity. What this pattern suggests is a conception of a "strong" commitment: It is a pattern of consistent behavior that resists change in the face of other opportunities.

Commitments generally develop in fits and starts. An activity may be tested by an individual to determine the configuration of benefits he can expect if he becomes further involved. Or he may develop an ambivalent attitude when his disposition to become fully involved conflicts with contrary temptations. A revolutionary dreams of total withdrawal from political activity, for example, and periodically vacillates between his desire to be in and out of revolutionary life. An individual can consequently occupy a transitional position for some time or indefinitely. Thus, we should not assume that the formation of a strong commitment is an inevitable feature of organized involvement. Nor should we assume that failure to reach goals necessarily leads individuals to abandon their loyalties.

It should be clear, however, that commitments form and are retained largely for economic reasons; that the attraction of one activity is a function of its potential for profit over and above current activities. In addition, outside forces may exert their influence in a way that will literally drive an individual further into the deep involvements that become enduring commitments. In this sense, a commitment is likely to develop strength, that is, resistance to change, when there are pulling and pushing forces influencing his behavior.

Pulling-Pushing Forces in the Commitment Process

Unlike commitments sanctioned by accepted social norms, conversion to a politically deviant perspective can be a threat to society. When a rebel is perceived as a threat, many agencies of society can combine their efforts to convince him to behave or coerce him into compliance. When I refer to pulling-pushing forces, then, I mean that the politically deviant activity is considered attractive by the person (a pulling force) while simultaneously action by societal agencies is pushing him further away from "legitimate" behavior and further into deviance (a pushing force). As Lemert has said of deviation in general: "In broad purview the societal reaction [to deviation] often presents a paradox in that societies appear to sustain as well as penalize actions and classes of people categorized as immoral, criminal, incompetent, or irresponsible."[32] The process through which transitional types are pushed into deviance is "stigmatization." According to Lemert, agencies of society attach "visible signs of moral inferiority to persons, such as invidious labels, marks, brands, or publically disseminated information."[33] By imputing a set of negative characteristics to the deviant, society forces a negative identity upon him. This "negative" identity, as seen from the perspective of societal agents, assumes a positive character for the deviant, who finds it easier to solve his problems in the deviant subculture than in "legitimate" society.

Stigmatization of political deviants can push individuals who are experimenting with varieties of political action further into revolutionary activities. However, a double stigmatization process operates in revolutionary settings. The rebel is depicted in negative terms by society, labeled "irrational," "degenerate," or at least "irresponsible." At the same time, the rebel stigmatizes non-revolutionaries in similarly negative terms, referring to the decadence and immorality of those who would stoop to defend the regime. This double stigmatization process produces both a strong pushing and pulling effect. By stigmatizing the rebel, society pushes him further into political excesses. By stigmatizing the non-revolutionary, the rebel imputes special moral virtues to himself and the revolutionary life, which increases the pulling power of the revolutionary organization. These two processes were quite effective, for example, in transforming Lenin from a serious student of law into a hardened revolutionary.

Lenin was depicted as a subversive figure by authorities long before he had actually become one. This was due to his brother's involvement in an attempted assassination of the Czar, an action for which he lost his life and Lenin his reputation. By association with his brother's political deviation, Lenin was stigmatized as "unreliable" and "dangerous," even though he had not yet become politically conscious, let alone politically active. This stigma made it difficult for him to gain admission into the university system, a surprising fact given his outstanding academic achievements. And after having started his university studies, he was expelled on the grounds that he was one of the organizers of a student demonstration, a charge that was never proven. It is of course quite possible that the negative identity that university authorities had created for Lenin was sufficient proof of guilt, part of the self-fulfilling prophecy that stigmatization seems to produce.

In time, Lenin developed similarly negative descriptions of the behavior of non-revolutionary types. It seems that, as commitments solidify, the politically deviant come to believe that their position is indeed the truly righteous one in an increasingly decadent society. It is through this stigmatization process that ideologies come to reflect leadership's concern with the purity of the soul.[34] For example, Lenin had been careful to condemn "slovenliness . . . carelessness, untidiness, unpunctuality, nervous haste, the inclination to substitute discussion for action, talk for work, the inclination to undertake everything under the sun without finishing anything."[35] This emphasis on moral virtue led Michael Walzer to the following assessment of the puritanical nature of Lenin's thinking:

> . . . Lenin's morality had little to do with the proletariat, and the "dissoluteness" he attacked had little to do with the bourgeoisie. He might as well have talked of saints and worldlings as the Puritans did. The contrast he was getting at was between those men who had succumbed to (or taken advantage of!) the disorder of their time—speculators in philosophy, vagabonds in their sexual life, economic Don Juans—and those men who had somehow pulled themselves out of the "unsettledness," organized their lives and regained control. The first group were the damned and the second the saved. The difference between them was not social but ideological.[36]

The tendency has been to focus on the organizational practices that encourage and sustain commitments, rather than on the pushing effect of society. For example, Kanter distinguishes between two commitment processes. The first is what she calls a "dissociative process," which encourages the new convert to terminate his commitments in activities other than those sanctioned by the community. This process works in conjunction with an "associative process," through which the new member is pulled into fuller organizational participation. The data show that successful utopian communities were distinguished from unsuccessful ones in their fuller utilization of these two processes. Successful communities were more likely to encourage disassociation by demanding the renunciation of competing loyalties as a price of membership. Furthermore, they developed rather elaborate procedures for binding individuals to the community. These procedures included various means of encouraging heavy investment and sacrifice, the use of communal activities to foster a commitment to the social group (sharing goods and labor, communal living and dining, ritual), the employment of mortification practices, such as public confession, and the use of techniques that would lead a member to surrender his rights to the social group.[37] In a similar context, Egon Bittner has enumerated a number of factors that are associated with the successful development of radical organizations.[38] The need to encourage total involvement in the life of the organization is one mechanism for insuring obedience from members. Becoming the convert's "family," "church," "school," the radical organization becomes a self-sufficient entity, reducing the probability that members will need to go elsewhere to satisfy their needs. Furthermore, a radical organization will increase its possibilities for survival to the extent that it can take advantage of the external sentiment against it. In this sense, the efforts of societal agencies to stigmatize political deviants can become a decided asset to protest organizations, for scapegoating is easier when an enemy makes himself clearly visible.

Pushed by the forces of society and pulled by the deviant subculture into new experiences in deviance, a transitional person can discover that the deviant life is better than expected, that profits exceed expectations. "Assuming that the person moves further toward deviance," Lemert suggests, "the abatement of his conflicts usually follows discovery that his status as a deviant, although degraded is by no means as abysmal as represented in moral ideologies."[39] For instance, the revolutionary who is anxious about making the transition to full-fledged membership in a subversive organization may discover that the use of violence is easier on the conscience than expected and that carrying a gun does not necessarily mean that one must use it frequently. Or, upon reaching full revolutionary status, he may find his new identity a more rewarding one than the old. For he is no longer required to alter his social face according to the different roles he assumes. Instead, his revolutionary identity becomes the organizing vehicle of his entire social existence. A sense of completeness emerges as he carries his unified revolutionary self into the many roles that formerly demanded artificiality and social lies.

Terminating Commitment

If investments and sacrifices have been heavy, even those who have become disillusioned with an activity may find that costs and rewards are balanced in a way that makes the decision to end a commitment impossible or, at least, traumatic. The person who has invested his time, energy, and youth in an occupation is unlikely to train himself for a new career, even though society does not condemn such efforts. Terminating activity in deviant political movements is even more difficult, however, especially if the movement is perceived as a threat to the values or institutions of society. Not only can societal agencies push the politically deviant further into a protest or revolutionary subculture, but they often arrange punishments in such a way that the disillusioned cannot escape from the movement and resume a normal life pattern. In the United States, for example, the Communist party member who has lost his faith and is anxious to leave the movement must face a cold and hostile public, not to mention the hardships placed on anyone known to be a former Communist, exclusion from many occupational and political roles for example. The stigma that contributed initially to the intensity of his dedication to the movement remains to haunt him when he tries to find a new place in society. Perceiving the costs of readmittance into society on these terms, party activity can continue long after the individual has lost faith in the cause, suggesting that a society that establishes punishments for sinners who want to return to the fold is apt to reinforce revolutionary commitments.[40]

Commitment to Rebel Leadership

In the preceding discussion, I emphasized the sequential factors that produce commitments in general. Now I want to examine more carefully the basis for a follower's commitment to leadership, for personal authority (where the follower's loyalty is primarily to the leader rather than the organization) is an especially important aspect of rebel leader-follower relations. Such authority is apt to develop if followers perceive that conformity to the personal initiatives of leadership will produce sound profits. Or it can flourish if the leader's use of threats and actual punishments creates fear, which fosters obedience even if the follower has no enthusiasm for the leader's initiatives.

Viewing the formation of commitments as a partial function of fear may seem strange because it denies that positive attitudes toward the leader are necessary. But this perspective can illuminate one of the problems associated with the analysis of rebel leader-follower relations, which is the tendency to assume that those individuals who develop a manifestly strong commitment to a leader, who demonstrate loyalty through public expressions of support and seem willing to conform to his initiatives, are devoted to him in a personal way. There are those persons who may thrust out their arms in rigid salutes to the leader, not out of devotion, but only because they fear that deviation from the norm might be interpreted by the leader or his lieutenants as treason.[41]

A study of the exchange aspects of commitment formation should include consideration of psychological relationships, the exchange of intangible goods that provide support for both the leader's and follower's ego. If commitments are formed to strengthen the ego's defense against the assault of the id and superego, they can become rather intense and may persist even in the face of heavy material losses. In this sense, the apparently "total" and "blind" commitment of followers to an ideology and rebel leader can function as an equilibrator, restoring the personality of the follower to a steady state by reducing personal anxiety and guilt to a normal and more tolerable level. It is from this general perspective that Hoffer argues that "faith in a holy cause is to a considerable extent a substitute for the lost faith in ourselves."[42] Immersion in a mass movement offers the follower a set of rigid moral standards and a "legitimate" target for aggression, which have the effect of minimizing ego deficiencies. Followers become converts to mass action, William Kornhauser adds, ". . . to replace an unwanted or unknown self with a collective image," which extends to "submissions to a leader and ideology."[43] These personality types, once they are ripe for a mass movement, are ". . . usually ripe for any effective movement, and not solely for one with a particular doctrine or program."[44]

The belief that rebel leaders who attain heroic stature are able to dominate and manipulate their followers presupposes that the follower's personality is submissive. In addition to his hold on the masses, such a leader, according to Hoffer, has the ". . . ability to dominate and almost bewitch a small group of able men."[45] In a similar vein, when the adjective "charismatic" is employed to describe the apparently heroic figure, followers are described as eager to accept the leader's initiatives, however demanding or extreme the sacrifices. Affected in some way by the leader's hypnotic powers, individuals seem ready to follow him wherever he bids, even to the grave, if need be. Assuming the "true believer" to be a personality type that could be applied to followers in general, this orientation has produced stereotypes of the "mass" and "crowd," both conveying impressions of those persons active in mass movements as irrational or nonrational automatons. Such activists are described as "disturbed," "rejects," and "goons." In short, organizations of militant protest are popularly seen as insane asylums for the refuge of the unsound in mind, or in Kurt Riezler's more complimentary terms, as a place for the "outcasts" and "fools."[46] But by overgeneralizing the distribution of strong psychological motives for the formation of commitments, we too easily dismiss the importance of purposeful behavior—the conscious and deliberate choices that affect the commitment process. A more balanced orientation would include a consideration of both conscious and unconscious exchange processes.

Bases of Commitment to Rebel Leadership

Too often, follower commitment to the popular rebel leader is arbitrarily linked to diffuse psychological factors and is explained as a strong and enduring emotional attachment. For those persons who are predisposed to accept this orientation, the tendency has been to grant magical qualities to the rebel leader, imputing affective motives to followers through the arbitrary use of charisma to explain the basis of their commitment. But if a single cause is considered sufficient to explain follower motives, the heterogeneous nature of a large collectivity is minimized and the different causes for commitment formation are blurred. As an alternative to this tendency toward overgeneralization and oversimplification, I propose that the charismatic basis of commitment is but one of three fundamental factors. The transactional and inspirational bases of commitment are the two additional dimensions that need serious consideration. A brief description of these three types of commitment shall be developed here, then, in later chapters, I will examine both the transactional and charismatic bases of commitments in greater depth, leaving the detailed analysis of the inspirational basis of commitment for a future study.

The Transactional Basis of Commitment

The term "transaction" has been used to refer to a process of exchange that is analogous to contractual relations in economic life. Obligations between individuals in a pattern of exchange are not binding in the contractual sense, but rather are contingent on the good faith of the participants. In this sense, the leader-follower relationship is developed on the basis of trust and stabilized through the existence of mutual benefits that accrue as a result of the exchange of tangible rewards, such as skills, information, decisions, material benefits, offices, status. And the investment of goods by a single person in a transaction is roughly related with expected returns. As George Homans has said: "Persons that give much to others try to get much from them, and persons that get much from others are under pressure to give much to them."[47]

From the transactional perspective, followers consciously weigh the balance of costs and rewards among a number of perceived options, either conforming to those of a leader's initiatives that offer the best returns or, if the leader is able and willing to punish deviants, conforming to his initiatives because of fear of reprisal for noncompliance. Therefore, two dimensions of the transactional basis of commitment can be identified and distinguished: *Positive transaction,* wherein commitment to leadership is based on expected rewards for obedience, and *negative transaction,* in which a manifest commitment is developed by threats of punishment, the promise to deliver negative goods or costs. In actual situations, both these types of transaction are likely to operate in creating consistent activity.[48]

Positive Transaction—The formation of a positive transactional commitment is closely related to the effectiveness of leadership in performing its instrumental functions. Through effective goal-setting, the construction and control of appropriate channels of communication, and through persuasion, leadership manipulates the reward system that is the basis for generating follower support. It is especially important that communication networks be well developed, for a leader-follower pattern formed through positive transactions is contingent on the leader's knowledge of follower demands and needs. At the same time, the leader must be willing to respond positively to follower expectations, since the relationship is based on his ability and willingness to deliver goods. In fact, when the leader is unable or unwilling to respond positively, the leader-follower pattern of exchange can be disrupted or broken entirely.

Rebel leaders who are in the market for a following must develop strategies (combining all areas of leadership functioning) that will make potential converts available for involvement in the exchange process and existing forces more eager to follow. Therefore, action initiated by rebel leadership should fall within each stage of the commitment process. First, for those who have already joined the movement, the rebel leader must encourage greater investments and sacrifices in order to strengthen their commitments. One way to accomplish this result is to create definite hierarchies of status that encourage individuals to invest and sacrifice to attain the next level of authority, with an eye on the ultimate status of the "inner circle." This aim can be achieved at the purely political level, wherein a political party is a vehicle to fame and fortune, as we see in the case of the Nazi movement. Or a similar result can be produced by the development of a military hierarchy, a strategy employed in guerrilla warfare with its definite emphasis on differences in military rank.

Rebel leaders must also present opportunities for those who are available for action. This result can be accomplished by diffusing the organizational apparatus, founding organizations in areas where people are ready to join them, by allowing a convert to pursue his subversive activity clandestinely, or by forming "front organizations," which conceal the real nature of their activity from other publics. In this last respect, it is interesting that 54 per cent of Almond's respondents reported joining a front organization as their first step to affiliation with the Communist party, as compared with 35 per cent who joined directly and 11 per cent who had first joined the Young Communist League. Apparently, the Communist leadership had provided opportunity in a way that recognized the additive feature of the commitment process. "For most respondents," Almond concluded, "joining the party cannot properly be described as a single act in time, but rather as a process involving a series of decisions stretching over a period of time."[49]

Through communication as well as specific actions, rebel leaders must also free individuals from time-consuming and restrictive commitments. They must develop goals and strategies that make those persons who are under tension more available to pursue revolutionary opportunities. To the extent that rebel leaders provide goods sufficient for a livelihood independent from normal occupations, the chances are greater that frustrated individuals will pursue the revolutionary course. If resources are scarce, then other goals can be effective, like encouraging unemployment in order to free workers from the social forces that make them reluctant to enter into new activities. By freeing the individual from his other obligations, rebel leaders are in a better position to begin the exchange of goods, providing food, shelter, and money in exchange for the convert's time, energy, and knowledge.

Finally, rebel leaders must develop strategies whose purpose is to expand and replenish their followings. At the most basic level, this process requires action that increases the level and extent of tension in the population by resorting to words or deeds. At the communication level, for instance, tension can be increased by showing individuals how their problems are the result of the bumbling and intransigence of ruling leaders. At the action level, tension can be increased and enlarged by attacking those parts of society whose loss would reduce the capabilities of the political and economic systems. The use of violence against industry, for example, can cause unemployment, which increases tension as well as availability. The danger, of course, is that those dispossessed by the terror or intimidated by the rebel organization may become available for action organized by leaders whose stated intention is to crush the revolutionary forces. A case in point is the Nazi revolution, which developed on the heels of rising leftist efforts to intimidate the public into commitments. Many ran, instead, to join the Nazis, who promised them nationalism without the Communists.

Negative Transaction—If positive transactions are insufficient for developing and maintaining commitments, leadership can threaten losses for noncompliance in order to preserve follower loyalty to its initiatives. Machiavelli recognized long ago the role of coercion in generating support. When a prince must choose between the love or fear of his followers, he is advised to abandon strategies that are intended to produce love for others that generate fear, for love of a leader is a bond easily broken, while "fear is maintained by the dread of punishment which never fails."[50] This Machiavellian strategy was central in Hitler's successful mobilization of servants for his cause, for, according to Allan Bullock: "stripped of their romantic trimmings, all Hitler's ideas can be reduced to a single claim for power which recognizes only one relationship, that of domination, and only one argument, that of force."[51]

Fear of the leader develops as the follower discovers that the leader is both able and willing to punish many varieties of deviation from his stated course of action. If rebel leaders such as Lenin, Hitler, or Castro gain sufficient control over the means of coercion, a transactional commitment can develop among those sectors most clearly disadvantaged by rebel goals. For these sectors, willingness to accept the rebel leader's initiatives, which an observer might interpret as a manifestation of the follower's devotion to the leader, might only be a façade rooted in the follower's fear of punishments.

The Charismatic Basis of Commitment

In a charismatic relation, a follower may consistently accept the initiatives of a leader when they are legitimized by the leader's association, directly or through a charismatic office, with a *manifestly* transcendental authority, be it God or the tribal ancestors, or when the follower *imputes superhuman qualities to the leader* and relates to him as a prophet. In the first case the follower's commitment is indirectly to the leader. The follower is attached first to the transcendental authority and secondarily to the leader because he is accepted as its chief spokesman. However, when no manifestly transcendental authority is present and the follower attributes mysterious and heroic qualities to a leader (considering him infallible or omniscient), it appears that commitment is directly to the person of the leader, the transcendental quality of his leadership having arisen in the mind of the follower to explain the leader's extraordinary successes or to rationalize the follower's commitment to the leader's moral claims.

Charismatic relationships can develop through three types of psychological exchange. These types are derived from my earlier analysis of the ego-support function of leadership as it pertains to the three agencies of the psychic apparatus. (1) A charismatic relationship can develop when a leader exchanges affection, encouragement, and security for deference and affection. Here the charismatic leader is the "comforter." For example, Dostoyevsky's "grand inquisitor" is a literary sketch of this type of charismatic leader. In such a relationship the leader reduces the distance between the follower's ego and ego-ideal by supporting his ego. (2) A charismatic relationship may also form when the leader offers the follower a new model of behavior in exchange for deference and affection. Here the charismatic leader is the "ideal." The leader who develops the charismatic relationship using this type of exchange helps the follower, for example, to overcome the distance between his ego and ego-ideal by offering him a new set of ideals that are more closely related to ego capacities and id dispositions. (3) Finally, a charismatic relationship can also emerge when the socialization patterns of society (or a subculture within it) inculcate deferential attitudes toward leadership as a part of the follower's conscience. Obedience to a leader who is chosen by custom as a spokesman for a transcendental authority has its rewards in the exchange process as well. These rewards are usually experienced as pride or as lowered levels of anxiety, especially when obedience to the leader insures immunity from the retaliatory potential of the gods, showing the influence of negative transactions as they reinforce the learning process. Here the charismatic leader is the "spokesman." This type of charismatic tie is not developed to reduce the distance that emerges between the follower's ego and ego-ideal, but is, instead, a socializing mechanism that attempts to integrate the agencies of the psychic apparatus so that excessive distance does not develop. It does so in two basic ways. (a) As spokesman for a transcendental authority, the charismatic leader supports a set of standards that incorporates obedience to his initiatives as an important feature of the superego. This condition is combined with everyday experiences in which the individual is able to demonstrate deference to the leader. This ritualization process minimizes the conflict between the follower's ego and superego, since it places the ego at the mercy of the superego in so many routine matters. (b) Relying on the charismatic leader's instruction the follower's ego and superego are able to team up, so to speak, in controlling the antisocial tendencies of the id. The result is a follower who depends on socially legitimized leadership as an external regulator of many of his activities. It is for this reason that charismatic ties that depend on the existence of a transcendental authority and that form through socialization processes should be the most enduring of the three types of charismatic relationships discussed.

The Inspirational Basis of Commitment

A rebel leader attempting to create a revolution must strive to give meaning to collective action and suffering, for he has to encourage his followers to invest and sacrifice if they are to develop strong revolutionary commitments. By asking his followers to invest and sacrifice, he is creating conditions in which they must act in the face of dangerous opposition and suffer numerous personal privations. He must therefore convince his following that there is meaning in what he asks them to do, that they can be part of a collective attempt to create a mutually shared vision of the "good" society through action. If he convinces his followers that there is meaning in revolutionary action and suffering, then he has inspired them; they will be ready to act and suffer bravely. Consider the testimony of one of Hitler's followers, for instance.

> I was attracted to the National Socialist party because it did not indulge in the high promises other parties made in their campaign literature. On the contrary, we were told that we must suffer and sacrifice; that the end of our striving must be a greater Germany rather than personal aggrandizement.[52]

How these appeals for suffering and sacrifice filled an existential void in the life of the individual is illustrated in the testimony of another party member: "The joy of fighting for Hitler's principle gave my life a new meaning. The philosophy of the movement endowed my hitherto aimless life with a meaning and a purpose."[53] In these two accounts there is no evidence that these followers had become psychologically dependent on Hitler, but rather that their membership in the party stemmed from their need for meaning in life.

In an inspirational relationship, the follower's willingness to accept the rebel leader's initiatives stems from his belief that the leader shares his social philosophy. There is no controversy about ends and means, for the leader personally represents the collective character and world view of his following. Therefore, he does not revolutionize his follower's soul by calling up magical powers as Weber said of the charismatic relationship, but merely represents the collective soul, or communal identity. He is not set off from his following as a new model of behavior to be deified, as is true for the charismatic leader. Rather, he is distinguished from the mass as a representative model of all followers, selected not for his God-like virtues but for his ability to inspire others.

Unlike a charismatic commitment in which the follower becomes psychologically dependent on the leader, an inspirational commitment is always contingent on the leader's continuing symbolic presentation of the follower's world view. In this respect, both the follower's critical capacity and his autonomy are maintained after the commitment is formed, and the leader may be rejected if he persistently acts in opposition to his role as representative of the group spirit. In an inspirational relationship such as this, respect is normally the deferential behavior that the follower accords the leader; whereas, the follower's deferential posture toward a leader in a charismatic relationship is apt to be one of awe. While all charismatic relationships will foster inspirational ties because charisma deals directly with meaning in life, it is important to note that not all inspirational relationships will be charismatic. It will become clearer in later chapters why it is necessary to distinguish the charismatic from the inspirational basis of commitment when assessing mobilization processes.

The Multiple Bases of Commitment

When a rebel leader mobilizes a large number of followers with outwardly strong commitments, we should consider (1) how they developed through the four stages of the commitment process, (2) how they were reinforced by the stigma assigned to political deviants, (3) how different motives can create strong commitments, and (4) how leadership coordinates the activities of followers with different motives so as to preserve and strengthen their commitments within a uniform organizational apparatus. Sensitized to the additive features of the commitment process and the multiple bases of commitment, the temptation should be avoided to offer a single explanation to account for the commitments of many individuals to a single leader.

Speaking of rebel leader-follower relations, this conclusion suggests that the use of the adjective "charismatic" must be abandoned because of the narrow perspective of follower motives it implies. Instead, the multiple bases of commitment should be assessed, identifying follower sectors whose relationship to the rebel leader can be categorized as a result of social transactions, the leader's charisma, or his ability to inspire. Furthermore, it is necessary to examine how each of these factors affects each follower's commitment and how each is related to the additive aspects of the commitment process.

Together, these three bases of commitment (which are pertinent for analyzing leader-follower relations in general) become an operational framework that should provide insights into the complexities of rebel leader-follower relations. However, while the formation of these three categories can be defended on practical grounds, they are not mutually exclusive. For instance, the formation of beliefs in the leader's superhuman qualities can actually be derived in part from a number of successes that, in terms of positive transaction, provide numerous rewards for the follower. In addition, a follower who relates to the rebel leader as a spokesman for some transcendental authority might consistently adhere to his initiatives because he fears the wrath of the gods or ancestors if he deviates, a negative transactional dimension. Finally, it is also reasonable to assume that when a follower relates to a leader on a charismatic basis he can fabricate or magnify a leader's successes and minimize his failures by attributing them to incompetent lieutenants. But while these analytic categories are not mutually exclusive, they should be· useful in the following chapters when I attempt to more carefully isolate and interrelate factors that bear on the formation of follower commitments.

Notes

1. Peter Amann, "Revolution: A Redefinition," *Political Science Quarterly,* 77 (1962), pp. 36–53.

2. Alexis de Tocqueville, *The Old Regime and the French Revolution* (Garden City, New York: Doubleday, 1955).

3. Howard S. Becker, "Notes on the Concept of Commitment," *American Journal of Sociology,* 66 (July, 1960), p. 33.

4. Rosabeth Moss Kanter, "Commitment and Social Organization: A Study of Commitment Mechanisms in Utopian Communities," *American Sociological Review,* 33 (August, 1968), p. 501.

5. Earl R. Carlson, "Attitude Change Through Modification of Attitude Structure," *Journal of Abnormal and Social Psychology,* 52 (1956), pp. 256–261.

6. John Lofland and Rodney Stark, "Becoming a World-Saver: A Theory of Conversion to a Deviant Perspective," *American Sociological Review,* 30 (December, 1965), p. 864.

7. Anthony Wallace, *Culture and Personality* (New York: Random House, 1961). Wallace refers to this problem as the "dilemma of immobility."

8. Howard S. Becker, "The Implications of Research on Occupational Careers for a Model of Household Decision-Making," in Nelson Foote (ed.), *Household Decision-Making: Consumer Behavior* (New York: New York University Press, 1961), p. 245.

9. Kanter, *op. cit.,* p. 500.

10. Neil Smelser calls this the "value-added" process. For a discussion of its features, cf. *Theory of Collective Behavior* (New York: Free Press, 1963), pp. 13–14.

11. Edwin M. Lemert, *Human Deviance, Social Problems, and Social Control* (Englewood Cliffs: Prentice-Hall, 1967), p. 55.

12. This quotation is taken from the case material in Theodore Abel's *Why Hitler Came into Power* (New York: Prentice-Hall, 1938), p. 260.

13. This is a point made by Lofland and Stark: "We suggest that acutely felt tension is a necessary, but far from sufficient condition for conversion. That is, it creates some disposition to act. But tension may be resolved in a number of ways (or remain unresolved); hence, that these people are in a tension situation does not indicate *what* action they may take." *Op. cit.,* p. 864.

14. Eric Hoffer, *The True Believer* (New York: Mentor Books, 1951).

15. Lofland and Stark, *op. cit.,* p. 870.

16. Gabriel Almond, *The Appeals of Communism* (Princeton: Princeton University Press, 1954), p. 226.

17. James W. Vander Zanden, "The Non-violent Resistance Movement Against Segregation," *American Journal of Sociology,* 68 (March, 1963), p. 546.

18. Quoted in Vander Zanden, *ibid.,* p. 547.

19. Lofland and Stark, *op. cit.,* p. 873.

20. *Ibid.,* pp. 871–872.

21. Almond, *op. cit.,* p. 226.

22. *Ibid.,* p. 221.

23. There is an interesting problem here that needs further study. No one, to my knowledge, has tried to assess the importance of broad-based versus narrow-based organization during the mobilization stage of revolution as it relates to the ease with which a regime consolidates its position. We can speculate that, had Lenin chosen to diffuse the Bolshevik organization more broadly, the problems confronted during the consolidation of power might have been less severe. And Stalin's efforts to collectivize the peasants might have been met with somewhat greater enthusiasm and considerably better local control. In terms of commitment formation, it is clear that the encouragement of activity is necessary if the individual is to become locked into an organization. By developing a strong commitment in the initial period of mobilization, rebel leaders may actually be investing wisely in their future. For a strongly committed member in the early stages is likely to carry his commitment over into the consolidation stage. This tendency might help to account for the successes of Hitler and Mao Tse-tung in consolidating their power against strong opposition, since both developed diffuse and broad-based organizations. If the opposition is almost nonexistent, as it was in Lenin's case, then a narrow-based organization might be sufficient to win, although possibly insufficient to maintain power over the long run.

24. Kanter, *op. cit.,* p. 506.

25. *Ibid.,* p. 505.

26. George Homans, *Social Behavior: Its Elementary Forms* (New York: Harcourt Brace Jovanovich, 1961), p. 18.

27. William F. Whyte, *Street Corner Society* (Chicago: University of Chicago Press, 1955).

28. Richard Crossman (ed.), *The God That Failed* (New York: Bantam Books, 1952), p. 88.

29. *Ibid.*

30. E. Abramson *et al.,* "Social Power and Commitment: A Theoretical Statement," *American Sociological Review,* 23 (February, 1958), p. 16.

31. Kanter, *op. cit.,* pp. 505–507.

32. Lemert, *op. cit.,* p. 42.

33. *Ibid.*

34. Egon Bittner has included this element as one of the important factors that contribute to the development of radical organizations. Cf. his article, "Radicalism and the Organization of Radical Movements," *American Sociological Review,* 28 (December, 1963), p. 937.

35. Lenin as quoted in Michael Walzer's, "Puritanism as a Revolutionary Ideology," *History and Theory,* 3 (1963), p. 86.

36. Walzer, *ibid.,* p. 87.

37. Kanter, *op. cit.,* pp. 504–514.

38. Bittner, *op. cit.,* pp. 936–939.

39. Lemert, *op. cit.,* p. 53.

40. This point, as well as others bearing on the problems of leaving the Communist party, is discussed by Almond, *op. cit.,* pp. 335–336.

41. Erving Goffman has recognized the importance of the negative side of the commitment process. He has distinguished between two types of obedience: "attachment," which refers to the commitment of one's "self-feelings" to a role and "commitment," which refers to the "forced-consequence" aspect of role performance. In this sense, an individual may play a role because it is personally satisfying (attachment) or simply because he has to (commitment). It is preferable, from my point of view, to discuss the commitment to roles in terms of cost and reward factors, noting the importance of rewards as they affect the enthusiasm of the person engaged in an activity and costs as they force a person to conform even when enthusiasm is nonexistent. For Goffman's point of view, cf. *Encounters* (Indianapolis: Bobbs-Merrill, 1961), p. 90.

42. Hoffer, *op. cit.,* p. 22.

43. William Kornhauser, *The Politics of Mass Society* (Glencoe, Ill.: Free Press, 1959), p. 112.

44. Hoffer, *op. cit.,* p. 25.

45. *Ibid.,* p. 106.

46. Kurt Riezler, "On the Psychology of Modern Revolution," *Social Research,* 10 (September, 1943), p. 321.

47. George Homans, "Social Behavior as Exchange," *American Journal of Sociology,* 62 (May, 1958), p. 606.

48. I apply the term "exchange" as a unifying concept to encompass both the social and psychological determinants of follower commitment. While it is clear that psychological exchanges can be discussed in transactional terms, I have chosen not to do so for analytic convenience. The term "transaction" is reserved for those aspects of the discussion that treat social exchanges of tangible goods, while psychological exchanges are discussed in terms of the charismatic basis of commitment.

49. Almond, *op. cit.,* pp. 224–225.

50. Nicolo Machiavelli, *The Prince* (New York: Modern Library, 1950), p. 61.

51. Alan Bullock, *Hitler: A Study in Tyranny* (New York: Bantam Books, 1958), p. 182.

52. Abel, *op. cit.,* p. 146. Most of Abel's respondents said that their positive orientation to the Nazi movement was due primarily to the fact that it appealed to their sense of obligation toward the common good of the nation, demanding sacrifices for the community rather than making promises that would have only benefited them as individuals.

53. *Ibid.*

4 □ THE TRANSACTIONAL
BASIS OF LEADERSHIP

□ There was a time when leadership was studied almost exclusively in terms of personal traits. It was believed that certain traits tended to accompany successfully initiated leadership; thus there was hope that potential leaders could be identified by the number of leadership traits they possessed. The lists of leadership traits soon reached such lengths that their utility and the validity of trait theory were openly questioned. Now, the tendency is to consider leadership as a product of environmental influences, especially of group norms and follower expectations. The traits of leadership that followers value are now understood to vary with the situation in which the leader and follower interact. Stressing this newer orientation toward leadership analysis, Bernard Bass has insisted that "any theory of leadership must take account of the interaction between situation and the individual."[1] Transactional analysis is one way of depicting this interaction process, wherein both leader and follower are viewed as bargaining agents trying to maximize their profits. And leader-follower relations are understood in terms of the exchanges that are attempted and consummated, beginning, extending, and maintaining commitments within the commitment process.[2]

The Transactional Pattern

There are several assumptions common to transactional analyses. First, it is assumed that individuals engage in action to obtain personal goals. Second, it is assumed that individuals behave "rationally," that they attempt to reach their personal goals in a way that, to the best of their knowledge, "uses the least possible input of scarce resources per unit of valued output."[3] Thus, according to James Coleman, a major aspect of socialization processes is the preparation of the individual for rational bargaining, which teaches him to calculate the consequences of his strategies in terms of his private interests.[4] But in specifying the operation of rational conduct, one must take into account the influence of long- and short-range goals in shaping the pattern of investment. Whether or not the individual is socialized to delay gratification in order to reap greater future profits is culturally determined to a great extent. Therefore, long-range planning should not be directly linked to a definition of "rationally." For example, while western man is taught to delay gratification, Arnhemland aborigines tend to be socialized to take immediate rewards in lieu of long-range benefits.[5] Both types of socialization do, however, produce men whose objective is to better serve their own interest, a course determined by customs and norms indigenous to their territory.

The third assumption of transactional theory is that behaviors that "pay off" are continued, while unrewarding activity tends to be terminated. And the final assumption is that social exchanges create debts that must be repaid at some time. In this respect, reciprocity is considered an important feature of the exchange process. In Alvin Gouldner's view, reciprocity makes two minimal demands on the actor: "(1) people should help those who have helped them and (2) people should not injure those who have helped them."[6] Furthermore, he argues, the norm of reciprocity imposes obligations only contingently. The obligation to return goods is apparently contingent on the value of the goods received, the extent of the receiver's need, the resource capacity of the donor, the donor's motive for giving, and the nature of the forces that may have influenced the donor to give.[7] Also, in social transactions it is seldom clear when one actor has reciprocated in kind to another. This ambiguity about whether or not obligations have been fully discharged tends to perpetuate the exchange process because it preserves a feeling of indebtedness that, in turn, becomes the stimulus for new transactions. And because obligations can be discharged in many different ways, a transactional pattern can become enlarged, encompassing many different social sectors and varieties of behavior.[8]

The transactional process is governed by a common motive to make profit within a loosely operating conception of justice. This standard of justice specifies that individuals "expect the rewards received for services to be proportional to investments, and that they do not seriously object if the rewards of others exceed their own *provided* that the investments of those others are correspondingly superior to their own."[9] In actual fact, unjust distributions of rewards are quite common in social life, especially in large collectivities wherein power is utilized to force individuals to accept less than others for their investments. This inequity is not without consequences, however, for "people whose standards of justice are violated feel angry as well as dissatisfied and give vent to their anger through disapproval of and sometimes hostility and hatred against those who caused it."[10] And when blatant distributive inequities exist in political life, men may come to see the political order as alien and when the opportunity is presented will oppose it.

While inequity in social exchanges can be the cause of frustration in many cases, it does not always lead to rebellious behavior. For there are several factors that increase the individual's toleration of inequity. One of these is the influence of moral principles, which apparently affect the perception and use of bargaining opportunities.[11] In this regard, an individual who believes in the equality of the races as a moral principle can tolerate an exchange pattern in which many goods are relinquished without commensurate rewards. Personal inequity is accepted as a price for establishing social justice. Research findings also suggest that individuals are more likely to tolerate inequity in transactions with friends than with strangers. In part, this willingness is due to the expectation that future exchanges with friends are probable, while contacts with strangers are uncertain.[12] The employment of negative transactions in the face of inequity can of course create toleration, but studies have shown this strategy to have no lasting effect on the individual in terms of his willingness and desire to cooperate.[13] A possible exception to this rule is the younger individual, who tends to be more cooperative with powerful leaders in performing tasks than older persons.[14] Those who are threatened by punishments may also tolerate inequity by identifying with the instigator of coercive influence, legitimizing punishing activity as the group norm. It was in this way that older inmates of the Nazi concentration camps came to grips with injustice. By assuming the behavioral patterns of the guards, prisoners came to believe that the oppressed must deserve the miserable treatment they received. If one can find a moral justification for inequity, it tends to minimize its ability to aggravate the soul.[15]

Those who receive less than they think they deserve in a transaction may overcome the disparity between their expectations and actual rewards by either (1) subjectively increasing the value of the rewards or (2) finding secondary rewards that prolong the transactional process. In the first case, Leon Festinger and James M. Carlsmith have shown that under experimental conditions the greater the dissonance created by an activity, the greater the probability that opinions will change to reduce dissonance. Their data support the claim that low rewards, which tend to increase dissonance, create conditions in which attitude change in the direction of supporting an unjust exchange is increased. Those subjects who received fewer rewards in the experiment tended to be more enthusiastic about their involvement than those subjects who received considerably greater rewards (and experienced less dissonance). Those subjects who accepted inequitable margins of profit were more prone to believe the tasks they were asked to undertake were enjoyable (even though they were meant to be boring), that the study of which they were a part had real scientific value, and that they would participate in similar experiments in the future.[16] On the second point described above, Elliot Aronson discovered that individuals engaged in a dissonance-producing task tended to select a secondary reward and magnify its importance. In an experiment in which respondents were asked to "fish" for colored containers, those who received no monetary rewards became attracted to the colors of the containers. Catching the preferred color became a compensatory reward that stimulated further activity even under conditions of obvious inequity.[17]

While research findings do point up various facts pertaining to the toleration of inequity, there is general agreement that inequity is not a preferred condition. On the contrary, most data confirm the operation of a standard of justice in social exchanges, albeit somewhat flexible and variable with local custom, that regulates the interactions of individuals in pursuit of their goals. This standard is all the more important in situations wherein followers are free to enter into transactions with leaders, unmolested by threats or actual punishments. If this is the case, a leader-follower pattern of exchange is likely to develop and persist when the parties to the transaction receive or are promised rewards that are at least commensurate with investments and sacrifices. The exchange of goods, which is undertaken to realize personal or collective goals, is regulated to some extent by norms that establish the value of various goods, the structure of the bargaining process, and the respective obligations of the individuals involved in the exchange. Initially, a follower may enter into limited transactions with a leader until the leader's honesty is established. And, at times, his reticence to plunge deeply into organizational activity initiated by leadership may stem from his ignorance of the bargaining situation. Small but numerous rewarding transactions with a leader will encourage increasing investments and sacrifices by the follower after he develops trust in the leader to discharge his obligations and after the situation becomes familiar to him. In the course of time, as I suggested in my analysis of commitment formation, a strong and enduring commitment to the leader can form.

The development of trust is essential in situations in which transactional relationships are free from coercion. For it is the mutual trust between bargaining agents that is the basis for the persistence of the exchange process. Trust is the positive evaluation of another person's willingness and ability to discharge his obligations. Because of the time lag between many transactions, trust provides the donor with an assurance that the receiver will reciprocate within a reasonable amount of time or when asked to do so. Furthermore, ambiguity concerning the worth of goods exchanged makes the trusting of others an important feature of the transactional process. "Since there is no way to assure an appropriate return for a favor," Blau notes, "social exchange requires a trusting of others to discharge their obligations."[18]

In a transactional setting, where the bargaining agents have negative evaluations of each other that create mutual distrust, transactions can still be made if a third party is recruited to negotiate differences. For the successful completion of the transaction, it is essential that both parties trust the negotiator. Trust in the third party's impartiality is assurance that they will receive a fair deal, that their reputations will not be tarnished (face-saving), and that agreements reached will be fully adhered to. These and other indirect transactions are a common feature of large collectivities and complex organizations.[19]

The importance of the third party in indirect transactions should not be overlooked, for often a follower may not be in direct contact with or have knowledge about important leaders distant from his locality. In such cases, he must rely on cues given to him by his associations. In fact, during revolutionary periods a follower's link to a popular rebel leader may be indirect, formed through his association with a group that either supports or acts in unison with the leader. For example, when the Bolsheviks captured control of the Petrograd Soviet toward the end of 1917, many who remained loyal to the Soviet were swept into line behind Lenin's plan to take power even though they had no great affection for him.

While trust mediates many relationships, concrete returns, not simply promises of profit, must be received by the follower if he is to maintain his trust in the leader. If benefits are received, trust is preserved and the right of the leader to lead is legitimized, be it by acclamation of a mob or by election. On this point, Blau has said: "If the benefits followers derive from a leader's guidance exceed their expectations of a fair return for the costs they have incurred, both by performing services and by complying with directives, their collective approval of his leadership legitimates it."[20] But approval of leadership is related in a significant way to the worth of the goods that the leader requests from his followers: The more valuable the goods requested, the more followers must be benefited by the leader's action. In this respect, Alfred Kuhn has argued that "if he [the leader] is content with praise and signs of deference, these may be easily arranged. If he wants personal services, money, or material goods from the group, then presumably he will have to satisfy rather substantial wants for his followers."[21]

A person's perception of the obligations of others in an exchange can be roughly determined by analyzing his expectations, which are his evaluations of how others ought to behave in discharging their obligations. Such expectations are ultimately influenced by reference to norms, the supply and demand for goods, standards of benefit in past social experiences, and, at times, by reference to what others of similar station receive in comparable situations.[22] If one wants to locate the goods transacted in a leader-follower pattern of interaction, the expectations of the bargaining parties should first be assessed, then the change in expectations should be traced as they are affected by changes in situations. Indeed, it would be difficult to understand changes in a leader's behavior without some knowledge of the constantly shifting priorities assigned to goods in the process of exchange. For example, a follower might expect a leader to behave in a compromising and cooperative spirit when scarcity is of minor significance. But when environmental conditions create adaptive crises, he may expect leaders to act aggressively and militantly in order to respond appropriately to the adaptive crisis.

However, when leaders will not or cannot deliver the required goods for meeting these new expectations (for example, they may not have the appropriate personal temperaments, beliefs, information, and skills for engaging in aggressive action), then the pattern of exchange can be either altered or terminated entirely. In the latter instance, followers may strike bargains with new leaders who are thought to have more appropriate goods for the situation. Here the transactional process continues as before, but with a change in leadership and corresponding shifts in leadership style.

An Application of the Transactional Framework

William Whyte's analysis of leader-follower relations in a street-corner gang illuminates the general transactional relationships described above, but in somewhat different terms. His data verify the operation of an exchange process, from which leader-follower obligations are created and follower commitments to leadership are formed. Acting as a participant-observer within the gang, he found that, through a rather elaborate process of interaction and exchange, there arose a system of mutual obligations based on trust that affected the strength of group cohesion. On closer examination, however, these obligations appeared to be more binding on high-status members. Those of low status could fail to meet some of their obligations in the exchange, but "Doc," the leader of the gang and a high-status member, was under strong pressures to live up to his obligations. Since the goods Doc contributed were indispensable for solving follower need problems, failure to meet his obligations resulted in serious disequilibrium for the group. Under these circumstances followers demonstrated a less than consistent willingness to accept his initiatives, manifest at times in open challenges to his leadership.[23]

Before attempting to locate the goods a single leader is obligated to bring to an exchange, the expectations of his followers must be considered carefully. With respect to street-corner society, follower expectations can be enumerated in order to specify the goods Doc was required to deliver to the gang. First, Doc was expected to spend money on his followers, an adaptive contribution to the followers' scarcity problem. Second, he was expected to unify various cliques within the gang when it was imperative to arrive at a collective decision. This expectation, shared by Doc and his followers alike, had definite behavioral manifestations: When Doc left the group, unity would give way to the divisions that were present before his appearance. Third, when a situation demanded action, Doc was expected to initiate it. The followers' general adherence to his initiatives was based on their perception that in the past his initiatives had paid off, "that his ideas were right."[24] Fourth, Doc was expected to keep his word to both low- and high-status members, providing predictability to the exchange and generating the necessary trust for creating positive orientations to leadership. Fifth, he was expected to demonstrate fairness in arbitrating disputes among gang members. Sixth, Doc was also expected to excel in activities undertaken by the gang. Thus, it was no accident that he was both a good street fighter and a good bowler, activities that were clearly important for all gang members. Finally, he was expected to keep the group informed about the activities of other gangs and clubs in the neighborhood.

Utilizing these expectations as clues, what goods was Doc obligated to bring to the exchange? In the appropriate sequence, they were: (1) money, (2) the ability to unify gang members, (3) decisiveness and the desire to lead, (4) trustworthiness, (5) objectivity in arbitrating disputes, (6) skill in group activities, and (7) information concerning the activities of other groups. More able than others to deliver these goods, Doc became the primary leader: As long as he was able to bring these goods to the group, followers remained willing to accept his initiatives consistently. But when he failed to meet these obligations for some reason, the intensity of the follower's transactional commitment to him was reduced, at times significantly so.

As we would expect, a normal pattern of exchange was maintained when adaptive pressures were minimal, making it easier for gang members to meet their respective obligations. It is important to point out, in this respect, that both leader and followers received psychological rewards in addition to more tangible goods when the transactional process was operating smoothly: All appeared to be comforted by the familiar and routine. Conversely, when a partner to the exchange failed to live up to the expectations of others, personal anxiety became apparent. For instance, when Doc was unable to bring his goods to the "bargaining table," he experienced "dizzy spells."[25] Such reactions should be expected, especially from those who receive considerable psychological "pay-offs" from their social relationships. One study has shown, for example, that leaders and followers who oriented more strongly to the social group than to its tasks reacted more sharply to criticism and group failure than those who were more task-oriented.[26] Any challenge to the group apparently shook the foundations that preserved personal equilibrium.

Boundaries of Discretion

At least two factors tend to limit the discretion of the leader in initiating action. First, follower expectations place limitations on leadership, as when followers expect that the initiatives of leadership should produce personal as well as group benefits; and, second, the instrumental functions of leadership can limit a leader by requiring certain actions for appropriate task performance. In the first instance, David Truman has argued that leaders must be ever mindful of the boundaries of discretion imposed by follower expectancies, for exceeding the limits of acceptability can produce criticism, then outright disaffection.[27] I should reiterate a point made earlier—that the formation of transactional commitments is contingent on the performance of the leader in his instrumental capacity, in which he responds to follower demands for tangible rewards. And when the response to one member's demands is made, the leader must face the almost inevitable rise in the general expectancies of other members.[28]

While a leader's behavior is influenced generally by follower expectations and task requirements, there are circumstances under which the boundaries of discretion are enlarged, allowing the leader to deviate more sharply from group norms. It has already been suggested in this regard that, during periods of adaptive crisis, followers may not only allow the leader to experiment with new modes of action, but they may make innovativeness a criterion for assuming leadership. But even in the absence of strong environmental pressures, leaders can still deviate from the group norm to some degree. For example, Hollander found that leaders tend to accumulate "credits" from successfully initiated action, which allow them to make departures from group norms. These "credits," which could as easily be considered units of trust, are won by the leader only after an earlier period of conformity to group norms. In Hollander's own words:

> So long as the person does not lose credits by sharp breaks with a past record of competence and conformity to expectancies, he rises to a level of credit which permits deviation from, and even open challenge of, prevailing social patterns of the group.[29]

However, when a leader exhibits nonconformity from the very outset, negative follower response—censure or rejection—may result.[30] Furthermore, a leader may overestimate the number of credits earned and thus, acting on overextended credit, he may increase the probability of negative feedback. For example, John Horrocks discovered that when an adolescent leader acted too far beyond the norms of his peer group he earned for himself "the dreaded appellations of 'droop' and 'drip.' "[31]

The value of a transactional perspective of leader-follower relations is in the emphasis it places on the mutual obligations, binding on both leader and follower, which arise from a rewarding process of exchange. From this vantage point, not only do we see that the leader's freedom to act is limited by follower expectations, but the follower's conscious, economic motives are given greater attention. In this respect, a follower can accept a broad range of leader initiatives quite consistently when they offer hope of solving problems, as the follower perceives them. His commitment, which is formed on the basis of anticipated rewards, is a pledge to deliver goods the leader values. To the extent that the leader expects much from the follower, an obligation will develop requiring the leader to return goods that are roughly commensurate with the investments and sacrifices associated with the follower's commitment. If the flow of goods is generally balanced, follower commitments will tend to be sustained. But in an exchange in which the leader demands goods without commensurate returns or the promise of acceptable future benefits, imbalance can result, forcing the leader to threaten punishments for deviation.

Having outlined the major dimensions of the transactional approach, a series of propositions will be presented in the following pages that, together, lend credence to the leader-follower pattern just described. For organizational purposes, each proposition will be separately introduced, followed by a brief analysis of the data that appear to be relevant. Where possible, the supporting data shall be drawn first from small-group studies, then from large-group contexts. In addition, studies of leader-follower relations in stable situations will be explored before considering similar relationships in crisis settings. In this way the transition to the later analysis of the transactional bases of rebel leader-follower relations will be facilitated.

Transactional Relations: Empirical Groundings

Proposition 1.1—In situations of stress characterized by ambiguity, the follower's demand for goods rises to a point where he is more willing to transact goods with leadership. When strain is especially intense, the follower becomes more receptive to exchanges with aggressive and powerful leaders who promise to reduce ambiguity and restructure the situation.

Aside from the personality differences that distinguish individuals in their tolerance of ambiguity, some security and order are essential for normal people engaged in the normal routine of life. Even the most creative persons, who appear to thrive on conflict and ambiguity, require some security to effectively participate in the creative enterprise,[32] a condition that is also necessary for leaders and followers engaged in bargaining processes. If the pattern of leader-follower exchange is disrupted by internal or external pressures, the predictability so necessary for creating a secure environment is lost and uncertainty and ambiguity are intensified. Under these conditions, restructuring the exchange becomes a pressing priority for followers: In such an emergency, they stress the importance of forceful leadership in order to impose "a redefinition or a new definition of the situation. . . ."[33] Since leadership becomes functionally necessary for restructuring the exchange, followers become more willing to accept the initiatives of others who attempt to restore order or who simply appear to have exact answers to complex questions. For example, one study has shown that individuals who perform tasks below the average tend, more than successful task performers, to rely on leaders to order their working environment.[34]

When ambiguity is intensified under experimental conditions, follower reliance on those who appear confident of their position increases. For instance, S. E. Asch's well-known research on visual perception and group conformity, which attempted to measure the relationship between group pressure and the distortion of judgments, demonstrated that, by regulating the length of lines (the test for measuring distortions of judgment), general conformity to a "false" group standard could be enhanced. As part of the experiment, the respondents were asked to select the line they thought to be the longest in a series that included lines of different lengths. In addition, stooges were included in the experimental group and were instructed to select as their preference a line that objectively was not the longest in the series. The likelihood that the respondents would choose the stooges' false preference was increased when several stooges had selected it in a sequence that preceded the respondents' choices. However, the important development with respect to the proposition resulted from Asch's alteration of the disparity between the length of the lines: The closer the lines approached equal length, the greater the ambiguity experienced by the respondents, thus the greater the probability that they would accept the "false" judgment made by the stooges. Since they were unsure of their own senses in selecting the longest line, they tended to rely on the judgments of others who appeared certain of their choices.[35] In a different study, a similar relationship was found to be operative: The less familiar respondents were with a situation, the more they oscillated in their behavior, thus the easier they were to influence.[36] Others have discovered that in children's groups the influence of deviant members rose when ambiguity was increased.[37]

Thus, during periods of crisis, when ambiguity is increased and followers become more malleable to leader suggestions, "usual rules are in abeyance and presumably the elite enjoys greater freedom in advocating new ideas."[38] At the same time, there is a tendency for followers to be swayed by the appeals of authoritarian leaders. For example, David Korten has shown that there is a positive relationship between crisis and the emergence of "power figures." Under conditions of stress, followers were more willing to accept the initiatives of the authoritarian leader whose function it was to control deviation and unite group opinion to facilitate the reduction of stress.[39] There is also substantial evidence that suggests that it was during the unstable periods in the evolution of labor unions that militant, decisive, and aggressive men rose to assume leadership.[40]

Since followers are likely to make greater demands on the single leader chosen to guide them through crises, they may feel bound to reciprocate by offering him goods commensurate with his heavy investments, including social deference, obedience to his initiatives, physical support, financial aid, and so on. Hence, deferential expressions of support and the granting of a broader range of discretion for the crisis leader may be conceived as the fulfillment of follower obligations arising from the benefits accrued from successful leadership or the promise of heavy rewards.

Proposition 1.2—A follower is more likely to transact goods with leaders whose bargaining proposals are compatible with his own experiences, needs, and beliefs.

In his extensive survey of innovation research, Everett Rogers has concluded that there is a positive relationship between compatibility and the rate of adoption. The greater the compatibility between an innovation and the experiences and needs of a follower, the greater the probability that he will adopt it. In more precise terms:

> *Compatibility* is the degree to which an innovation is consistent with existing values and past experiences of the adopters. An idea that is not compatible with the cultural norms of a social system will not be adopted so rapidly as an idea that is compatible. Compatibility ensures greater security to the potential adopter and makes the new idea more meaningful to him. . . .

> An innovation may be compatible not only with cultural values but also with previously adopted ideas. Compatibility of an innovation with a preceding idea that is evaluated unfavorably may retard its rate of adoption. . . . Old ideas are the main tools with which new ideas can be assessed. One cannot deal with an innovation except on the basis of the familiar and old fashioned. The rate of adoption of a new idea is affected by the old idea that is superseded.[41]

For example, birth control innovations have been largely rejected in those cultures in which they have been incompatible with religious beliefs. As well, beef production has been unacceptable as an innovation in India because it is clearly incompatible with the cultural and religious prohibitions against killing cattle and eating meat.[42]

In addition to the influence of compatibility in the adoption process, an individual's needs may also increase his willingness to accept innovations. As Anthony Wallace has argued in the general context: "the criterion of acceptability is the conviction, on the part of potential recipients, that the innovation will, in sum, contribute more importantly to the satisfaction of a network of wants and needs than to their frustration."[43] Thus, if needs are intensified during periods of crisis, the adoption process is likely to accelerate. For example, the threat of the Berlin situation in 1961 accelerated the construction of fallout shelters in the United States by focusing attention on their advantages.[44]

In addition to the many studies that confirm this position there is some evidence from research on Chinese-controlled prisoner-of-war camps in North Korea that suggests that the degree of collaboration with the enemy, a rough indicator of innovation adoption, was directly related to the compatibility of the Chinese initiatives with the experiences and needs of the collaborators. The differences between the collaborators, who cooperated with the Chinese leaders, and the resisters, who openly refused to cooperate, could not be explained in terms of psychological variables. Edgar Schein and his associates found, for example, that collaboration was unrelated to personality differences: On a range of personality tests, collaborators and resisters always deviated from the neutrals in the same direction.[45] By focusing more closely on the social background of the twenty-one men who stayed to live in China after the peace settlement, a somewhat different explanation can be offered.

For the twenty-one who stayed there appeared to be: (1) compatibility between the Chinese criticisms of American society and their own experience and (2) susceptibility to the innovative initiatives because they offered a direct satisfaction of needs that had been unsatisfied in the United States. Virginia Pasley conducted personal interviews with the friends and relatives of the men to determine which situational factors might have prepared them for a new ideological orientation. She found that of the twenty-one, eighteen had grown up in poverty, with eight knowing real deprivation; sixteen had come from homes broken up by death, divorce, or separation; nineteen were the eldest or only boy in the family; and fifteen were under twenty-one years of age.[46] These men appeared to have the requisite experiences and needs to make them first sympathetic, then supportive, of the Chinese argument that there was no social, political, and economic equality in the American system. Having to perform an adaptive function for their families as the eldest or only son, in most cases in which fathers were not present in the home, placed these men face to face with the harsh realities of poverty and inequality. That they were young, another factor heightening susceptibility to change,[47] enhanced their willingness to accept Communist initiatives.

The personal accounts given by collaborators to explain the basis for their cooperation with the Chinese tend to confirm this view: They said that they were influenced by the Chinese arguments because what was said "seemed true" and "made sense." In short, they were attracted to Communist ideology and leader initiatives because their own experience confirmed the "truth" of that ideology and the feasibility of those initiatives.[48] As Bass has pointed out in this regard, in any attempt to mobilize followers the leader must take into account the experiences and tendencies of those to be influenced.[49] Through this knowledge, the leader is able to develop innovative initiatives that promise the delivery of goods known to be in demand by the follower, thus increasing the chance that a transaction will be consummated. In this sense, leaders are apt to influence others to accept their initiatives and to form new commitments, when those to be influenced are already on the brink of change.

Proposition 1.3—The greater a leader's competence as perceived by the follower, the greater the probability that the follower will transact goods with him. Here, it is postulated that followers will attempt to choose as leaders those who they perceive to be most able to grant them their most preferred choices. In this sense, we should expect the leader's information, skills, and personal temperament to be important factors influencing the formation and maintenance of follower commitments.

Competence to cope with the instrumental tasks of the group is an important criterion in selecting leaders, for it is through the leader's successful performance of his instrumental functions that rewards are accumulated by individual followers. In the most basic sense, "the leader is followed," Bass has argued, "because this is seen as the way to achieve the group's goals, resulting, in turn, in reward for the membership."[50] Reviewing the findings from several of his leadership studies, Hollander has concluded that in work units in which group rather than individual performance was rewarded, competence to achieve the group's goal was one of the most crucial determinants of selection to leadership.[51] Furthermore, there appeared to be an evaluation of the leader's "potential for performance largely independent of the dimension of friendship."[52] This suggests that when the tasks of the group are altered in such a way that new goods are required of leaders, there is likely to be a change in leadership positions. This hypothesis was tested by W. Warner Burke in his examination of the relationship between group tasks and leadership selection.

In Burke's experiment, two groups of college pledges were offered monetary rewards for solving two tasks—decoding a message in Morse Code and selecting important requisites for survival on the moon (the latter to be determined through group discussion and consensual decision-making). Two types of leaders initiated action: those who felt somewhat removed and unaccepted ("high social distance leaders") and those who felt close to and accepted by the group members ("low social distance leaders"). In both contexts, followers tended to accept the initiatives of the leader who they felt had the most appropriate information, skills, and personal temperament for producing the greatest monetary reward. For example, followers were more willing to accept the initiatives of the high social distance leaders on the code problem because their goods, which were more authoritative in nature, seemed more appropriate for the decoding task, a problem that required expertise rather than cooperation. Conversely, the initiatives of low social distance leaders, who appeared to be more competent for consensual politics, were clearly accepted by the members of the discussion groups, whose aim was to arrive at collective decisions concerning the moon survival task.[53]

Further data bearing on this proposition can be found in the research findings of George A. Heise and George A. Miller. Quite in conformity with Burke's results, they found that the nature of the tasks faced by a group was an important determinant of the type of leadership followers were willing to accept.[54] This point is borne out further in a study of prison inmate leadership. The inmates of a prison were able to nominate leaders, and the prisoners most often preferred were those serving long sentences for crimes of violence. They were also those who had frequently broken the regulations of the prison. Since the relations between the prisoner and managers of the prison are often characterized by conflict and hostility, the prisoners were choosing as leaders inmates who were potentially better able to carry on the struggle with management.[55] In sum, it appears that followers attempt to select leaders who are best able to respond to adaptive pressures through goal-setting and the efficient mobilization of resources. For instance, followers in street-corner society tended to select as leaders those members with the goods appropriate for effective adaption. The three recognized leaders of the gang were respected by their followers "for their intelligence and powers of self-expression," as well as for their ability to outmaneuver and defeat competing gangs in street fights.[56]

The tasks confronting a group appear to affect the selection of leaders in another important way. When an individual recognizes his goods are inappropriate for realizing group goals, there is, in fact, less likelihood that he will pursue leadership.[57] This fact should surprise no one, however, for when an individual believes that others will be unwilling to reciprocate if an exchange is initiated, he will be reluctant to begin a transaction that would clearly fail to bestow on him the rewards of leadership. Such reluctance is a result of rational forces underlying individual choice, for it would be irrational (given our previously stated view of rationality in decision-making) for an individual to expend more in an exchange than he expected to receive.

Proposition 1.4—Leaders who have succeeded in developing an exchange pattern with followers must continue to meet their obligations or the exchange will break down. The leader who fails to provide the goods followers expect tends to be replaced by someone else who will.

To insure the permanence of their positions, leaders must successfully respond to follower needs, which requires sensitivity and responsiveness to follower expectations. From one perspective, the leader attempts to discover the opinion of the group as a whole, then tries to communicate his conception of the group norm to deviant members.[58] But as Bass has shown, even "the member with power or ability may fail in his attempt to lead through confusion concerning what is wanted or expected of him."[59] Such confusion can cause a leader to take action that fails to satisfy completely the wants and needs of his followers, thus conceivably reducing or even terminating the transactional commitment the followers have formed with their leader. Fillmore Sanford has stated this position quite precisely:

In any given situation, we can conceive of determining with reasonable accuracy what are the principle needs of followers. And once we know these needs we can predict what the leader must do to meet them, for the function of the leader, in order to win acceptance, is to meet the needs of followers. If he meets these needs successfully, he is accepted. If he does not, he is merely tolerated or, if the followers are free, rejected.[60]

Follower rejection of leaders is most probable when the leader—because of confusion, incompetence, or outright intransigence—fails to adjust his behavior to changing group goals. For instance, if a leader is unable to reduce stress within his group because of internal conflict or external pressures he will be rejected in favor of one who will.[61] This assertion is supported by the conclusions from a shuffleboard experiment conducted by

Robert Hamblin, in which group stress and crisis were artificially created in order to gauge the variable relationship between crisis and the tempo of leadership change. The experimental setting included a college and high school group, which were to compete against each other in learning the rules of shuffleboard by a process of trial and error. Red and green lights were to designate incorrect and correct responses and each group was to be scored according to the number of correct choices. The group with the highest final score was to be declared the winner. Early in the game the college group dominated the competition, as the college players had expected. But at this point Hamblin induced stress in the college group by arbitrarily changing the rules of the game: To their dismay, the college players began receiving red lights for responses that had already been approved. And, in order to intensify stress still further, the rules were arbitrarily changed each time a new rule was learned. These conditions produced a sense of crisis as the college group watched their score falling sharply behind the high school group's. Comparing the non-crisis and crisis situations, Hamblin found a much more frequent rejection of leaders during the crisis period. While leaders were not replaced immediately (we should expect a phasing out), during the crisis stage the leader of the college group who failed to reduce stress and end the crisis was rejected. In the college group, when crisis was induced, nine out of twelve leaders were rejected; for the same total in non-crisis control groups, only three leaders were replaced.[62]

While our knowledge of leadership in mob situations is fragmentary, there is some evidence to suggest that leaders who fail to alter their behavior to conform to mob norms will be rejected for someone who will. For example, by artificially inducing mob action among a group of college pledges, Frederich Elkin, Gerald Halpern, and Anthony Cooper produced an almost instantaneous change in leadership. The established leader (the pledgemaster) was immediately rejected for new leaders who, by proposing immediate action, were able to meet the new expectations originating from the crisis situation. In order to produce the mob climate, the researchers instructed a stooge to break into a pledge meeting and announce in the most urgent terms that a rival fraternity had stolen its trophies. This claim was given credence a few moments later when a second stooge proceeded to announce the theft in the same fashion. Having received this confirming report, follower interest in the formal meeting waned and soon the pledge-master was unable to maintain control over the group. Under new leaders the pledges burst from the meeting, leaving their pledgemaster behind, in order to recapture their trophies. An additional interesting observation is that the leaders in the artificially induced mob situation were the same ones who initiated action during a goal post mob scene after a football game. Regular changes in leadership seemed to occur when the goals and tasks of the group were altered, necessitating a rejection of established leaders when they appeared to be unwilling to respond positively to the new set of follower expectancies. In this case, when aggressive action was required followers accepted the initiatives of those individuals they thought had the necessary goods, which involved the same individual leaders in comparable situations; the pledgemaster could demand their loyalty under normal conditions when his goods were appropriate.[63] Thus, as mentioned earlier with regard to sharing leadership functions and as Hamblin has discovered in his own work, it may be necessary and desirable to think in terms of a "distribution of labor" within a leadership structure wherein "different members . . . lead in fulfilling different functions."[64]

These general findings are reaffirmed in Robert Myers' case study of anti-Communist mob activity, action which began as a peaceful demonstration by veterans' groups against the appearance of a Communist speaker in Trenton, New Jersey. The organizers of the protest demonstration had originally intended to allow the speaker to air his views and then at the conclusion of his remarks to boo what he had said. However, once the meeting hall was filled to capacity and emotions had reached a high level of intensity, support for the original leaders deteriorated. Instead of conforming to the leaders' initiatives, when any one of the three Communists who were present rose to speak followers shouted, booed, and stamped their feet. Acting on the basis of their original plan, the leaders attempted to restore calm and mobilize support for their position, but without success, as the dialogue demonstrates:

Plea: (A leader of one of the original veterans' groups) "Listen to me fellows. I'm one of the men that started this thing. Now we didn't intend to deny anyone free speech, but simply to boo what these rats said *after* they said it. So let's all be quiet for a minute, and let these rats talk."

Answer: You're probably a damn Commie yourself. Why don't you get up there with them, you god-damned Stalin-lover? (At this sally the veteran leader blanched with the shock of the clear realization that a definite schism had taken place; that he and the other leaders had lost all control, and that other and perhaps more sinister leaders had taken over.)

Plea: "Men, that's certainly no way to talk to the command of a respected [veterans'] group here in Trenton."

Answer: "Tell him to keep his mouth shut, then."[65]

As demands increased for more aggressive action, the leaders who resisted the change were replaced by others who were willing and able to act aggressively.

Proposition 1.5—A follower's field of group associations influences his willingness to enter into exchanges with available leaders. Commitment to a leader will tend to begin or will be increased in intensity when the follower's group affiliations reinforce his acceptance of the leader's bargaining initiatives. Conversely, when cross-pressures develop, the follower will tend to avoid exchanges with the leader or will reduce or terminate his commitment if it has already been formed.

Group pressures are critical in pushing followers to accept innovative leaders. Rogers has shown, for example, that for the majority who ultimately adopt new ideas the influence of peer groups is clearly fundamental, especially for the late adopters who often accept innovations because of pressures from their group associations. "The weight of public opinion must definitely favor the innovation before the later majority are convinced. They can be convinced of the utility of new ideas, but the pressure of peers is necessary to motivate adoption."[66] When the acceptance of one leader's initiatives disturbs other group commitments or when those groups react by escalating costs for deviation, then the formation of a transactional commitment to that leader, even though his initiatives are personally attractive, becomes improbable unless it is clandestine.

Through group associations a personal ideology develops—a system of values and beliefs for governing perceptions and actions—which, according to Robert Lane, "is almost always a rationalization of group interest."[67] Thus, personal preferences and modes of action tend to conform quite naturally to the standards of groups, although selected associations, which become points of reference, may assume a disproportionate influence over the follower's judgments. One writer defines a "reference group," for example, "as that group whose perspective constitutes the frame of reference for the actor,"[68] which may include membership groups like the family or groups the individual simply aspires to join. Functioning as frames of reference, these groups may bring their weight to bear rather heavily on follower choices and ultimately influence the formation of commitments.

That groups influence individual choices and commitments when they function as points of reference is clearly illustrated by Melvin De Fleur and Frank Westie in their study of verbal attitudes and overt behavior. After measuring respondents' attitudes regarding racial integration, the researchers presented an overt action opportunity to determine the degree to which action corresponded to expressed attitudes. In order to create the opportunity for action, the all-white subjects were asked if they were willing to have their photograph taken with a black person of the opposite sex, the photograph then to be used in a variety of situations, ranging from a laboratory experiment, where only professors and students would see it, to a nationwide publicity campaign advocating the end of racial segregation in which their private judgments would be fully exposed. Immediately following their responses to the seven possible situations, which were rank-ordered by degree of public visibility, the subjects were asked to identify any person or group of persons who might have influenced their decision. A large majority needed no prompting in naming key individuals and groups: "Nearly three-fourths of them (71.8 per cent) invoked some type of reference group when faced with this problem. . . ."[69] Furthermore, a third of the respondents behaved in a manner quite inconsistent with their earlier expressed attitudes toward blacks as their choices approached full public visibility, which suggests that they were responding to reference group expectations and the possible negative reactions to their public behavior when it ran contrary to those expectations.[70] But if group orientations are not mutually reinforcing, how will these cross-pressures affect the consistency of action, and thus commitment formation?

When group orientations run at cross-purposes, each group testing the loyalty of the individual, that individual may in fact be unable to develop consistent lines of activity. When these cross-pressures are intense, the follower tends to be hesitant, inconsistent, and/or apathetic, all indicating his inability to form a strong commitment. In American voting studies, for example, we learn that the individual experiencing cross-pressures tends to form his voting preference late in the campaign and to cast his vote with less enthusiasm, that he is more prone to split his ticket; and that he is somewhat less likely to vote than others. White-collar Catholics, who are subject to cross-pressures between their religious (Democratic bias) and occupational (Republican bias) group attachments, demonstrate less consistent partisan attitudes and behavior than people whose group orientations are mutually reinforcing.[71] Thus it appears that commitments are more than a collection of lower-level choices derived from a private set of attitudes and beliefs. They arise as well from the individual's perception of sanctions and reinforcements from groups in his field of associations. The intensity of the follower's transactional commitment to leadership must be understood, then, in terms of the support or resistance within or among his group affiliations. And, in reference to rebel leader-follower relations, it is also necessary to consider the pushing effect of society as it stigmatizes the follower and forces him deeper into the deviant subculture.

Applying the Transactional Approach to Rebel Leader-follower Relations

Extending the transactional explanation to cover rebel leader-follower relations should be undertaken cautiously. For while small-group leaders may perform many of the same functions as rebel leaders, there are decided disparities between small groups and collective movements that must be considered if we are to avoid the errors of over-simplification. Drawing from Herbert Blumer's leading essay on collective behavior, Neil Smelser has outlined five areas of divergence that must be noted at the outset: These include differences in physical size, in psychological currents, in the nature of communication and interaction, in mobilization processes, and in the amount of support given to cultural norms. Small groups and large collective movements produce essentially different psychological reactions, manifest in different feelings of self-control among the respective individuals involved. In small groups the individual is apt to feel that he has more control over his environment than in collective action, where his prerogatives and the environment in general may seem under the influence of a transcendental power. Small groups can also be distinguished from collective movements in terms of communication and interaction: In the small setting individuals engage in a two-way communication pattern in which information evaluation and feedback are possible; collective behavior, on the other hand, encourages or even necessitates a single direction of communication and a pattern of interaction that creates "the uncontrolled circular reaction of the psychological crowd." Small-group members and those engaged in collective action are also recruited through essentially different types of mobilization. Small groups utilize direct, simple methods of recruiting new members; large collective movements operate on the basis of mobilization strategies that incite and agitate, manipulating discontent and providing group symbols. Finally, small groups and collective movements are distinguished according to their relationship with the cultural milieu. Small-group behavior tends to reflect the norms and values of the cultural system, while collective movements can occur outside cultural prescriptions.[72]

Especially crucial are the differences Smelser describes between the communication and interaction patterns of these two settings, for positive transactions require that communication channels be open to the extent that followers are able to receive accurate information regarding leader beliefs, goals, and action; that such channels be sufficiently well developed so that feedback is possible; and, that leaders be willing and able to respond to that feedback, whether directly or indirectly received. In small groups these conditions are fairly easily satisfied, while in large collective movements communication patterns between rebel leaders and followers are complicated by geographical separation, social distance, or sheer size. Under these conditions, direct communication with the rebel leader may be reserved for a select few and information concerning the leader's activity is apt to be either scarce or distorted by those persons controlling the media of indirect communication. When these indirect channels are controlled by the leader in his gatekeeper capacity, he assumes a degree of control over the content of information that increases his ability to develop myths about the fruits and style of his leadership. For example, by controlling information he might publicly fabricate the compatibility between his position and his followers' beliefs, goals, and general expectations. While the follower is relating positively to his leadership in terms of this myth, the leader can act contrary to this public image without incurring public wrath since his private behavior is not open to public scrutiny. Furthermore, through such control, myths can be developed depicting the superhuman powers and magical gifts of the leader in order to create the basis for forming a charismatic commitment among those removed from direct contact with or knowledge of the leader. "It is sometimes asserted," James Davies tells us, "that it is the distance itself which lends enchantment, that no man can be great in the eyes of his intimates."[73]

Bridging the Communication Gap in Large Collectivities

We should expect to find a communication void in collective movements similar to the one that exists between national political leaders and the electorate in the American political system. In both cases, geographical separation, social distance, and size produce information shortages among followers, especially about the *real* beliefs, goals, and activities of leadership. In this environmental setting, how do followers engage in meaningful exchanges with leaders? If information of questionable validity is released or information volume is reduced, on what basis will the follower accept or reject leader initiatives?

When communication gaps develop between leaders and followers in large collectivities, the follower's orientation to leadership may be determined by his "trust associations," those reference groups the follower believes operate from a system of values and interests consistent with his own and have more accurate information concerning the leader's orientation regarding those values and interests. These "trust associations" function to cut information gathering and evaluation costs, when more direct means of collecting information are not utilized or are unavailable to the follower. In this sense, the influence of "trust associations" can be an intervening factor affecting the formation of transactional commitments to leadership when the follower is geographically or socially removed from direct contact with the leader. Under these conditions, the transactional process is still operative but it is complicated and modified by this two-stage communication network, a structure similar to the "two-step flow of communication" described by Elihu Katz and Paul F. Lazarsfeld.[74]

In order to bridge the communication void between rebel leaders and followers, we must consider the role that the follower's "trust associations" play in setting his preferences, focusing especially on the transactional relations between primary rebel leaders and the leaders of those associations, which I shall call secondary leadership.[75] In order to mobilize sufficient strength to overthrow the political order, primary rebel leaders may have to win and maintain the loyalty of secondary leaders by engaging in mutually beneficial exchanges; thereby indirectly creating the basis for the formation of transactional commitments among a large number of followers who might not otherwise have been mobilized for action against the state.

Rebel Leader-follower Relations: Inferences from the Propositions and from the Commitment Process

On the basis of the preceding transactional perspective of leader-follower relations in small groups and large stable systems, and referring back to the theory of commitment developed in Chapter III, I have drawn the following inferences about rebel leader-follower relations. The propositions that resulted are ordered sequentially in terms of the four stages of the commitment process and correspond by number to the propositions offered above. This second set of propositions will be discussed in the next chapter.

Stage I: Tension

Proposition 2.1—In situations of intense structural strain characterized by ambiguity, individuals will experience extreme tension and will become susceptible to the influence of those who promise to restructure the situation. In the political context, followers expect ruling leaders to act in a way that would rectify structural problems, leading to a satisfaction of their needs and a reduction of personal tension. If established leaders fail in their efforts, then followers will become mistrustful of those leaders and predisposed to act in a deviant fashion under the guidance of rebel leaders.

Stage II: Availability

Proposition 2.2—Individuals experiencing extreme levels of personal tension will become more available for transactions with rebel leaders when they are between activities; when the initiatives of those rebel leaders are compatible with their own experiences, beliefs, and moral systems; and when their personal resources are adequate for engaging in politically deviant action.

Proposition 2.5—An individual's field of group associations will influence his disposition to enter into transactions with rebel leaders. Availability for beginning a commitment to a particular rebel leader will increase to the extent that his group ties reinforce his desire to follow. When cross-pressures exist, the potential follower may avoid entering into exchanges with the rebel leader, may break off his ties with the countervailing groups in order to pursue a preferred course of action, or may conceal his activities in behalf of the rebel leader from those groups who oppose them.

Stage III: Opportunity To Act

Proposition 2.6—The success of the primary rebel leader in expanding his popularity to new follower sectors depends on his ability to provide organizational opportunities for those who are available for action and on the support he receives from secondary leaders who facilitate the follower's access to the movement. The greater the opportunity for action and the broader and more intense the support from these secondary leaders, the greater the probability that followers will enter into transactions with the primary leader, although they may be indirect transactions through secondary leaders or "trust associations."

Stage IV: High Profit Potential Accompanied by Rising Investments and Sacrifices

Proposition 2.3—Followers are most likely to develop a transactional commitment with those rebel leaders whom they perceive to have the most appropriate information, skills, and personal temperaments for reaching personal and group goals. However, once a movement has developed, its structure may limit the number of potential competitors for leadership positions, for example, by requiring special access to a transcendental authority. An established leader who has the trust of his followers has an advantage over potential competitors because he has proven his competence over time and has developed mutual obligations with his followers.

Proposition 2.4—Once the exchange between leader and follower has begun, the follower's transactional commitment will be strengthened initially when increasing investments and sacrifices are extracted from him by the rebel leader and/or when rewards are received which make him dependent on the rebel organization for social status, opportunities, and honors. Reciprocally, rebel leaders who have succeeded in developing a persistent pattern of exchange must continue to satisfy the follower's expectations or, despite the follower's investments, sacrifices, and organizational dependence, the exchange will become strained and may even break down entirely if other options for profit appear.

Notes

1. Bernard Bass, *Leadership, Psychology, and Organizational Behavior* (New York: Harper & Row, 1960), p. 18.

2. We have come to a point in this work where the focus narrows and more concrete components of behavior are identified and analyzed. By isolating the factors that bear on the development of transactional relations, I shall expand my earlier discussion of the commitment process, wherein the individual assesses the potential profits of an opportunity for action. This should put into a more empirical context the operation of leadership as it attempts to perform its mobilization function, a factor that directly affects its general responsibility for the coordination of social systems.

3. Anthony Downs, *An Economic Theory of Democracy* (New York: Harper & Row, 1957), p. 5.

4. James Coleman, "Collective Decisions," *Sociological Inquiry,* 34 (Spring, 1964), p. 168.

5. Kenneth H. David and Stephan Bochner, "Immediate vs. Delayed Reward among Arnhemland Aborigines," *Journal of Social Psychology,* 73 (December, 1967), pp. 157–159. The authors concluded: "Although there was a tendency for the older Ss to choose the delayed reward, there was no significant difference between age groups. This congruence of choice between age groups indicates that one-half of Ss chose the delayed reward, the other half chose the immediate reward, irrespective of their ages. This is in contrast to western culture, where children learn at an early age to choose a larger delayed reward over a smaller immediate reward."

6. Alvin W. Gouldner, "The Norm of Reciprocity: A Preliminary Statement," *American Sociological Review,* 25 (April, 1960), p. 171.

7. *Ibid.*

8. *Ibid.,* p. 175.

9. Peter M. Blau, "Justice in Social Exchange," *Sociological Inquiry,* 34 (Spring, 1964), p. 195.

10. *Ibid.,* p. 199.

11. The influence of moral principles in bargaining processes is one aspect of Philip W. Blumstein's and Eugene A. Weinstein's, "The Redress of Distributive Injustice," *American Journal of Sociology,* 74 (January, 1969), pp. 408–418.

12. William R. Morgan and Jack Sawyer, "Bargaining, Expectations, and the Preference for Equality Over Equity," *Journal of Personality and Social Psychology,* 6 (June, 1967), pp. 139–149.

13. One study especially shows significant differences between rewarding and punishing strategies in effecting cooperation. One cluster of 15 groups included a leader whose strategy was to reward but not punish and a cluster of six groups in which the opposite strategy was employed. In all 15 groups in which rewards were given, a high level of cooperation was achieved; whereas, in only one of the six groups where punishment was used was this the case. In other groups in which both rewarding and punishing strategies were utilized, cooperation developed only after punishment ceased and rewards were given. David R. Schmitt and Gerald Marwell, "Reward and Punishments as Techniques for the Achievement of Cooperation Under Inequity," *Human Relations,* 23 (February, 1970), pp. 37–45.

14. Marginal support for this hypothesis can be found in D. Kipnist and C. Wagner, "Character Structure and Response to Leadership Power," *Journal of Experimental Research in Personality,* 2 (1967), pp. 16–29.

15. For extensive treatment of this issue, cf. the leading essay by Bruno Bettelheim, "Individual and Mass Behavior in Extreme Situations," *Journal of Abnormal and Social Psychology,* 38 (1943), pp. 417–452.

16. Leon Festinger and James M. Carlsmith, "Cognitive Consequences of Forced Compliance," *Journal of Abnormal and Social Psychology,* 58 (March, 1959), pp. 203–210. For further confirmation of this point, cf. also Jack W. Brehm, "Increasing Cognitive Dissonance by a *Fait Accompli,*" *Journal of Abnormal and Social Psychology,* 58 (May, 1959), pp. 379–382.

17. Elliot Aronson, "The Effect of Effort on the Attractiveness of Rewarded and Unrewarded Stimuli," *Journal of Abnormal and Social Psychology,* 63 (September, 1961), pp. 375–380.

18. Peter M. Blau, *Exchange and Power in Social Life* (New York: John Wiley & Sons, 1964), p. 94.

19. Blau, "Justice in Social Exchange," *op. cit.,* p. 205. For an interesting application of transactional theory to the problem of political integration and arms control, cf. Ralph Goldman, "A Transactional Theory of Political Integration and Arms Control," *American Political Science Review,* 63 (September, 1969), pp. 719–733. Transactional theory has also been usefully applied to political processes in R. L. Curry, Jr., and L. I. Wade, *A Theory of Political Exchange: Economic Reasoning in Political Analysis* (Englewood Cliffs: Prentice-Hall, 1968). Finally, the dimension of trust as it affects political relationships has been fully explored by William Gamson in his work *Power and Discontent* (Homewood, Ill.: Dorsey Press, 1968).

20. Blau, *Exchange and Power in Social Life, op. cit.,* p. 202.

21. Alfred Kuhn, *The Study of Society: A Unified Approach* (Homewood, Ill.: Dorsey Press, 1963), p. 499.

22. Blau, *Exchange and Power in Social Life, op. cit.,* p. 143.

23. William F. Whyte, *Street Corner Society* (Chicago: University of Chicago Press, 1951), pp. 256–257.

24. *Ibid.,* pp. 258–259.

25. *Ibid.,* p. 265.

26. Paul Ninane and Fred E. Fiedler, "Member Reactions to Success and Failure of Task Groups," *Human Relations,* 23 (February, 1970), pp. 3–13.

27. David Truman, *The Governmental Process* (New York: Alfred A. Knopf, 1951), p. 192.

28. Cabot Jaffee and Richard Furr, "Numbers of Reinforcements, Conditioned Leadership and Expectancy of Reward," *Journal of Social Psychology,* 76 (October, 1968), pp. 49–53. Data showed that rewarding any member of the group resulted in an increase in the expectancies of all other group members.

29. E. P. Hollander, *Leaders, Groups, and Influence* (New York: Oxford University Press, 1964), p. 27.

30. *Ibid.,* p. 28.

31. John Horrocks, *The Psychology of Adolescence: Behavior and Development* (Boston: Houghton Mifflin, 1951), p. 91.

32. Eric Hoffer, *The Ordeal of Change* (New York: Harper Colophon Books, 1963), p. 38.

33. Norton Long, "The Political Act as an Act of Will," *American Journal of Sociology,* 69 (July, 1963), p. 3.

34. Lauren G. Wispe and Kenneth E. Lloyd, "Some Situational and Psychological Determinants of the Desire for Structured Interpersonal Relations," *Journal of Abnormal and Social Psychology,* 51 (July, 1955), pp. 57–60.

35. S. E. Asch, "Effects of Group Pressure upon Modification and Distortion of Judgments," in Harold Guetskow (ed.), *Groups, Leadership and Men* (Pittsburgh: Carnegie Press, 1951), pp. 177–190.

36. Roger G. Barker, Beatrice A. Wright, and Mollie R. Gonick, "Adjustment to Physical Handicap and Illness," *Social Science Council, Bulletin 55* (1946), pp. 32–44.

37. Marian Radke Yarrow, John D. Campbell, and Leon J. Yarrow, "Interpersonal Change: Process and Theory," *Journal of Social Issues,* 14 (1958), pp. 60–63.

38. Snell Putney and Gladys Putney, "Radical Innovation and Prestige," *American Sociological Review,* 27 (August, 1962), p. 548.

39. David Korten, "Situational Determinants of Leadership Structure," *Journal of Conflict Resolution,* 6 (September, 1962), pp. 222–235. For further confirmation of this position, cf. Mauk Mulder and Ad Stemerding, "Threat, Attraction to Group, and the Need for Strong Leadership," *Human Relations,* 16 (November, 1963), pp. 317–334.

40. Benjamin M. Selekman, *Labor Relations and Human Relations* (New York: McGraw-Hill, 1947).

41. Everett Rogers, *Diffusion of Innovations* (New York: Free Press, 1962), pp. 126–127.

42. *Ibid.,* p. 127.

43. Anthony Wallace, *Culture and Personality* (New York: Random House, 1961), pp. 129–130.

44. Rogers, *op. cit.,* p. 125.

45. Edgar Schein *et. al.,* "Distinguishing Characteristics of Collaborators and Resisters Among American Prisoners of War," *Journal of Abnormal and Social Psychology,* 55 (September, 1957), pp. 197–201.

46. Virginia Pasley, *21 Stayed* (New York: Farrar, Straus, & Cudahy, 1955), pp. 245–248.

47. In his treatment of scientific revolutions, Thomas Kuhn has argued that young men have been the great innovators primarily because they felt less bound by the norms of the established scientific schools. This attitude gave them enough freedom to develop new theories. Cf. *The Structure of Scientific Revolutions* (Chicago: University of Chicago Press, 1962).

48. For an interesting collection of personal accounts, cf. Edward R. Murrow's presentation, *The Prisoner of War,* a documentary report of P.O.W. camp Number Five.

49. Bass, *op. cit.,* p. 302.

50. *Ibid.,* p. 123.

51. Hollander, *op. cit.,* pp. 25–26.

52. *Ibid.,* p. 73.

53. W. Warner Burke, "Leadership Behavior as a Function of the Leader, the Followers, and the Situation," *Journal of Personality,* 33 (1965), p. 71.

54. George A. Heise and George A. Miller, "Problem Solving by Small Groups Using Various Communication Nets," *Journal of Abnormal and Social Psychology,* 46 (1951), pp. 327–335.

55. Clarence Schrag, "Leadership Among Prison Inmates," *American Sociological Review,* 19 (February, 1954), pp. 37–42. For further data supporting the proposition, cf. M. Kent Jennings, Milton C. Cummings, Jr., and Franklin P. Kilpatrick, "Trusted Leaders: Perceptions of Appointed Federal Officials," *Public Opinion Quarterly,* 30 (Fall, 1966), pp. 368–384; Leonard V. Gordon and Frances M. Medland, "Leadership Aspects and Leadership Ability," *Psychological Reports,* 17 (1965), pp. 388–390; and R. J. House and A. C. Filley, "Leadership Style, Hierarchical Influence and the Satisfaction of Subordinate Role Expectations," *Proceedings of the 76th Annual Convention of the American Psychological Association,* 3 (1968), pp. 557–558.

56. Whyte, *op. cit.,* p. 12.

57. John K. Hemphill *et al.,* "A Proposed Theory of Leadership in Small Groups," *Second Preliminary Report* (Columbus, Ohio: Ohio State University, 1954).

58. E. Borgatta, L. Cottress, Jr., and L. Wilker, "Initial Expectations, Group Climate, and the Assessments of Leaders and Members," *American Psychologist,* 5 (1950), p. 311 (abstract).

59. Bass, *op. cit.,* p. 316.

60. Fillmore Sanford, *Authoritarianism and Leadership* (Philadelphia: Stephenson-Brothers, 1950), p. 4.

61. Carolyn Sherif and Muzafer Sherif, *Groups in Harmony and Tension* (New York: Harper & Row, 1953), p. 438.

62. Robert L. Hamblin, "Leadership and Crisis," *Sociometry,* 21 (December, 1958), pp. 322–335. For further confirmation of this position, cf. George A. Theodorson, "Elements in the Progressive Development of Small Groups," *Social Forces,* 31 (1953), pp. 311–320.

63. Frederich Elkin, Gerald Halpern, and Anthony Cooper, "Leadership in a Student Mob," *Canadian Journal of Psychology,* 16 (September, 1962), pp. 199–201.

64. Hamblin, *op. cit.,* p. 323.

65. Robert Myers, "Anti-Communist Action: A Case Study," in Ralph Turner and Lewis Killian, *Collective Behavior* (Englewood Cliffs, N.J.: Prentice-Hall, 1957), p. 115.

66. Rogers, *op. cit.,* pp. 170–171.

67. Robert Lane, *Political Ideology* (New York: Free Press, 1962), p. 397.

68. Tamotsu Shibutani, "Reference Groups as Perspectives," *American Journal of Sociology,* 60 (May, 1955), p. 563.

69. Melvin De Fleur and Frank Westie, "Verbal Attitudes and Overt Acts: An Experiment on the Salience of Attitudes," *American Sociological Review,* 23 (December, 1958), p. 672.

70. *Ibid.,* p. 673.

71. Angus Campbell, Phillip Converse, Warren Miller, and Donald Stokes, *The American Voter* (New York: John Wiley & Sons, 1960), pp. 80–88.

72. Neil Smelser, *Theory of Collective Behavior* (New York: Free Press, 1963), p. 6.

73. James Davies, *Human Nature in Politics* (New York: John Wiley & Sons, 1963), p. 283.

74. Elihu Katz and Paul F. Lazarsfeld, *Personal Influence* (Glencoe, Ill.: Free Press, 1955).

75. "Primary" and "secondary" are arbitrary categories for distinguishing different sectors of leadership. The primary leader stands at the apex of a coalition of subgroups and initiates most of the action for lower level leadership. The secondary leader heads a subgroup and tends to accept the initiatives handed down by the primary leader. In actual fact, several leaders may share the responsibility to initiate action. Thus, secondary leaders may be given the opportunity to initiate action when their talents are appropriate for the situation.

5 □ THE DEVELOPMENT OF POLITICALLY DEVIANT COMMITMENTS: AN ANALYSIS OF FOUR CASES

□ The fortunes of rebel leaders are the object of much conversation and study these days. Yet the development of myths concerning their rise to influence has had a marked effect on our understanding of the reasons why men and women develop politically deviant commitments and how some of these commitments assume a revolutionary character. The common tendency has been to assume that those who accept the initiatives of a rebel leader have either been mesmerized by the leader's charismatic powers or coerced into submission. However, this over-simplification, as well as the use of negatively charged stereotypes to describe rebel leaders and followers, has deep roots in the western political tradition, which has been outspokenly opposed to revolutionaries who call for the use of violence. Those who are prone to think in these terms are deluding themselves, of course. For, if one is truly opposed to revolutionary violence and is seeking ways to prevent it, then it is imperative to focus on the social and political weaknesses that give rise to personal tensions that signal the first stage in the formation of a revolutionary commitment. We have to know what structural strains contribute to rising tension, how the individual becomes available for a revolutionary commitment, how the revolutionary organization provides opportunities for action, and why the rebel finds greater rewards in political deviation than in continued conformity to the norms supported by ruling leadership.

Instead of viewing revolution as a manifestation of the crowd mind, in the tradition of Gustave LeBon, we should see it as men acting collectively to solve problems that the old order could not resolve by normal means. In this respect, we might take Leon Trotsky more seriously when he suggests that revolution is really only politics carried to a more extreme level, or as a colleague of mine has said, it is "normal politics plus violence." Given this view, it is absurd to think that revolutionary commitments can be prevented from forming by exercising force or by using stereotypes intended to belittle those thought to be enemies of society. On the contrary, the use of force and stigmatization is likely to push the committed revolutionary deeper into the politically deviant subculture while simultaneously convincing others to join. Instead of worrying excessively about how to control or put a stop to rebellious political behavior, we might spend more of our time wondering how society produces rebels, how structural strains drive men out of desperation to add violence to normal politics.

From the multitudinous forms of deviant group behavior that have occurred as collective movements, four especially relevant cases have been selected for comparative study: an "end of the world" movement, whose small membership and brief time span make possible an analysis of individual relationships and events; the Black Muslim movement, which produced an autonomous, nonviolent cult within an established society; the Bolshevik revolution, which succeeded in overthrowing and replacing an established political system by force; and the Nazi revolution, which fulfilled revolutionary designs by subverting a political system from within. By including two instances of non-revolutionary deviation, it is possible to gauge the extent to which the transactional pattern outlined in the preceding chapter can be applied to leader-follower relations in general. Finally, I chose these four particular cases because the primary leaders in each movement are either connected to a clearly specified transcendental referent or have come to be popularly regarded as "charismatic" leaders.

The development of the four stages of the commitment process will be traced in each case, linking the transactional pattern to the sequential theory of commitment formation. With this in mind, propositions are arranged in line with those stages thus the reader should be warned that the propositions will not conform to the normal numerical order. Following the statement of each proposition, a brief summary of its relationship to the commitment process and the transactional pattern is presented. Each case is then examined separately in terms of the specific proposition in question, beginning with the "end of the world" movement and concluding with the Nazi revolution.

The Formation of Politically Deviant Commitments: A Comparative Study

Stage I: Tension

Proposition 2.1—In situations of intense structural strain characterized by ambiguity, individuals will experience extreme tension and will become susceptible to the influence of those who promise to restructure the situation. In the political context, followers expect ruling leaders to act in a way that would rectify structural problems, leading to a satisfaction of their needs and a reduction of personal tension. If established leaders fail in their efforts, then followers will become mistrustful of those leaders and predisposed to act in a deviant fashion under the guidance of rebel leaders.

Structural strain can be said to increase within a political system when a regime's capabilities[1] decline while the demands of individuals, groups, and other nations increase. The strains resulting from this disparity between capabilities and demands are distributed as costs to the various sectors of the population, sometimes by design of political leaders but often fortuitously. Sometimes strain may arise from the weakening only of a single capability or it can multiply as all of a regime's capabilities decline. Furthermore, the costs of strain can be concentrated in a single sector, or even group, of society or they can be generalized to several sectors. How many of a regime's capabilities decline and how the resulting strains are distributed are critical factors in assessing the specific character of a collective movement as well as changes that might occur in its character over time. For example, when a political system has concentrated the costs of strain from extractive and distributive problems in one sector but maintains a high regulative capability, the expectation is that sporadic outbursts, such as riots, or cults are likely to develop, rather than revolutionary movements. If those costs are concentrated in the military sector, seriously diminishing the regime's regulative potential, a *coup d'état* is probable. When all capabilities decline, the accompanying strains are likely to become displaced to many sectors of the population to some degree, creating a diffusion of personal tension that leads to the dissolution of political obligations and to revolutionary change.

As I have already said, coordination is the most general responsibility of political leadership in maintaining the political system's ability to serve, thus to survive. Effective coordination depends on the creative ability of leaders whose goal must be to develop the political system's capabilities to a point where strain is controlled and maintained at a low level. Through the performance of instrumental and expressive functions the capabilities of the regime are enlarged, increasing the probability that human needs will be gratified. And when environmental pressures intensify as a result of demographic changes, or the like, leadership must behave in a way that reduces structural strain (and the resultant personal tension) through instrumental action, such as changing goals, communicating to followers what the source of the problem is, or mobilizing new resources through the exercise of power. This effort can be combined with expressive behaviors in an attempt to create a social bond with followers that would minimize collective tension even in the face of strain on organizational capabilities.

Ruling leaders who may have contributed to the decline of a political system's extractive, regulative, and distributive capabilities often emphasize what remains of their responsive potential by turning to the use of established myths and symbols, which had previously been a source of social solidarity. Indeed, when ruling leaders threatened by rebellion make repeated references to myths and symbols, it is sometimes a sign that they are losing their legitimacy, that feelings of trust in the regime are falling to a dangerously low level. Riots and other forms of collective behavior are the early signs of this decreasing trust and indicate that myths and symbols are usually not good substitutes for tangible changes.

When collective tensions become severe and the use of myths and symbols fails to produce sufficient cohesion, the tenure of ruling leaders may depend on their ability and willingness to initiate sharp departures from the status quo, which might have to include basic changes in the values and norms that govern the pattern of exchange. Under conditions of intense structural strain, even "normal" personalities will accept the initiatives of those leaders—be they rebel or ruling—who recommend radical departures from common practice, recognizing that such innovations will lead to more rewards than deprivations for themselves. Ruling leaders who fail to initiate changes that would reduce strain and generally restructure the exchange pattern are apt to lose the respect and trust of those who, in more normal times of abundance, felt obligated to obey their orders. These feelings of disrespect and mistrust mark the beginning of the ruling leadership's loss of legitimacy and are grounded in the follower's perception that he is not getting his share of goods in the network of social transactions. This belief that distributive justice has been denied and the corresponding tendency to develop a rebellious attitude occur under the following conditions: when environmental difficulties lead to sharp deprivations for followers; when new information increases their awareness that they are not getting their share of goods; or when those who are satisfied with their share become fearful that they will lose it. As mistrust of ruling leaders reaches the point where their promises are no longer believed, obedience becomes strained and followers become susceptible to the appeals of rebel leadership; and, to the extent that they are available, new transactional commitments form.

The "End of the World" Movement

In the 1950's Leon Festinger, Henry Riecken, Stanley Schachter, and their research assistants observed and participated in a contemporary social movement in the United States whose leader prophesied the occurrence of a cataclysmic flood, an event with supposedly dire consequences for mankind. *When Prophecy Fails,*[2] the published findings of their research, provides a rich body of data linking the small-group studies discussed previously to rebel leader-follower relations that develop during episodes of revolutionary change.

In this particular collective undertaking, the position of primary leadership was assumed by Mrs. Marian Keech, a suburban housewife about fifty years of age, who had been active in studying the occult and was engaged as well in private readings for those interested in knowledge of the transcendental world. Her personal history was marked by a growing fascination for "cosmic knowledge," for the mysteries of the flying saucer phenomenon, and for "scientology," an art or science that prepares the individual to trace life stages back to their beginnings. Through careful study, Mrs. Keech had been able to return to the day of her conception.

One morning Mrs. Keech began to feel a tingling in her arm and, after a period of bewilderment, became conscious of someone trying to communicate with her. Intuitively she picked up a pencil and paper and, to her amazement, began writing messages in someone else's handwriting. After asking the unknown source for identification, she received word that it was her deceased father. Soon thereafter, she began receiving communications from "Elder Brother," then from "spiritual beings" residing on the planets of "Clarion" and "Cerus." But her most important link came to be with "Sananda," who was identified as Jesus in a different "age of light."

Through her communications from Sananda, Keech was given "lessons" covering all aspects of life, which were to be shared with those she considered ready to accept spiritual enlightenment. One of her first, and most important, contacts was with Dr. Thomas Armstrong, a physician living in a nearby city, who was actively studying mysticism and was well versed on the flying saucer question. From their first meeting Keech and Armstrong formed a consensus on questions of the occult. Almost without hesitation, Armstrong accepted both Keech's role as a medium and her spiritual "lessons."

Even before meeting Keech, Dr. Armstrong had organized a group of college students who called themselves "The Seekers." Formed originally to discuss religious, metaphysical, and personal problems, under Armstrong's leadership they began investigating and discussing the flying saucer phenomenon and related subjects. Assuming major responsibility for the mobilization function of leadership, Armstrong began successfully recruiting members of "The Seekers" to follow Mrs. Keech, some of whom became strongly committed to her, accepting many of her initiatives consistently, even the outlandish ones without question or criticism.

Seeming to be encouraged by Armstrong's interest in her work, Keech began receiving messages that promised "visitation" from outer space. These general promises were put in more concrete form when a communication was received saying that a space ship would land at a nearby military base, an event she was instructed to witness. On Keech's initiative, Dr. and Mrs. Armstrong and nine other spectators joined her on the appointed day to await the space vehicle that had been promised, but it never materialized. For several of those present the fact that the spacemen failed to appear was sufficiently compelling evidence to disconfirm Keech's ability to prophecy, for, of the eleven observers, only five remained within Keech's sphere of influence after this disconfirmation. Yet, Keech's faith, while surely tested, was not shattered by any means. On the contrary, in the ensuing days the number of communications from outer space increased and her activities in behalf of the movement were multiplied significantly.

Approximately one month later, on August 27th, the word of the flood was received from Sananda. Except for certain mountain ranges, on December 21st the greater part of the land area was to be submerged. Those who accepted Keech's lessons and were convinced of the flood prophecy would be saved by spacemen sometime before the day the flood was to commence. Accepting the message as authentic, Keech and Armstrong immediately informed their followers and, for the first time, sought to make the public at large aware of the prophecy. Dr. Armstrong composed and distributed a news release announcing the impending flood, which was picked up by the major wire services and circulated to news media across the nation. Yet in spite of this broad news coverage, in two months' time the number actively involved in the movement had reached less than magnificent proportions—a total of eighteen had become committed, with varying levels of intensity.

At first glance it may appear that strain in the American political system had no bearing at all on the development of this collective movement. There is no evidence to suggest that the participants suffered excessively from the government's extractive, distributive, and responsive weaknesses. In fact, most of them were young students who had few direct contacts with political life, and the young males were not even threatened by the draft. The older participants were either employed in good jobs or were housewives. However, we should remember that the 1950's was the decade of the Cold War, when the development of nuclear bombs, intercontinental ballistic missiles, and the acceleration of the arms race with the Soviet Union generated widespread collective tension. The structural strain that was the source of this tension was regulative in nature, resulting from the huge gap between the demands for peace and the national government's obvious loss of control over international affairs. Thus, while the regulative capability of the political system was relatively strong in the domestic setting, in the international system it was excessively weak.

Unable to regulate the international environment so as to force the Soviet Union to accept its proposals for disarmament, the U.S. government mounted a national effort to reduce anxiety by encouraging state civil defense units to develop air raid shelters. Thousands of private bomb shelters were also constructed by homeowners in order to reduce the level of risk even further. But most people knew that within the area of impact no one would survive the blast, shelter or not. On top of this was the ambiguity stemming from the uncertainty of the moment of attack. It could come any minute, next week, or not at all. And the air raid sirens that were tested periodically and that sometimes started accidentally contributed further to collective uneasiness. Out of this anxious situation some people found solace in their bomb shelters, others in the debate about whether they would prefer to be "red or dead," or neither, and many just became cynical and resigned themselves to the fact that the days of the human race were numbered. Such times are also conducive to the rise of collective movements for they intensify already existing personal anxieties. These movements often divert attentions away from the sources of structural strain and hold out hope for salvation. This, we can speculate, was one function of the "end of the world" movement, for Keech introduced a third party, the Guardians from space, who would intentionally destroy the world and punish the wicked but would also rescue the "pure in heart." This was a more pleasant alternative for those who feared that the whole human race would be destroyed by misunderstanding or accident. Thus, in turning to Keech, her small band of followers may have been looking unconsciously for an explanation that would help them to cope with the ambiguities created by the Cold War. The personal tension stemming from the regulative weakness of the political system was displaced onto the impending flood by those who chose to follow Keech; thus the political system was not assumed to be responsible for their problems, which may help to explain why the movement failed to assume a political character.

For those who accepted Keech's prophecy of the flood, the possibility of such total destruction contributed to a rise in tension, as did the ambiguity surrounding their rescue. It is significant that as the day of the expected flood approached and they became increasingly uncertain about the place and time of their rescue, Keech and her followers became very receptive to leadership from other quarters. Quite in line with Asch's findings, during the last days especially, when ambiguity was at its peak, there occurred "a persistent, frustrating search for orders."[3]

In an attempt to reduce collective tension stemming partially from ambiguity, the group of believers (including Keech) sought and received initiatives for action from various sources. Caught up in a collective craze for guidance, many accepted initiatives that were absurd. During the later stages of the movement, for example, Keech received a telephone message from a prankster, who identified himself as "Captain Video," informing her that spacemen would pick them up that afternoon. Ready to grasp at initiatives from any source whatever, she relayed this information to her followers, who "took it seriously and began to make preparations for the trip."[4] Without even questioning the authenticity of this communication, she instructed her followers to remove all objects of metal from their person. This was necessary, Captain Video had told her, because any metal on board the space craft would disturb its flight control mechanism. Conforming to Keech's initiative, everyone promptly removed metal zippers, buttons, eye glasses, and, in one case, even the foil from gum wrappers. This precaution was all in vain, of course, for even without metal, the promised rescue did not materialize; in fact, no space craft was even sighted. It is interesting that those who expressed the strongest faith in the flood prediction, resulting in a heightened feeling of tension, were the first to tear the metal from their clothing in order to prepare themselves for the space flight, demonstrating a somewhat greater propensity to accept Keech's initiatives than those of lesser faith.

Even more desperate for orders after the first disconfirmation, Keech received a group of four college-aged men at her home who introduced themselves as "The Boys from Clarion." After questioning them for some time, Keech decided that they were indeed spacemen. Those who strongly believed in the prophecy accepted Keech's decision without question, even adding observations of their own that confirmed her arguments that the boys were from outer space. On the other hand, those who doubted the authenticity of her flood prophecy expressed open skepticism concerning Keech's conclusion that the boys were spacemen. Because they were less convinced that the flood would come and less worried about being rescued, the skeptics were more selective in their choice of outside initiatives and less willing than others to accept Keech's effort to persuade them that such initiatives were authentic.

And a few days before the flood was to commence, an even more crisis-ridden group jumped at a youngster's invitation: "We have a flood in our bathroom and we're going to have a party. Would you like to come over?" Ready for leadership from any source, "Marian hesitated not for a moment; she took down the address, and very excitedly, called to the other believers."[5] All those present responded to her call to action, for, wanting to escape the anxiety of an ambiguous situation, they were willing to enter into transactions with anyone who promised to deliver them from their fear of impending doom and from their uncertainty. "All the members, but especially the leaders, were floundering. Still fast in their beliefs, but more and more directionless as each succeeding prediction failed, they searched desperately for guidance, for some sign or some person to tell them what to do next."[6]

The Black Muslim Movement

Cults can be regarded as collective movements with revolutionary potential that turn inward. Weak in relation to the political system's regulative capability, they become isolated from contact with the ruling elite instead of staging futile assaults against the political order. The Black Muslim movement—a religious cult with important revolutionary aspects—has developed in this fashion. Indeed, the roots of the Black Muslim movement run deep in a black nationalist tradition of protest, episodic outbursts of activity caused by the frustrations of black men and women in a color-conscious society.

Even though the Marcus Garvey movement with its "back to Africa" slogan had been effectively stifled as an organization of protest by the 1930's (the victim of governmental regulation of political deviance), black nationalism as a way of thinking and an embodiment of aspirations remained. The way was prepared for Wallace D. Fard, a man whose origin and lineage were unknown but whose appearance was decidedly foreign. In the summer of 1930 Fard began selling silks and satins from door to door in the black ghetto of Detroit, warning those persons he met to avoid certain foods and drink and to abandon Christianity for Islam, which he insisted was the black man's true religion. It was not long before he had established a Muslim temple where he delivered sermons embracing popular themes from the black nationalist heritage. His followers were told repeatedly that "white men cannot be trusted" and that "the so-called American Negro must rediscover the black man's glorious past, a history white men have carefully concealed." Appealing to blacks suffocating in overcrowded slums or suffering from the deprivation arising from unemployment and Fifth Avenue rents, in a short time Fard had mobilized a sizable following. With these followers he founded a University of Islam, a home economics class for training Muslim women, and a quasi-military organization, the Fruit of Islam.

Once the foundations of the Nation of Islam had been firmly established, Elijah Muhammad, one of Fard's first converts, was appointed to the position of Chief Minister of Islam, a status he still occupies today. Then, shortly after bestowing authority on Mr. Muhammad, Fard "vanished as mysteriously as he arrived,"[7] never to be seen again. Mr. Muhammad teaches that Fard was sent as a Prophet of Allah and, because of his close association with Fard, he has assumed the distinction of the Prophet's Messenger. "To this day," says Louis Lomax, "the wellspring of Muhammad's power flows from the fact that he was with Fard in life and possibly in death."[8]

The Black Muslim movement is partially a collective response to the concentration of structural strain that has been passed down into the black community from the political system and elsewhere. Its development and growth can be largely traced to distributive and regulative strains that developed in the 1950's when, encouraged by white liberal leaders and some signs of change, blacks began to make extensive demands on the political system for goods, services, positions, and opportunities. By the beginning of the 1960's, however, disillusionment in the black lower class became apparent as the general rise in expectations was followed by insufficient realization. Bonds of obligation between these disillusioned and the white ruling leadership began to erode when trustful relationships were shaken by the unwillingness or inability of white leaders, especially at the state level, to deliver the goods that had been promised. Capitalizing on this deflation of trust, "the Black Muslims came to power during a moral interregnum, at a time when it seemed that this nation would refuse to obey its own desegregation laws."[9]

Distributive problems constitute the greatest obstacle to the development of trust between ruling leaders and the black population. While some progress has been made, our national, state, and local governments have failed to make strenuous efforts to reverse a long history of distributive injustice in which blacks and other minority groups have persistently been denied their share of goods, services, honors, statuses, and opportunities. Consider, for example, the fact that, while the enrollment of whites and nonwhites in school achieved percentage-wise parity only in 1950, far fewer nonwhites finished high school and college. In 1957, for instance, 18.4 per cent of nonwhites 25 years and older finished high school as compared to 41.6 per cent of white youth. And only 2.9 per cent of nonwhites as compared to 7.6 per cent of whites finished college.[10]

Discouraged by whites and some blacks from going on to college to train for professional occupations, some blacks, like Malcolm X, leave school and turn to marginal jobs on the street. Many others, untrained for skilled work, fall into low-paying, low-status jobs in the unskilled and semiskilled labor market. In 1950, only 10.2 per cent of nonwhites were employed in white-collar occupations, which includes professional and managerial roles, as compared to 40.3 per cent of the white population. Nonwhite employment was concentrated in blue-collar jobs or in service occupations. In the latter case, nonwhites dominated clearly, for 33.8 per cent of nonwhites performed service roles in 1950 in comparison to only 8.5 per cent of the white population.[11] While these figures are based on data collected for the group of nonwhites, similar findings for blacks as a narrower category turn up in occupational distribution figures in the military services in the 1960's. Many blacks end up in the infantry (16.4 per cent, although in Viet Nam blacks sometimes constitute as much as from 40 to 45 per cent of infantry units), the medical corps and dental services (11.8 per cent), or in service and supply roles with the Navy's food service or with the quartermasters (16.9 per cent). As we would expect, few blacks are assigned to skilled jobs in the field of electronics (only 5.5 per cent are electronic equipment repairmen), crafts (9.3 per cent), and communications and intelligence (only 6.7 per cent).[12]

Untrained and vulnerable to economic fluctuations that hit the unskilled reservoir of labor heavily, blacks and nonwhites in general are the first to be placed on the unemployment rolls. In every year from 1948 to 1967, the percentage of unemployed nonwhite males, aged 16 and over, has been twice as high as for the corresponding white group. In 1954, for instance, 10.3 per cent of nonwhite males as compared to 4.8 per cent of white males were unable to secure permanent jobs. Hardest hit in both groups were the younger men, although, beginning in 1956, the percentage of unemployed nonwhite males between 16-19 years of age rose rapidly; whereas, the unemployment rate for white males of the same age remained fairly constant. For example, among nonwhite males in the 18-19 age group, 14.7 per cent were unemployed in 1954 versus 13 per cent of the white group; yet, by 1958, the disparity between the two groups had become very great. By that year, 26.7 per cent of 18-19-year-old nonwhites were jobless, almost twice as many as only four years earlier, as compared to 16.5 per cent of whites, a meager increase of only 3.5 per cent for the same period. It is also important that for the 20-24 age group the rate of unemployment has been about twice as high for nonwhites as for whites, starting as early as 1948.[13] The significant difference in unemployment rates, but especially the growing disparity among the young males, is one source of distributive injustice that generates mistrust of leadership and encourages the disillusioned to seek out new leaders. Thus, it is not surprising that, according to C. Eric Lincoln, the followers of Mr. Muhammad tend to be young, up to 80 per cent of a typical congregation's membership falling between the ages of seventeen and thirty-five. Congregations are also predominantly male, unlike typical Christian churches, and come primarily from lower-class backgrounds, with low incomes and low educational achievements.[14]

It is true that the nonwhite family's median income has increased steadily since the end of World War II, but it still remains about half as large as the comparable figure for the white family. Thus, while the white wage-earner was making an average of $4,605 in 1955, his nonwhite counterpart was making only $2,549. This difference would probably be understandable, and even tolerable for the nonwhite worker, if it was only a function of the different occupational statuses they occupy. But major disparities of income exist as well within the same occupations. In 1959, we discover that the median income of bakers as a whole was $4,633, but for nonwhite bakers it was only $3,354. Nonwhite carpenters made an average of $2,320 that year, almost $2,000 less than the total of $4,271 for the occupation as a whole. And, while tinsmiths, coppersmiths, and sheet metal workers had average incomes of $5,542, nonwhite workers in the same occupation had to be content with $4,710.[15] In conditions of relative deprivation, such as these figures suggest, frustration rather than contentment is apt to develop, for when rewards are so unevenly distributed among individuals in comparable statuses, the party receiving the smaller share of goods can hardly close his eyes to the inequity, even though he may tolerate it out of necessity.

The intervention of politics into economic and social life that began in the 1930's appears not to have lessened distributive injustices in the black community very much. In education, housing, and employment the regulative capability of the political system has been relatively weak and in some areas, such as income and employment, it has not been able to regulate the activities of businesses or labor unions to insure advancements for blacks. Consequently, income and occupational opportunities have actually deteriorated if we compare them to rather large gains made by whites. And the changes that have taken place have come only very slowly and with the constant prompting of federal officials trying to enforce civil rights legislation. Part of this problem lies in the racist attitudes that have pervaded our mental life so long, but we should not underrate the influence of political decentralization. The delegation of powers to the states, especially the police power, and the further fragmentation of power through the granting of "home-rule" charters to counties and cities has seriously weakened the ability of the federal government to enforce national law. It has had to bargain with governments that outwardly resisted when ordered by the Justice Department to enforce civil rights legislation. Aid to southern schools and matching grants for public works construction were not very subtle rewards intended to gain southern compliance. The threat to withdraw federal contacts from areas in which there was resistance to federal efforts was met with cries of "black mail." To insure that the voting rights bill would be enforced, federal marshals were sent into the South to prevent deliberate registration and election irregularities. And more than once, force has had to be used to bring law-breaking state officials to heel, even though none, to my knowledge, spent time in prison. On the surface, these threats and the use of force by the national government may seem to be indications of a growing regulative ability. Yet the fact that threats and force have had to be used is testimony that there are weaknesses in the system's responsive capability that make threats and force necessary.

While the national government has been relatively ineffective in enforcing civil rights laws, local social control agencies and courts have been fairly successful in filling our prisons with blacks and members of other minority groups. Thus, while the nonwhite population constituted only 10 per cent of the total U.S. population in 1950, nonwhites made up 34.8 per cent of the total prison population.[16] The concentration of criminal activity in nonwhite neighborhoods is a function of the concentrated social strains that are present in nonwhite communities. For where unemployment is high, income low, and opportunities few, crime becomes a profession of necessity. Those who made their living through crimes against society had been well prepared by the social strains of ghetto life to accept the teachings of Mr. Muhammad, and many of those who were detained in prison did so. Indeed, the Black Muslim movement made significant gains in mobilizing black prisoners, for, at the peak of its success, six hundred were joining the Nation of Islam each year.[17]

Accompanying the structural strains that were concentrated in the black community were two factors that greatly increased the ambiguity of the black's situation in the 1950's. First was the Supreme Court's 1954 decision to forbid segregated schools, the implications of which held out hope that other types of segregation would be abolished in their turn. On the one hand, we could point to this decision as the turning point in the political system's effort to rectify distributive injustice, but, on the other hand, it was also the source of increasing uncertainty and personal tension for the black citizen. For once the Court had decided that segregated public facilities were not in harmony with the U.S. Constitution, it destroyed the legitimacy of the old racist norms that had governed the nature of transactions between blacks and whites. While equality was intended to be the normative umbrella under which new transactional patterns were to be protected, the failure of the executive branch of the national government to effectively regulate the political behavior of state officials, local leaders, and subordinates in its own bureaucratic structure made it apparent from the beginning that "equality" was a "hunting license" rather than a viable norm for the formation of a new transactional pattern. Given the decay of the old racist norms and the weak adherence to equality, social and political exchanges between blacks and whites became somewhat haphazard as they had no stable normative moorings. Also, considerable uncertainty developed among blacks about which social and political barriers would give way under pressure and there was also serious doubt about the means to be used and how to react to possible forms of retaliation. The failure of procedural means and the increasing search for some understandable and predictable relations with whites is partially what led many blacks to finally embrace the ideology of "black power" in the 1960's and, even earlier, to join the Nation of Islam.

The migration of blacks from the farm and the South to the city and the North is the second factor that contributed to a rise of ambiguity. In the search for better opportunities, blacks began moving in great numbers to the urban and northern parts of the nation as early as 1930. The magnitude of this demographic change is reflected in the fact that the percentage of blacks living in urban areas rose from 43.7 per cent in 1930 to 73.2 per cent in 1960. The migration of blacks to the various regions of the North is not so striking but is nonetheless significant, for, while they made up 78.8 per cent of the South's population in 1930, in 1960 they constituted only 60 per cent. In the Northeast, the percentage of blacks in the population rose from 9.6 per cent in 1930 to 16 per cent in 1960. Similarly large increases occurred in other regions as well.[18] Those blacks who went North seeking an escape from the distributive and regulative abuses of the southern social and political systems were bewildered by what they found there.

> Many came North seeking "a way out" of their miseries in the South. Subsequent experience taught most that the Northern city was far from being the "promised land"; because they lacked education and skills, their employment and the cultural opportunities were limited. They found that discrimination in jobs and housing in the North, just as in the South, is sanctioned custom. These migrants were strangers not only to the white society but also to the urbanized Negro community. The established Negro residents resent them because of fear that the "ignorant" migrants would inundate their neighborhoods. They fear that the newcomers' rustic ways would impede the "advancements of the race," check the "gains" which they have already made in race relations, and impair their acceptance by whites. They are ashamed of the newcomers—aptly described by a Negro reporter as the "unwanted from Dixie."[19]

For the "unwanted from Dixie," "unemployment, broken homes, and sickness are their common experience. Bitterness, frustration, and disillusionment are the constant ingredients of their daily life."[20] We should add ambiguity to this list, for the insecurities of their condition, which seriously eroded the capacity to predict, made many blacks susceptible to the suggestions of rebel leaders whose views helped them to give structure and definition to their lives. Lincoln is referring to this causal relationship when he writes: "The lynchings, the danger of being killed under arrest, the unevenness and uncertainty of justice in the courts, the continuing problem of simply finding a decent place to live—all are contributory to the making of a Muslim and to the propagation of a mass movement of protest."[21]

Yet for those blacks who moved from the South there was an additional source of ambiguity. In the North, the outward appearances of segregation were gone but racist feelings still dominated white attitudes, creating more subtle forms of discrimination. These subtle forms of discrimination, as opposed to the blatant forms in the South, prevented a clear definition of relationships between blacks and whites from forming, thus breeding confusion about what behaviors were truly expected in a variety of social and political exchanges. The increasing ambiguity of the norms governing black-white relationships made exchanges a source of considerable personal tension for members of both races. One could even argue that the black ghetto, the physical manifestation of concentrated social strain, became a convenient mechanism used by both races to avoid contact and thereby reduce ambiguity. And racial separatism, a feature of the Black Muslim ideology, is meant to reduce that contact and the accompanying ambiguity even further. Furthermore, the normative code of the movement provides its members with clear guidelines for relating to whites, which provides a predictable and stable pattern to racial relationships that the events of the 1950's had altered.

The Bolshevik Revolution

Lenin was in exile when Czar Nicholas II was removed by force of arms and a bourgeois government donned the discarded mantle of authority. But this change, the so-called "February Revolution," was in fact only an adjustive change in leadership, as the Provisional Government demonstrated by supporting basically czarist policies. When Lenin returned to Russia in April, 1917, attacking the position of the legal government and offering proposals for radical political and economic innovations, he was criticized openly by sectors of the worker, military, and peasant populations that were not yet ready for a second revolution. Insufficiently disillusioned with the war against Germany, for instance, many soldiers thought Lenin's position an outrage and expressed their opposition in direct and forceful terms: "'Ought to stick our bayonets into a fellow like that,'" one soldier shouted in response to one of his first speeches.[22] On into May, and especially after Lenin had been accused of collaboration with the Germans, the tide of public feeling against the Bolsheviks was rising. "The names of Lenin and his companions-in-arms, daily spattered with filth, were still heard with hatred and suspicion by the ignorant masses," recalled N. N. Sukhanov.[23] Yet within a few months' time, many of those who had been openly hostile toward Lenin would be standing with the Bolsheviks acknowledging him as the head of a new state.

The Bolsheviks were able to eventually overthrow the Provisional Government not because they were inordinately strong but because the regime's capabilities were excessively weak. Structural strains resulting from this weakness were generalized to most sectors of the population, although peasants, soldiers, sailors, and workers were hardest hit by the costs of ineffective political structures and political mismanagement. Indeed, as the months of 1917 wore on, increasing demands for change originating in those four sectors, and the erosion of the political system's capabilities, created such enormous strains that the regime collapsed from the sheer weight of them. However, the truth of the matter is that very little weight was necessary to topple the government, for its middle-class basis as well as the counter-vailing power of the Soviets doomed it almost from the moment of its inception.

Out of the chaos created by the unexpected collapse of czarism, two separate centers of political authority developed, which we have come to know as the dual system of government. First was the Provisional Government, whose function it was to prepare the way for elections to the Constituent Assembly and the formation of a permanent government. An evolutionary extension of the old State Duma, it was essentially bourgeoisie in character, representing the propertied and liberal elements of Russian society, most of whom had taken no responsibility at all for leading the February revolution. Alongside this bastion of the middle class was the Soviet of Workers' and Soldiers' Deputies. Resurrected from the unsuccessful 1905 revolution, the Soviet was the political body of the masses of peasants, soldiers, sailors, and workers, most of whom outwardly distrusted the provisional leaders that the socialists had placed in power as a historical necessity. Ironically, both these governments held their meetings in the Tauride Palace, which was probably the closest they came to being integrated political structures. For conflicts between them were present from the beginning, and the fact that the Soviet had both organizational and popular support gave it an advantage that it never relinquished. Thus we can speak of a dual system of government in theory only, for, in actual practice, political power was concentrated in the Soviet, a fact that accounts for the Provisional Government's low capability for effective rule. Already by March, War Minister A. I. Guchkov could write:

> The Provisional Government possesses no real power and its orders are executed only insofar as this is permitted by the Soviet of Workers' and Soldiers' Deputies, which holds in its hands the most important elements of actual power, such as troops, railroads, postal and telegraph service. It is possible to say directly that the Provisional Government exists only while this is permitted by the Soviet.[24]

Extractive weaknesses in the Provisional Government can be traced to its inability to mobilize goods and popular support among the peasants, workers, soldiers, sailors, and police. We know that under czarist rule peasants were forced to pay astonishingly high taxes: "It was calculated when the redemption payments came to an end that the value of the lands allotted to the peasantry in 1861 had already been paid three times over."[25] In order to meet these heavy extractive demands many peasants were forced to sell their land in order to make their payments to the government. Thus, between 1861 and 1905 "the average size of the peasants' holdings diminished by one-third."[26] Under czarism the ruling leadership had demanded taxes with no accompanying rewards for the peasantry. Now, under the Provisional Government, peasants were recruited to fight in the trenches while members of the government promised to study the land distribution problem rather than to make changes that would rectify the inequity. Under czarism, but also under the hand of the bourgeois leadership, the peasants "became increasingly conscious of the state as an alien and hostile force, which made demands without conferring benefits."[27] Unwilling to work to meet governmental demands for food and preoccupied with land seizures, which usually occurred during the harvest season, the productivity of the peasant community fell considerably behind consumer demands. Food shortages became so excessive that the Provisional Government "proclaimed a state monopoly of grain, decreeing that all grain which was not required for the nourishment of the agriculturists and their domestic animals and for seed should be sold to state organizations at fixed prices."[28]

Combined with food shortages was an extractive weakness in the regime's capability to gain the support of the mass of workers, especially for carrying on the war. Committed to the continuation of the war for the sake of honor, the government depended on full-scale industrial production to supply the front with adequate materials. Yet, by March, workers who had long considered the eight-hour day a guarantee of the revolution took things into their own hands. The Petrograd workers, in league with the Soviet, unilaterally instituted the eight-hour day for industrial workers and the Provisional Government could do nothing. The implications of this change in terms of industrial output were fairly clear, for in 1913 only 119,000 of the 2,218,000 industrial workers were enjoying an eight-hour day, while the bulk, or 1,351,000, were required to work ten or more hours each day.[29] The effect of the Petrograd workers' action thus meant, at the very least, a loss of some 2,600,000 hours of production each day, a reduction in productive capacity whose magnitude can only be gauged in terms of the already pressing shortages of supplies at the front.

Had the provisional leadership had support among the soldiers, sailors, and police, there might have been a faint glimmer of hope for the regime. But all indications are that it was unable to extract promises of allegiance, except from the numerically small group of Cadets, who had become the chief military advocates of war and conservatism. Appeals to the peasant soldiers at the front, who were anxious to return home after the fall of czarism, were empty and unsuccessful. In the first few weeks after the February revolution the attitudes of these soldiers toward the provisional leadership became quite apparent as over 1 million left the trenches to return home. Neither was the Provisional Government able to mobilize support among the sailors. At the Kronstadt base, 55,000 sailors were led in revolt against their officers, some of whom they killed, while 200 were held as hostages. Declaring their independence from the government, the sailors would not listen to the provisional leaders and even refused to recognize the Petrograd Soviet.[30] To make matters worse, policemen of the czarist era, who were despised by the public for their resistance to the revolution, had been dismissed from their posts. Potential allies of the provisional regime, these professional defenders of the state were replaced by an amateurish and unreliable militia.

With little support from military and police quarters, and hampered by its dependence on the Soviet, the Provisional Government's regulative attempt to allocate and integrate roles and control deviation was nothing short of a disaster. Operating in an atmosphere of mistrust, its only hope of building credits was to propose goals that promised peasants, soldiers, and workers the goods they expected from a "revolutionary" government—a redistribution of land, an end of the war and of outdated military restrictions,[31] and a reorganization of the economic system that would force factory owners to make some major concessions to the workers. As representatives of the propertied class, these were changes that the provisional leaders could not and would not support. Neither would the peasants, soldiers, and workers be content to play the roles assigned to them under czarist rule, which the provisional leaders foolishly insisted they were duty-bound to perform. This ideological impasse, created by the provisional leadership's unwillingness to follow, had numerous regulative consequences.

Peasants turned to rebellion when they realized that the Provisional Government intended to do nothing about their demands for a more equitable distribution of land. Reports of peasant disorders were recorded as early as March 22 and on March 30 a statement was issued by the government that argued that land seizures were no way to solve the land question and promised to begin collecting material that could be put to legislative use by the permanent government they were working to create. Over one month later a Main Land Committee was appointed by the government to carry out its promise. The reluctance to act in a forthright legislative fashion, which was obvious in this case, was generally indicative of the frame of mind of the provisional leaders, who were apparently not even convinced that they constituted a government. Unwilling to wait for the formation of a permanent government to rectify distributive injustice, the peasants turned to confiscation and plunder. By September the countryside was in constant ferment and the government was too weak to stop it. In Tambov, for example, one estate was pillaged and twenty-five were razed to the ground by torch-carrying peasants. Cattle were stolen, land and forests divided, and granaries emptied on estates at Sartov. And in Voronezh, numerous estates were reportedly destroyed, over a thousand tons of grain burned, and irreplaceable antique furnishings smashed.[32] And so it went from one peasant community to another. Beyond patience, the peasantry had decided to take politics into its own hands.

The Russian army, with inadequate equipment, insufficient supplies, and ebbing morale, had fared very poorly against better equipped German forces. Hoping to turn the tide of war and enhance the morale of his soldiers simultaneously, Alexander Kerensky, then Minister of War, ordered the army to begin a massive offensive in July in order to break through the Germans' stalwart defenses. Caught by surprise, the German forces offered little resistance to the attack, allowing Russian soldiers the opportunity to move ahead along a solid front. However, the Russian generals, elated by what appeared to be a major victory, eventually watched the enemy regroup, cease retreating, and turn what they hoped would be a striking victory into a staggering defeat. Beaten at the very peak of its strength, the morale of the Russian army collapsed. One telegram from the front described the mood of the soldiers: "The majority of the troops are becoming more and more demoralized. No one listens to authority or orders. Persuasion and pleading are in vain and are answered by threats and even by shots."[33]

These regulative problems within the army had a political source, for in March the representatives of the Soldiers' Soviet had paved the way for insubordination by adopting a new manifesto—the Declaration of the Rights of Soldiers. Its effects were far-reaching. Among its provisions were articles that abolished an officer's right to impose disciplinary punishments on his subordinates, and abolished compulsory saluting, political censorship of mail, and rules restricting the right of soldiers to organize. The consequences of these provisions on military operations are conveyed in a letter from General Alekseev to the War Ministry on April 29:

> Discipline in the army is declining every day. . . . The authority of the officers has fallen, and there is no power to reestablish it. The spirit of the officers' corps is falling more and more as a result of the undeserved insults and acts of violence which are inflicted upon officers, under the influence of their removal from actual power over their subordinates or the transfer of this authority to the soldiers' committees. . . .[34]

By September, the soldiers' rebellion against the war and their officers became both more generalized and more intense. Four officers were shot and killed by their own subordinates in Helsingfors and, at Vyborg three generals and a colonel were thrown into the river to drown. Furthermore, clashes occurred between rebel soldiers and troops loyal to the provisional regime, one such incident having taken place at Elisavetgrad, where several men were killed and twenty-one wounded.[35]

In the first days of October, soldiers on the northern front, who had lost all respect for their officers, were becoming increasingly aware that deviation would not be punished. Aside from the weakening resolve of their officers to make arrests, social control mechanisms were also made inoperative by military courts that were unable to function properly in an atmosphere of extreme hostility. Encouraged by this weakening regulative capacity, soldiers continued to rebel against authority. The Provisional Government received special abuse among the soldiers of the 12th Army, one regiment having declared Kerensky, by then the head of the Provisional Government, a traitor to the February revolution. On the western front, 8,000 soldiers being transferred to enemy lines demanded that they be sent home instead. Provoked to action when their request was denied, they stormed the armory and assaulted two officers whose sympathies were with the government. Similar events transpired on the southwestern front, where the main theme of conversation had become "peace at any price and under any condition." There, the soldiers of the 2nd Army passed a resolution expressing no confidence in their officers and began invading estates to secure provisions that were in short supply.[36]

Regulative problems in the urban areas were aggravated by the increasing intensity of two strains that the provisional leadership had seemed to push into the background while preoccupied with the war. First there was a shortage of food in the city, owing both to peasant unrest that reduced productivity and to the higher priority soldiers were given in the distribution process. Having to assume the costs of the war in this way generated tension among city-dwellers, resulting in collective outbursts. Food riots, while not everyday occurrences, were frequent enough to remind the uncommitted urban masses of the failings of the ruling regime. When bread and flour prices were increased in Azov, adding to the already widespread scarcity, a mob broke into the city's food department, summarily throwing a public official who had intervened down two flights of stairs. Similar riots in Omsk became so serious that a military detachment was deployed to the scene, but only after several shops and private homes had been destroyed and the chairman of the city's food administration had been killed.[37]

The labor-management dispute was another source of strain that affected the regime's regulative capability in the urban areas. Having failed to gain the necessary concessions from their employers, workers turned their attention to a more dangerous objective—wresting control from the bourgeoisie and assuming command over the means of production. When the general urban crisis had immobilized the police machinery, reducing the effectiveness of law enforcement, the workers' aspirations were suddenly accompanied by bold action. "Shots were fired at factory administrators, they were arrested for refusing to raise wages, executives were ousted or barricaded in their offices. . . . The government could do little to stem the tide."[38]

Racked by extractive and regulative weaknesses, it is almost a foregone conclusion that the provisional leadership's ability to distribute goods, services, honors, statuses, and opportunities would decline accordingly. But its low distributive capability has to be linked to its own lack of concern for the domestic issues around which demands for redistribution revolved. "Their first object was to restore order, to get the Dark People under control, and after that they were all for going on with the war." In contrast, the Executive Committee of the Soviet was concerned primarily with domestic problems, such as the eight-hour day and the general improvement of working conditions.[39] In a time when distributive injustices were uppermost in the minds of the masses, the Provisional Government had chosen a reckless course to follow.

A further weakness of the Provisional Government lay in the liberal ideology of its leaders. Committed to the forms of western democracy, at the outset they granted amnesty to political prisoners, guaranteed freedom of speech and assembly, and promised to ensure equal rights for all citizens (whether of foreign nationality or not). Such guarantees had the effect of stimulating the development of many new political organizations and activities.

> The first weeks of the new regime were characterized by feverish organization and an endless flood of talk. Socialist parties and trade-unions, proscribed or barely tolerated under Tsarism, sprang into life and activity. With the long crust of censorship and repression broken, people of all classes felt the impulse to meet, discuss, pronounce speeches. The fullest liberty of speech and press had been decreed; and there was no power that could have enforced restrictions, even if any had existed. So meetings and speeches went on everywhere, at congresses of parties and organizations, on public squares and street corners.[40]

This increase and proliferation of new political groups had serious effects on the Provisional Government's responsive capability. First, as the number of political associations multiplied, so did the number of demands for governmental decisions. Obliged to postpone legislative action on domestic problems until the formation of a permanent government, and with little power to legislate or execute new laws, the provisional leaders could not respond to the tide of new demands that their generous granting of rights had produced. The resulting disparity between the level of demands and the ability to meet them had the consequence of enlarging the authority of the Soviet, for the new political groups, expecting no decisions from the provisional leaders, took their demands to the Soviet instead. Thus, it was that "the Soviet more and more became the centre of Russian political life. It was to the Soviet, not to the Provisional Government, that delegates swarmed with greetings, proposals, complaints."[41]

Under the protection of these democratic guarantees, new Soviets began springing up in every city, town, and village. Alongside these popular assemblies, the commissars appointed by the Provisional Government were powerless. In many places, the Soviet alone was the seat of government. Even against the wishes of the Petrograd Soviet, for example, the Kronstadt Soviet declared itself the sole governing power in the city; and in the town of Krasnoyarsk, the local Soviet was already a fully operating government. "It introduced a rationing system, not only for food but also for manufactured goods, granted furloughs to soldiers, regardless of the protests of the commander of the military district, interfered in local labor disputes to the point of handing over to the trade-union sawmills and flour-mills where the employers refused to satisfy the demands of the workers."[42] The inability of the provisional leadership to secure a foothold in these areas added further to its already diminished responsive capability by reducing the integration of local and national governing units necessary for the smooth operation of government. To make matters more serious, the minority states of Finland,

Estonia, Lithuania, the Ukraine, the Caucasus, and Siberia took the provisional leadership's statements about equality at face value and immediately demanded independence from the state.[43]

It should be clear by now that the political impotence of the Provisional Government can only partly be attributed to the mismanagement of its leaders. We have to remember that the Socialists had encouraged the bourgeoisie to assume political office in a climate of suspicion and mistrust, then withheld the resources of power that were necessary for the rudimentary operations of government. Therefore, it was not just from the intransigence of the provisional leadership that the Soviet, and later the Bolshevik party, attained its great popular following, but from the structural inadequacies of the political system with its dual governments. Amidst the contradictions and conflicts of this political arrangement it is little wonder that the provisional regime's capabilities could not develop. More than this, the existence of two independent governing bodies with such competing purposes added considerable ambiguity to the already rampant uncertainties surrounding mass unrest and protest. In this regard, we should expect that the success of the Bolsheviks stemmed not only from their promises to rectify the distributive injustices maintained by the provisional leaders, but also from their promise to end the ambiguities of the dual system of government by the exercise of force.

The Nazi Revolution

The Nazi movement developed out of structural strains that became generalized throughout most of German society in the late 1920's and early 1930's. In this period, diminishing capabilities of the Weimar regime went hand-in-hand with a sharp rise in demand for goods, statuses, and services. Almost from the beginning, the leaders of the Weimar government were forced into the paradoxical position of having to distribute the costs of reducing strain in one sector onto other sectors, thereby diffusing structural strains to the society as a whole, instead of confining the costs to one or two sectors they could control. By distributing strain back and forth between sectors, they generalized personal tension and mistrust, which are the antecedents to the breaking up of transactional patterns and to the search for new leadership.

The extractive capability of the Weimar regime was low in relation to the demands for material resources, a source of strain that touched more than one sector of the population. Bound by the Treaty of Versailles, Germany was required to make material retribution to the Allies in cash, goods, machinery, and the like, to the tune of 132 billion gold marks, or approximately 32 billion dollars. While the Allies were draining capital from the government's treasury, the United States was floating sizable loans to the Republic, most of which aided the industrial barons in their campaign to enlarge the industrial plant. Yet this expansion failed to increase the productive output of industry. Even during the peak of the economic boom of 1929 heavy industry fell far below its actual productive potential and the output of goods deteriorated rapidly by the end of that year. The result was a sharp decline in national income, from 72 billion marks in 1928 to 48 billion in 1932. In addition to reparation payments, the Weimar leadership found itself subsidizing the huge economic cartels, trusts, and agricultural estates. To diminish the economic crisis, the cost of reducing the pressure on faltering industrial and agricultural interests was distributed to lower- and middle-class taxpayers in the early 1920's. To make matters worse, the regime persisted in levying a heavy tax even though wages and salaries fell from 44 billion marks in 1929 to 25 billion in 1932. Mistrust of ruling leaders mounted as "the worker became aware that a share of his tax payments was being diverted to subsidize agriculture on the estates of the large landowner."[44] Middle-class investors were also hit hard by the extractive policies of the regime. By borrowing heavily from the Reichsbank to pay national debts, the government was caught in a spiraling financial shortage that could only be solved by issuing new notes. The result was rampant inflation even by 1923 (the dollar was worth 3 to 4 billion marks in that year). Small middle-class investors paid heavily in savings, stocks, bonds, and mortgages as the mark dipped sharply in value.

The Weimar Constitution, the politicization of the *Reichswehr,* the right-wing bias of the judges, and the clashes between the Communist and Nazi forces posed serious obstacles to the leaders of the Republic in their efforts to allocate and integrate roles and to control political and criminal deviation. From the beginning, the regime's regulative capability was undermined by the provisions of the constitution that created a pluralist political system. In this regard, Franz Neumann suggests that "compromise among all social and political groups was the essence of the constitution. Antagonistic interests were to be harmonized by the device of a pluralistic political structure, hidden behind the form of parliamentary democracy."[45] At the time, it was hoped that the sharp divisions that had existed between the dominant classes would be lessened by a political framework whose success depended on the participation and cooperation of special interests in each class.

To insure that each important interest group had a stake in the political marketplace, the principle of proportional representation was employed in the election of representatives to the *Reichstag,* which meant that political parties secured legislative seats in proportion to their electoral strength. The consequence, of course, was a highly fragmented legislature in which no single political party could secure majority control for itself. In order to rule, coalitions were necessary both in the *Reichstag* and in the Cabinet, but political ties among the strongly ideological factions of the Left, Center, and Right were quite tenuous and short-lived. Furthermore, "there was little sense of loyalty among the Party members to their representatives in the Cabinet and no Chancellor or Minister could ever be sure that he would not be stabbed in the back by his own followers."[46] Unable to resolve the disagreements institutionalized by pluralism, and hampered by disloyalty, coalition governments were formed, fell from grace, and were dissolved so rapidly that governmental stability was never achieved. The government leaders could neither integrate nor control the legislature, with the predictable effect—serious problems of extraction, regulation, and distribution were left in abeyance.

Had the leadership of the *Reichswehr* remained loyal to the Republic or to their apolitical tradition, Hitler's aspirations for dictatorial control would probably have been unrewarded. But among the generals there were those who regarded the Republic almost as if it were a government imposed by foreign occupation. Nor were the generals ready to forgive the Allies, who had pressed for the adoption of new governmental forms, for having drastically reduced the size (to 100,000 men) and influence of the army through the provisions of the Treaty of Versailles. As heads of a smaller professional army, the generals felt diminished in status and power, at least in comparison with former times.

Although there had been a long-standing nonpartisan political tradition in the military, the desire to regain their former position of prominence in the Reich enticed a few ambitious generals to enter into political intrigue, thinking they would use Hitler to restore the influence of the *Reichswehr,* not to mention their own. The most notable of these generals was Kurt von Schleicher, a man who "dreamed not only of restoring the conservative military caste in Germany but also of reviving that old spirit of Prussian military-socialism which could unite the Army with the Trade Unions and thereby provide a ready reservoir of manpower upon which the military direction might draw at will."[47] Von Schleicher felt that he, among those in positions to lead the government, was chosen by destiny to guide the faltering Republic between the warring Communist and Nazi movements and then to safety. His strategy was very simple and very military in its origin: Divide the two political camps, then conquer each in turn.

Von Schleicher had two major resources in his move for power: President von Hindenburg trusted him almost to excess, and he commanded great influence among the officers of the General Staff. Using his persuasive skills with the President and threatening to withdraw the support of the *Reichswehr* when necessary, von Schleicher worked behind the collapsing façade of the Republic, applying his influence to make Chancellors and then to oppose and remove them. The last in a long line of men who met this fate was Franz von Papen, who, in a fit of revenge against von Schleicher, collaborated with Hitler and drew on his good will with the President to pave the way for Hitler's appointment as Chancellor.

Von Schleicher's Chancellor-making exploits seriously reduced the regulative capability of the regime, first by creating ambiguity about the *Reichswehr's* willingness to defend the government and, second, by forcing rapid changes in executive leadership upon the government. If that were not enough, his policy of divide and conquer was a disaster because it was partially successful: In Prussia he succeeded in splitting the Left by removing the trade unions from the influence of the Social Democratic party, but his attempt to create permanent and devastating fractures in the Nazi ranks was a total failure. His strategy underestimated Hitler's personal power within the Nazi party and seriously overestimated the potential influence of the head of organization, Gregor Strasser. He knew that Hitler had insisted that he would not join a coalition government except as Chancellor with dictatorial powers. This was not a closed issue within the Party, however, for several leaders, Strasser being one, were of the opinion that Hitler's demands would not be met, thus leaving infiltration the only practical avenue to power. Conscious of this conflict, von Schleicher offered Strasser the Vice-Chancellorship, thinking that he might accept and thereupon wreak havoc on the party. He was wrong, of course. Instead of accepting the appointment, Strasser preferred to resign from his official position in the party rather than confront Hitler directly on the issue. As was his customary tactic, Hitler turned on Strasser, discrediting him in public as the man who had stabbed him in the back. Thus, with his usual cunning in crisis situations, Hitler turned Strasser into a scapegoat that he could conveniently use to rally his followers behind him. Such was the consequence of von Schleicher's plan: Instead of dividing the party he had given Hitler the incident he needed to consolidate his support for the final assault on the regime. But the generals "may well have had it in their power in those fateful January days to combat the final consummation of that National Socialist rise to power, which they, by their own equivocal policy, had helped to promote; but they did not wish to do so."[48]

Further regulative weakness was imposed on the regime from within the court system, which had concentrated extensive power in the hands of judges, many being considerably less than impartial in the administration of justice. For, like the leaders of the *Reichswehr,* the judges tended to sympathize with nationalistic groups of the Right and to be hostile toward those with leftist leanings. Neumann exposes these ideological biases in the judicial system by referring to the court's decisions in three important political cases, which I will only mention briefly. First, when the Bavarian Soviet Republic collapsed in 1919 the court was swift in imposing stiff penalties for those of the Left: 407 persons were sentenced to fortress imprisonment; 1,737 persons were sent to regular prisons; and 65 persons were assigned to imprisonment at hard labor. In contrast, the right-wing participants in the unsuccessful Kapp Putsch of 1920 suffered only the inconvenience of the fifteen-month delay incurred by review of their cases by the Reich Ministry of Justice: 412 cases were dismissed under the amnesty law of 1920, even though, according to Newmann, the law had intentionally excluded the putsch leaders; 108 cases were declared obsolete owing to death or other circumstances; 174 cases were not pressed; and 11 cases were still pending. Similar judicial tolerance of the Right can be found in the court's handling of the Nazi Putsch of 1923. Not only did the presiding judge allow Hitler "to deliver a two-hour harangue packed with insults against high government

officials and threats against his enemies, without being arrested for contempt,"[49] but relatively light sentences were handed down for the leaders
of the conspiracy. Hitler and three others received five-year sentences, while
five others were given sentences of one year and three months. Most significant in terms of regulation, however, was the judge's unwillingness to
deport Hitler under section 9 of the Law for the Protection of the Republic,
which required the deportation of every alien convicted of high treason
(Hitler was an Austrian citizen). The depth of the judge's nationalistic
sympathy was clear when he exempted Hitler from the provisions of the
law, after accepting his argument that, while he was not officially a German
citizen, he considered himself to be German.

Given the regulative strains originating from within the Weimar constitution, the *Reichswehr,* and the judicial system, groups on both ends of the
political spectrum were able, almost at will, to organize along military lines.
From the early 1920's the courts had tolerated the operation of various
reactionary military groups, and the leadership of the *Reichswehr* viewed
this military resurgence with approval. Within this permissive setting, the
military arms of the Nazi party, the SA and the SS, flourished. Working
under the legitimizing cover of legality, Hitler used his influence to insure
that the SA operated inside the law as much as possible, but his control
over the local units was often too tenuous to prevent armed clashes with
the Communists and the general use of strong-arm tactics against other
political enemies. The regime's inability to deal with the militarization of
political struggle is demonstrated by the steady rise in the number and
magnitude of incidents of political violence. Thus, in 1929, 42 deaths from
political warfare were reported. The figure rose to 50 in 1930 and in the
first half of 1931 the number reached 100. In the months of April and May
alone, political violence resulted in 15 dead, 200 serious casualties, and 1,000
minor casualties.[50]

After President von Hindenburg defeated Hitler for another term as
President in 1932, the leadership of the Reich government finally took the
initiative and dissolved the SA, the SS, and the affiliated Hitler Youth, and
prohibited them from wearing their uniforms,[51] a move that had been
encouraged for some time by the federal states and the Social Democratic
party. But at this late moment, such a prohibition was ludicrous, for Nazi
party electoral support had already made it the largest party in the *Reichstag*.
Therefore, when the Nazis soundly defeated their political opposition in the
Mecklenburg local elections in June, winning 29 seats, as many as all other
political parties combined, von Hindenburg was forced to reconsider and
finally rescinded his ban of the Nazi military forces ten days later. The
regulative problems aggravated by this reversal are pointed out by Wheeler-
Bennett:

> . . . at once a wave of political violence and assault swept through the
> country. Nazis and Communists responded with avid enthusiasm to the provo-

cation which each offered to the other, and bloody disputes ensued in all parts of the Reich. They were equally violent against the Social Democrats, breaking up their election meetings and the parades of the *Reichsbanner,* and attacking the editorial offices of *Vorwärts.*[52]

The best the Cabinet could do at this point to meet the calls for a restoration of order was to ban political demonstrations and parades: this in the face of a large increase in the ranks of the SA that, according to SA sources, had expanded by 100,000 from December, 1932 to February, 1933. At the same time, the *Reichswehr* leadership "was forced to admit its own impotence to meet armed revolt within the Reich, or, rather, its unwillingness to fire on the youth of Germany as represented by the SA."[53] The result of this shift in power was the creation of militarized politics, which substitutes violence for authority and chaos for order. In such times, ambiguity and insecurity begin to affect the masses of people trying to carry on business as usual, forcing them to pay attention to politics. In the last days before Hitler, says Wheeler-Bennett:

> The ordinary law-abiding German citizen went in terror of his life under this "Government of the President's Friends" which von Schleicher and the Reichswehr had brought into being. Not only were the streets rendered unsafe by frequent conflicts between armed hoodlums of the Right and Left, but the criminal class did not hesitate to exploit the situation created by the political extremists, and among the outrages were many cases of burglary with assault, highway robbery and the settling of private feuds.[54]

The personal tension growing from the ambiguities caused by the regime's regulative failures would lead many of these ordinary law-abiding Germans to clamor for order even under the Nazis if necessary.

Extractive and regulative inadequacies directly affected a large part of the German population, but they also created further problems within the political system itself. Unable to mobilize adequate funds and to integrate the *Reichstag,* executive leadership faced an extremely severe distributive crisis as their control over the allocation of goods, services, honors, statuses, and opportunities dipped sharply. Especially critical was the incapacity of the leadership to cope with economic problems affecting the distribution of goods and statuses. Owing to the fragmented legislative system, laws could not be developed to rectify economic inadequacies of the kind that directly affected the private lives of millions of workers, professionals, farmers, and students. Physical deprivation accounted for the political awakening of large numbers, but, for the Nazis, the largest base of support centered in the middle-class where the expectation of losing goods and statuses turned people away from the regime in search of a new leader who would secure what they had and who promised them new opportunities for upward mobility.

A sense of distributive injustice became generalized in German society as people became aware that they were getting less than they thought they deserved in transactions with the leaders of the Republic. A look at some of the distributive injustices of the Weimar regime will show why the masses no longer felt bound to obey and why many who experienced extreme tension began to develop revolutionary commitments. In the urban areas, unemployment should be mentioned as the most pressing problem the government failed to cope with, for, by 1929, the unemployment rate was climbing rapidly. In that year the monthly average reached 2 million and, in 1930, the figure rose to 4.5 million. About one-tenth of the total population, or 6 million citizens, was unemployed by the beginning of 1932. To relieve the personal suffering of the mass of unemployed, the ruling leaders might have chosen to drastically increase unemployment benefits, but instead unemployment compensation was cut.[55] Nor would they "support a large-scale works program lest it revive the declining power of the trade unions, whose funds were dwindling and whose membership was declining."[56] These actions created the conditions described by an unskilled worker who joined the Nazi party in 1930:

> Thousands of factories closed their doors. Hunger was the daily companion of the German workingman. Added to this was the artificial whip of scarcity, wielded by the Jews, which sent workingmen scurrying from their homes to beg for food from the farmers. For no German family received more than twenty to thirty pfennigs dole per head in the terrible year of unemployment. Housewives will readily appreciate what it means to rear a family on that. The government carried its measures against the public so far that many an honest workingman had to resort to theft to obtain food. A case in point is the extensive pilfering of potatoes all through harvest time. Burglaries, too, became daily occurrences, and the police had their hands full protecting the citizens' property. All fellow citizens, with the exception of the Communists, yearned for better times. As for me, like many another, I had lost all I possessed through adverse economic conditions. And so, early in 1930, I joined the National Socialist party.[57]

With scant income, the consumer could buy little and small shopkeepers, too, began to feel the economic pinch quite early. The seriousness of this generalization of structural strain to the small shopkeeper is magnified by the fact that between 1882 and 1907 the number of small shopkeepers had grown at a faster rate than the population, as people moved to the city from the farm hoping to exploit the rising living standards by opening tobacco shops, groceries, drug stores, and delicatessens. This increase in small shops did not abate either, for between 1907 and 1925, the number of small businesses rose from 695,800 to 847,900 (a 21 per cent increase) and it is estimated that close to 45 per cent of those shopkeepers were only earning workers' wages in 1925.[58]

In the rural areas, desperate economic conditions hit the small landholders and the owners of large estates alike. According to David Schoenbaum, agricultural production was drastically hampered by the relatively small and unmechanized peasant farms. Around Kassel, he notes, 40 per cent of the landholdings were under 12½ acres, only 4.7 per cent of all the farms had power-driven machines, and 75 per cent had no machines at all. In addition to this narrow productive base, agricultural output fluctuated severely from bumper-crop to subsistence levels, so that rural areas experienced cycles of labor shortage and unemployment. To eliminate the insecurities and ambiguities generated by these cyclical changes, the farmer intensified his use of the land in order to increase production and hopefully his income. Production increased, but income did not, however. Between 1919 and 1930 wheat yields per hectare (equal to 2.471 acres) surpassed comparable American yields by 100 to 150 per cent. Overproduction, coupled with inflation, produced a 50 per cent decline in the price of wheat by 1933. Other agricultural products underwent similarly steep declines in price: Milk prices fell almost 50 per cent, swine by nearly 65 per cent, and cattle 55 per cent, all in 1933. Furthermore, the farm debts that had developed out of the early intensification of production skyrocketed with the losses caused by surplus and inflation, so that the farmers no longer were confident in the leaders of the Weimar regime.[59]

The general decline in goods and services seemed only to have vaguely concerned the ruling leadership, even though the resulting economic strains accounted for high levels of personal tension and a tendency to develop transactional relationships with emerging rebel leaders. Among those who joined the Nazy party in Abel's sample, for instance, 20 per cent mention inflation and its effects as the major crisis of their lives. Also, the general level of economic insecurity is reflected in the fact that 14 per cent had changed jobs two or more times and that 20 per cent became perpetual wanderers searching for better opportunities to make a living. Especially hard-hit were the young, 21 per cent of whom were unemployed for more than a year.[60] Even as early as 1923, the effect of unemployment on the conversion to Nazism was fairly obvious, for 30 per cent of the charter members had been unable to secure jobs.

With the economic collapse and the reduction in size of the *Reichswehr,* statuses and opportunities also became scarce, leaving the ruling leaders in a position where they could not reward followers adequately for their services or loyalty to the regime. Talented working-class youth had almost no hope for advancement within the crippled economy and turned increasingly to politics where upward mobility was still possible through merit. Others, who were able to secure jobs in industry or government, often found their salaries incommensurate with their training and had few expectations of rapid promotion. For example, a university graduate, who had studied four to six years at a cost of from 5,000 to 9,000 marks, was rewarded with a meager starting salary of from 200 to 400 marks per month. At such a rate, he could not expect to achieve a financial level in line with his family obligations and social status until he was about forty or fifty years of age.[61] The sense of distributive injustice that he must have felt was surely understood by the professional soldier or sailor of the *Reichswehr,* who had been socialized to believe that his place in society and his mark on history had to be earned through military advancement and adventure, yet had no hope of promotion in the dwindling armed forces and little chance for heroics in a military establishment demilitarized by the Allied powers.

In discussing the extractive, regulative, and distributive weaknesses within the Weimar political system, I have suggested implicitly that its responsive capability was also quite low, for the governmental structures could not adequately respond to the demands of various associations, political parties, and bureaucracies operating under the principle of proportional representation. The effect of this electoral mechanism was excessive fragmentation of both the executive and legislative bodies, resulting in a drastic decline in policy output, while demands for change grew. The government's responsive capability was also impaired by the political intrigues of von Schleicher, which had the effect of accelerating the circulation of leadership, both in the Cabinet and *Reichstag,* to a point where governmental continuity and permanence were seriously jeopardized. To add further to this responsive inadequacy was a court system whose judges had forsaken their oath to uphold the law in order to defend and protect their own political convictions, a charge, by the way, that can be leveled as well against both the executive and military leadership.

How effective the leaders of the Weimar regime were in using symbols we can only surmise. There are several indications that the symbols of the new parliamentary democracy—especially the Constitution and flag—did not strike a responsive cord with a large part of the population that was still guided by the cultural imperatives of their Prussian and imperial past. How ineffective these new symbols were in creating social solidarity is reflected in the fact that, from the beginning, nationalistic groups rejected the black-red-gold flag symbolizing the new regime for the imperial black-white-red standard or a variant. Also, the leader of the government who was most able to spark a sense of unity among the masses was President von Hindenburg, who in appearance and sentiments, stood as a symbol of the old imperial order. Indeed, one gets the impression that one source of instability within the political system lay in the fact that most of its leaders did not believe in the parliamentary democracy they helped to create. Even though they may have paid lip service to the symbols of democracy, their presentation of self gave off a number of definite symbolic impressions of the glorious past. This may account for the fact that the ruling leadership made no conscious, well-planned attempt to use symbols to rally the people around the new democratic forms of political life. Contrast this with the Nazi leadership's deliberate manipulation of symbols: "The name for the new movement was created with great deliberation: *National-Socialist-German-Workers-Party.* Each word had special significance for certain groups. The red on the party banner preserved a color dear to the Socialists; its combination with white and black recalled to the Nationalists the imperial colors. The swastika reminded all of the common enemy—the Jew. The party salute, the Heil Hitler greeting, gave short-cut identifications to members of the movement, and also represented breaks from the past."[62]

To attribute Hitler's success to certain personal, magnetic qualities or to his genius for organization would simplify the complex set of interrelated social factors discussed above. As is the case with all revolutions, the Nazi movement succeeded in mobilizing a mass following not solely by the designs of revolutionary strategists, but because of weaknesses inherent in the German political system that seriously reduced the capabilities of the governing regime. Indeed, it would not be an exaggeration to say that Hitler could not have had much better allies than the numerous leaders of the Weimar government, but especially von Schleicher, who had assumed the challenge to guide the nation through its first experiment in parliamentary democracy. By their inept handling of the affairs of state, these leaders succeeded in generating widespread mistrust of their rule, so much so that in the general elections of 1932, 90 per cent of the vote was registered against the presidential Cabinet,[63] which had assumed a dictatorial character under the emergency powers granted by Article 48 of the Weimar Constitution. With this fact in mind, it would not be unfair to argue that the ruling leaders of the regime had a large hand in making the Nazi revolution, playing no small part in creating conditions in which ordinary citizens began to look for new leadership that promised to rectify a bad situation. In this respect, I would agree with Schoenbaum's conclusion: "The Nazis came to power by miscalculation [of the ruling leadership] rather than by some exclusive popular demand focusing on the person of Hitler or his Party."[64]

Stage II: Availability

Proposition 2.2—Individuals experiencing extreme levels of personal tension will become more available for transactions with rebel leaders when they are between activities, when the initiatives of those rebel leaders are compatible with their own experiences, beliefs, and moral systems, and when their personal resources are adequate for engaging in politically deviant action.

Not only do structural strains contribute to the intensification and generalization of tension, but the social dislocations they produce, such as unemployment and demographic changes, free those individuals who had been previously locked into the normative structure of society and make them available for starting new activities. Those who are forced by circumstances to end their commitments within the traditional social fabric do not necessarily turn to rebel leaders when they are between activities, however, for many other options in the economic or political sphere may exist. And sometimes the ruling leadership may maintain the loyalty of the dislocated through a reward structure that provides benefits, such as unemployment insurance. It is normally when opportunities and governmental support decline, as in the Nazi case, that those individuals freed by social dislocation begin to consider deviant courses of action. Just as collaborators in the Chinese prison camps in North Korea cooperated with their interrogators when opportunities and rewards were scarce, so do dislocated individuals who have been cut off from opportunities and benefits in unstable societies begin listening intently to the words of rebel leaders who promise to change their situation.

In the Chinese Communist prison camps, you will remember, those who cooperated fully with their interrogators had had experiences and possessed beliefs and moral systems that were compatible with Communist ideology. This compatibility made the prisoner much more willing to accept new leadership that, in his view, uttered words that "made sense." In a similar way, individuals who have been directly deprived by structural strains in society will tend to listen to those rebel leaders who are able, through their speeches, writings, or by manipulating symbols, to reinforce their own political impressions and judgments. Much as in small-group processes, transactional patterns are reinforced when, to use Theodore Newcomb's language, both leader and follower co-orient to the political situation, producing symmetry and the tendency to increase social exchanges.[65]

Resource potential is another factor to consider in assessing the extent of the individual's availability for deviant political action. Here should be included such resources as time, energy, intelligence, courage, knowledge of the proposed field of action, skills appropriate to that field, and the like. The possession of such resources has at least two effects on the disposition of the potential follower: It gives him confidence that he can meet the expectations of the rebel leader if he chooses to follow, and gives him hope that he will be able to advance to higher positions within the movement. To the extent that he feels confident that he can meet his obligations and can find new opportunities for advancement, the individual experiencing extreme levels of tension will be more predisposed to follow and may do so if the opportunity is present.

The "End of the World" Movement

In this movement, followers became available for action in various ways. Bob Eastman, one of the most committed of the group of eighteen, was recruited into the local flying saucer club and into Dr. Armstrong's group while he was making the transition between army service and college. However, Eastman appears to be an exception in this respect, for most of the remaining members were firmly established as student or bread-winner. For most of those who ultimately joined, the most significant factor increasing their availability for action was the compatibility of their own experiences, beliefs, and moral systems with Keech's teachings and initiatives.

It is fairly clear that the prior experiences of Keech's followers had a direct bearing on their willingness to accept the flood prophecy and seemed to affect the intensity of their beliefs concerning Keech's lessons and her ability to communicate with men from outer space. For example, Daisy Armstrong, Dr. Armstrong's wife, had made an independent prediction of the date of the flood, so she uncritically accepted Keech's prediction because it corroborated her own. In fact, all who accepted Keech's lessons and thought her communications authentic had been prepared by previous activities in occult groups and were convinced that flying saucers were present in the earth's atmosphere. For instance, we know that, of the eighteen followers, sixteen believed in flying saucers before they were mobilized to the movement. And those who most consistently accepted Keech's initiatives had had personal histories of involvement in occult activities. Therefore, when Dr. Armstrong met with "The Seekers" to explain Keech's prophecy and the accompanying belief system, the disposition to accept her initiatives had already been cultivated. "Much of what he said fell upon fertile ground, for most of his hearers were already convinced (or at least ready to believe) that messages from the spirit world and visitors from other planets were not only possible but actual."[66]

Additional support for this view is apparent in the somewhat lesser availability of Hal Fischer, which resulted from an earlier experience that made him more reluctant than others to believe Keech's flood prophecy and to conform to her initiatives for action. Previously, he had accepted as authentic a message warning of an impending flood that had supposedly been received by a fellow student from a source somewhere in space. But after they had prepared for the disaster, the flood failed to materialize. "His intimate connection with this incorrect experience," the authors note, "had made Hal cautious. . . . One of the most vocal discussants of the ideology, he was also one of the most challenging and doubting."[67] Although he became committed to the movement this earlier experience led him to be critical and skeptical of Keech's initiatives, reducing his willingness to make heavy investments and sacrifices.

Many who ultimately joined were also able to devote considerable time and energy to the movement. This was especially true of the younger participants, most of whom were college students with flexible time schedules. More broadly speaking, one of the reasons why the young play such a large role in collective movements is that they have usually not been locked into occupations and therefore are more available for starting new activities. With more time on their hands and less to lose through action, the young are considerably freer to run the social and physical risks that accompany collective movements. Even those in the movement who had full-time jobs were not consumed by them, for all conserved time and energy for activities outside their normal working day. For example, Dr. Armstrong's job at the college medical facility was routine and failed to spark the type of dedication that leads to a consuming career. Thus, his mind and time were free to pursue occult interests.

Keech's success as a leader stems partly from the fact that, through Dr.

Armstrong and by her own efforts, she was able to tap a source of potential followers who had been conditioned by experience to accept the truth of her personal claims. Quite unconsciously she increased the availability of these followers by demanding very few investments and sacrifices from them during the initial stage of mobilization. All were able to maintain their educational and occupational obligations. Therefore, potential followers, who were not yet able or willing to make heavy investments and sacrifices for the movement, were invited to participate only as much as their time and energy allowed. As we shall see later, Keech encouraged her followers to take small steps on their way to more costly choices.

The Black Muslim Movement

If tension were a sufficient condition for the development of a politically deviant commitment, then Mr. Muhammad, through his secondary leaders, should have succeeded in recruiting many more black people from the lower class than he did. But, of course, many blacks who have been materially deprived by distributive injustices are not available for entering into transactional relationships with rebel leaders that could lead to new commitments. For example, those lower-class blacks who are dependent on whites for their daily bread, or who are into heavy drugs or mysticism, are not apt to be as free as others to follow a black nationalist leader like Mr. Muhammad who is openly defiant of "white devils" and who espouses the causes of clean living and racial separation. This leads one to the tentative conclusion that those who have chosen to follow Mr. Muhammad are distinguished from many other lower-class blacks not necessarily by their greater level of tension, but by their greater availability for forming new commitments.

Looking at the composition of the movement, there are several inferences that can be made about the importance of availability in preparing blacks for the teachings of Mr. Muhammad. First, there is some indication that many who chose to become Black Muslims were between activities when they were attracted to the movement. We should recall that many converts had been recent immigrants from the South, many of whom were unemployed and most of whom were alienated in the northern ghettos from established black residents and leaders. Unemployment not only increased the level of personal tension, it also freed these immigrants from the occupational restraints that can inhibit the development of politically deviant commitments. For example, the unemployed black is no longer dependent on the white manager or foreman; therefore he is somewhat freer than blacks employed by whites to accept the strong anti-white component of the Black Muslim ideology.

Availability can also help to explain why the Black Muslims were so successful in mobilizing black convicts. For detention in prison has the effect of dislodging black inmates from forces in the ghetto that would militate against involvement in black nationalist movements. Unless detained for life without parole, or sentenced to death, individuals in prison are forced into a transitional state that makes them freer to begin new activities. Of course most do not in fact begin new commitments on their release because opportunities are normally not offered to them. Black Muslim leaders have given black inmates an opportunity and, because they are in a transitional stage, this helps to explain why over 600 joined the movement each year during the peak of its growth.

Black Muslim appeals have received their widest acceptance among lower-class blacks with low incomes and educational achievement, a fact to keep in mind when considering the extent of availability for politically deviant commitments. For the lower-class black is more clearly preconditioned than the middle-class black to accept the truth of the Black Muslim criticisms of the white majority. Black Muslims argue, for example, that, while white men have freed the black man from chattel slavery, they continue to keep him in a state of mental servitude. Black people "have been systematically and diabolically estranged from their heritage and from themselves,"[68] losing their native language, their traditional names, and, because the white man wants black people to accept an image of inferiority, their history as well.

> The black child in Harlem learns about the Revolutionary War but he does not learn that the man who set it off by leading the Americans in the Boston Massacre was a Negro, Crispus Attucks. The black child sees the clock work but he does not know that Benjamin Bannaker, a Negro, invented the pendulum. The black child visits the blood bank but he does not know that a Negro, Dr. Charles Drew, discovered how to preserve blood and thus made the bank possible.[69]

Not content to stop here, the white man duped the black man into accepting his religion with its blond-haired, blue-eyed, white-skinned Jesus.[70] Unlike Islam, the "true" religion of the black masses, the white man's religion has made black men patient, waiting for happiness in heaven, when they should be coming to grips with their hell on earth.

Furthermore, Black Muslims learn from Mr. Muhammad that estrangement of the black man from himself has been partially achieved by the white community's monopoly of control. The Black Muslims agree that:

> The white man still owns the so-called Negro because the white man owns the factories, the land, the houses and everything else needed for survival. . . . The so-called Negro is no more than a "free slave," for he dares not assert his manhood, no matter what indignities are heaped upon him or what atrocities are directed his way.[71]

The white man "now hopes that by integrating with the rising black man, he can avoid paying for a long list of crimes he has perpetrated against humanity."[72]

In the first years of the movement, as today, conditions in the South and in the northern ghettos have made the dispositions of many lower-class blacks compatible with these teachings of Mr. Muhammad. And the same was apparently true under Fard's leadership, where the environmental situation in Detroit made his messages meaningful for many. As Lomax has said:

> The black Detroiters who heard Fard were starving, living in overcrowded slums. They were the victims of police brutality, the continuing symbol of the power of the white establishment. They were bitter toward the white workers who took over "Negro jobs" as work became more scarce. Even the white welfare workers in Detroit . . . deliberately abused Negroes by making them wait long hours in line before passing out pitiful supplies of flour and lard. All this fear resulted in deep resentment and despair. The words of Fard began to make more sense than ever before.[73]

Malcolm X's commitment to Mr. Muhammad was similar to that of other Black inmates serving prison sentences. In substance, the large number of convicts who have converted to Islam can be explained partly as a consequence of their more thorough preparation by society for Mr. Muhammad's verbal attacks against the white community. In Malcolm's view, the black convict has been very well prepared by social conditions to accept the statement, "the white man is the devil." His readiness to accept this description of the white man results from the fact that the convict comes from the bottom of the pile, where he is kicked about and treated like a child by whites.[74] The action undertaken by whites Malcolm had known seems to have prepared him for rebellion against the political order, as his own testimony suggests. "I think that an objective reader may see how when I heard 'The white man is the devil,' when I played back what had been my own experiences, it was inevitable that I would respond positively. . . ."[75]

Later, when Malcolm assumed chief responsibility for the mobilization function of leadership, there were few systematic procedures for actively recruiting followers. At first, Malcolm sought contact with people on the ghetto streets in a random fashion, thinking that poor blacks trying to live from hand to mouth would jump at the chance to hear the truth about the white man's abuse of the black race. But he soon learned that tension is not enough to convert people to a politically deviant perspective. Thus, almost instinctively, he began to search for public places where the more available lower-class blacks could be found, blacks whose experiences and beliefs were generally compatible with those shared by the members of the movement. Before long he had located two such places, one at the fringes of other black nationalist street meetings and another outside store-front Christian churches. In both instances the Black Muslim Minister could distribute leaflets to blacks who were already half-way prepared to make initial investments in the movement. Those on the fringes of the crowds who had stopped to listen to other black nationalist speakers were being tuned in to the general outlines of black nationalist themes and consequently could understand and empathize with the basic content of Mr. Muhammad's teachings. On the other hand, those gathered outside the store-front churches, usually older, southern migrant people, were steeped in religious practices and beliefs that made them more able to accept the religious underpinnings of the Nation of Islam, with its strict moral code and rituals.

In the case of both groups, the attempt of the Ministers of Islam was simply to encourage attendance at Muslim meetings in order to hear the teachings of Mr. Muhammad. This strategy was an effort to offer potential followers a choice with a very low initial investment. Many of those in the store-front churches responded positively to this tactic because they were always ready to listen to "good preaching," Malcolm tells us. But of course this modest investment of time became a lower-level commitment for some who had come to listen out of curiosity, which led to other more costly investments and sacrifices.

The Bolshevik Revolution

The importance of experience in making persons available for politically deviant commitments can be found particularly in the respective case histories of Lenin and Trotsky, both having had earlier personal experiences that prepared them to accept the initiatives of rebel leaders, whom they ultimately replaced. In Lenin's case, the experiences that made him available for a revolutionary commitment were: (1) the execution of his brother by the czarist government and the abandonment of his family by the Liberals; (2) his unjust arrest and expulsion from Kazan University; (3) the arbitrary and continual rejection of his applications to travel abroad; (4) his experience as a land owner in Samara, which heightened his distaste for exploitation; (5) the police raid on the Committee of Literacy, an organization in which he served; (6) and his period of imprisonment, which functioned as his baptism into revolutionary life. Lenin's experiences seem to have confirmed the arguments of the more radical leaders of his early years, leading him first to embrace populism, then Marxism, and later the "permanent revolution."

Trotsky's background is similarly marked with experiences confirming the radical arguments of others. For, being Jewish, Trotsky's family faced persecution at the hands of the czarist regime. Before the turn of the century, for example, his family was deprived of most of its land and, because several participants in the assassination of Czar Alexander II had been Jewish, a decree "forbade Jews to rent, lease or buy further land."[76] Familiar with his father's debts and losses as a farmer, Trotsky recognized at an early age "the hardness of a system which left the rural laborer almost nothing to tide him over the enforced idleness of winter."[77] On the farm, he came to understand and identify with the views of the hired help, often taking their side in disputes with his father. Then, as a young man, he left the farm and resided with a family [the Shpentsers] whose master used Trotsky as a sounding board for his criticisms of the barbarism of Russian society. Later, he was to confirm these criticisms in his own experience, finding it difficult to gain admission into school because he was Jewish, then being expelled for being implicated in a mild student outcry against a French teacher. Bertram Wolfe's description of Trotsky's preparation for a revolutionary commitment is worth including at length here.

> The episode of the "concert" for the French teacher was followed by a conflict of lesser scope with a new Russian teacher, who failed to read and mark the themes he exacted from his pupils. Both incidents suggest that in Tyova Bronstein [Trotsky] there was growing up a feeling of indignation of injustice. Imperceptibly this feeling had been nourished by a whole series of childhood experiences at Yonovka, experiences which were evaluated increasingly with the criteria supplied by the attitude of the Shpentsers and the ideals of the masterpieces of Russian literature. His contact with the servants and laborers had made him aware of their humble viewpoint. He remembered a woman's walking seven versts and sitting submissively a whole day on his father's doorstep to collect a ruble; a sit-down strike of the farm help—no worse treated than most—because they did not get enough to eat; a man pleading with his father for the release of a cow that had trespassed on the Bronstein field; the shame he felt when old Bronstein failed to tip a porter adequately and the latter cursed at him; the spectacle of an overseer striking a shepherd with a knout because he kept the horses out late, with Shpentser standing by, face pale, hissing between his clenched teeth, "how shameful."[78]

The type of experience that had made Lenin and Trotsky revolutionaries later became generalized throughout Russian society and began to turn the tide of public sentiment toward revolutionary change and the Bolsheviks.

Loss of control on the battlefront was an important factor increasing the availability of soldiers for political deviance. For ruptures in the structure of military authority created a serious social dislocation as thousands upon thousands of soldiers fled the front to return home. Within a few weeks of the fall of czarism, for example, about 1 million soldiers had already deserted.[79] Most were peasants returning home to participate in the redistribution of land, but many returned to the cities as well. With few economic or political opportunities available in the urban areas, these soldiers were not locked into statuses that might have given them an investment in the new regime, and thus they remained free from strong attachments. Between commitments, they were ready for involvement of some kind and many found it with the Bolsheviks. More important, perhaps, was the growing compatibility of Lenin's outline for revolution, his April Theses, with the experiences and beliefs of the masses of soldiers, sailors, peasants, and workers.

Speaking before a gathering of Socialists shortly after his return to Russia, Lenin set forth his April Theses, a testament that would become increasingly important to the masses as tensions mounted. He proposed the following: (1) The war with Germany had to end by all means available, which would necessitate the overthrow of the bourgeois government whose stake in the crisis had been determined by imperialist designs; (2) support should be withdrawn from the Provisional Government and given directly to the Soviets, "the only possible form of revolutionary government"; (3) Soviets should be developed that would include Agricultural Laborers' and Peasants' Deputies from all parts of the country; (4) land should be nationalized and managed by Soviets of Agricultural Laborers' and Peasants' Deputies; (5) all banks should be merged into one general national bank, over which the Soviet of Workers' Deputies would have control; (6) the Soviet of Workers' Deputies should immediately be placed in "control of social production and distribution of goods . . ."; (7) a party convention should be called to shift the base of the party program to a more radical level; and (8) the Communist International had to be reorganized for carrying the Socialist revolution abroad.[80]

At first, Lenin's Theses were not very warmly received. In fact, E. H. Carr's account of this situation indicates that the reaction to his proposals was quite hostile.

> It was on this last occasion that Lenin for the first time read the famous "April Theses" which summarized his views; that Bogdanov interrupted with cries of "Delirium, the delirium of a madman"; that Goldenberg, another former Bolshevik, declared that "Lenin had proposed himself as candidate for a European throne vacant for 30 years, the throne of Bakunin'; and that Steklov, the editor of *Izvestiya* and soon to join the Bolsheviks, added that Lenin's speech consisted of "abstract constructions" which he would soon abandon when he had acquainted himself with the Russian situation. . . . On the same evening he reread the theses to a gathering of Bolshevik leaders, and once more found himself isolated.[81]

When Lenin's Theses were published in *Pravda,* not a single Bolshevik organization, group, or individual had joined him, and the editors were quick themselves to discredit his position by labeling it "unacceptable."[82] Most thought that he would not stick to his abstractions, nor could they imagine that using them "Lenin would be able to conquer not only the revolution, not only all its active masses, not only the Soviet—but even his own Bolsheviks. We were cruelly mistaken . . . ," recalled Sukhanov.[83]

The increasing gravity of the strains running through Russian society and the Provisional Government's inability and unwillingness to respond to public pressures for change created experiences for the masses that led them to see value in Lenin's position. Lenin's appeal for land reform and the transfer of some control to peasants had a positive impact on those in rural Russia who had become impatient with the Provisional Government and who were becoming weary of the constant turmoil and confusion generated by peasant disturbances. Lenin's proposed reforms held out some hope that order would be restored and the land problem solved to their benefit.

Changing conditions at the front also brought a large part of the military into the Bolshevik sphere of influence. Undertaken on Kerensky's orders, the Galicia offensive proved to many soldiers what Lenin had long argued, that the war was imperialistic in nature. Many saw this offensive to be a blatant and unconcealed effort by the government to annex Constantinople. Furthermore, after the attempted military coup in July (the Kornilov Affair), many more soldiers, who at that time still supported the existing government, began to see their own officers as counter-revolutionaries, thus adversaries. The recognition that their sacrifices at the front were serving some leader's dreams of imperialist expansion increased the availability of some soldiers for action against the government, while the Kornilov Affair made others available for action against their officers. Indirectly, both were becoming increasingly available for Lenin's initiatives.

Tensions were also rising rapidly in the urban areas during the early months of 1917. Pressures generated by food shortages and the resistance of factory management in granting concessions to workers increased workers' availability for deviant political action. Turning to the revolution as an alternative way of solving their personal problems, many workers fell into line with Lenin's claim for worker control of production and the distribution of goods. As the experiences of the masses became compatible with Lenin's Theses, the Bolsheviks began to receive endorsement from "the city workers, the soldiers, and vast illiterate hordes who had nothing much to lose and a great deal to gain from the breakup of the established order."[84]

Bolshevik fortunes improved significantly between April and July. In the first two months following Lenin's return to Russia, the membership of the party more than doubled, increasing from 15,000 in April to 32,000 in June. Another sign of its growing strength could be seen in the steady expansion of its control within the Petrograd Soviet. While it was far from a majority, by the first days of May it had captured about a third of the seats. Successes, while not on a grand scale, were steady and began eroding the support of the provisional leadership at the lower organizational level from the earliest moment. Going to the areas where availability was greatest, the Bolsheviks began to get positive results. For instance, a May conference of Factory Committees of Petrograd adopted Lenin's proposal for greater worker control over governmental action by an 86 vote margin (421 to 335).

Yet, while the Bolsheviks were finding strength at the lower organizational levels and almost exclusively with workingmen, their success with the general population was minimal. Even in conjunction with ideologically allied groups, the Bolsheviks were able to win only 137 out of 1,000 seats at the First Congress of Soviets, which convened on June 16. In fact, it was their relative weakness in the Soviets that led the Bolsheviks to the Factory

Committees for support. They recognized the necessity of building an independent base of power from which they could supplant the Soviet.

In July the Bolshevik strategy was to force the Soviet to move against the Provisional Government and assume total power. But the Soviet, composed largely of moderate Mensheviks and Social Revolutionaries, could not be persuaded or intimidated and remained loyal to the regime. So, in order to test the capabilities of the political system as well as to put pressure on the Soviet, the Bolsheviks organized armed demonstrations against the Provisional Government. Although the demonstrations failed to topple the government, they were successful enough to make the ruling elite and moderate Socialists wary of the Bolshevik organization's capabilities for waging an insurrection in the future.

Retaliation against the Bolsheviks was inevitable and, when it came, it was swift. An attack was first initiated against *Pravda*. After officials had forcefully confiscated manuscripts and documents, a mob completely destroyed the editorial offices, smashing equipment and furnishings and setting fire to the debris. Later the same evening, the government began making wholesale arrests, seizing soldiers, workers, and sailors who were suspected of inciting riots, and confiscating weapons where they could be found.

Moving in a more insidious manner, governmental agents began circulating what were apparently slanderous statements concerning Lenin's loyalty to Russia. For example, "several of the Guards regiments, which had not taken part in the demonstration, were informed . . . that the Minister of Justice had documentary proof that Lenin was a German agent."[85] On the government's initiative, charges of treason were widely published in the newspapers and a warrant was finally issued for Lenin's arrest. As a consequence, the movement was brought to a temporary halt, for "the whole force of anger and 'patriotism' was . . . coming down on the Bolsheviks." In fact, "the word 'Bolshevik' had become synonymous with scoundrel, murderer, Judas. . . ."[86] But although the July events had virtually exhausted the strength of the movement, at a time when the availability of the masses for revolution was increasing, the actions of the Provisional Government would breathe life into it again.

The Nazi Revolution

Military and economic dislocations account for a good part of the increasing availability of the German masses for revolutionary activity. In the military sector, for example, dislocation was caused by both the Treaty of Versailles and the shortsightedness of the Weimar leadership. When the treaty was signed the German army was 400,000 strong. But within a span of about two years, the Weimar government was forced to dismiss over a quarter of a million officers and men to meet the Allied demand for a standing army not to exceed 100,000. Hardest hit by this mass firing were those who had been conscripted into the army. In contrast, career soldiers were maintained in their military statuses as long as possible, although a large number were ultimately relieved of duty. The 300,000 soldiers who were dislocated as a consequence of the treaty returned to the cities at a time when unemployment was rising rapidly. With few occupational opportunities, these ex-soldiers became the backbone of the *Freikorps,* an illegal military organization with patriotic zeal and revolutionary intentions. "Without income, without status, without power, their only hope," says Daniel Lerner, "was to win these things for themselves and the only method open to them was violence."[87]

The fact that the government had tolerated the *Freikorps* and that officers of the *Reichswehr* had assumed positions of leadership within it gave the technically illegal organization a degree of legitimacy and, although somewhat tenuously, the members were tied into the political system. But after the participation of the *Freikorps* in the abortive Kapp Putsch of 1920, the government moved to disband it. By destroying the *Freikorps,* the Weimar leadership reduced its potential to coopt and thus to control it. In effect, the government's action duplicated the dislocating results of the Treaty of Versailles. For by forcing these men to terminate their commitments within the *Freikorps* without at the same time offering legitimate opportunities to form new ones, the government placed them in a transitional stage that essentially freed them for joining other right-wing military organizations that had no ties with the political system whatsoever. "Their aspirations were not changed; a new instrument for fulfilling them had to be forged. The instrument was the Nazi movement."[88]

In the three years between 1930 and 1933, unemployment figures nearly doubled, rising from 3,218,000 to 6,014,000. Those 6 million Germans, dislocated by the foundering economy, were thus freed from their dependence on the occupational structure and, facing governmentally imposed decreases in unemployment benefits, they began looking elsewhere for solutions. The increasing availability of these unemployed is reflected in the fact that during those years of rising unemployment, the vote for political parties on both extremes of the ideological continuum rose dramatically. In 1932, alone, the Communist vote rose over 6 per cent, from 10.6 to 16.9 per cent. In the preceding year the Nazis had surprised everyone, including themselves, by accumulating 18.3 per cent of the total vote and winning 107 out of the 577 seats in the *Reichstag.*[89]

While unemployment initially frees the individual from certain restraining forces within the occupational structure, it can also make him a slave to physical necessity. His concern with the day-to-day problems of eking out a living may inhibit the development of a revolutionary commitment by depleting the resources, especially time and energy, which are necessary for pursuing a revolutionary way of life. Even when a revolutionary commitment is formed, however, unemployment may still pose an obstacle to those who are ready to make huge investments and sacrifices as signs of their dedication and loyalty. Under such circumstances, the unemployed revolutionary must try to free himself from the pressures of physical necessity. For example, if he is married, he may become dependent on his wife, assuming of course that she shares his convictions. Thus, one unemployed Nazi was able to devote all his time and energy to party work by shifting the occupational burden onto the shoulders of his wife:

> My wife underwent untold hardships throughout these years. To enable me to pay my party dues, and spend an occasional penny, she worked hard at sewing, constantly harassed to provide a meager living for me and the family. Frequently, if I returned late at night from a meeting or a propaganda trip, I still found her bent over her work, happy to see me come home unharmed. This went on for weeks, months, and years. But she willingly endured it, for she too could not be robbed of her faith in the ultimate victory of National Socialism.[90]

Unemployed by choice, another member of the party reduced the problem of physical survival by consuming his savings, borrowing from others, and economizing.[91] Through connections within the Nazi ranks, some were also able to secure jobs. Giving an account of his successful effort to find employment for a comrade, a member of the party conveys the impression that physical necessity must have been a greater inhibiter of action than working an eight-hour day. For, by securing his comrade a position as an assistant in the post office, he freed him from the struggle to feed himself, his wife, and two children, thereby allowing him to concentrate more of his energies on party work.[92]

The availability of the German population was also enhanced by the fact that Hitler's social philosophy was compatible with the experiences and socialization of important social groups. His appeals to nationalism, for instance, struck a resonant cord with many who had been trained to believe that the community should always be placed above private interests. Thus, most contributors in Abel's sample reported that strong feelings of patriotism had been developed in their youth through the influence of their families, schools, and youth organizations. They were encouraged by Hitler's promise to overcome the conflicts that had arisen from geographical disputes, political fragmentation, religious differences, and class distinctions. Above these historically powerful divisive forces, Hitler promised to construct a national community (*Volksgemeinschaft*) which would accord status, not in terms of class, education, or occupation, but in terms of one's service to the German people and the German race. Through the unity forged by national consciousness, Germany would achieve its greatness and the German people its destiny.

Within this national community that Hitler promised to create, the state would loom large as a militaristic and hierarchical power structure. He would assume dictatorial powers, he told the German people, not to rule over them, but to rule in their name. He could not fail to incorporate the nation's interests in his leadership because he was the personal embodiment of the German nation and the German people. When he spoke, the German people spoke; when he acted, the German people acted. There could be no conflict of interest.

Repeated time and time again in his speeches and in those of his subordinates, these simple themes found their mark in those who had not yet been socialized to democratic norms and who had already observed at first-hand the disastrous consequences of the experiment in parliamentary democracy. "I heard Hitler in Bonn, in 1926," recalled a member of the party. "What he said, in clear, concise phrases, had long since agitated the feelings of every good German. The German soul spoke to German manhood in his words."[93] Apparently, the restoration of a militaristic and authoritarian power structure was an aspect of the "German soul," for most of those in Abel's sample repeatedly stressed their shock in learning that, under the Weimar Republic, they would have to participate in government, vote for a political party, and pass judgment on their leaders. They were accustomed to autocratic government, and their army service had socialized them to follow orders. Thus, when Hitler spoke of submission to his leadership as an act of national necessity and the need for "soldiers" of industry and labor, those who had been socialized in the Prussian tradition nodded their heads to show that they understood.

There is some indication that compatibility of beliefs was an important determinant influencing the individual's choice between the competing Communist and Nazi movements. For instance, workers who had been inculcated with strong feelings of nationalism could not sympathize with the Communist party's emphasis on internationalism. "I felt a deep-seated aversion to the idea of an 'International,'" are the words of a worker who joined the Nazi party. "I was brought up as a nationalist, and I could never develop any enthusiasm for the utopian idea of a 'unity of nations.'"[94]

Just as in the other collective movements, youth was also a significant factor in the Nazi revolution. In 1930, for example, over 60 per cent of the Nazi party membership was under 40 years of age and 36.4 per cent fell in the 21–30-year-old category. Indeed, in some party groups in Berlin over 40 per cent of the members were between 21 to 30 years of age. Moreover, this general youthfulness of the movement was reflected in the Nazi delegation in the *Reichstag*, 60 per cent of the Nazi deputies being under 40, as compared to less than 10 per cent of the Social Democratic party membership.[95] This disproportionate representation of younger people in the party, which some might attribute to a general rebellion against authority, is best explained in terms of their greater availability for deviant political action. Not yet deeply invested in occupations and families, these young Germans were freer to apply their energies to movement politics. Even before the Nazi party had become an important political force, the young, as well as the older people uprooted by social dislocations, possessed the time that makes the development of revolutionary commitments possible. In these early counter-revolutionary groups and later in the Nazi party, we find large numbers of individuals with a general lack of strong social ties, who had yet to settle into a career or to start a family. Most were young people, although there were many older men whose lives had been uprooted by social strains and who felt they had nothing to lose by joining a revolutionary venture.[96]

> *Proposition 2.5*—An individual's field of group associations will influence his disposition to enter into transactions with rebel leaders. Availability for beginning a commitment to a particular rebel leader will increase to the extent that his group ties reinforce his desire to follow. When cross-pressures exist, the potential follower may avoid entering into exchanges with the rebel leader, may break off his ties with the countervailing groups in order to pursue a preferred course of action, or may conceal his activities in behalf of the rebel leader from those groups who oppose them.

The importance of the cost-reward calculation in the formation and maintenance of commitments is accentuated when we take into account the reinforcements and cross-pressures that affect an individual's availability for starting a new commitment or extending one already begun. Especially when forming a new commitment, the actor must consider the possible effects it will have on his constellation of commitments. He must weigh the rewards offered from one line of action against the possible losses in other areas of activity. Thus, if reaction from his group associations threatens heavy losses, the individual under tension will be restrained from starting new commitments. Or he can begin them surreptitiously, like the card-carrying Communist who conceals his party affiliation so as to preserve the rewards flowing from his traditional associations. If, on the other hand, the individual's group ties mutually support him in a particular line of action, then there is a much greater probability that he will form a commitment openly. Yet, even when a commitment has been established, external group pressures can still intervene in the commitment process, forcing the actor to weigh the merits of conforming to the deviant leader's initiatives against pressures from competing groups.

The "End of the World" Movement

Social ties were as important a factor as time and compatibility in enhancing the availability of followers for starting their commitments to Mrs. Keech. Even before she had received her powers of communication, Keech had been in close association with several of her followers in various occult activities. Through these personal ties she mobilized six recruits directly into the movement. Most of the other active members were also mobilized through their personal connections with someone in the movement. Notable cases were Cleo Armstrong, Mark Post, and Kitty O'Donnell. Cleo was encouraged to join under pressure from her parents. Mark was a tag-along who followed his mother into the movement and remained steadfast in his desire to conform to her wishes. And Kitty was led into the movement as a consequence of her emotional ties to Bob Eastman.

Of all the active members of the movement, Dr. Armstrong was the least free from external attachments. His affiliation with an eastern college as a staff member of student health services made him vulnerable to harsh criticisms and possible expulsion. Cognizant of this threat to his occupational status and livelihood, he attempted to preserve his anonymity by maintaining a degree of secrecy about his occult interests. That Dr. Armstrong relied on this mechanism is clearly documented by his early suspicion about inviting interested persons into his group. For example, when a young woman called him concerning Keech's prediction and expressed a desire to attend one of his meetings, he refused to grant her permission. This refusal was based on his suspicion that she was a "stooge" of the college administration who was being planted to spy on the group. To preserve his freedom to act within the movement he was forced to shield himself from those who were in positions to cut off his financial resources, especially since there was no alternative source of funds to be had within the movement.

Dr. Armstrong's effort to conceal his occult activities demonstrates how, even once a commitment has been formed, the actor must preserve his freedom to engage in actions involving even heavier investments and sacrifices. Thus, availability will be a factor in the commitment process even into the later stages. Kitty's case is possibly the most interesting illustration of this point. Totally convinced that the flood would come, she quit her job and moved from another town to be closer to the center of action. By breaking the ties that had restricted her freedom to respond to Keech's initiatives, she was able to devote more of her time to the movement in preparation for the impending crisis. In other instances, spokesmen for society can intervene, against the person's will, and dislodge him from a position within the system, pushing him deeper into the movement by freeing him for further actions. Thus, college officials made Dr. Armstrong more available for exchanges with Keech when they dismissed him from his post at the college. Indeed, Armstrong seemed to have understood how the action of the college administration had given him more freedom, for he came to believe that his expulsion was "a 'part of the plan' of the Guardians—an indication that he was being shaken loose from the ties of this world in order to make more ready to leave it for a better one."[97]

Now, what was the impact of cross-pressures on the commitments of those who maintained contacts with groups or individuals hostile to Keech's initiatives? The weakening of Bertha Blatsky's commitment during the latter days of the movement demonstrates rather clearly how cross-pressures affect the strength of commitments. Blatsky had been one of the most active participants in the movement and at one stage she fell into a trance and began to receive rather incoherent messages from God. Before she had assumed her role as the Creator's confidante, Blatsky had purposefully refrained from informing her husband (a non-believer) about her activities in the movement, as Dr. Armstrong had concealed his from his employers. However, her newly acquired position of leadership as a competing medium to Keech made her so confident that she felt compelled to tell him of her talents as God's link to mankind. To win his admiration she fell into one of her trances. Immediately, the Creator began to give her husband orders and threatened to strike him dead if he disobeyed. Contrary to Bertha's expectations, instead of obeying her orders he went into a rage. He ordered her not to leave the house without his permission and threatened to question her mental stability if she continued participating in the movement. The countervailing pressure had the predictable consequence: She immediately lost her confidence within the movement and found it more difficult to receive messages from the Creator. The apparent effect of cross-pressures on her commitment is highlighted in her own testimony: "'In this house [Keech's] it's easy not to have doubts, but when I get home alone or when I'm with my husband, I'm full of doubt, and I just don't know what to do.'"[98] Under pressure from her husband, Bertha finally withdrew from the movement altogether.

Other members of the movement were also directly affected by pressures from their group associations. Family pressures forced May Novick to terminate her activity in the movement. Arthur Bergen's commitment was reduced to infrequent contacts with the movement as a result of pressures from his parents, who had openly criticized him for his involvement. And Kitty's ultimate rejection of Keech can partially be explained by the fact that she had come under the influence of Ella Lowell, a competing medium. In Bob Eastman's view, Kitty had fallen into a "negative environment."

The Black Muslim Movement

As is true for most mass movements with formalized organizations, the Black Muslim organization attempts to eliminate points of pressure working against the potential convert or active member. To increase availability for action, the organization urges younger members to marry other Muslims, and those married to non-Muslims are expected to convert them. Moreover, by rejecting integration into white society, Mr. Muhammad attempts to eliminate the white community as a positive reference group. For Black Muslim leaders know very well that in order to win and hold converts they must overcome multiple counter-pressures working against black nationalism within the black community. As Lincoln has said:

> Many counterpressures exist . . . to restrain the lower-class Negro from active participation in black nationalist movements. The Christian church is still powerful, though its magic has been seriously eroded. Personal friendships with white men, where they exist, make the absolute generalizations of black nationalism difficult to accept.[99]

Because he accepts the white community as a positive reference group, the black Christian minister is especially resistant to Black Muslim appeals.

As we know, Malcolm X was firmly committed to Mr. Muhammad until isolated within the movement in the last months of 1963. His initial step in prison, which culminated in a strong commitment, was possible because he was both free from strong competing loyalties and received encouragement from his family to join. Having identified so completely with ghetto life, Malcolm had abandoned the white community as a positive reference group, thereby eliminating a restraining force that could have modified or even prevented his commitment. His social ties with his family had the similar effect of increasing his availability for conversion, for his brothers and sisters had joined the movement before he was imprisoned and he was under pressure from them to do the same. Through these ties he was finally led into the movement and within the movement he married a Muslim woman, Betty X, a further reinforcement for his commitment. From Malcolm's own testimony, it is clear that few cross-pressures existed to prevent the formation of his commitment or, once formed, to effectively challenge it.

While there is little evidence available to show the effect of cross-pressures on the reduction or termination of commitment within the Nation of Islam, there is some data demonstrating this relationship in the civil rights movement. Robert Coles, staff psychiatrist for the Student Non-Violent Coordinating Committee, examined the forces affecting commitments within the civil rights movement and found cross-pressures to have a significant effect on the follower's choice to terminate action. After "weariness" occurred, a depression that results when the few rewards of action are measured against the correspondingly heavy investments and sacrifices, the individual's reference groups were altered so that the commitment could be terminated without strong feelings of guilt. During this stage, when the follower was looking for some way out, other pressures began to influence his behavior. Some became more sharply aware of parental disapproval. Others felt pressures to return to school or work. For many leaving the movement, these countervailing forces appeared to have taken their toll: "Working against continued involvement may be family pressures, public ones, or private wishes—the desire to be a doctor; a fiancee who opposes this kind of life; an ill father who needs his son at home to take up new financial responsibilities. . . ."[100] These kinds of pressures are not likely to influence the behavior of followers who have become insulated within a movement. But for those who have not severed ties with groups that stand as countervailing threats to the organizations' goals, such conflicts are likely to create the doubts that lead one to question motives and directions. In this sense, Malcolm could escape doubt because he had become fully insulated from the outside world, but Bertha Blatsky could not, owing to the contacts with her husband, who posed a constant threat to her peace of mind.

The Bolshevik Revolution

Through their associations in study groups and action organizations, individuals with revolutionary inclinations sometimes find the reinforcements they need to break away from the old order. Thus, in addition to the ideological and organizational impact of revolutionary groups on social action, there is the less visually dramatic effect that they have on the individual's constellation of commitments. To successfully mobilize new converts, such groups must undermine and destroy the ties that bind the individual to the traditional social fabric. By cutting these ties, the revolutionary organization frees the frustrated from forces that restrain them from making the transition to strong revolutionary commitments.

As historical accounts point out, both reinforcements and diminishing cross-pressures help to account for the increasing availability of Lenin and Trotsky for revolutionary action. For both men, there were many group reinforcements encouraging them along the path of the revolutionary life. First of all, we should remember that the status of a revolutionary in Russia before the February uprising was not as socially stigmatized in intellectual circles as it was in other societies and as it had been at other times in Russian history. Indeed, for many intellectuals, the revolutionary life was considered quite proper, for it provided an outlet for the mental energy and training that might have ordinarily been applied to the tasks of another occupation, had one been available. "Russia of the time was going through a prodigious industrial and commercial expansion," Adam Ulam tells us, "and a new class of millionaire entrepreneurs was springing up. Still a career in business was thought possible only for a Jew or a member of the lower classes. The only occupations open to a gentleman and an *intelligent* were those in the civil service, the free professions, and . . . the revolutionary."[101] The social value that was assigned to a revolutionary status must surely have given Lenin and Trotsky a greater sense of freedom in pursuing a revolutionary profession.

There are also times when the behavior of ruling leaders actually reinforces the inclination toward revolutionary thinking. Imprisonment for political crimes can have this consequence, as can banishment or exile. For Lenin this was certainly true. Penal detention not only furnished him with the time and materials to document his criticisms of existing institutions, but it put him into close contact with others who were, in spirit, members of an enlarging revolutionary family.

Even more consequential was Lenin's banishment to Samara. Because of its geographical remoteness and its lack of a university, ruling leaders assumed that this town in Siberia would effectively isolate political rebels from the revolutionary elements that moved around metropolitan universities. Yet while this plan did succeed in reducing the opportunities for rebellious behavior, it inadvertently increased availability for such action. For it placed these disillusioned rebels together where they could reinforce their own ideas and spawn even more revolutionary feelings. Thus, in Samara, Lenin became more thoroughly convinced than ever of his own assessments of Russian society and more dedicated to the task of organizing a revolutionary struggle against the bourgeoise. Only twenty-one years of age at the time, he was already beginning to develop a reputation as a scholar and debater. Other radicals began to respect him as one who could hold his own in the discussions that filled their days. In these lively exchanges over beer or tea, Lenin would argue the case of Marx against what were the last gasps of a form of populist socialism. Others listened with respect to what he had to say and some were converted to the Marxian revolutionary view.

In another part of the country, Trotsky listened to others peddling their radical political ideas, although he was still quite serious about an academic career. Although his previous experiences had made him critical of existing institutions, he had not yet developed a revolutionary disposition. On the contrary, at first he insisted that he was apolitical. But decisions that might have seemed inconsequential led him into situations that changed the course of his life. For these choices put him in touch with radical intellectuals who were the agents of change. At first these contacts were made quite unexpectedly. For example, in 1896, he was introduced to Socialist thinking while boarding with a family whose sons were eager to convince him of the truth of their Socialist views. "For several months they seemed to make no headway. He superciliously dismissed their 'Socialist Utopia.' Assailed with arguments, he would adopt the posture of a somewhat conservative young man, not devoid of sympathy with the people but distrusting 'mob ideology' and 'mob rule.' His passion was for pure mathematics and he had no time or taste for politics."[102] But by the middle of his semester, he openly admitted he was wrong and, thereupon, assumed the Socialist stance vigorously.

After his conversion to socialism, Trotsky began attending a small discussion group for radical students and workers. There he argued the Socialist position against a rising Marxist sentiment. These social exchanges, which were usually quite heated, pried him from his Socialist position and freed him even further from the obligations he felt toward the old order. The effect that these small group discussions had on his availability for a revolutionary commitment is clear in Isaac Deutscher's account of the process by which he was moved from one philosophical position to another.

> He is confronted with a new idea to which up to a point he is conditioned to respond; yet he resists at first with stubborn haughtiness; his resistance grows with the attraction and he subdues incipient doubt and hesitation. Then his inner defenses crumble, his self-confidence begins to vanish; but he is still too proud or not convinced enough to give any sign of yielding. There is no outward indication yet of the struggle that goes on in his mind. Then, suddenly, the new conviction hardens in him, and as if in a single moment, overcomes his spirit

of contradiction and his vanity. He startles his erstwhile opponents not merely by his complete and disinterested surrender, but by the enthusiasm with which he embraces their cause, and sometimes by the unexpected and far-reaching conclusions which he draws from their arguments.[103]

These innocent social gatherings, which Trotsky had chosen to attend quite capriciously, led him first to socialism, then to revolutionary Marxism. We can find no better testimony for the additive features of the commitment process, where seemingly inconsequential choices lead to more dramatic ones, or for the effect of the social group as it frees the individual for heavier investments and sacrifices.

In contrast to Trotsky's readiness to change in accordance with prevailing group opinion, Lenin steadfastly resisted the attempts of others to shape his thinking or behavior. And, unlike Trotsky, who seemed to relish debate with philosophically opposed parties, Lenin preferred the company of like-minded comrades. Partly as a mechanism to avoid cross-pressures that might have forced him to reassess his position, Lenin avoided meeting with people whose views were too markedly different from his own. For example, when Maxim Gorky invited him to meet with a group of unorthodox Marxists, Lenin refused on the grounds that it would be useless and harmful to him. He said that he would have nothing to do with anyone who sought to unify Marxism and religion, which apparently was the objective of the group. In his view, there was no use arguing with such people, for it was quite absurd to become upset for nothing.

This tendency to avoid conflict situations can be explained from another point of view: He was simply unwilling to waste his time with those who were outside the range of his influence. For, as an instrumental type, he was first and foremost an organization man and only when it served a useful purpose would he enter upon a course of conflict. Both these explanations are probably correct in part and it would be difficult, if not impossible, to say whether his need for reinforcement influenced his views on organization or his organizational principles incidentally reinforced his views. We must be content with the conclusion that, both for personal and organizational reasons, Lenin wanted to be surrounded by loyal comrades who shared his vision and agreed with the means he proposed. "For health and political effectiveness," Louis Fischer writes, "Lenin needed a small party united in obedience rather than a larger organization hiding divergent elements under a blanket of unity."[104]

Both Lenin and Trotsky preserved their right to follow a revolutionary course by marrying women who shared their Marxist stance. Had they chosen to marry women of more moderate or even opposed views, the chances are that either Russian history would have taken a different turn or both marriages would have collapsed under the weight of revolutionary circumstances. But they did not share the problem of Bertha Blatsky, who was faced with a hostile spouse who had threatened sanctions if she did not discontinue her activities within "the end of the world" movement. As it happened, the marriages reinforced the revolutionary activity of Lenin and Trotsky in the same way that Malcolm X's commitment to Mr. Muhammad was strengthened by his marriage to Betty X.

Even before he had married his first wife and Marxist mentor, Alexandra Sokdovskaya, Trotsky was preparing himself for revolution by dissolving the ties that bound him to the past. As a Socialist, for example, he had openly talked to his father about the need to overthrow the czar. His father, alarmed by such radical thinking, succeeded in learning the location of his small discussion sessions and ordered him not to attend in the future. Trotsky, exerting his right to be free, left his father's house and moved in with his radical friends. That this decision freed him for heavier political investments and sacrifices is clear from his response to his new-found independence. "The change was exhilarating; freedom at last! Gone was the neat and dutiful bourgeois son, the object of admiration and envy to other boys' parents. His place was taken by a real *Narodnik,* who, like the pioneers of old, 'went to the people' to become one of them, lived in a little commune where everybody dressed like a farm labourer, put his few *kopeyeks* into the pool, drank the same thin soup, and ate the same *kasha* from a common tin bowl." [105]

The choices that Lenin and Trotsky made from day to day reinforced their initial revolutionary direction and diminished the cross-pressures that might have checked them as they acted out their revolutionary thoughts. But luck and even accident must be taken into account by anyone who wishes to convey a total picture of their increasing dedication to revolution as a way of life. Where formalized organizations fail to emerge in revolutionary circumstances to direct the mobilization process, chance factors must be assumed to play a more important role in making a revolutionary. In a contrasting light, we have seen in the international Communist movement an organizational effort to minimize the influence of luck and accident on the conversion process. To accomplish this goal, insulation techniques akin to those used in the Black Muslim movement are applied to reduce the effect of countervailing forces on the newly converted. Such was the experience of Ignazio Silone when he joined the Communist party, for example. He was required by organizational order to sever ties with those groups that might still have maintained a hold on him, someday possibly to compete with the party for his loyalty. By insulating the member effectively from the outside world, it is no wonder that the party could become the follower's "family, school, church, barracks. . . ." [106]

The Nazi Revolution

Whether a German citizen was converted to Nazism or not depended to a great extent on the nature of his existing affiliations. Those who maintained ties with groups that outwardly opposed Hitler were much less available for making investments in the Nazi movement than those whose groups either reinforced their initial contact with the Nazis, or at least remained neutral.

Given the concentration of structural strain in the worker and agricultural sectors, we would have expected workers and farmers to be especially vulnerable to Nazi appeals. Yet the evidence suggests that these two important social classes were strikingly underrepresented in the party from its inception to its seizure of power. In 1930, for example, workers constituted only 26.3 per cent of the party's total membership, while they made up more than 40 per cent of the population at large; and farmers, who represented about 30 per cent of the total population, constituted only 13.2 per cent of the party's rank and file. By 1933, the percentage of workers in the party did rise by 5.2 per cent to 31.5 per cent, but the proportion of farmers declined to 12.6 per cent. Compared with their absolute numbers, says Schoenbaum, both workers and farmers were still significantly underrepresented on the Nazi rolls in 1933,[107] even though the "band wagon" effect was in full swing and Hitler was beginning to make the worker and farmer the *volk* heroes of the *Volksgemeinschaft.*

It is impossible to explain the reluctance of these two groups solely in terms of beliefs, for while many workers who had embraced Marxist internationalism were unsympathetic with Hitler's notion of a national community, farmers as a whole were quite nationalistic in their orientation, a fact revealed in the traditionally heavy rural vote for conservative political parties. A second, and possibly more powerful, explanation is that many workers and farmers maintained commitments within organizations that had taken steps to stop the growth of the Nazi movement. For the worker, his trade union was a source of countervailing pressure militating against involvement with the Nazis, while the farmer with traditional religious ties to Rome was restrained by the urging of the Catholic Church.

Opposed to Nazism on principle, trade unions as well as factory workers made it clear that Nazi sympathizers and adherents would "pay their dues." For example, trade unions refused to admit as apprentices anyone known to be an advocate of Nazism. The unions were able to exclude Nazis from occupational positions, even when shop owners might have hired them, because control over hiring procedures fell within the unions' sphere of authority. The effectiveness of this control is conveyed best in the personal testimony of an unemployed Nazi who was rejected for apprenticeships because of his beliefs: "I was unemployed," he begins, "but I managed to get through somehow. I found some kind German brothers who helped me from time to time, even though, not being masters in their own workshops, they couldn't give me a job. Vacancies in each case were filled by trade unions."[108] As another personal account illustrates, Nazis who were lucky enough to secure employment faced social exclusion by their work peers:

> I found work again as an electrician. I tried to talk to my fellow workers
> about Hitler. At first they listened in silence. I was more eloquent now, and

I could answer the *whys* and the *wherefores.* Suddenly they began to curse me, and one day I found I was ostracized. I greeted them as I entered the shop, but they all became silent and turned to their work. This was the most unpleasant experience in my life.[109]

For the worker who might have been inclined by family training to sympathize with Hitler's appeals, these outward signs of oppression and ostracism must have made him stop and think twice about following a similar course. The cross-pressures that he and other workers must have felt might explain in part why Hitler's major organizational effort to win the support of urban workers in the latter half of the 1920's was such a miserable failure.

Between 1926 and 1928 Hitler initiated a major organizational change within the party in order to more effectively compete with the Socialist parties (Social Democratic party and Communist party) for the loyalty of the working class. Party organizations were strengthened in all the urban areas of the country and, although it did not materialize, there was even serious talk of developing a parallel Nazi union structure to rival the Socialist-dominated trade unions. To coincide with this concentration of organizational effort in predominantly worker districts, Hitler shifted the propaganda emphasis of his speeches toward anti-capitalist and Socialist themes when he spoke in urban areas. However, unable to mobilize enough workers to assume positions of leadership in the working districts, lacking a militant counterpart to match the Communist party's street fighting force, the *Rotfrontkämpferbund,* and without a union structure to compete with the existing trade unions, in 1927 Hitler already had sensed the futility of his plan and thereupon shifted his appeals toward university students and civil servants. The failure to dislodge the workers from their Socialist party alliances was reflected in the national elections of 1928, when the Nazis lost heavily in most urban sectors. "In a very real sense," Orlow notes, "the electoral results and the party's organizational efforts showed a very high degree of negative correlation. Basically, the party had been unable to disengage any significant number of politically articulate Germans in the urban areas . . . from the pluralistic values of Weimar."[110] To Hitler's surprise, the party fared much better in the small-scale, marginal farming areas and small towns where party organization was almost nonexistent. Wasting no time, he changed the organizational thrust of the party once more by ordering the expansion of the party's districts to include these areas and the development of a technical branch of the party whose function it was to advise farmers on agricultural problems.

In the rural areas of Germany, Hitler's appeal had its greatest impact on Protestants, and much less influence on Catholic farmers. According to Schoenbaum, "German Catholics, a large minority of the population with a susceptibility to Fascist ideas at least equal to that of their neighbors, resisted Hitler with impressive unanimity until at least 1933."[111] Just as workers were held in line by their trade unions, so the Catholic Church restrained the Catholic farmer from acting out his beliefs. While the unions' success was determined in part by their control over hiring practices, the Church's influence lay in its control over the sacraments and other sacred rituals. For example, those Catholics who joined the Nazi party and then refused to resign at the Church's request were barred from the sacraments. And fallen Nazis, profane in the eyes of the Church, were denied a resting place in sacred ground.

More available than workers and Catholic farmers, who were restrained by cross-pressures, were those whose groups either reinforced or did not openly oppose involvement in the Nazi movement. Individuals whose reference or primary groups were infused with conservative and patriotic sentiments were quite easily induced to take the rather short step further to the right along the ideological continuum. Nazi party strength in the *Reichstag* was bolstered by the early move of these conservative nationalists into its ranks, as the election results of 1930 demonstrate. The German Nationalist People's party (DNVP), the traditional mainstay of the *völkisch* movement, lost over 1.9 million of its voters to the Nazi party, whose total vote jumped sharply from the 810,127 registered in 1928 to 6,379,672 in 1930. In comparison, the non-Catholic middle-class parties lost only 700,000 votes, an obvious indication that the middle class had not yet made up its mind to support Hitler. Somewhat later adopters of Hitler's political innovations, the middle-class Germans waited until 1932, when it was fairly clear that Hitler was apt to be a winning contender, before declaring their full support for Nazism. This middle-class shift to the Nazi party is revealed in the 1932 electoral decline of the non-Catholic middle-class parties when they lost almost 6 million of their voters, slipping from 22.3 per cent of the vote in 1930 to a meager 5.2 per cent in 1932. It is important that the Socialist parties and the Catholic Center party maintained their electoral strength at about the same level through these years, testifying again to the countervailing influence of the trade unions and the Catholic Church.[112] In contrast, those bound by *völkisch* sentiments within the DNVP had positive reinforcements for voting the Nazi ticket and non-Catholic, middle-class Germans were relatively free from strong negative group influences comparable to those that affected workers and Catholics.

So far, the influence of groups in the commitment process has been analyzed only in terms of data bearing on the composition of the Nazi party and on general electoral shifts that strengthened the Nazi hold on the *Reichstag*. Yet, as Trotsky's conversion shows, individuals are often encouraged to make investments and sacrifices in a movement through social ties with those who have already been converted. Encouraged to attend a meeting for the sake of friendship or out of curiosity, an individual can be led through small increments of action to the point of real dedication. How this process operated in the Nazi revolution is conveyed in the personal account of one who was led into the movement through a friend:

. . . in 1928 I became acquainted with a colleague of my own age, with whom I had frequent conversations. He was a calm, quiet person whom I esteemed very highly. When I found that he was one of the local leaders of the National Socialist party, my opinion of it as a group of criminals changed completely. My new attitude was further confirmed through my contacts with other National Socialists, after I had attended a meeting at the instigation of my friend. I came to value many of them as good comrades and honest, sincere fellows.[113]

But possibly a more interesting example of interpersonal influence in the formation of commitments is the case of the Communist who was a neighbor of the Nazi whose words I quote:

At the back of my house there lived a functionary of the Communist party who was rather ill disposed toward me. The man had a dog, and so did I. Consequently we often met in front of the house, since we were in the habit of taking our dogs out at the same hour. One day the dog, to which he seemed very much attached, was hit by an automobile. When I heard his cry I went outside, and offered to bandage the dog. This was the more welcome, as the Communist seemed quite lost, while I had the necessary first-aid material in the house.

From that time on we were friends. I continued to discuss political questions with him, and finally I got him to the point where he consented to attend a meeting of the N.S.D.A.P. [the Nazi party] and listen to the "quacking," as he put it. The meeting was at Hasenhaide, Comrade Dr. Goebbels speaking. As we parted after the meeting, my friend the Communist said very little. I noticed that he seemed different from his usual self, and that he seemed to have heard something new at the meeting. Still it took some time before he came to the conclusion that the views he had previously held were not right.

One day he came to me, and told me he was sick of the crookedness of the Communist party and that he had become a member of the N.S.D.A.P.[114]

These case histories convey two impressions that are worth noting as I close this section. First, there is the appearance of an accidental factor in the conversion of the Communist, like that which occurred in the development of Trotsky's commitment. For it was purely accidental that his dog was struck by an automobile and that his Nazi neighbor would be home to help him in his moment of personal crisis. It is unlikely that a personal bond would have developed between them had there been no accident, thus the Communist might not have attended a meeting of the Nazi party. One is also left with the impression that for a revolutionary movement to mobilize large numbers of people its leaders must encourage followers to take initiative, rather than training them to wait for orders. For as the cases above illustrate, it is through the interpersonal influence of followers assuming leadership that the primary leader is able to mobilize the energies of those who are available but geographically or socially distant.

Stage III: Opportunity To Act

Proposition 2.6—The success of the primary rebel leader in expanding his popularity to new followers depends on his ability to provide organizational opportunities for those who are available for action and on the support he receives from secondary leaders who facilitate the follower's access to the movement. The greater the opportunity for action and the broader and more intense the support from these secondary leaders, the greater the probability that followers will enter into transactions with the primary leader, although they may be indirect transactions through secondary leaders or "trust associations."

It should be clear by now that an individual who is available for deviant political action is only a potential source of energy. Rebel leaders must tap and convert that energy into forms of power that can be utilized for organizational purposes. Both through communication and organizational strategies, such leaders must provide opportunities for action. While the traditional view has enshrined the heroic leader as the chief ingredient in successful mobilization efforts, we know that there is more to it than that. Indeed, the careful observer must admit that the development of a large rebel following is the result of many people cooperatively sharing the instrumental and expressive functions of leadership.

Examining each of the four movements, one is struck by the fact that two leaders, not three or four, stand out as organizationally responsible for mobilizing followers, although even the unknown follower may convert his neighbor through interpersonal influence. Even more dramatic is the division of labor between leaders as it pertains to the instrumental and expressive modes of action. If the primary leader is predominantly expressive, as were Mrs. Keech, Mr. Muhammad, and Hitler, the secondary leader is apt to possess instrumental talents, as we see in the cases of Dr. Armstrong, Malcolm X, and Goebbels. On the other hand, we find that in the Bolshevik revolution Lenin, the instrumental leader, was able to complement his own style with the expressive talents of Trotsky. The effect of this cooperation is to compensate for a single leader's organizational deficiencies, which consequently enhances organizational capabilities and accomplishments.

Moreover, when primary rebel leaders attempt to mobilize followers over geographic distances, "trust associations" become essential for bridging communication gaps with potential and actual followers. Many followers who have no direct contact with the primary leader are mobilized through groups and secondary leaders who are trusted, that have faithfully lived up to their obligations in previous transactions. Thus, the primary leader's ability to mobilize a large following is dependent in part on his skill in selecting his lieutenants and in capturing control over groups that provide more immediate access to the movement for those available for action. This view suggests that the mass support behind a popular rebel leader's position need not be the result of his magical qualities or even of the follower's direct emotional attachment to him, but can grow indirectly through the follower's transactions with others who are trusted. In fact, a revolutionary leader who engineers a successful insurrection may find his newly won position surprisingly tenuous as he discovers that many, who were active in the movement and pressing in essentially the same direction, were not following him at all, but were simply acting in unison by joining the tide of protest, although with different motives and toward different ends.

The "End of the World" Movement

Keech's role as goal-setter was complemented by Dr. Armstrong's position as chief mobilizer and communications specialist. As the secondary leader, he took the organizational business of the movement more seriously than Keech, who apparently felt very little obligation to convert others. "Her function, as she saw it, was to pass along information given her by the Guardians. Those who were 'ready' would see and heed the warning; those who were not would be swept away in the swirling waters of Great Lake."[115] This posture threw the organizational burden on Dr. Armstrong's shoulders. Taking the place of Keech on such matters, he sought followers in his own town and became a "relay station" in the communication process, passing on information from Keech to members of "The Seekers" and drawing on his own "credits" to persuade those who trusted him to accept Keech's lessons and initiatives. A significant number of followers, who had come to trust Dr. Armstrong, were led indirectly to start transactions with Keech. Of the eighteen mobilized, seven members were recruited through direct contact and loyalty to him.

By relaying Keech's instructions back to his own group, Dr. Armstrong diffused the organizational structure of the movement, providing easier access for those who were available for action. The opening of these channels was combined with the relative ease with which believers could travel to Keech's home, for the distance between the two cities was apparently not very great. Also Keech had made it a rule not to bar any of the chosen ones from her home, which had assumed the character of an operational headquarters. The fact that neither Keech nor Dr. Armstrong insisted on attendance at the headquarters as a condition for deliverance was quite significant in terms of organizational maintenance. For followers who were removed from the center of things could still take steps to prepare themselves for their eventual rescue. In this sense, the opportunity to act was always available for those who believed in Keech's lessons and prophecy. How far the leadership was willing to go in encouraging followers to invest and sacrifice is exemplified by the response to the geographical dispersion of student followers at the advent of Christmas recess. In order to maintain the opportunity level of each follower in the face of increasing separation, it was decided that the chosen would be picked up by spacemen individually, wherever they were at the appointed time. By this device, all followers were assured that they would be rescued. Such a guarantee was essential for maintaining their transactional commitments, for, without any promise of rescue, there would have been no potential profits for conforming to Keech's initiatives.

In closing, I should emphasize the role that Dr. Armstrong played as "gatekeeper" in the communication process. For his own followers, he was the chief link with Keech, and even in adverse weather he was assured of a full audience of followers who listened intently for their instructions. Furthermore, he was also a key link with the world of nonbelievers. As disciples are wont to do, it was Dr. Armstrong's decision to write the first press release to tell the world of Keech's flood prophecy. Spreading the word and explaining the movement to members of the media in interview situations was also his primary responsibility. In fact, his leadership in communication was so well established that when Keech met with reporters she tended to imitate Dr. Armstrong's style of presentation.

As we should expect, Dr. Armstrong's efforts to open up action opportunities for the mass of nonbelievers was far from successful, for only a small number of persons are apt to be available for occult activities. The lone exception in this case was Manya Glassbaum, who was mobilized through one of his press releases, but who left the movement after only a brief visit to headquarters. Here, Dr. Armstrong's heavy commitment distorted his judgment, for the decision to inform the world to gain converts in the face of low availability made the members of the movement vulnerable to public ridicule. While public stigma seemed to have little effect on the followers' commitments up to the day of the expected flood, it apparently affected levels of involvement after the flood failed to materialize. For Keech, also, this was apparently the case, for after the final disconfirmation she went into hiding to escape public reactions.

The Black Muslim Movement

It would probably not be unfair to say that Malcolm X was responsible for the growth of the Black Muslim movement. For his organizational talents were largely responsible for the development of the Nation of Islam into a mass movement. Like Dr. Armstrong, he assumed primary responsibility for the communication and mobilization functions of leadership, although his ability to generate enthusiasm through expressive modes of conduct is also well known. Lincoln has captured the essence of Malcolm's leadership:

> Malcolm is an indefatigable organizer and speaker. Whereas Muhammad speaks almost exclusively to the black masses, Malcolm frequently appears at colleges and universities, and he is a popular radio and television discussant. He also visits temples in every part of the country with the regular frequency of a salesman. He organizes new temples, pumps spirit and encouragement into the missions or newly founded cell groups, conducts rallies and fund-raising campaigns and serves as Muhammad's general trouble-shooter and spokesman.[116]

Malcolm's success in mobilizing lower-class blacks into the ranks of the Nation of Islam can be partially attributed to his skill in providing organizational opportunities for those on the fringes of black nationalist meetings and outside store-front Christian churches. For example, while selecting building sites for Muslim temples, he was careful to pick or approve locations that would make the Muslim organization easily accessible to the available masses. Leaders of the various temples were also encouraged to live in the black ghettos, close to their base of support. Furthermore, each Muslim was encouraged to make new opportunities for action available where none existed. Thus, when members moved to another city they were expected to plant seeds for Mr. Muhammad.[117] Some of those seeds grew into Muslim temples.

Through their communication and mobilization efforts, secondary leaders sometimes draw followers into a movement who have little direct loyalty to the primary leader. The fact that Malcolm left the Black Muslim movement in 1964 gives us a chance to gauge the importance of this two-step communication and mobilization process. Although exact figures are not available, it is known that, after Malcolm's formal split with Mr. Muhammad, a sizable number of followers from Malcolm's Mosque Seven announced their own break with the Nation of Islam, followed by Black Muslims in other cities who apparently felt little direct obligation to Mr. Muhammad. This development suggests that secondary leaders not only contribute directly to the growth of mass movements, but they may also capture the loyalty of many followers who are assumed to be exclusively committed to the primary leader.

The Bolshevik Revolution

Trotsky returned to Russia from exile in May, just one month after Lenin. Although he was not yet a member of the Bolshevik party, his political position had taken on a new character in exile, such that he differed very little from Lenin on the substantive issues of the movement. In his first speeches, he opposed the efforts of the moderate Socialist groups to develop ties with the Provisional Government, arguing that such cooperation could only prolong the dual power situation wherein the Soviets and government shared political authority and, consequently, neither was in a position to rule effectively. What was needed to accelerate the process of social change, he thought, was to consolidate power behind the slogan, "All Power to the Soviets!" As was his tendency, Trotsky again had radically altered his political thinking, and this time he had joined Lenin on common political ground. Having arrived at a similar ideological view of the Russian situation, it was not long before Trotsky had joined the Bolshevik party and joined hands with Lenin in solving the enduring problems of leadership. Between them, the functions of leadership were performed, cooperation having enhanced the capabilities of the Bolshevik organization at the same time that it ensured the fulfillment of their own private ambitions. They needed each other and the Bolshevik movement needed them both.

Historical accounts show that Trotsky's role in the events leading up to the October insurrection was much greater than Lenin's, although we must remember that Lenin was in hiding much of this time, avoiding certain arrest. Still, it is a bit ironic that while Trotsky's organizational and oratorical skills paved the way for a successful revolutionary assault, Lenin inherited not only the revolution, but state power as well. By utilizing Trotsky's secondary leadership, and by using the Soviet as a point of access for revolutionary activity, Lenin was able to indirectly mobilize the active masses.

Securing the talents of Trotsky was a windfall for Lenin and the Bolshevik party, for he was exceptionally gifted both as organizer and orator. Possibly even more than Lenin, Trotsky can be regarded as a "heroic" figure, since he was extremely effective in the instrumental and expressive areas of leadership. Lenin's brilliance was partly in his sensitivity to talent and his readiness to incorporate gifted people, like Trotsky, into the movement where they could serve to reach organizational goals. For instance, even though he had differed sharply with Trotsky many times in the past, once they had reached an ideological consensus he was willing to share the revolutionary stage with him. On hearing Trotsky's analysis of the political situation in May, Lenin decided that Trotsky and his friends must be encouraged to join the Bolshevik party immediately. Inside the party, "he was willing to accord them every democratic right, to share with them his influence, and, as the record shows, to allow himself to be outvoted on important occasions." As more concrete enticements to join, Lenin offered them key positions on the important governing bodies within the party, including participation on the editorial staff of *Pravda*. "He did not ask Trotsky to renounce anything of his past; he did not even mention past controversies. He himself had put these out of his mind and expected Trotsky to do likewise—so anxious was he to join hands with anybody who could promote the common cause."[118]

Trotsky's capacity to move the masses through the spoken word is well known. Often, he would be swept away by the atmosphere of the crowded hall, leaving his prepared remarks in order to develop ideas that better represented the mood of his audience. His objective was always to persuade, even those who were known to disagree with him. In contrast, Lenin aroused anger and division in his audiences by haranguing his political enemies. While Lenin had a tendency to narrow the base of support for the party along rather rigid ideological lines, Trotsky sought to enlarge the potential source of energy from which the Bolsheviks could draw. Even against Lenin's preference, he tried to preserve access to revolutionary action for many who were not yet ready to accept the Bolsheviks as the vanguard of the pro- letariat. It is quite understandable, then, that Lenin wanted to make the revolution only in the name of the Bolshevik party, while Trotsky insisted that it must be made under the direction of the Soviets, the political bastions most trusted by the active masses. After considerable controversy over how to proceed in announcing the sponsor of the coming revolution, Lenin compromised, agreeing that the revolution would be made in the name of both the Bolshevik party and the Soviets. Such a concession was, of course, an organizational triumph for Trotsky. More than that, with Bolshevik fortunes improving significantly within the Soviets, Lenin would be able to use these "trust associations" to catapult his party into power.

By mid-September, the Bolsheviks had obtained a strong majority in the Petrograd and Moscow Soviets, and they were fast becoming the dominant influence in many provincial Soviets as well. Solidifying their position still further, Trotsky was elected chairman of the Petrograd Soviet in early October. "The party of Lenin was strong," we are told, "not only in the two capitals, but also in the Volga towns, the industrial centers of the Urals, the Donets Basin, and in other industrial towns of the Ukraine. Moreover, the Bolsheviks had as allies the Left Socialist Revolutionaries, who had a considerable following in the army and among the peasants."[119] Furthermore, the Bolsheviks had successfully eroded the regime's regulative capability, while enlarging their own striking power. Through the efforts of Trotsky, as head of the Bolshevik Military Organization, the Petrograd 1st Machine-Gun Regiment had repudiated the Kerensky government and had shifted its support to the party of Lenin. Then, on October 21, the entire Petrograd garrison acknowledged the Soviet as the sole power and the Bolshevik Military Revolutionary Committee as its authority.

Contrary to popular belief, Lenin's apparent success in mobilizing the support of the peasants, workers, soldiers, and sailors was not based primarily on their devotion to his person or even to his political party. In fact, there is considerable evidence to show that a significant number of those who participated in the October revolution were mobilized through points of access in the Soviets or through contact with the Left Socialist Revolutionaries. As a result of Trotsky's initiative in enlarging the opportunities for revolutionary action, many who felt little loyalty to Lenin or the Bolsheviks joined the tide of protest against the Provisional Government. The Soviet, as a "trust association," was the crucial intermediary link in the two-stage transactional process. This is clearly revealed in Trotsky's own account:

> In those millions upon whom the party legitimately counted it is necessary to distinguish three layers: one which was already with the Bolsheviks on all conditions; another, more numerous, which supported the Bolsheviks insofar as they acted through the soviets; a third which followed the soviets in spite of the fact they were dominated by Bolsheviks.[120]

Thus, Lenin's success in mobilizing followers to the revolutionary cause hinged on Bolshevik control over the Soviets, which Trotsky had insisted was the best course and which he was prepared to take full advantage of. Through Trotsky's wise counsel, Lenin was able to align the masses behind the Bolshevik move, although many had little sympathy for the Bolsheviks and little allegiance to Lenin personally. This situation is clearly demonstrated by the poor showing of the Bolsheviks in the November, 1917, election for control of the newly formed Constituent Assembly. As Carr has noted:

> Of the 707 elected members of the assembly . . . the SRs [Social Revolutionaries] could claim a comfortable majority—410 in all. The Bolsheviks secured just under a quarter of the seats, i.e., 175. Most of the eighty-four members of the "national groups," of which the Ukrainians formed the largest, were strongly anti-Bolshevik. . . . If this could be read as a verdict on the government set up by the October revolution, it was a crushing voice of non-confidence.[121]

Lenin's personal appeal, if we take the election results as an indicator, was more limited than is generally assumed in discussions of his place in the revolution. It must be recognized that when a large following is mobilized for revolutionary purposes, many individuals recruited through the opportunity structures provided by secondary leaders or "trust associations" may only be acting in unison with the primary leader. After the revolutionary attempt succeeds, the primary leader's task, as Lenin discovered, is not simply one of coping with known enemies of the revolution, but of winning the loyalty of those thought to have been friends.

The Nazi Revolution

Like Trotsky, Hitler can be described as a heroic leader, for he combined in a powerful way both instrumental talents as an organizer and expressive sensibilities that allowed him to play on the emotions of certain sectors of the German population. There are those who would undoubtedly argue that the growth of the Nazi party and its ultimate conquest of power were rooted primarily in Hitler's magnetism or charisma. Alone, this explanation is quite weak, for it fails to take into account the historical evidence that shows that Nazi successes stemmed largely from Hitler's ability to create an organizational network and plan of operation that offered the available masses opportunities to act. By constructing a highly visible and easily accessible organizational structure, Hitler was well prepared to receive the multitudes of middle-class Germans who, fearing that they would lose their income and social status, began to look for some radical solution to the problems of strain that the Weimar government was impotent to deal with.

Hitler joined the German Peoples' party in September of 1919. His public speaking ability and concern for organizational growth immediately won him a seat on the executive committee of the party and the post of Chief of Propaganda. Within this early embryo of the National Socialist party Hitler was to learn promotional strategies and organizational principles that would be vital to the evolutionary development of the party's organizational apparatus.

In the beginning of his promotional campaign, Hitler randomly distributed leaflets announcing meetings to passersby on the streets of Munich. Operating in this way, he produced rather dismal results, just as Malcolm X had produced using random methods on the ghetto streets. At the first meeting under Hitler's leadership, only seven people were present and, after several months on the street, no more than thirty had been mobilized. A dramatic change in the party's fortunes came after Hitler was able to collect enough money through penny contributions to advertise his meetings in the newspaper. Through the media he was able to reach many Germans who were available for starting commitments but who had not yet been contacted because of the more limited nature of the sidewalk confrontations. The impact of this first advertisement was impressive, for 100 people attended the meeting following its appearance. To increase the visibility of the party still further, Hitler proceeded to recruit a few well-known nationalist leaders to speak at a mass meeting. Drawn by popular names, 2,000 Germans made their first contact with Hitler and the movement.

As was characteristic of his organizational thinking, Hitler did not abandon the use of street contact when other promotional devices proved to be more effective; rather he maintained it as one in a widening arsenal of organizational weapons. Thus, all three of the strategies mentioned above were included in the operating procedures of the party. Street contact by local members of the party, the use of news media and placards, and the training of party orators to promote the growth of district and local branches of the party became distinctive features of the movement through its mobilization stage and after the seizure of power.

Until the unsuccessful Nazi *putsch* of 1923, Hitler and the movement were relatively unknown outside of Bavaria, the nucleus of nationalist activities. As his paid advertisements had increased the party's visibility within Bavaria, so too did Hitler's trial on charges of conspiracy publicize the Nazi cause throughout the nation. The newspaper accounts of the trial gave the party national exposure free of charge and repeated references to Hitler as the organizer of the *putsch* etched his name on the minds of the available masses, many of whom would ultimately cast their lot with him in defiance of the Weimar system. Abel reports, for instance, that a large number of his contributors had established contact with the movement through these early press accounts of the *putsch* trial.

Hitler's imprisonment in the Landsberg fortress was a respite from the pressures of party activity that allowed him time to assess the weaknesses in organizational strategy leading up to the abortive *putsch* and to crystallize his own thinking about the state of the nation and his struggle for power. The government had assumed that by isolating Hitler from his followers and by outlawing the party, the Nazi movement would collapse; but, just as Lenin's revolutionary zeal and work were nourished by imprisonment, so too were Hitler's. With the help of Rudolf Hess, Hitler gave the movement its first political testament, exposing many who had escaped the touch of the expanding party apparatus to the full range of his political ideas and aspirations. Printed in 1926, *Mein Kampf* was to greatly increase the visibility of the party. Many who were prepared by their own training to accept the ideological tone of the book were led into the movement after reading it. The following is one example of conversion by testament:

> My greatest political experience occurred when I bought and read a copy of Hitler's book. I saw therein a confirmation of the very views I had cherished, but which I could not express properly. Now I had the necessary equipment to take up the quarrel with my political opponents. I had found the cause to which I could devote my life, and I availed myself of every opportunity at the club, the office, and at home, to spread the ideas of Hitler.[122]

For those who had already found their way into the movement, Hitler's testament of faith, much like Mao Tse-tung's little red book of quotations, became the central focus for group discussions and study, through which members of the party derived inspiration and guidance.

Contemplating the future of the movement in the calm atmosphere of prison life, Hitler made basic decisions whose impact on mobilization far exceeded the influence of his book. Realizing that he could not succeed without the majority of the nation behind him, he decided to turn the movement away from illegal ventures and into a legal course of action. Instead of relying on the *putsch* to achieve political domination, he resolved to use elections as an instrument of revolutionary change. This decision was to affect the Nazi party's organizational operations in two fundamental ways. First, in order to overthrow the government through voting power, the Nazi organization had to be more diffusely distributed throughout the whole nation, with functioning units in each electoral district. Second, the use of elections as a means to power meant that Hitler could rely on the electoral machinery financed by the government in order to offer the German people an opportunity in their own neighborhoods to take the first incremental step, in the election booth, toward revolution.

When he was released from prison in November, 1924, Hitler was prohibited by the government from making public speeches. Designed to stifle the growth of the movement, the government's action had just the opposite effect, for Hitler was freed by this act from the obligations to make public appearances, which would only have diminished the time and energy he had committed to the tasks of organization. He was thus more concerned about the ban on party activities than he was about the inaccessibility of the public podium. After assuring governmental leaders in Munich that he had forsaken violence for legal procedures, he was able to secure a lift of the ban on the party in Bavaria and thereupon set out to organize a mass party that eventually covered all of Germany.

Between 1924 and 1929, Hitler's chief organizational goal was to build a bureaucratic apparatus with clear lines of vertical responsibility and communication. He realized the need to expand the number of local party units in order to make the movement more accessible to potential followers, but he also wanted to concentrate decision-making control at the top. He resolved this dilemma by distributing leadership functions to all three of the party echelons, allowing a large degree of autonomy for local leaders, while securing control over planning and finance for himself and his administrative subordinates within the *Reichsleitung,* the command group at the apex of the bureaucratic pyramid.

Below the *Reichsleitung* in the administrative hierarchy were the party districts (*Gaus*). The administrative leader in each district (the *Gauleiter*) was appointed by Hitler as his personal executive representative. He was subject to instant dismissal, although such action could be undertaken only with Hitler's consent.[123] Aside from carrying out administrative orders from the *Reichsleitung,* district leaders assumed the important function of collecting local dues, which were sent to the top echelon to be redistributed according to existing developmental plans. In order to insure that district matters were being administered according to plan, Hitler developed rather unique control mechanisms. He created new administrative positions—the state inspectors and the roving ambassador—whose functions were to watch over the interests of the *Reichsleitung.* State inspectors could carry out surprise inspections at any time of the day or night and roving ambassadors were sent into districts under Hitler's orders to handle serious crises. Through his power of dismissal and with the help of his loyal state inspectors and roving ambassadors, Hitler effectively controlled the activities of his district leadership.

Below the district leader, and under his jurisdiction, lay a complex of local leaders heading party units that were the chief instruments in mobilizing the yet uncommitted masses. At first, Hitler allowed the local cells of the party extensive autonomy, but the appearance of local obstructionism, such as the withholding of monies and the attempt to expel district leaders without appropriate clearance, forced him to take a harder line. Hence, in October, 1926, he empowered district leaders to appoint sub-leaders as additional control agents to watch over the activities of local units.[124] Hitler's success in constructing clear and dependable lines of responsibility between the three echelons of the party is indicated by the fact that by 1929 he was able to withdraw almost completely from the day-to-day problems of administration.

A mass-based revolutionary organization is not apt to grow or adapt to rapidly changing circumstances if its primary leader does not encourage or at least allow followers to initiate leadership when conditions demand immediate responses. Although Hitler was obsessed with bureaucratic responsibility and efficiency, out of necessity he was forced to leave areas of organization slack in which the local representatives of the party could find room for independent and creative political action. The following personal account illustrates this point very well:

> We, the early simple champions of the Third Reich, fought largely of our own accord. Ready to do all in our power, we frequently did things without being told to do so; in fact, there were a great many things no command could have foreseen. Action, after all, is the outstanding preoccupation of the true fighter; but his action must be such as to serve the great cause to which he has pledged his support.[125]

Through the interpersonal influence of these secondary leaders at the local level, Hitler was able to swell the ranks of the party, yet his use of the party apparatus to provide opportunities for action cannot compare in importance to the use he made of elections.

As weapons of revolutionary change, elections possess certain positive features that make them especially valuable for mobilizing the support of those with lower levels of availability. Polling places are normally quite accessible and the secret ballot, if such exists, allows the voter to support extremist political parties without fearing public reprisals. In general, voting is a very lost-cost investment that can bring together the voting power of those who are frustrated but who are not yet free to make heavy investments and sacrifices within a collective movement.

Hitler's decision to take power through elections meant, in effect, that he could provide an opportunity for thousands of Germans who were ready to support an extremist solution but who were still too restrained by their commitments within the system to make contact with one of the many local branches of the party. This fact is clearly documented by comparing the percentage of women in the Nazi party to their role in the general elections. In 1932, at a time when the party's membership was rising rapidly, women constituted only 3 per cent of the total membership, while they comprised up to half of the Nazis' electoral support that same year.[126] Locked into the family and restrained by social custom, women were simply not so free as men to invest their time and energy in the movement by assuming membership in the party. In essence, the elections allowed them the opportunity to support Hitler without having to make a commitment. Sympathetic but not yet committed, these women, as well as others similarly stationed, were not viewed by Hitler as followers, but only potential converts. To transfer this sympathy into real dedication, Hitler broadened the horizontal structure of the party after the 1930 elections. He launched the development of many new front organizations and instructed his subordinates to step up the infiltration of existing organizations in an attempt to capture control. Through these methods, he hoped to ease into party activity those who had cast their votes for the Nazis out of sympathy rather than conviction.

For those who were not able or ready to assume full-fledged membership in the party, the Nazi front organizations had a definite appeal. They provided local opportunities of an economic and social nature for those who did not want to take the social risks that might have accompanied the stigma of being a card-carrying Nazi. Starting in 1931, Hitler began to stimulate the development of parallel front organizations for each major association in the country. Individuals who had voted the Nazi ticket in 1930 were encouraged on purely economic grounds to join the National Socialist Association of Pharmacists, the National Socialist League of Munich Coal Dealers, the Association of National Socialist Police Officers, and other similar organizations. During this same period, Hitler also reactivated and expanded the Hitler Youth organization in an attempt to play on the sympathies of parents who were beginning to fear that their children had no future under republican rule. Indeed, how front organizations recruit members through a veil of deceit and then isolate them from the outside world is nicely illustrated in Orlow's account of the mobilization strategy of Hitler Youth:

> The HJ emphasized its apolitical, nationalist image (its Jungvolk units did not even carry swastika flags), but its functionaries, too, were not allowed to forget the political object of their work. The apolitical image was a façade to lure the uncommitted; once organized in any party group, no member was allowed to cooperate with those still on the outside.[127]

Paralleling the development of these Nazi front organizations were well-planned attempts to take over control of established interest groups. By controlling these "trust associations," the Nazis hoped to influence the behavior of many Germans who were either neutral or unsympathetic toward the party. Following the course of the Bolsheviks, who achieved power by gaining supremacy in the Soviets, the Nazis made serious inroads into farming groups (especially the *Landbund*), into various guilds and business associations, and into civil service organizations. These efforts, combined with the expanding network of front organizations, appear to have accomplished Hitler's organizational goal to transform the sympathizers of 1930 into card-carrying members of the party. For from 1930, when the horizontal development of the party was accelerated, to 1932, the number of members in the party increased from 389,000 to 1,000,000.

Stage IV: High Profit Potential Accompanied by Rising Investments and Sacrifices

Proposition 2.3—Followers are most likely to develop a transactional commitment with those rebel leaders whom they perceive to have the most appropriate information, skills, and personal temperaments for reaching personal and group goals. However, once a movement has developed, its structure may limit the number of potential competitors for leadership positions, for example, by requiring special access to a transcendental authority. An established leader who has the trust of his followers has an advantage over potential competitors because he has proven his competence over time and has developed mutual obligations with his followers.

Politically deviant commitments are constructed on a rational basis if, from the actor's point of view, such deviation promises greater potential profits for him than other perceived opportunities. While the enumeration of "profits" is relative in terms of the particular individual, there are structural aspects of the commitment process that allow us to generalize beyond the individual to the group of followers. Followers who may actually be experiencing different types of personal tension, some tensions based on biological deprivation and others on status deprivation, can become available for politically deviant commitments in different ways and jump at the chance to begin action when the first opportunity presents itself. The spectrum of different motives that can energize the commitment process at the individual level can converge into a uniform set of behaviors that conform to the norms established by rebel leadership. In this context, followers with different motivations are apt to develop different types of transactional relations with leaders, who, as a condition for each separate bargain, demand that each follower behave according to a set of rules no matter what his motives. From a long list of possible effects, such rules can establish uniform styles of dress, rituals governing the interactions between followers, or basic authority relationships between leaders and followers, specifying the range of appropriate responses that followers are allowed to make to the leader's orders and the correct deferential posture they must assume in his presence to preserve the social distance he demands as his right.

When followers are able to choose between rebel leaders who essentially share the same beliefs and goals, they will place their loyalties according to their estimate of the relative competence of those leaders in reaching goals. As in small-group processes, we expect followers to change their leadership preferences to conform to the particular tasks that have received high priority within the group. When revolution is the goal of a group, for example, followers may place great value on hardheadedness, aggressiveness, heroism, and the ability to unify divergent forces. A leader who can demonstrate that he possesses such attributes is apt to win the support of many who are judging and choosing among available leaders.

Often, the structure of the situation can affect the follower's evaluation of competence. For instance, if leadership is legitimized in relation to a transcendental authority, followers may judge as competent only those who have a close relationship with the higher authority. In such circumstances, a prospective leader's proximity to such an enormous source of power is likely to heavily influence the follower's choice of a leader. Those leaders with transcendental contact have a sharp advantage over those without, for followers see the decisions of these leaders as the work of divine providence.

In such cases, those who are chosen to lead must be able to speak with the gods, a "good" in the transactional process that is indispensable for those aspiring to leadership.

Geographic distance can also affect the selection process. This is especially true in mass movements, where often there is no electoral mechanism to eliminate much of the confusion stemming from geographic dispersion. Balloting may occur in the private atmosphere of party caucuses, but usually there is no way to determine precisely which leaders have captured the support of the masses, the Nazi movement being an exception. For example, the tendency is to see Lenin leading the masses in the October revolution, when actually he was able to control only his own political faction. The most that we can expect to discover is how he gained and maintained primary leadership within the Bolshevik party, especially in the face of Trotsky's great popularity.

By placing the emphasis on the competitive nature of the leadership selection process, there is a danger that the primary and secondary categories of leadership will become overly rigid and formal. While useful for highlighting the relative dominance of leaders in mass movements, these categories should not be considered as positions for which leaders fiercely compete, although they might in some cases. Rather, it is apparent from our earlier discussion that leadership is shared. Thus, as information and skill demands are altered by adaptive pressures, shifts in leadership occur in order to more appropriately regulate the organization's response to strain. Who initiates action for the group will thus depend on the problems needing resolution and the particular "goods" that are required to successfully resolve them. In this sense, we should speak of competence as it applies to the selection of more than one leader, sharing the functional responsibilities of leadership.

The "End of the World" Movement

Bertha Blatsky's attempt to assume leadership within the movement helps us to determine the weight that followers attach to competence when selecting leaders. In addition, it points out how the connection with a transcendental source of authority (in this case, the spiritual forces in space) can be an avenue to leadership. Moreover, Blatsky's effort to initiate action for the group can be understood as a response to the leadership void left by Keech. In this sense, we should see her effort to assume leadership as compensatory, taking up the slack in Keech's own style and organizational effort. For Keech's command of the first meeting at headquarters lacked direction and resolve, owing to the fact that she had failed to adequately explain why the believers had not been picked up by spacemen as she had predicted. Keech's uncertainty about the exact time and place of their rescue created a situation wherein new leadership was necessary. Seizing the opportunity, Blatsky fell into a trance and was given "the power of speech" through which she was capable of receiving messages from outer space. Her source of information was not Sananda, however, but the "Creator" himself. Blatsky's trance not only established her direct connection with the source of transcendental power, but her choice of contacts directly challenged Keech's authority. Sananda, Jesus in a different age of light, was upstaged by God. Faced with the ambiguity of Keech's behavior, there was an immediate acceptance of Blatsky's new role, for she had gained access to information that promised to clarify the situation and reduce the intensity of the crisis. Yet, while Blatsky's ascension to a position of leadership resulted from her potential for receiving information vital for reducing tension, she proved to be an amateur and consequently failed to maintain the enthusiasm of the followers. Her messages from the Creator, which were usually incoherent, tended to intensify the collective tensions that Keech was feeding. Thus, after several hours of "tedious, painful monotony," Dr. Armstrong quietly suggested to Mrs. Keech that Blatsky was "off the beam."[128] Unskilled in receiving communications from outer space, she could not bring information to the group that assured the members of a profitable course.

Blatsky's attempt at leadership failed to secure a permanent role for her as the chief initiator of action, yet she remained an important source for corroborating the messages that Keech continued to receive from outer space. As such, her secondary position in the leadership structure had the effect of further legitimizing Keech's leadership. Not only could Keech speak for Sananda, but, through Blatsky's trances, she could call on the Creator to verify her own messages. Such confirmation must surely have enlarged the general feeling of trust in Keech's instructions, at least for those who were convinced that she was a competent medium. But as Blatsky's experience shows so clearly, even those who pretend to speak for the gods can be rejected for incompetence.

A follower who is skeptical of a leader's ability to reach goals that promise tangible profits is not so likely to make the investments and sacrifices that lead to strong and enduring commitments. Hal Fischer's attitude toward Mrs. Keech points this out very well. He was quite skeptical of her ability as a medium and vacillated in his willingness to follow orders. His reluctance to accept her initiatives consistently, we are told, partially "revolved around the relative inexperience of Mrs. Keech, who had, he pointed out, been receiving messages for less than a year."[129] In sum, his wavering commitment resulted in part because he had little confidence in Keech as a medium, which, in turn, led him to question the validity of her messages. In this case, the feeling of trust was insufficiently strong to lead Fischer into heavier investments and sacrifices and he left the movement knowing his judgment had been correct all along. Further evidence of the relationship between competence and willingness to follow is found in Cleo Armstrong's relationship to Ella Lowell, a competing medium. She was skeptical of her competence as a medium and behaved very much as Fischer had toward Mrs. Keech. She consistently rejected and belittled Lowell's initiatives.

The Black Muslim Movement

As suggested above, the close relationship between a leader's association with a transcendental source of authority and his ability to rule is endemic to a religious charismatic office. Within the Nation of Islam, for example, one of the goods necessary to consummate transactions with followers is the ability to mediate between the transcendental source of authority and the secular realm. This position, which could be granted to both Keech and Blatsky in the "end of the world" movement, is held by Mr. Muhammad within the Black Muslim organization. Since all important decisions are sanctioned by reference to Allah's will, Mr. Muhammad's closer proximity to Allah through his office and through his contact with Fard has given him the goods required for effective expressive leadership and the means for instrumental control over the decision-making apparatus.

Because we are speaking of a religious charismatic office, the circulation of primary leadership is facilitated only if others claim close proximity to the transcendental source of authority and are in positions to effectively compete with the leader whose claim to speak for the gods or ancestors has already been validated by the group. In the "end of the world" movement, for instance, Blatsky's trance, because it provided a link with God, gave her the transcendental contact so essential to compete with Keech for the primary position. But in the Nation of Islam, Mr. Muhammad has largely eliminated the possibility that others can effectively compete with him as a spokesman for Allah, a tactic that has not been without consequences. In the earlier stages of the movement, after Mr. Muhammad had appointed a Haitian, Theodore Rozier, as Chief Minister of the nation, "dissident factions repudiated Rozier on the ground that he 'never saw the Savior' and that his 'second-hand revelation' was not sufficient qualification for the role." Moreover, there was an effort, which failed, to challenge Mr. Muhammad's identification of himself "as the only channel through which Fard's 'truth' could be brought to the sleeping Black Nation."[130] As the only contact with Fard's "truth," Mr. Muhammad has created a monopoly over spiritual information that excludes the possibility of competitors, such as people like Blatsky, from opening up their own channels. Because he has effectively closed other avenues to Allah, Mr. Muhammad has been able to control the extractive, regulative, and distributive activities of the movement. In the distributive context, especially, he has effectively manipulated the rewards and punishments that have ensured that strong commitments would develop behind his leadership.

Malcolm X's leadership remained secondary largely because he had no contact with Fard and thus could not develop sufficient proximity to Allah to legitimize an expressive role beyond that which he assumed in his organizational work. While he initiated action with respect to instrumental tasks, his decisions had to be approved by Mr. Muhammad and could be vetoed by him. They shared leadership functions, as I mentioned previously, but

Malcolm could not effectively compete with Mr. Muhammad for the primary position because he was unable to gain access to the spiritual information necessary for rule. It is important that Malcolm perceived his own limitations with respect to ability and information. Recognizing that he did not possess the appropriate goods for the situation, he made no attempt to compete with the Messenger for primary leadership. Like Rozier, who was rejected by followers because he had not known Fard, Malcolm sensed that they would similarly reject any attempt of his to make claims to the primary position because he, too, had not directly received the Savior's "truth."

The Bolshevik Revolution

Lenin's position as primary leader within the Bolshevik party was earned in competition with others for organizational control. Since there was no transcendental source of authority to legitimize his position as founder of the party, he had to prove, to the satisfaction of his comrades, that his organizational skills, information, and personal attributes were more appropriate for the revolutionary situation. His dominance in the party and the movement was achieved, in Carr's view, by "clear-headed genius, confident persistence and polemical temperament. . . ."[131] And Sukhanov recognized Lenin as "an extraordinary phenomenon, a man of absolutely exceptional intellectual power; he [was] a first-class world magnitude in calibre."[132] Indeed, Lenin took revolution as a profession seriously and prepared himself for revolutionary leadership as a young man might spend years grooming himself for elected political office.

Lenin spent most of his life preparing for revolution, gathering information concerning revolutionary strategies and environmental conditions wherever he lived and traveled. As a young man in Samara, for example, he was eager to ask questions of the retired revolutionaries: "How had they themselves come to the movement and how won recruits for it? . . . How did one 'go underground' and what could they tell him of the technique of conspiracy? What of chemical inks, secret codes, signals, false passports, jailbreaks, escapes from exile?"[133] During the same period he digested volumes of statistical reports dealing with the major problems of Russian society. For six years, "he thought, studied, questioned, examined, soaking up knowledge like a sponge. . . ."[134] This period of exploration into the basic causes of agrarian and worker problems led Lenin, more than his contemporaries, to deeply understand the tempo of the agrarian movement and the nature of the worker's plight.

Coupled with his vast information about the social strains in Russian society, Lenin had also developed skills appropriate for a revolutionary situation. His writing skills, reflected in his major critiques of Russia and of capitalist societies, won him followers at the outset of his career. And, while not an orator to match Trotsky, the force of his arguments was irresistible for many. Even without the full range of oratorical skills, he dominated his audiences by the strength of his intellect and personality.

Sukhanov remembers listening to Lenin "breaking down complicated systems into the simplest and most generally accessible elements, and hammering, hammering, hammering them into the heads of his audience until he took them captive."[135]

In a different light, Trotsky places emphasis on the importance of Lenin's intuition and consistency in mobilizing the support of followers inside and outside the party. In his biography of Lenin, he recalls that Lenin had "the ability to grasp appearances correctly at once, to distinguish the essential and important from the unessential and insignificant, to imagine the missing parts of a picture, to weigh well the thoughts of others and above all the enemy, to put all this into a united whole and the moment the 'formula' for it comes to his mind, to deal the blow."[136] The boldness and consistency of action, once undertaken, endeared Lenin to the workers, for they appreciated those leaders who pointed out the "path of progress" and followed it without hesitating.

In addition to Trotsky's willingness to concede the role of party chief to Lenin, we know that Paul Axelrod had stepped down from his position as chief theorist and organizer in the formative stage of the movement, recognizing that "for the practical work of organization Lenin had both more talent and vastly more concern and energy."[137] This relationship between Lenin's competence and the willingness of others to accept his initiatives is dramatized in M. N. Pokrovsky's personal testimony:

> I frequently had occasion to differ from him [Lenin] on practical questions but I came off badly every time. When this experience had been repeated about seven times, I ceased to dispute and submitted to Lenin even if logic told me that one should act otherwise. I was henceforth convinced that he understood things better and was master of the power denied to me, of seeing about ten feet down into the earth.[138]

At least within the Bolshevik party, competence seems to have been a crucial factor in the selection of a leader. But it still remains for us to try to understand why Trotsky, who played such an important role in the days before the insurrection and had achieved such widespread popularity with the masses, failed to openly compete with Lenin for the primary position. Malcolm X, you will remember, did not attempt to replace Mr. Muhammad because he had no contact with the transcendental source of authority judged by followers to be necessary for anyone occupying the position of primary leader. Since Trotsky was not faced with this problem, we must look further for an explanation of his decision not to compete with Lenin as head of the party.

The act of founding an organization or movement apparently gives the founder an organizational advantage over others. Why this is true, I cannot say for sure. But numerous cases besides the Black Muslim movement and the Bolshevik and Nazi revolutions substantiate such a view, for example,

Mao Tse-tung's preeminence as the father of the Chinese Communist revolution, Fidel Castro's undisputed command in Cuba as the founder of the July 26th Movement, and Emiliano Zapata's special place as the originator of the Mexican peasant revolution that took place in this century. One explanation for this phenomenon is that "fathers" of organizations or movements perform a special integrative function that others in positions of power realize they cannot perform in the same way and with the same success. Another possible explanation is that long tenure as primary leader creates multiple opportunities that can be capitalized on to develop strong transactional commitments with many followers. Such commitments solidify the primary leader's organizational strength to such an extent that encroachment by a competing leader is infinitely more difficult. Together, these conditions can discourage even the most ambitious men, since they are unlikely to attempt to take leadership when the possibilities of failure militate against their own aspirations for greatness. For Trotsky, this was apparently the case.

In contrast to Lenin's long tenure as founder and chief of the Bolshevik party, Trotsky was a newcomer who had had no hand at all in shaping the character of the organization. On the contrary, as an active Menshevik he had been one of Lenin's chief mentors and an enemy of the party. Although Lenin was eager to recruit Trotsky and his friends, others within the party felt differently, for his history of anti-Bolshevism was the source of considerable mistrust and suspicion. "Trotsky's feud with Lenin for nearly fifteen years seemed insignificant in comparison with the things he would do in fifteen minutes for the Bolshevik party. . . . Yet in the inner circle of the party there were, naturally, men from whose memories nothing could efface the past feud."[139] Even on Lenin's initiative, Deutscher continues, Central Committee members had been unwilling to grant Trotsky an important role in governing the Bolshevik press. Although he was finally given a post as chief editor after his release from prison, those within the party who had dedicated their life to it, "looked with instinctive distrust upon former emigres, especially the one who was the most proud, colourful, and eloquent of all."[140]

Although Trotsky was the shining light in the days preceding the revolutionary coup, as the discussion above indicates, he was in no position to challenge Lenin's primary role. Lenin had founded the organization and had developed a following within the party that respected his instrumental talents and had grown to trust him. Against these strong transactional bonds Trotsky had very little chance, since he had little time to turn the tide of feeling against Lenin and create trustful relations that are the basis of organizational control. Trotsky accepted this secondary role in the revolution, not because he lacked the organizational genius for the primary position, but because he had entered the contest after Lenin had already led the members of the party to develop strong commitments behind his leadership, commitments that locked them into the Bolshevik organization almost as securely as a career civil servant who has made periodic advancements in a governmental bureaucracy becomes a slave to his job. In short, while the active masses were available for Trotsky's initiatives, the members of the Bolshevik party were not.

The Nazi Revolution

Personal rule can develop in several different ways. In the cases of Mrs. Keech and Mr. Muhammad, for example, it originated from their direct association with a religious and transcendental source of authority. On the other hand, Lenin's personal rule appears to have developed primarily from his organizational skills, for his claim to power was not made in terms of a transcendental authority or by reference to special personal attributes that led him to expect obedience from others as a right. Finally, Hitler's personal authority neither flowed from a transcendental source of power, as it did for Mrs. Keech and Mr. Muhammad, nor was it based on strictly organizational skills, as in Lenin's case. Rather it developed as a logical outgrowth of the organizational forms deduced from the *Führerprinzip*. As distinct from these other leaders, his personal rule was an integral part of what I shall call, for want of an existing phrase, *secular charismatic organization*. This organizational type is unique in the sense that the structural features of the organization tend to support and maintain personal rulership.

The most obvious feature of a secular charismatic organization is the concentration of decision-making power in a leader whose instrumental and expressive attributes are considered extraordinary. He is not chosen through divine intervention but earns his central place in the organizational network by commanding the support of others in terms of his competence. Hitler's rise to power began in this way. When he demanded unconditional control over the German Workers' party in 1921 there was strong opposition from the older members of the executive committee, who were fearful of his excessive personal ambition. Yet, Anton Drexler, one of the founders of the party and its leader at the time, was even more fearful that Hitler would leave the party, as he had warned, if dictatorial powers were withheld from him. Realizing that the party owed its rapid growth to Hitler's skills in mass mobilization, and recognizing the necessity of continuing those lines of action, Drexler chose to forsake his own ambitions by urging the executive committee to concede to Hitler's demands. It did and the membership followed suit by electing Hitler chairman of the party by a vote of 553 to 1. The first step in the concentration of decision-making power was taken at the next party congress when the by-laws were rewritten so as to secure Hitler's personal control over the entire organization and its administration, as the head of a three-man executive committee (the remaining two members being his appointees).[141]

From the moment that he seized control of the party, Hitler's goal was to make the *Führerprinzip* the primary operational norm of the Nazi party. At the 1923 party congress, for instance, he persuaded the members to voluntarily relinquish the democratic rights they had enjoyed under Drexler's leadership. Only through discipline and obedience to his personal authority, he argued, could the party develop the strength that was necessary to overthrow the Weimar Republic and initiate the millenium of the Third Reich. Further changes in the party's by-laws were approved by the members during the 1926 congress, which essentially placed Hitler above the executive committee and extended his power to expel individuals and organizations from the party. Furthermore, within the congress itself it was understood, through indirect communications from Hitler, that the function of the delegates was to ratify his initiatives, not question them or propose courses of independent action. As a consequence, by 1929 party congresses were devoid of any great political significance, save as symbolic demonstrations of party unity and Hitler's personal control. The extent of Hitler's success in making the *Führerprinzip* the organizing norm of the party is seen in the fact that by 1929 he did not have to attend the business sessions of the congress any longer. Secure in his position, he was able to send executives of the *Reichsleitung* as his personal representatives to accept the routine endorsements of the party rank and file.

Hitler's absence from party congresses is indicative of changes that had occurred as a result of organizational growth within the party between 1924 and 1929. By constructing vertical lines of authority between the three echelons of the party, he became increasingly dependent on his subordinates at lower levels to make contact with the masses, and at the top to act as his emissaries at meetings of the party's leadership. As a result of this increasing differentiation of function, his major organizational problem was maintaining control over his functionaries in order to chart the course of the movement. He used various organizational techniques to accomplish this goal, as, for example, when he applied financial controls to reward leaders who had religiously executed his policies or when he used his personal authority to name subordinates as candidates on the party's list for the *Reichstag* elections, which was both a reward for good behavior and a way of tying the district leaders into the *Reichsleitung*. "Increasingly," notes Orlow, "he named *Gauleiters* as candidates so that they, quite literally owed their personal incomes to the central office in Munich."[142]

A second important characteristic of a secular charismatic organization is the increasing dependence of the organizational network on personal authority as an integrative force, as a feedback mechanism for gauging the extent of organizational achievements, and as a source of material support for organizational growth. Two integrative aspects of personal rule within the Nazi movement are especially worth noting. The process used by Hitler in selecting leaders made them dependent on his continuing approval for social status within the party. As Hans Gerth has pointed out, Hitler utilized no objective criteria in selecting members for specific tasks. To gain entrance into the "inner circle" of the party one had to win Hitler's personal confidence, and to maintain his favor all means of flattery and deferential behavior had to be bestowed upon him.[143] By placing the selection process on this subjective basis, Hitler created considerable ambiguity about the criteria for entrance, thereby forcing ambitious men to take their cues from him. This meant quite literally predicting his expectations as much as possible and conforming to them excessively. The integration of the leadership corps that resulted from this process reached back to their respective organizations, for the best way of proving their loyalty to Hitler was to perform their subordinate organizational functions in complete conformity to his directives. Paradoxically, the nature of the selection process fostered excessive competition among members of the inner circle and their organizations, as the Goebbels diaries illustrate so well, yet it was also a source of integration. For however much competition raged, secondary leaders and their organizations were united through common loyalty to Hitler's personal authority. Without the mutual ties to Hitler as the personal ruler, the competitiveness of the secondary leadership might have degenerated into chaos. Here, both the secondary leaders and their respective organizations came to depend on personal rule as the vehicle for preventing "the war of all against all."

More objective criteria were developed for estimating an organization's success, such as its responsibility in paying dues, its success in electoral efforts, its growth, and so on. Yet because the secondary leaders derived their status from Hitler's approval, organizational achievements took on social and political significance primarily through his public recognition of them. His presence was a sign that an organization had performed well; his continual absence, a reprimand for incompetence. Fully aware of this organizational dependence, Hitler consciously used his personal appearances as a source of control. He refused to enter a town in which the party had fared poorly in elections, but he would visit more successful units of the party several times to indicate his approval of their work. Possibly the greatest tribute that Hitler could make to an organization within the party was to deliver a speech within its field of operations. A Hitler speech was both the most visible affirmation of an organization's achievements and a stimulus for its growth, for the large crowds that characteristically came to hear him significantly improved the economic standing of the organization.

As these points indicate, there are numerous control mechanisms operating within a secular charismatic organization that insure the continuation of the leader's decision-making power and the organizational dependence on his personal rule. In theory, the most general purpose of these mechanisms is to prevent the formation of countervailing concentrations of individual or organizational power that might pose threats to the leader's authority. The operation of these mechanisms within the Nazi movement helps to explain why Hitler had almost no competition from his secondary leaders within the party. In addition to the controls noted above, there were two other mechanisms operating to prevent the rise of powerful competing leaders.

The use of overlapping jurisdictions was one type of control employed by Hitler to avert rebellions against his authority. By assigning more than one member of the inner circle to a problem area, such as propaganda or police administration, he generated rivalries. Such competition secured his personal authority in two basic ways. When a conflict over jurisdictional authority arose, as it did frequently between the SA and SS, Hitler was able to act as arbitrator, thereby securing the power of decision for himself. These rivalries also prevented leaders in the inner circle from forming coalitions that might have led to serious challenges to his rule.

The absence of effective coordination between the leaders of the inner circle was another control that worked quite well to assure Hitler's influence. Instead of forming an advisory council or cabinet, he preferred to deal separately with each member, which had the effect of perpetuating intraparty rivalries. And by allocating specialized functions to each leader he effectively prevented any one of them from securing adequate knowledge of the general situation, which he, alone, possessed. Goebbels recalls in his diary, for instance, that he seldom met with other members of the inner circle and he constantly laments the fact that he was kept in ignorance of events outside his specialized field of activity. The general absence of coordination between the leading figures of the movement reduced the number of informal connections that could have led to political alliances.

In the advanced stages of its development, the greatest danger to the existence of a secular charismatic organization is likely to come from threats that would remove the leader. Indeed, when such a point is reached the leader may enlarge his own base of power by taking advantage of his organization's dependence on him. He may threaten to resign. Or, what is worse perhaps, he can threaten to commit suicide, a strategy employed by Hitler in 1932 in an attempt to rally the party behind him against the Gregor Strasser revolt. By this ploy, he successfully mobilized the party's leadership and "in twenty-four hours had smashed the powerful political machine in Berlin which Strasser had for so long ruled with semi-independence."[144] Similarly swift and even more merciless action was taken by the party organization following the July, 1944, attempt on Hitler's life. The broad reach and excessive use of organized violence against the conspirators can be viewed not simply as an emotional reaction to the threat on Hitler's life but to the danger such an attempt posed to the life of the Nazi party organization.

Much has been made of the fact that Hitler seldom received blame or criticism for organizational setbacks, which is essentially correct. His failure to unseat President von Hindenburg, for example, was attributed to inadequacies in the lower and middle echelons of the party. Later, when the war effort was experiencing difficulties his lieutenants bore the brunt of criticism. This reluctance to blame or criticize the leader in a secular charismatic organization is understandable in strictly organizational terms, given the arguments above. For any verbal attack on the personal ruler, just as threats against his life, has much broader organizational implications. To blame or criticize Hitler, for instance, would have called into question the legitimacy of the entire Nazi party organization; whereas, to place the responsibility for failure on some part of the organization or on the shoulders of a lieutenant only raised the issue of the efficiency of a single link in the organizational chain of command.

> *Proposition 2.4*—Once the exchange between leader and follower has begun, the follower's transactional commitment will be strengthened initially when increasing investments and sacrifices are extracted from him by the rebel leader and/or when rewards are received which make him dependent on the rebel organization for social status, opportunities, and honors. Reciprocally, rebel leaders who have succeeded in developing a persistent pattern of exchange must continue to satisfy the follower's expectations or, despite the follower's investments, sacrifices, and organizational dependence, the exchange will become strained and may even break down entirely if other options for profit are present.

Commitments grow in strength, not in spite of the follower's investments and sacrifices, but because of them. Leaders who realize this fact are apt to develop strategies to encourage those who have shown an interest to make, initially, low-cost investments and sacrifices. As the cost of the follower's investments and sacrifices increases, we should suppose that he will work harder for the group's goals in order to secure the "pay-offs" that meet his expectations for profit. Under these circumstances, conformity to the initiatives of leaders that specify rules and procedures for reaching those goals is a rational attempt on the follower's part to secure profits.

It should not be assumed, however, that all rewards come through delayed gratifications, for the very act of joining a movement or organization is likely to generate immediate "pay-offs" that make the follower dependent on the organizational apparatus for his livelihood or social status. Those who accept official positions within a movement, but especially those who reap financial benefits, are likely to conform to the rebel leader's initiatives in exchange for continuance in their positions.

In revolutionary situations, rebellious outbreaks of the active masses should not be regarded as a good indicator of the existence of revolutionary commitments. For individuals can participate in riots and the plundering of estates without a revolutionary idea in their heads, with the result that they shift their loyalties one way and then another as self-interest dictates. Those who make heavy investments and sacrifices or assume organizational roles within a movement, on the other hand, are more likely to develop commitments that are resistant to competing options for action. When members of a revolutionary organization conform to a leader's initiatives, the resulting unification of purpose and action gives them an advantage in directing the revolution. However, there may be occasions when even those who are strongly committed cannot contain collective outbursts of anger against the ruling regime that have no organized purpose. Especially in terms of the consolidation of power after the revolution, the spontaneous demonstrators are the available, but as yet weakly committed, masses whose energies need to be tapped and put under control if revolutionary promises are to be converted into revolutionary changes. Indeed, it is only after the revolutionary organization gains access to the resources of the state that the small band of strongly committed revolutionaries can begin to enlarge their own capabilities for rule. Through extractive, regulative, distributive, responsive, and symbolic behaviors they begin to make revolutionary cadres out of angry mobs.

Once followers have developed commitments to a rebel leader that resist change, the maintenance of loyalty depends on the strength of the pulling attraction of the rebel organization in combination with the pushing influence of society. In the first respect, the rebel leader must meet a sufficiently large number of his followers' demands to reduce the severity of collective tension. His right to lead may be questioned to the extent that he fails to generate profitable returns for those who have demonstrated their loyalty. When the rebel leader secures access to the resources of the state, the pulling influence in the commitment process increases for the available masses, for conformity to the norms established by the rebel leader becomes the main vehicle for claiming a right to status in the new regime. The "bandwagon effect" that precedes and follows successful revolutions is a measure of the strength of this pulling influence on the formation of commitments. In contrast, when a rebel leader fails to achieve the general goals of a movement, he still may be able to retain the support of his followers if the achievement of some of the group's goals has secured a steady flow of profits for some followers that makes participation in the political subculture attractive as a way of life. Society can also reinforce politically deviant commitments, pushing members further into subcultural patterns of behavior, if social stigma prevents an easy escape and if points of entry into the larger society are blocked so that those who have become disillusioned with a movement can find no easy way out.

The "End of the World" Movement

Through their day-to-day choices, several members of this movement locked themselves securely into a pattern of behavior that was consistent with Keech's lessons and instructions. Those who developed the strongest commitments, that is, those whose commitments resisted the challenge posed by the disconfirmation of Keech's prophecies, had consistently followed orders that increased their investments and sacrifices. And on their own initiative, several of the strongly committed members had made decisions that were as costly as those required by Keech's instructions. In fact, the mark of Keech's success as a leader was that she intensified the strength of her followers' commitments quite gradually, first requiring low-cost activities and moving only to more costly ones as the movement approached its peak. Initially, followers were mainly encouraged to attend meetings, to discuss the spiritual lessons received from space, and, for several members, to wait for their rescue, after having removed all metal from their clothing in preparation for space flight. As the day of the expected flood approached, followers tried to minimize their own doubts by proving the strength of their beliefs through decisions that drastically escalated their investments and sacrifices. It was also during these last days that Keech made greater and greater demands on their resources and required heavier sacrifices as preparation for their deliverance.

In early December, Keech began to receive messages from the Guardians that demanded more of her followers. For example, Edna and Mark Post were instructed to move into Keech's home to care for her. Their help was needed because she had been on a three-day fast and was beginning to show physical signs of hunger. (Even leaders must make sacrifices to conserve their own commitments in the face of doubt and numerous countervailing pressures.) Moreover, to ensure a community of suffering, the Guardians ordered Edna and Mark to join Keech in fasting for one day. All three were forbidden to leave the house for any reason. Not only did Edna and Mark conform to these initiatives, but, during her internment, Edna refused to leave the house against the Guardians' orders to visit her mother, who had fallen seriously ill. By resisting this alternative course of action, Edna demonstrated how strong her commitment was. Even then, it was not the end of her sacrifices.

Next, the believers were ordered to quit their jobs. Dr. Armstrong had already been forced to resign from his post at the college and Kitty O'Donnell had left a good job and withdrawn from school to move closer to the hub of activities. However, Keech's orders, coming through the Guardians, did affect some followers who had yet to cut their remaining ties to society. Conforming to these orders, Edna resigned as director of the nursery school; Mark gave up his job at the hardware store; and Bertha Blatsky quit her job as a clerk. Although not under instructions to do so, several student members of the group stopped studying for their classes. Among these followers who were in the process of uprooting themselves from old commitments, the cases of Bob Eastman, Susan Heath, Fred Purden, Laura Brooks, and Kitty best illustrate the importance of rising investments and sacrifices in the formation of strong commitments.

A quick review of Bob Eastman's investments and sacrifices suggests why, even at the end, his commitment was resistant to change. He had invested great amounts of time and energy, attending every meeting of "The Seekers" and spending a great deal of time at the Armstrong home. Under Dr. Armstrong's supervision, he read all of Keech's lessons, extending his study to include numerous other works dealing with mysticism. In addition, he contributed heavily to the production of Keech's lessons as they appeared in mimeographed form, and assisted Daisy Armstrong as editorial aid. He also made heavy sacrifices, for he gave up smoking, drinking, swearing, and other bad habits as a price for his rescue. Although he still attended classes to keep up appearances, he sacrificed his academic standing since he had quit studying for his courses and fully expected to fail at least one of them. And in order to pay off some debts incurred during his involvement, he sold some highly valued property. While he did not sell his car because he still needed transportation, he drove it harder than usual to use it up before the 21st deadline. Even during Thanksgiving recess, when other students were working or playing, Bob was straightening up the rest of his affairs and saying good-bye to his parents.

The development of Susan Heath's commitment ran a similar course. She attended the meetings of "The Seekers" regularly and actively sought converts among her acquaintances. In November, she increased her level of investments by giving systematic instructions to a few students living in her dormitory with hopes of converting them to the movement. She was also willing to make sacrifices in defense of her beliefs. For example, she chose to terminate her affiliation with the Community Church after Dr. Armstrong's teachings were rebuked by church officials. Then, in a dispute with her roommate over the flood prediction, she chose to sacrifice her friendship rather than her commitment. Similar things can be said about the commitments of Fred Purden and Laura Brooks. Both attended meetings regularly, had quit studying for their classes, and had made sacrifices of a tangible kind. Fred argued violently with his parents who threatened to throw him out of the house and Laura, convinced that the flood would come, threw away many of her personal possessions.

Possibly because she had more to give up, Kitty O'Donnell made greater investments and sacrifices than her student counterparts, many of whom were still dependent on their parents for financial support. She attended all the meetings of "The Seekers" and assumed tasks that invested her in the group. She accepted the responsibility for telephoning members for special meetings, for instance, and often baked cakes for the refreshment periods after meetings. Like Bob, she successfully gave up drinking and tried hard to stop smoking. She also went on a vegetarian diet. In addition to the fact that she quit her job and withdrew from school, she sacrificed important social relationships by speaking openly about her beliefs. Her parents thought her demented and her friends at the plant where she had worked scoffed at her beliefs and new life style. Her investments and sacrifices had reached such a magnitude that on December 4th she could say: "'I have to believe the flood is coming on the 21st because I've spent all my money. I quit my job, I quit comptometer school, and my apartment costs me $100 a month. I have to believe.'"[145]

On the morning of December 20th Keech received a communication saying that a space vehicle would land in front of her home and those stationed at headquarters would be summoned by a spaceman who would appear at the front door. Keech and several of her followers gathered in her living room to wait for the expected visitation, knowing that this was finally going to be the real thing. Anticipating the historic moment with reserved joy, members of the group exchanged thoughts and feelings concerning the events that had transpired. But, as midnight approached, the quiet but animated conversation diminished into silent anticipation as the attention of each person shifted to the front door. However, midnight came and the hopes of this silent band of believers began to sink. After a period of quiet desperation, waiting for the minutes beyond midnight to verify their fears, the morale of the group fell sharply as members of the movement experienced the full force of their disappointment. Some broke down completely and cried; others expressed their disenchantment by withdrawing into complete silence. Mrs. Keech, unable to face her followers, quietly left the room to reopen communication with Sananda, hoping that somehow this final disconfirmation could be explained as earlier ones had been. She returned to the living room a short time later with her spirits renewed, for she had heard from Sananda and had eagerly returned to read his "Christmas message" to her followers. In effect, the message said that the cataclysm had been called off. Their faith had spread so much light, she told them, that God had intervened to save the world from destruction. Through their unswerving commitments, they had all contributed to the rescue of mankind.

The reading of the "Christmas message" marks the end of the movement. Several followers, thinking Keech a false prophet, left the movement completely disillusioned. Even a few of those who had made heavy investments and sacrifices began to sense their commitments giving way to new activities. While Susan Heath's first reaction was to support the group, she later became a skeptic and withdrew her services completely. Fred Purden and Laura Brooks also joined the disillusioned and Laura was heard saying that she was sorry she had disposed of so many of her possessions. Kitty O'Donnell expressed similar sentiments: " 'I just regret that I made such an ass of myself giving away my money and stuff. . . .' "[146] Yet, there were others, like the three Armstrongs and Bob Eastman, who had also made heavy investments and sacrifices but who accepted Keech's rationalization for the final disconfirmation and remained convinced of the authenticity of her lessons and messages from space. Seeming more convinced than ever, Dr. and Mrs. Armstrong began a national speaking tour to tell others of their experience. Thus, for a sizable number of followers (about ten out of the original eighteen), the disconfirmed prophecies had not seriously affected their beliefs. Why this was so can be partially explained by the ambiguity of "proof" when a leader's prophecies deal with transcendental themes and by the fact that losses that follow heavy investments and sacrifices work to reinforce commitments in the face of such ambiguity when other attractive alternatives are not available.

According to the authors, the data appear to support the conclusion that the disconfirmations of prophecy intensified, rather than weakened, the follower's commitment to Keech's initiatives. When confronted with undeniable evidence that his beliefs are wrong, "the individual will frequently emerge, not only unshaken, but even more convinced of the truth of his beliefs than ever before. Indeed, he may even show a new fervor about convincing and converting other people to his view."[147] Yet it is reasonable to argue that the believers who remained committed to Keech did so because the disconfirmations had not, in fact, fully negated their beliefs.

The authors argued that the disconfirmations were "unequivocal and undeniable." However, the beliefs of the more committed followers—beliefs in the presence of superior beings on other planets, in flying saucers, and in Keech's ability to communicate with men from outer space—were neither directly nor fully negated. When belief systems incorporate transcendental themes, the follower's commitment to leadership may be sustained even when the leader's prophecies fail to materialize, because the development of an "unequivocal" proof negating such beliefs is probably impossible. For example, it is currently impossible to refute the assertion that superior beings reside on other planets, just as the U.S. Air Force has been unable to disprove the claim of private citizens that flying saucers exist. Because it is difficult, even impossible, to totally negate such beliefs, it should come as no surprise that those in the "end of the world" movement with histories of occult activity, who had held transcendentally grounded beliefs for some time, were more faithful in maintaining their commitments to Keech after the last disconfirmation than were those without occult experience. We might suspect, then, that if a leader has legitimized his position in relation to a transcendental source of authority and relies on transcendental themes as part of the organizational ideology, the commitments of his followers may persist even in the face of some tangible failures.

How difficult it is to invalidate transcendentally grounded beliefs can be seen in Fred Purden's response to the last disconfirmation. He was critical of Keech's ability as a medium but maintained his belief that superior beings on other planets were in touch with her. "He said that he did not believe as some believed that Mrs. Keech was a hoax: her messages were genuine, though she might not have been getting some of them right."[148] Thus, the disconfirmations had forced him to admit that Keech was not as competent as he had previously thought, but they did not unequivocally disprove his beliefs. His decision not to attend any more meetings must have been based on his reevaluation of Keech's leadership in the light of the disconfirmations. It is understandable why others who had not drawn similar conclusions about Keech's abilities could remain committed. The ambiguity surrounding the meaning of the disconfirmations and their heavy investments and sacrifices made several members even more ready than ever to disseminate her lessons.

The Black Muslim Movement

Many more thousands heard the teachings of Mr. Muhammad than joined him in the Nation of Islam. Even though Malcolm X realized the value of leading potential converts by small increments to heavier investments and sacrifices, he was disappointed after public meetings when only a few were willing to stand in order to affirm their desire for membership. Yet virtually the entire audience would rise to their feet when asked if they agreed with the Black Muslim view of white racism. Most of those who made the low-cost decision to attend in order to hear the "good preaching" that Malcolm promised could not make the heavy sacrifices that the norms of the movement required upon assuming membership. In fact, Malcolm was very much aware of the impact of the code and strict discipline on those shopping around for a new political orientation. Many were virtually scared away when they were told that the followers of Mr. Muhammad were forbidden to eat pork, to use cigarettes, alcohol, and narcotics, to dance, to date, to go to movies, to participate in sporting events, among other things. Hearing such a long list of sacrifices, all of which had to be accepted as a price of membership, it is understandable why the available masses would come to hear Malcolm, but chose not to join the movement. Yet while this code and discipline restricted Malcolm's mobilization effort, they were a source of organizational strength. In those who joined, accepting the norms and accompanying sacrifices, strong commitments emerged that resisted competing options for action. By making huge sacrifices a condition for membership, Mr. Muhammad created the conditions for a limited but dedicated following. In terms of organizational effectiveness, such a move had decided advantages.

Upon entering the movement the new member is bombarded with organized activities and rituals that extract their toll on his resources. Each week night a different event is scheduled which requires investments of time and energy. According to Malcolm's account, on Monday evening the Fruit of Islam train, learning military drill, judo, and karate as part of an instructional program designed to teach the male participants the art of self-defense. Unity Night is on Tuesday evening. This is a social occasion where the brothers and sisters of the movement enjoy one another's company and refreshments. Wednesday night is set aside for the instruction of new recruits into the doctrine and rituals of the Nation. Thursday night is devoted to the education of women, which means learning how to keep house, how to raise their children, how to care for their husbands, and how to cook and sew. Friday night is called Civilization Night because, at that time, interpersonal relations are explored in depth, especially as they pertain to an understanding of the different natures of men and women. Although Saturday night is a free night, it is common practice for Muslim brothers and sisters to meet at one anothers' homes. Then on Sunday, Muslim temples hold their regular religious services. With this range of organized activities, it is little wonder that members become heavily invested in the movement.

During the day, rituals are performed that invest members even further, creating uniform patterns of behavior even among those with different motives for joining. Malcolm's description of the rituals at his brother's home supposedly typifies practices required of all members. Let me briefly relate his account. His brother, as the father of the household, was the first to rise in the morning, preparing the way for the rest of his family. Before beginning the morning ablutions, he was required to say aloud, "In the name of Allah, I perform the ablution," then he proceeded to wash his right hand first, followed by the left. He then brushed his teeth thoroughly and rinsed his mouth three times. His nostrils were rinsed out three times also. To complete the purification process, a shower was taken and the body carefully cleaned. Later, when the wife and children rose, each was required to follow the same ritual. Once the family had purified itself, the prayer rug was spread out and each member of the family took his place in preparation for morning prayer. Facing East, all members in unison stepped from their slippers onto the rug and knelt in prayer to Allah and all recited a standard prayer. At breakfast no solid food was taken, only juice and coffee. Later in the day, first at noon and then at three in the afternoon, wherever they were the members of the family were required to rinse their hands, face, and mouth and then meditate quietly.

The development of Malcolm's strong transactional commitment to Mr. Muhammad illustrates how such investments and sacrifices strengthen the ties between leader and follower. Even before he was aware of it, Malcolm was taking the first step in prison toward serious choices that would ultimately lock him into the Nation of Islam. For when he received a letter from his brother, Reginald, telling him to stop smoking cigarettes and eating pork, he assumed that such sacrifices must be part of a con to get him out of prison. So he immediately abstained from both practices. Here, Reginald was encouraging Malcolm to make a fairly low-cost choice that would lead him by increments to heavier ones, just as Malcolm would learn to entice the members of store-front churches to attend his public meetings by using the bait of "good preaching." In both instances, the leader's goal is to prepare people for new commitments before they are even conscious of it themselves. Thus, when Malcolm decided to quit smoking and to quit eating pork he had no idea that such a decision was the initial sacrifice that would be the start of a new style of life.

Later, Reginald explained to him why such sacrifices were a small price to pay for enlightenment through the teachings of Mr. Muhammad. It was during this time that he explained to Malcolm the Messenger's teachings, emphasizing the role of the white devil in the oppression of blacks. Once Malcolm had accepted these teachings, he was ready to take the next steps on his way to a strong commitment. His decision to begin praying to Allah was his first step. Then, in order to improve his writing skills, he began a heavy investment by copying the dictionary from cover to cover. At the same time that he was filling his tablet with new words, he began consuming books one after the other, sacrificing his good eyesight in the process by studying after hours in the light that dimly flooded his cell from the hallway. Through these heavy investments of time and energy, Malcolm was able to significantly improve his vocabulary and grammar, at least to a point where he could write a decent letter. This was important to him because he was writing daily to Mr. Muhammad, an investment that continued for the remaining years of his detention.

Through these initial investments, Malcolm prepared himself for a new role—that of propagandist and mobilizer for Mr. Muhammad's teachings. After a period of isolation, in which he prayed, memorized, and read, he was prepared to make the next important choice. "My reading had my mind like steam under pressure," is the way he characterized this turning point. To relieve that pressure he decided to put his name down to debate so he could tell the white man something about himself face-to-face.[149] From then on he participated in the prison's weekly debating match, but only after tracking down and reading every book he could find on the subject.

Debating led him to the next step, culminating in a decision to actively proselytize for the movement. In addition to telling other black convicts the truth about the white devil, he intended to convert them to the teachings of the Messenger in hopes of recruiting them for the Nation of Islam. Remember, in comparison, that Susan Heath had become heavily committed to Mrs. Keech's lessons and prophecy by a similar route. However, the parallel does not stop there, for both Malcolm and Susan also sacrificed an important personal relationship as a price for maintaining their beliefs. While Susan had accepted the loss of her best friend over the controversial flood prophecy, Malcolm sacrificed a very close relationship with his brother, Reginald, who had been suspended by Mr. Muhammad for misconduct. Had he been forced to make this sacrifice before he had become heavily invested through his earlier choices, it is questionable whether his commitment to Mr. Muhammad would have developed at all. Here, again, we see accident emerging as a factor in the formation of a commitment.

After he was released from prison, Malcolm continued to make decisions enlarging his investments and sacrifices. Almost immediately after his release he began attending Black Muslim meetings and, looking over the audience, he became concerned over the number of empty seats. Seeing this, he made his next incremental step by deciding to volunteer as an aide to the Minister of Detroit Temple Number One. By this move, Malcolm invested his evening hours in the movement, responding to Mr. Muhammad's call for an expansion in membership. This decision to assume an official position within the Black Muslim organization prepared him to make more costly decisions, for it set him on his course up the organizational hierarchy. Thus, in 1953, he accepted an appointment as Assistant Minister in Detroit Temple Number One. Then, in order to increase his availability for heavier investments and sacrifices, he quit his job. Not only did this move make him freer to act, it also made him dependent on the movement for his income, for not long after he retired from his job, he was named to the important post, Minister of Temple Number Seven in New York City. By accepting financial support from Mr. Muhammad in exchange for his services, profits were beginning to accumulate that would further solidify Malcolm's transactional commitment.

As a further pay-off for his services, Malcolm was given a special status within the Nation as Mr. Muhammad's organizational arm and official spokesman. Accepting this challenge meant continual traveling, both in the process of organizing new temples and speaking publicly on college campuses and in the news media. By this time, he had married Betty X and established a home for himself. So his new assignment not only included new investments, but a correspondingly heavy sacrifice on the home front, as he says.

> Awakening this brainwashed black man and telling this arrogant, devilish white man the truth about himself, Betty understands, is a full-time job. If I have work to do when I am home, the little time I am at home, she lets me have the quiet I need to work in. I'm rarely at home more than half of any week; I have been away as much as five months.[150]

As a further sacrifice during the years as an official in the Black Muslim organization, Malcolm accepted no payment for his services beyond that required for living and traveling. Even against the urgings of his wife, he would not put money into the bank for his and his family's future. (In fact, as proof that he had sacrificed his financial security, he was forced to borrow money to make his journey to Africa after his expulsion from the movement.) That Malcolm had developed a strong commitment is suggested by his resistance to his wife's attempt to change his pattern of investment and sacrifice. His own account conveys this very well:

> My attitude toward money generated the only domestic quarrel that I have ever had with my beloved wife Betty. As our children increased in number, so did Betty's hints to me that I should put away *something* for our family. But I refused, and finally we had this argument. I put my foot down.[151]

When he was expelled from the movement, Malcolm came to regret the fact that he had made these financial sacrifices, just as Laura Brooks ultimately lamented her decision to dispose of her worldly possessions.

When you combine heavy investments and sacrifices with tangible profits you get a commitment like Malcolm's that resists change. When a commitment of this type is altered, as it was for Malcolm when he was expelled by Mr. Muhammad, it is often modified rather than abandoned entirely. Remember that for most of those who left the "end of the world" movement there was a continuance of their beliefs and some, like Fischer, continued their occult activities after the movement collapsed. Similarly, Malcolm not only carried over many of his religious beliefs into his new organization, but his heavy investments and sacrifices for the sake of reaching black nationalist goals made his choice predictable. "What was I going to do?," he asked himself at this critical moment. "My life was inseparably committed to the American black man's struggle."[152] Therefore, while his transactional commitment to Mr. Muhammad was terminated against his will, his commitment to black nationalism was hardly shaken.

The Bolshevik Revolution

Conversion to a revolutionary point of view is usually gradual. Events and choices narrow the alternatives for action so that a revolutionary course can develop even before the individual is really conscious of being a revolutionary. Yet there is a point in the development of a revolutionary commitment when the actor finally admits to himself, and then says in defiance, "I am a revolutionary!" Such a proclamation is more than a statement of fact, for his decision is not simply to *be* a revolutionary, but to *become* one through choice and action. With respect to the development of a strong commitment, the acceptance of a revolutionary identity is a promise to increase investments and sacrifices in order to produce revolutionary changes. In a sense, it is much less important to know at what point the negative stigma of being a revolutionary is accepted by the individual as a compliment, than it is to understand how this choice accelerates and shapes the process of choosing that culminates in a strong revolutionary commitment. What makes a revolutionary, I would argue, is not his decision to be one, but the subsequent decisions he makes which invest him in the identity he has claimed in his mood of defiance.

In revolutionary situations, choices that make a person's private grievances public are likely to have heavy consequences in creating an irrevocable course of revolutionary action. Because they were highly visible, certain events in the Russian situation set individuals from the agrarian, military, and worker sectors on a revolutionary course. For example, the plundering of estates and the confiscation of land in the rural areas made the active peasants highly visible, making them vulnerable to serious reprisals by the land barons and governmental officials had the revolution failed. Soldiers at the front who deserted their units and fired on their officers made a similar investment in revolutionary change, for court martial hung in the balance had the Provisional Government survived the revolutionary assault. Workers who fired on factory managers and participated in the food riots placed themselves in an equally dangerous position. Through their participation in these events individuals made rather large incremental moves that invested them in the revolution, for not only did they have reason to hate the regime, they now had cause to fear it.

Ruling leaders who test their regulative capability by arresting those who are publicly defiant of their rule may inadvertently lend a hand to rebel leaders who are preparing the masses for more forceful action. Indeed, by arresting a demonstrator the ruling regime may push him further into political deviance. For imprisonment not only closes off future opportunities within the society, either by social stigma or by the conscious designs of law-makers, but forces the demonstrator to make a heavy sacrifice for the movement. Thus, in July, when leaders of the Provisional Government ordered the wholesale arrest of soldiers, sailors, and workers for their participation in the armed demonstrations against the regime, they were sealing their own fate by creating the type of sacrifice that can strengthen a revolutionary commitment. You will remember that Lenin's first prison term and his later banishment to Samara made him more, not less, willing to invest his resources in the revolutionary life. The solitude of the prison cell may even lead some political criminals to realize that they have become revolutionaries: Leon Bronstein assumed his revolutionary identity in prison by borrowing the name Trotsky from one of his jailors.

Arrest and imprisonment for political crimes can also become a ritualized event in which rebels prove the strength of their commitments. Status within a revolutionary movement may even depend on the periodic prison terms handed down by the regime. Especially for those who aspire to be leaders, detention may be one of the prices that they must pay to make it to the top. Thus, by arresting Lenin and Trotsky, first the czarist leaders then the Provisional Government helped assure them positions of leadership with the active masses. This should lead us to suspect that ruling leaders play as large a role as rebel leaders in mobilizing the masses for revolution. But maybe this is to overestimate the influence of leadership in the revolutionary process, for once a revolution begins leaders and followers alike may simply be swept along by the force of events.

The need to satisfy the expectations of followers can put both rebel and ruling leaders at the mercy of the revolutionary motion created by random events and collective outbursts. For example, during June and July, there is a good indication that the Bolshevik leaders followed the revolutionary masses as much as they led them. At that time both Lenin and Trotsky were aware that an insurrection was not yet right for the situation. "But their following in the capital, seething with restlessness," we are told, "began to view with distrust their tactics. The Anarchists denounced the waiting game and the treachery of the Bolsheviks, as the Bolsheviks had denounced the hesitations and the treachery of the Mensheviks and Social Revolutionaries. Finally, a number of regiments confronted Bolshevik headquarters with an accomplished fact and called an armed demonstration for 3 July."[153] At first the Bolsheviks attempted to cancel the demonstration, but seeing that they could not stem the tide of public anger, their next move was to try to assume leadership over the demonstration in order to impose controls on it. But even the latter course of action failed, for the leaders were unable to hold in check the collective emotions that were stirred by the huge assembly of people. As in small-group activities, here we see leaders assuming a follower orientation in order to preserve their leadership. In this sense, the key to successful leadership is knowing when and how to follow. Apparently, the Bolshevik leaders were better followers than their Socialist counterparts.

Just as Plekhanov had been displaced within the Socialist faction during the early stages of the movement because he would not follow the larger public in its demands for immediate revolutionary options, so, too, did the Mensheviks and Social Revolutionaries reduce their capabilities by refusing to listen to followers mocking their alignment with the government. "They were spoken of just like the Provisional Government: The Menshevik-SR majority had sold itself to the bourgeoisie and the imperialists. . . ."[154] Apparently, those Socialist leaders who failed to follow the active masses in their attempt to secure "Land, Bread, and Peace" lost their right to lead and were bitterly rejected by many. But Lenin had wisely avoided alignments with other Socialist factions from the beginning and had tried to keep up with the masses even against his own judgment. As a consequence, in the days before the October revolution, "only the Bolsheviks were trusted. . . ."[155]

At the end, the balance of political and military power had shifted so swiftly toward the Bolshevik party that the Provisional Government was overthrown with virtually no bloodshed. Sukhanov argues, in fact, that "by October 21st the Provisional Government had already been overthrown, and was nonexistent in the territory of the capital."[156] But what had been accomplished so quietly on the 21st still had to be announced to the masses and the provisional leadership by a successful insurrection on the 25th. Lenin, who had been ridiculed in April as a "madman" and was despised as a German agent in July, was appointed to lead an all-Bolshevik government as Premier without portfolio. "Even those nearest, those who knew well his place in the party, for the first time fully realized what he meant to the revolution. . . . It was he who had taught them; it was he who had brought them up."[157]

The Nazi Revolution

Assuming membership in the Nazi party was probably the most critical step a discontented German could take in the formation of his revolutionary identity and revolutionary commitment, for it was a turning point that forced him to see himself as a political enemy of the Weimar republic and what it stood for. Combined with membership was the oath of allegiance to Hitler, which forced the convert to make an even stronger identification with the revolutionary way of life and to make a clean break with groups and individuals that would try to conserve his former commitments. In his new identity and with these points of resistance broken down, he could engage in action that he had previously avoided. This sense of freedom is conveyed in the testimony of a party member who could recall how he felt after taking the party oath: "Now I felt as though I were a National Socialist, for I had taken the oath. . . . I realized for the first time how easy it was to act according to National Socialist ideas."[158] Unlocked from the existing social fabric, the new member was freer to increase his investments and sacrifices.

Although membership in the party did not require it, many who were initiated made their political convictions a matter of public record by wearing the Nazi uniform and insignia and by adopting the party salute in public places. This behavior pushed them deeper into the movement, for it made them the brunt of public ridicule and the target of social sanction. As we saw in an earlier section, Nazis who were willing to shoulder the negative stigma of membership were excluded from occupational apprenticeships, from civil service positions, and from the rites and sacraments of the Catholic Church. These measures had the effect of increasing the level of sacrifice for those who joined, which apparently increased, rather than decreased, their dedication to the movement and their determination to fight against the republic.

> The world often does not understand and is astonished that it was possible for the National Socialists to conquer the state. They cannot see how we, the old fighters, again and again worked up the courage and the energy to overcome all obstacles. Who knows the sacrifices and privations of those years of battle, who knows the inner feeling of those party comrades who sacrificed everything in constant faith to the idea and to its first soldier, Adolf Hitler? Was that opportunism or chauvinism? As an old fighter, I maintain it was neither. It was renunciation and sacrifice in a belief in the great cause.[159]

The negative stigma attached to the Nazi label and the accompanying exclusion from normal opportunities thus pushed the convert deeper into the movement in search of social support and new opportunities, status, and honors. Such were possible within the party as it expanded rapidly after 1926, but the price that followers had to pay in return was deference and complete loyalty to Hitler. Through such bargains many Nazis were locked securely into the party apparatus.

As the personal leader of the Nazi party, Hitler was given extensive powers to reward and punish, which he used arbitrarily to increase the party member's dependence on him for opportunities, status, and honors. Social status and opportunities for upward mobility were possible within the party, you will remember, only when Hitler was personally gratified with a follower's performance. Thus, his decision to speak in a particular geographic area was consciously intended as a reward for conforming to his initiatives and for accomplishing his organizational goals. In exchange for their loyalty and good services, Hitler's appearance gave district and local leaders both higher social standing in the eyes of their comrades and money for their organizations, which enhanced their reputation with the ministers of the central headquarters and greatly increased their potential for control within their own field of operations. Further reinforcement of his subordinate's already strong sense of loyalty was achieved through the allocation of honors such as appointment to the privileged positions of state inspector, roving ambassador, and candidate to the *Reichstag*. For example, the *Gauleiter* who was appointed by Hitler to the party's electoral list and who subsequently assumed a seat in the national legislature became indebted for the honor bestowed on him and financially dependent, to the extent that his legislative appointment was his only, or major, source of revenue. Through these and similar transactions, Hitler produced strongly committed subordinates within the party's chain of command. Such strong commitments were the basis of the movement's organizational strength, for they were the building blocks upon which Hitler developed the elaborate set of horizontal structures that drew hundreds of thousands of sympathizers into the party's sphere of influence.

By developing a horizontal structure that facilitated action, Hitler created the conditions in which investments and sacrifices could be extracted from those who were being driven to find an alternative to the Weimar Republic. By using elections and front organizations as aggregating devices, he provided these frustrated Germans with less socially stigmatized avenues of action that could draw them eventually into Nazi party membership. As the earlier portions of my analysis show, this approach encouraged those who sympathized with the Nazis to take the first step toward fuller involvement. These small steps were fundamentally important as contributing factors in the expansion of the movement after the 1930 elections. As later adopters of innovations are wont to do, the newcomers to the party after 1930 were swept into the movement by the bandwagon effect and the accompanying anticipation of a Nazi victory.

The fact that Hitler had chosen to use elections as a means to power turned out to be a double-edged sword. Not only did elections provide an opportunity for sympathizers to make a very low-cost investment in the movement, they also became an important barometer of Hitler's popularity. The steady and, at times, dramatic Nazi party successes at the polls, combined after 1930 with extensive press coverage of its activities in the *Reichstag,* gave the indication of a huge groundswell of public support that produced the bandwagon effect. That such an effect occurred is indicated by the fact that in the three years after 1930, when the electoral barometer was indicating a sharp rise in Hitler's popularity, party membership rose over 650 per cent.[160] The thousands who joined the party during that period in hopes of riding the crest of the Nazi wave of popularity had not yet developed strong revolutionary commitments, however, for they had not yet made the heavy investments and sacrifices that early advocates of Nazism had made through years of struggle.

The bandwagon effect had positive financial consequences for the Nazi party, for large sums of money were received through application fees and the sudden rise in demand for advertising in the party's newspapers. With this turn in the party's fortunes, it was able to pay off its enormous debts, putting it on a solid financial basis for the first time. Still, the rising costs of organizational expansion and of campaigning put the party into debt again by 1932. To ensure the party's financial strength, Hitler negotiated an exchange with a prominent group of industrial magnates. "In return for certain 'promises to pay' on the part of Hitler, if and when he came to power, the Rhenish-Westphalian magnates were persuaded to shoulder the burden of the Party's debts and to put the NSDAP back into the political arena as a fighting force. Without the formidable assistance of the industrialists, the Nazi party would have foundered on the rocks of bankruptcy."[161] These barons of industry, like the masses of middle-class Germans, were ready to begin transactions with Hitler, believing that the Nazi take-over was inevitable and wanting to be on the winning side.

Yet, just a few months prior to Hitler's agreement with these industrialists, the party's electoral strength began to wane, as the percentage of its vote slipped to 33.1 per cent. About 2 million votes were lost to other parties. Even though the party rolls continued to increase, the November 1932 election results show that over 65 per cent of the electorate had voted against the Nazis.[162] Therefore, when Hitler was named Chancellor in 1933 through the efforts of von Papen, a large majority of the population had still not indicated any sympathy toward him. Even after assuming power, he still could not capture a majority of the electorate in the first, and last, general election under his leadership. Thus he faced the task, which had dominated his organizational energies from 1926 to 1933, of having to convert resisters into sympathizers, sympathizers into party members, and new party members into strongly committed followers. His seizure of power in 1933 produced few radical changes in organization; rather, his regime simply carried forward the organizational techniques, using the resources of the state, that had already been proven effective by 1930. The character of the Nazi state was only a more fully developed representation of the organizational model that Hitler had created to mobilize the masses for the conquest of power. The totalitarian state he created after 1933 was intended to finish the job he began in 1921—to make every German into one of his strongly committed followers.

How Hitler rose from obscurity to the Chancellor's office in a little over a decade cannot be explained adequately by alluding only to the concept of charisma. Indeed, his personal rule appears to have been derived more directly from the operations of the Nazi party organization than from weaknessess in the German personality. His success in mobilizing a sizable part of the population was an organizational triumph more than it was a triumph of the will. Yet, while the concept of charisma by itself cannot help us to understand Hitler's success, there were undoubtedly a large number of followers who developed charismatic commitments to Hitler. Why and how such commitments develop are the concerns I want to pursue in the following chapters.

Notes

1. I am referring here to the extractive, regulative, distributive, responsive, and symbolic capabilities discussed in Chapter 1.

2. Leon Festinger, Henry Riecken, and Stanley Schachter, *When Prophecy Fails* (New York: Harper, 1956). The primary concern of this study was the impact of disconfirmation on the maintenance of beliefs.

3. *Ibid.,* p. 192.

4. *Ibid.,* p. 140.

5. *Ibid.,* p. 179.

6. *Ibid.,* p. 180.

7. C. Eric Lincoln, *The Black Muslims in America* (Boston: Beacon Press, 1961), p. 15.

8. Louis Lomax, *When the Word is Given* (New York: Signet Books, 1963), p. 47.

9. *Ibid.,* p. 75.

10. Thomas F. Mayer, "The Position and Progress of Black America: Some Pertinent Statistics," in Howard Gadlin and Bertram E. Garskof (eds.), *The Uptight Society* (Belmont, Calif.: Brooks/Cole, 1970), p. 109.

11. *Ibid.,* p. 112.

12. Richard Stillman II, "Negroes in the Armed Forces," *Phylon,* 30 (Summer, 1969), p. 145.

13. Mayer, *op. cit.,* p. 113.

14. Lincoln, *op. cit.,* pp. 22–26.

15. Mayer, *op. cit.,* p. 110.

16. *Ibid.,* p. 106.

17. Louis Lomax, *The Negro Revolt* (New York: Signet Books, 1962), p. 190.

18. Mayer, *op. cit.,* pp. 103–104.

19. E. U. Essien-Udom, *Black Nationalism* (New York: Dell, 1962), pp. 201–202.

20. *Ibid.,* pp. 202–203.

21. Lincoln, *op. cit.,* p. 8.

22. N. N. Sukhanov, *The Russian Revolution, 1917,* Volume I (New York: Harper, 1955), p. 276.

23. *Ibid.,* Volume II, p. 371.

24. Joel Carmichael, *A Short History of the Russian Revolution* (New York: Basic Books, 1964), p. 55.

25. Christopher Hill, *Lenin and the Russian Revolution* (London: English Universities Press, 1947), p. 78. "The poll tax, totaling 42 million roubles a year, was levied exclusively on the peasants and of the remaining 166 million roubles direct taxation, they paid 153 million" (p. 80).

26. *Ibid.,* p. 79.

27. *Ibid.,* p. 80.

28. William Henry Chamberlin, *The Russian Revolution 1917–1921,* Volume I (New York: Macmillan, 1952), p. 104.

29. *Ibid.,* p. 105.

30. Alan Moorehead, *The Russian Revolution* (New York: Harper, 1958), p. 160.

31. According to Chamberlin, "under the rules of service for 1913 the private soldier was forbidden to ride inside streetcars, to eat in public restaurants, except in the third-class buffets of railroad stations and passenger-boats, to receive books or newspapers without the permission of his commanding officers, to belong to any societies with political ends, to attend lectures or theatrical performances, unless permission was secured from a superior officer." *Op. cit.,* p. 106.

32. A. L. Popov, *Oktinabrskii Perevot,* pp. 81–83 in John Shelton Curtiss, *The Russian Revolutions* (New York: D. Van Nostrand, 1957), pp. 148–149.

33. Reich, Nos. 160 and 161, July 24 and 25, 1917, in Curtiss, *op. cit.,* pp. 135–136.

34. Quoted in Chamberlin, *op. cit.,* p. 107.

35. Popov, *op. cit.,* pp. 85–88.

36. From the Belevsky Papers, Hoover War Library, Stanford University, in Curtiss, *op. cit.,* pp. 146–148.

37. Popov, *loc. cit.*

38. Curtiss, *op. cit.,* p. 64.

39. Moorehead, *op. cit.,* p. 159.

40. Chamberlin, *op. cit.,* p. 109.

41. *Ibid.,* pp. 110–111.

42. *Ibid.,* p. 113.

43. Moorehead, *op. cit.,* p. 160.

44. Hadley Cantril, *The Psychology of Social Movements* (New York: John Wiley & Sons, 1963), p. 222.

45. Franz Neumann, *Behemoth: The Structure and Practice of National Socialism 1933–1944* (New York: Harper & Row, 1966), p. 10.

46. John W. Wheeler-Bennett, *The Nemesis of Power: The German Army in Politics 1918–1945* (London: Macmillan, 1964), p. 198.

47. *Ibid.,* p. 182.

48. *Ibid.,* pp. 285–286.

49. Newmann, *op. cit.,* p. 23.

50. Wheeler-Bennett, *op. cit.,* p. 251, ff. 1.

51. Dietrich Orlow, *The History of the Nazi Party: 1919–1933* (Pittsburgh: University of Pittsburgh Press, 1969), p. 252.

52. Wheeler-Bennett, *op. cit.,* p. 251.

53. *Ibid.,* p. 265.

54. *Ibid.,* p. 251.

55. Cantril, *op. cit.,* p. 223.

56. Neumann, *op. cit.,* p. 30.

57. Theodore Abel, *Why Hitler Came Into Power* (New York: Prentice-Hall, 1938), pp. 126–127.

58. David Schoenbaum, *Hitler's Social Revolution: Class and Status in Nazi Germany 1933 1939* (Garden City, N.Y.: Doubleday, 1967), pp. 4–5.

59. *Ibid.,* pp. 12–13.

60. Abel, *op. cit.,* pp. 121–122.

61. Schoenbaum, *op. cit.,* p. 10.

62. Cantril, *op. cit.,* p. 262.

63. Wheeler-Bennett, *op. cit.,* p. 260.

64. Schoenbaum, *op. cit.,* p. 1.

65. Theodore M. Newcomb, "An Approach to the Study of Communicative Acts," *Psychological Review,* 60 (November, 1953), pp. 393–404.

66. Festinger, *op. cit.,* p. 65.

67. *Ibid.,* pp. 83–84.

68. Lincoln, *op. cit.,* p. 69.

69. Lomax, *When the Word is Given, op. cit.,* p. 44.

70. Malcolm X, *The Autobiography of Malcolm X* (New York: Grove Press, 1964).

71. Lincoln, *op. cit.,* p. 123.

72. *Ibid.,* p. 125.

73. Lomax, *When the Word is Given, op. cit.,* p. 44.

74. Malcolm X, *op. cit.,* p. 183.

75. *Ibid.,* p. 378.

76. Bertram D. Wolfe, *Three Who Made a Revolution* (New York: Delta Book, 1964), p. 169.

77. *Ibid.,* p. 175.

78. *Ibid.,* p. 191.

79. Moorehead, *op. cit.,* p. 160.

80. Curtiss, *op. cit.,* pp. 121–123.

81. E. H. Carr, *The Bolshevik Revolution, 1917–1923,* Volume I (Baltimore: Penguin Books, 1966), p. 90.

82. Sukhanov, *op. cit.,* Volume I, p. 289.

83. *Ibid.*

84. Moorehead, *op. cit.,* p. 227.

85. Curtiss, *op. cit.,* p. 44.

86. Sukhanov, *op. cit.,* Volume II, p. 470.

87. Daniel Lerner, "The Nazi Elite," in Harold D. Lasswell and Daniel Lerner (eds.), *World Revolutionary Elites* (Cambridge, Mass.: M.I.T. Press, 1965), p. 261.

88. *Ibid.,* p. 262.

89. Eliot B. Wheaton, *Prelude to Calamity: The Nazi Revolution 1933–1935* (Garden City, N.Y.: Doubleday, 1968), p. 94.

90. Abel, *op. cit.,* p. 88.

91. *Ibid.,* p. 90.

92. *Ibid.,* p. 79. From these three cases one could draw the inference that individuals with large families are likely to be less available than those with small families for developing intense revolutionary commitments. Taking this idea one step further, we should expect single persons to be the most available of all since they would not be heavily invested in family life. If this is correct, then single people should be represented in collective movements in proportions considerably larger than their average in the population as a whole.

93. *Ibid.,* pp. 152–153.

94. *Ibid.,* p. 139.

95. Schoenbaum, *op. cit.,* pp. 28–29.

96. Abel, *op. cit.,* p. 152.

97. Festinger, *op. cit.*, p. 86.

98. *Ibid.*, p. 202.

99. Lincoln, *op. cit.*, p. 49.

100. Robert Coles, "Social Struggle and Weariness," *Psychiatry,* 27 November, 1964), pp. 314–315.

101. Adam B. Ulam, *The Bolsheviks* (New York: Macmillan, 1965), p. 96.

102. Isaac Deutscher, *The Prophet Armed* (London: Oxford University Press, 1954), p. 22.

103. *Ibid.*, pp. 22–23.

104. Louis Fischer, *The Life of Lenin* (New York: Harper & Row, 1964), p. 41

105. Deutscher, *op. cit.*, p. 29.

106. Ignazio Silone, in Richard Crossman (ed.), *The God That Failed* (New York: Bantam Books, 1949), p. 88.

107. Schoenbaum, *op. cit.*, pp. 3, 28, 36–37.

108. Abel, *op. cit.*, p. 98.

109. *Ibid.*, p. 97.

110. Orlow, *op. cit.*, p. 131.

111. Schoenbaum, *op. cit.*, p. xv.

112. Karl O'Lessker, "Who Voted for Hitler? A New Look at the Class Basis of Nazism," *American Journal of Sociology,* 74 (July, 1968), pp. 64–65.

113. Abel, *op. cit.*, p. 116.

114. *Ibid.*, p. 82.

115. Festinger, *op. cit.*, p. 59.

116. Lincoln, *op. cit.*, p. 189.

117. Malcolm X, *op. cit.*, p. 223.

118. Deutscher, *op. cit.*, pp. 257–258.

119. Curtiss, *op. cit.*, p. 65.

120. Leon Trotsky, *The Russian Revolution* (Garden City, N.Y.: Doubleday, 1959), p. 416.

121. Carr, *op. cit.*, p. 120.

122. Abel, *op. cit.*, p. 72.

123. Orlow, *op. cit.*, p. 81.

124. *Ibid.*, p. 86.

125. Abel, *op. cit.*, p. 82.

126. Schoenbaum, *op. cit.*, p. 35.

127. Orlow, *op. cit.*, p. 231.

128. Festinger, *op. cit.*, p. 95.

129. *Ibid.*, p. 84.

130. Lincoln, *op. cit.*, p. 182.

131. Carr, *op. cit.*, p. 19.

132. Sukhanov, *op. cit.*, p. 290.

133. Wolfe, *op. cit.*, p. 95.

134. *Ibid.*, p. 96.

135. Sukhanov, *op. cit.*, p. 280.

136. Leon Trotsky, *Lenin* (New York: Capricorn Books, 1962), pp. 193–194.

137. Wolfe, *op. cit.,* p. 219.

138. *Ibid.,* p. 363.

139. Deutscher, *op. cit.,* p. 288.

140. *Ibid.,* p. 289.

141. Orlow, *op. cit.,* pp. 29–30.

142. *Ibid.,* p. 83.

143. Hans Gerth, "The Nazi Party: Its Leadership and Composition," *American Journal of Sociology,* 45 (January, 1940), p. 521.

144. Orlow, *op. cit.,* p. 269.

145. Festinger, *op. cit.,* p. 80.

146. *Ibid.,* p. 218.

147. *Ibid.,* p. 3.

148. *Ibid.,* p. 220.

149. Malcolm X, *op. cit.,* p. 184.

150. *Ibid.,* p. 233.

151. *Ibid.,* p. 291.

152. *Ibid.,* p. 309.

153. Deutscher, *op. cit.,* p. 270.

154. Sukhanov, *op. cit.,* Volume II, p. 395.

155. *Ibid.*

156. *Ibid.,* p. 587.

157. Trotsky, *Lenin, op. cit.,* p. 292.

158. Abel, *op. cit.,* pp. 268–269.

159. *Ibid.,* p. 278.

160. Schoenbaum, *op. cit.,* p. 36.

161. Wheeler-Bennett, *op. cit.,* pp. 273–274.

162. Wheaton, *op. cit.,* p. 149.

6 □ CHARISMA AS A PSYCHOLOGICAL EXCHANGE

□ Few concepts in the analysis of leadership have produced as much theoretical confusion as charisma, a term borrowed from the Christian legacy by Rudolf Sohm, the Strassburg church historian and jurist. Max Weber incorporated the concept into this theoretical formulation of authority, which included the traditional, charismatic, and rational-legal bases of rule. Since then, few concepts in the social sciences have gained as much notoriety as charisma and few have been as indiscriminately applied to describe the emergence of popular leaders. Yet a concept that is applied so indiscriminately loses its usefulness for analytic purposes, except as a residual category for describing what we cannot fully understand or explain. In revisiting the concept of charisma, my first objective is to discuss how the concept has been used in the social sciences and how misused. Then I want to offer a psychological interpretation of the concept that will be derived from the earlier assessment of expressive functions. In the broadest sense, commitments based on charismatic relationships will fall within the ego-support category of leadership functioning, wherein the expressive tie arises from ego weakness and discontent. In a later section, charisma will be considered an affective relationship through which the leader and/or follower exchange intangible goods in an attempt to minimize or resolve basic conflicts within the personality. Such exchanges are assumed to influence the development of consistent lines of action within the commitment process.

Weber's Perspective of Charisma

A follower's commitment to a leader in a charismatic relationship is toward the person of the leader and is expressed in strong, emotional sentiments. From Weber's frame of reference, the charismatic leader's power to act "springs from faithful devotion. It is devotion to the extraordinary and unheard-of, to what is strange to all rule and tradition and which therefore is viewed as divine. It is a devotion born of distress and enthusiasm."[1] The follower's recognition of the other-worldly quality in a leader fosters "complete personal devotion to the possessor of the quality . . . ," which Weber clearly sees as the psychological readiness to obey. "Psychologically," he says, "this 'recognition' is a matter of complete personal devotion to the possessor of the quality, arising out of enthusiasm, or of despair and hope."[2] Furthermore, once the charismatic leader is accepted, he is seen by the follower as the "master,"[3] and may simply disregard the "attitudes of the masses toward him."[4] For the charismatic leader's legitimacy to act is not derived from the follower's consent, nor from custom or law, but from a transcendental realm, which Weber describes only vaguely, from which the leader rightfully specifies the follower's obligations and duties. The leader lays claim to the loyalty of his following through his personal magnetism rather than by articulating an ideology that offers a concrete program of action. Shunning the material rewards available to the ambitious and terminating his traditional ties in social life, the charismatic leader becomes singularly bound to the fulfillment of his personal hopes from which he legitimizes his right to demand obedience from his followers. Thus, in Weber's words, he "demands obedience and a following by virtue of his mission."[5]

Weber's Intention

Weber's formulation of charisma attempted to account for the basis of personal authority and was distinguished from rule based on custom (traditional authority) and law (rational-legal authority). In his analysis of charisma, he emphasized the conditions that tend to encourage the emergence of authority residing in a single person. Under such conditions, the right of the leader to rule is determined by the follower's recognition of his God-like qualities, either imputed to him by the follower in the heat of social change or bestowed on him through ascension to a charismatic office. This line of thinking is naturally derived, as Hans Gerth and C. Wright Mills have argued, from "Weber's conception of the charismatic leader as a continuation of a 'philosophy of history' that, after Carlyle's *Heroes and Hero Worship,* influenced a great deal of nineteenth-century history writing."[6]

A major source of confusion that has developed from the discussion of charisma arises from the integration of two distinct analytic orientations. Most writers tend to combine haphazardly both the social and psychological aspects of leader-follower relations, a tendency begun by Weber himself. In fact, the social and psychological dimensions of Weber's analysis of charisma are neither clearly distinguished nor fully discussed, a situation that has produced a dispute concerning his real intention. From the social perspective, Weber recognizes that charisma is associated with certain conditions of structural strain that are especially pronounced during periods of accelerated social change. Also, he alludes to the fact that charismatic leaders must produce concrete returns for their followers or they will lose their right to lead. From the psychological perspective, on the other hand, charisma is described as an affective sentiment that springs from the follower's belief in the extraordinary or superhuman powers of the leader. Which of these two approaches is most likely to enlighten our thinking about the nature of the charismatic commitment?

A social approach to leader-follower relations cannot hope to explain in precise terms the basis of the follower's devotion to a leader. When Weber introduced the concept of charisma to explain the basis of personal rule, it might have been his intention to emphasize the social conditions that give rise to the formation of charismatic ties. But the nature of his focus on personal rule led him to the study of personality. For how else can one explain a relationship between leader and follower that is personal and affective? Yet, K. J. Ratnam discounts the central importance of Weber's concern for the psychological aspects of the charismatic relationship, arguing that his "emphasis on personality constitutes a definite point of deviation from the main points of his analysis."[7] As we shall see, the confusion within Weber's own thinking has been carried over into the more recent literature dealing with charisma.

Trends in the Literature

The concept of charisma has been discussed in rather diffuse terms and applied with only a margin of discrimination in some cases. Usually it is used to describe leaders who have gathered large, avid followings, although it has also been attributed to political structures such as political parties. Using the concept in this general manner, its distinctiveness as an analytic category is impaired, at times conveying impressions about the underlying motives or causes of commitment that are misleading and often wrong.

An observer may perceive avid support for a leader and, with only scant knowledge concerning the nature of his following or the intensity of commitment, conclude that the leader must indeed be a charismatic type. For instance, David Apter described Kwame Nkrumah during his reign of leadership in Ghana as an "almost mythical person" who had gathered a "faithful flock." In Apter's view, this qualified him to be called a charismatic leader.[8] The outward manifestations of charisma might very well be indicated by the apparent faithfulness of a group of followers, but are we to call all who follow charismatics? Is it to be assumed that all impute God-given gifts to the leader and that all are equal in their adoration of him? Or is it possible for a follower to form an intense commitment to the leader, to develop a consistent line of action that resists change, because he agrees with the leader's policy position and considers it clearly in his interest to support him? It is also possible that a manifest commitment to the leader might be the follower's compromise to escape from punishments for non-compliance, whether meted out through a governmental system of terror or by the more immediate and enduring process of social group pressure.

There are three analytic tendencies in the literature that must be mentioned before I begin my critique. First, there is the tendency to develop a modal personality, which attributes uniform, rather than multiple and disparate, motives to followers as the basis for their commitment to the popular rebel leader. Second, if a distinction is drawn between motives that are grounded in personality and those that are grounded in social structure, those who prefer the social orientation tend to claim the leader's appropriate response to social strains as the basis of charisma (which I would not call charisma at all, only support based on confidence in the leader's ability to meet needs). In both these tendencies, charisma is over-generalized. The third tendency is to confuse the non-institutionalized and institutionalized aspects of charismatic authority.

The Emphasis on the Transcendental Character of Charisma

At a highly abstract level, John Marcus argues that charisma emerges from man's desire for transcendence, an ideal that he describes as "beyond-self." This is the individual's basic aspiration to rise out of his condition, to become something more noble, something more worthy. Best typified in religious belief systems, this inclination for metaphysical change prepares followers to accept leaders who identify with transcendental objectives. Leaders who successfully support the follower's identification with a transcendental ideal, he asserts, develop an aura of charisma. Furthermore, the leader imbued with charisma becomes indispensable to a movement because followers believe "that he can control the forces of history and achieve its transcendental objective."[9] The leader comes to be seen as the embodiment of the follower's aspirations: The basis of the follower's commitment to the charismatic leader lies in his "emphatic identification with a hero personality *seen as the transcendental self.*"[10] In this context, the leader's personality does not have to express "flamboyant emotionalism," as was the case for Calvin and Robespierre, for the psychological intensity of the follower's commitment to the charismatic leader is to the person of the leader in only a secondary sense. The primary focus of the follower's attention is the transcendental authority the leader represents. Marcus concludes that the "psychological intensity of charisma" is fostered by the follower's perception that the leader has a special relationship with the transcendent ideal.

While Marcus is obviously sympathetic to the psychological interpretation of charisma, his analysis, like so many, considers the symptoms rather than the underlying determinants of charisma. For the fact that a leader's charisma is derived from association with a transcendent ideal is symptomatic of a deeper, psychological urgency for transcendental contact, be it culturally implanted or generated by conditions of stress. To go deeper than an enumeration of the symptoms of the charismatic relation, several questions should be asked. What follower types are most likely to identify with a transcendental state? What are the conditions that may make followers susceptible to transcendental appeals from leadership? And how can the imputation of special gifts to the leader be explained if no transcendental ideal is apparent?

Like Marcus, Carl Friedrich embraces the transcendental features of charisma, but in a much narrower sense. For him, charisma applies to governments whose rule is legitimized by a "higher being," suggesting that charisma emerges only if a government or political movement has religious overtones. From his perspective, charismatic leadership is similar to other leadership types in its ability to inspire confidence, but "it is distinguished from them by its close ties to religion."[11] Attacking Weber's central thesis that "gifts" can be imputed to strictly political leaders, Friedrich asserts that charisma should not be loosely applied to all categories of inspirational leadership. He rejects the view, for instance, that the relation between the demagogue and his followers is a charismatic one, for the demagogue is not divinely inspired. Similarly, he argues, charisma should not be applied to describe totalitarian leaders, who are typically preoccupied with power, while charismatic leaders who found religions are not.

It is apparent in purely political movements that a select group of followers may impute God-given gifts to the leader. For example, in Richard Fagen's analysis of Castro's leadership, evidence is offered to suggest that even though religion was not a legitimizing force, Castro was seen by his followers as an individual with divine qualities. In a survey of 1,000 respondents, 86 per cent were found to be Castro supporters; of these, 43 per cent were classified as "fervent" believers. Among his fervent followers Castro was seen as a man with ideas similar to Jesus Christ, and in many Cuban homes the resemblance of Castro's portraits with those of Christ were striking.[12]

Friedrich's insistence that charisma should be reserved as a concept for analyzing movements in which religion is clearly present denies the salience of the follower's imputation of divine gifts to the strictly political leader. In fact, he suggests that "the introduction of the concepts of authority and legitimacy as Weber understands them tends to exaggerate the psychological aspect of systems of rule or patterns of government."[13] But how else can we explain a follower's tendency to believe that a strictly political leader is God's representative, except in psychological terms? On this point, Friedrich remains silent.

Locating the transcendental sources of charismatic authority appears to be mainly intuitive and arbitrary. While Marcus is unwilling to specify a single, concrete source and Friedrich anchors charisma to the Gods, another author places his emphasis squarely on the "nation," at least in the new states. Beginning with the premise that the "nation" is the transcendental source of authority from which the legitimacy of the leader is derived, Edward Shils concludes that the extent of one's personal authority is determined by proximity to the "nation." Because "the nation is the ultimately significant entity, only those who rule . . . are endowed with the charisma of the nation." Businessmen and tribal chiefs, because they are further removed from rule, are outside the "circle of the charisma of nationality."[14] The concentration of charisma in the nation has a negative consequence for political development, according to Shils, because it alienates the businessman from the source of legitimacy, thus minimizing his effectiveness in creating sound economic policy that would be acceptable to the public. The apparent connection between nationalism and charisma is assumed by Shils without verification, however. It is unclear, for instance, how the follower's affection for the nation is transferred to the leader. Nor are we told what empirical base underlies the argument that the nation is the sanctifying source of authority.

In a companion discussion of charisma, Shils turns his attention more specifically to the analysis of "institutional charisma" in which the transcendental referent is "power" rather than the "nation." His main thesis is that charisma is produced as a deferential tendency when the individual relates to those occupying power roles. In fact, charismatic qualities come to be attached to the power roles themselves and may remain for some time after they are vacated. Proof for this position is found, he argues, in the awe people show simply standing before the desk of the President of the United States. This mystique exists because the role that exercises great power over our lives is considered transcendental. Linking power and charisma, he suggests that the "main recipients of deference are those who exercise authority in the central institutional system and those who occupy the main positions in the central value system."[15] In this sense, charisma is dispersed to persons occupying authority roles, such as civil servant, administrator, and judge, because "the particular incumbent of that role . . . is perceived as a manifestation of a larger center of tremendous power."[16] Taken one step further, the power of the masses is assumed to generate a charisma of its own, which, if accepted by leadership, creates a sense of civility indispensable to the on-going social and political order.

Conceptualizing the basis of institutional charisma in these terms raises a number of analytic problems. First, if charisma is to be equated with deference and awe, then Shils would have to consider other deferential relationships (besides power relations) as charismatic. For example, does it make any sense to allude to the charisma of the wealthy or the aged, since both often receive deferential treatment? Second, Shils assumes that awe and deference of power roles will create obedience to initiatives undertaken by those filling such roles. While one might stand in awe before the

President's desk, this feeling of deference to the power role must affect the individual's willingness to accept the political initiatives of the President, if it is even to approximate the charismatic relationship that Weber's analysis implies. For example, there is some evidence to suggest that congressional deference to the President's power role is socially prescribed and does not necessarily affect the set of relationships in the political arena. In short, deference to power roles affects *social* relations because no interests or values are at stake, but this does not seem to affect *political* relations drastically.[17] Third, Shils' formulation of institutional charisma, as with all such emphases, creates some difficulty in determining the exact basis of the follower's commitment. Does awe of a civil servant's power increase the individual's willingness to accept the bureaucratic initiatives? Or does the follower orient to the authority role in terms of universal standards or the threat of sanctions for noncompliance?

The consideration of charisma in its institutional form can be found in two separate analyses of the charismatic qualities of political organization. For both W. C. Runciman and Irving Horowitz attribute charisma to political parties. Runciman argues that, in Ghana, "even without a leader of Nkrumah's qualities, the first party victorious was likely to remain the embodiment of the charisma derived from achieving the national aim."[18] Faced with a weakening traditional structure and an insufficiently strong rational-legal base of authority, the Convention Peoples' party (CPP) had to sustain itself charismatically, which, according to Runciman, perpetuated conditions of political uncertainty and arbitrary decision-making. Viewing charisma as a transitional element in political development, he perceives that the routinization of the CPP's charisma was necessary in order to enhance structural stability.

In a similar vein, Horowitz conceives of party charisma as a midpoint between revolutionary charisma (the pure personal type) and rational authority. In the emergent nation-states there are contrasting trends toward personalism, on the one hand, and toward mass participation and mass domination, on the other. Party charisma provides a resolution of these tendencies by assuming the "God-like" features of leadership. As a result, the party is viewed as the most significant instrument for limiting the caprice and wickedness of pure personal charisma. But it is basically stronger than a charismatic leader because the party can more readily absorb defeats. The role of the party in the Third World, Horowitz concludes, is to establish a basis of authority that combines both personal and legal aspects of rule, wherein loyalty is extended to the party rather than to the individual leader or the law per se.[19]

Attributing charisma to political parties leaves one somewhat bewildered. Neither Runciman nor Horowitz offers a precise meaning of charisma and, at times, one might wonder whether they have not deviated rather sharply from Weber's original conception. For example, one author has suggested that Horowitz's concept of "party charisma" is impaired by the vagueness of the concept of charisma itself.[20] Two other criticisms can be advanced against Horowitz's position, however. First, he utilizes the Weberian analysis of personal charisma to describe what is essentially an institutional dimension, without first considering the analytic problems that emerge when factors associated with personal rule are applied indiscriminately to a situation in which authority resides in a political party. This approach leads him to the questionable conclusion that the God-like features of leadership, which are personalized qualities derived from a personalized God, can be assumed by political parties. Second, he diverges from Weber's analysis of institutionalized charisma by arguing that party charisma can modify or inhibit the strength of personal charismatic authority. In terms of Weber's formulation, charismatic office is routinized personal rule but it is personalized authority nonetheless. Weber's analysis of routinization implies continuance of personal authority, leading one to question whether Horowitz would not be well advised to abandon the notion of charisma entirely for a more precise discussion of the political party as an institutionalizing force, as a political embryo with a decidedly rational-legal basis that may inhibit or counteract the influence of personal authority.

The Emphasis on the Structural Determinants of Charisma

Runciman makes a departure from the transcendental emphasis that should be brought out: For him, charisma adheres to both personal and impersonal objects. For the charisma of the leader or political party is produced by essentially separate orientations to and successes in achieving independence.[21] Here, success in meeting follower demands and expectations is the concrete source of legitimacy, rather than the leader's personal mystique or a transcendental office that legitimizes his leadership. In short, the legitimacy of action undertaken by the leader or party is a result of the follower's recognition that adherence to leader or party is personally beneficial. In this sense, commitment appears to be rooted in the follower's political and economic interests, factors that should be considered in the light of the transactional basis of leader-follower relations.

The tendency to consider the foundations of charisma as being rooted in the follower's self-interest is most distinct in the separate studies of K. J. Ratnam and William Friedland. Emphasizing the rational aspects of the follower's commitment, Ratnam argues that

> the type of leader we generally call "charismatic" gets his support very largely from the issues he is associated with, the grievances he seeks to put right and the manner in which he proposes to do so, and the time he chooses for making these issues and grievances the passionate concern of those whom he thinks will be his followers.[22]

Discounting the importance of the transcendental aspects of leadership, Ratnam prefers to emphasize the leader's behavior as it relates to issues, pressure group demands, and skills. He appears certain "that the type of popularity generally associated with 'charisma' relies at least as much on the issues taken up by a leader as on his personality."[23]

Drawing on data collected in Tanganyika,[24] Friedland's findings generally confirm Ratnam's more diffuse observations. In Friedland's view, charismatic leadership derived its legitimacy from: (1) the expression of sentiments that were publicly salient; (2) the assumption of risks by leaders in articulating their views; and, (3) the perception by followers that the leaders were successful in activities undertaken. The rise of charismatic authority was directly related to the leader's success in developing positions that synchronized with the dissatisfactions of followers.[25] In this sense, the followers' willingness to accept the leader's initiatives was not the result of blind faith in or devotion to the leader as a spokesman or embodiment of a transcendental source of authority. Rather, it was a product of his perception that the leader's initiatives would provide solutions to his personal problems. From Friedland's perspective, if a leader's message is "meaningful to a group of people, they will provide support by expressing agreement through some form of deferential behavior."[26]

The issues raised by Ratnam and Friedland are crucial, although their conclusions are likely to perpetuate the indiscriminate use of charisma, which is the very problem they are attempting to remedy. Given their arguments and data, it seems more beneficial to argue that charisma *should not* be utilized to describe a leader-follower relationship that is essentially transactional in nature, that it is fallacious to equate charismatic leadership with popular leadership, and, that, while a sector of a leader's following may be committed on a charismatic basis, a sizable number may follow because the leader proposes to solve their problems or threatens to terrorize them for disobedience. In this sense, the different bases of the followers' commitment to seemingly popular leaders must be appraised more carefully. Yet the failure to distinguish between different sectors of followership is only one of several weaknesses that are apparent in the general application of charisma to describe the emergence of popular rebel leaders.

Weaknesses in the Literature

The arbitrary imputation of charisma to popular leadership is the source of considerable confusion concerning the proper place of the concept in the analysis of leader-follower relations. If charisma is considered the sole basis of personal rule, then any manifestation of personal popularity has to be explained in charismatic terms. Instead of formulating a new view of the determinants of personal rule, scholars have persisted in using the term "charisma" even when it appeared to fit badly. Some have attempted to broaden its meaning to include factors Weber had scarcely mentioned (the transactional determinants of commitment), while others attack his analysis for its unnecessarily heavy emphasis on the psychological aspects of the charismatic relationship. It is apparent from the literature that the basis of personal authority has been much too narrowly conceived. Too many have overlooked the other possible bases of personal rule, especially the aspects of patrimonial leadership discussed by Weber.

What we have called the transactional basis of personal rule can be found in fact within the context of patrimonial authority. According to Guenther Roth, patrimonial leadership remains one of the most neglected aspects of Weber's conception of authority. Applying this dimension of Weber's thought to leadership in the new states, Roth depicts patrimonial leaders as men attempting to maximize their personal control for purposes of nation-building. He distinguishes between two types of patrimonial rule. The first, which appears in Ethiopia, Roth calls "traditionalist patrimonial regimes," and the second is more closely associated with what I have described as the transactional basis of leadership. Regarding the second type of patrimonial relation, Roth says:

> The second type of patrimonialism is personal rulership on the basis of loyalties that do not require any belief in the ruler's unique personal qualification, but are inextricably linked to material incentives and rewards. *This second variant has been submerged in much of the literature through the indiscriminate use of the term "charismatic."*[27] [Emphasis added.]

As a basis of personal authority, patrimonial regimes need have neither a personal charismatic appeal nor a sense of mission—factors associated with the psychological aspects of follower commitment. Rather, the personal patrimonial leader legitimizes his rule by responding appropriately to the problems of his society and by providing rewards for his followers. "Neglect of the patrimonial dimension of government," Roth correctly points out, "has . . . led to a tendency to interpret all political leadership as charismatic."[28] This indiscriminate use of charisma has been especially apparent in the analyses of leadership in the new states. Disputing the over-ambitious use of charisma, he argues that:

> Most heads of government in the new states do not have the magic of charisma for many groups in the society, nor do they have the kind of impersonal, institutional charisma that Edward Shils has stressed as a basic requirement for organizational stability. The political situation in many African and Asian countries is so fluid exactly because leadership is merely personal and lacking in both charismatic qualities, that is, personal as well as office charisma.[29]

Given these problems, it should be profitable to develop a perspective of personal rule, an undertaking I will leave for the final chapter, which includes the charismatic, transactional, and inspirational bases of personal authority. Not only will this perspective reduce much of the confusion, it may also minimize the tendency to view a popular leader's following as a large collection of disturbed personalities hungering for faith and commitment to a cause. In this sense, the proportion of a rebel leader's following that accepts his personal rule because of severe personality disturbances can be compared with the proportion who are inspired by him and who accept his initiatives largely because of his position on issues and who anticipate that adherence to his personal directions will produce concrete rewards. In examining weaknesses in applying the concept it is clear that much of what has been passed off as charisma is more appropriately included as the popular manifestations of appropriate and successful leadership.

Since most works have discounted the multiple bases of personal rule, no adequate criteria have been developed for deciding which leaders should qualify for inclusion in the "charismatic" category.[30] To assume the existence of a charismatic relationship when there is a devoted following is so arbitrary that it intensifies rather than alleviates the problems of classification. For example, as one writer argues, since both Hitler and Robespierre had devoted followers, both could be classified as "charismatic" leaders.[31] Here, the boundaries of charisma are so broad that the term simply fails to distinguish these leaders in a meaningful way. As Alex Simirenko has suggested, there must be something wrong when a concept like charisma is applied with the same ease to such varied types of men as Caesar, St. Francis, Calvin, Hitler, Gandhi, and Stalin.[32]

If we assume a more narrowly conceived psychological interpretation, however, charisma can be more usefully equated with fanatical commitments and studied more precisely as growing out of ego discontent. This suggests a scalar view of charisma based on the proportion of a leader's following that relates to him in terms of ego-support functions. Thus, the question is not who is a "charismatic" leader, but how many individuals in a leader's following may be classified as charismatics? Since we might expect any popular leader to attract such types, leaders might be classified according to the size of their charismatic following.

Accepting charisma as if it were the only basis of personal rule has led to another problem. Once a leader is designated a charismatic type, the tendency has been to minimize the importance of the non-charismatic segments of his popular support. For instance, in Nazi Germany which follower sectors expressed beliefs in Hitler's God-given talents and identified with him? Which accepted his initiatives because they feared punishments for deviation? How many followers were neither mesmerized by his personal mystique nor subjugated by their fear of punishments, but accepted his initiatives because they perceived his issue positions, skills, and information to be most appropriate for the situation? And, how many followed Hitler because he was able to give meaning to action and suffering? Through such questions, followership categories can be developed that clarify the subtle differences in leaders' relations with follower sectors whose willingness to accept personal rule is determined by essentially different forces.

In this context, a popular leader maintains the support of his following in different ways. Why was Nkrumah overthrown in Ghana? One might argue that charismatic leadership had become dysfunctional in an increasingly rational-legal system. But this position simply begs a number of questions. How extensive was his charismatic following in the first place? Were those who had accepted Nkrumah on a charismatic basis in the forefront of the protest against him? Or did deviation originate among those who had accepted his leadership in terms of positive and negative transactions? In the latter context, what changes had occurred that affected his ability to wield power against antagonists and what policies had he executed which resulted in discontent? From those oriented toward Nkrumah on a charismatic basis, we might expect a rejection of evidence disconfirming his "gift of grace." Under such conditions, the sector of charismatics is apt to remain loyal to the leader during and after a crisis. What might appear as a decline of charisma (by those who conceive of charisma in the broadest sense) might be simply a decline in popularity (oriented to issues), coupled with an inability to coerce. In any event, to understand the decline of a leader's personal authority we should recognize that his following is likely to be heterogeneous in terms of commitment; thus the kind and quantity of evidence necessary to terminate the follower's commitment will differ from sector to sector.

Since charisma is usually defined broadly in terms of a transcendental referent from which leader choices are legitimized, little attention has been paid to those choices as the *leader's choices*. For Shils, the leader's successes are not the result of the soundness of his decisions, but are derived from their closer proximity to the "charisma of nationality." Conversely, the initiatives of businessmen are rejected by the public, not because their initiatives are possibly inappropriate or unacceptable, but because they are further removed from the "nation." The assumption is that most followers do not attempt to analyze the leader's successes and failures, but orient to the leader in relation to some higher source of authority. In the same respect, leaders in closer proximity to the source of legitimacy must be assumed to possess an almost infinite number of possible choices, since followers appear not to judge the appropriateness of their actions. Thus, Nkrumah's success in making a relatively smooth transition in Ghana is attributed to his charisma, not to his choices in setting collective goals appropriate for the moment.[33]

The tendency to equate popular rebel leadership with charismatic leadership has produced a misleading impression: The rebel leader is too often seen as a millenarian prophet, acting freely and forcing his will upon an adoring audience. This view of personal power, which appears to grant the rebel leader an extensive realm of freedom and control over his followers, must be critically evaluated in much the same way that researchers have surmounted serious misconceptions about presidential power in the United States. There is, in fact, a striking similarity in our current assessment of personal power and the dominant view of presidential power less than two decades ago. In both cases, surface impressions are accepted at face value in explaining the leader's ability to carry the articles of his faith into effect. Through new insights into power relations and more carefully refined investigations of presidential decision-making, we have come to better understand the complexity of presidential action.[34] A more careful investigation into the relationships between rebel leaders and their followers should result in a similarly productive clarification of personal power.

During times of social stress, followers are likely to increase their commitments to leadership (in terms of role) because, in such times, leadership becomes the functionally prominent element for revising goals and restructuring situations. Thus, while it appears that followers are devoted to the person of the leader, it is also quite likely that many are positively oriented to leadership roles because of their perception that new goals are absolutely necessary for overcoming structural discontinuities. When the social structure is restabilized, when subsystems can again carry their functional burdens, a personal type of leadership becomes less functionally significant and lines of activity come to be influenced increasingly by other political sectors. This reduces the follower's adherence to the initiatives of a single leader. Thus, Winston Churchill, considered a charismatic leader by many, failed to maintain his personal authority after World War II because his personalized style of leadership was no longer necessary in the post-war situation. This suggests that the willingness of most followers to accept his initiatives during the war was the result of necessity, not of any magical quality of the leader or the recognition of such qualities. This case substantiates the claim that commitment to the popular leader is far from total and compulsive for many followers. Rather, it appears that commitment formation is contingent on the follower's changing view of rewards and his perception that leadership, as a creative status, is necessary in times of rapid social change for setting goals and reestablishing social harmony.

A Psychological Perspective of Charisma

While my analysis of the literature might seem a bit excessive, I wanted to leave no doubt in the reader's mind that confusion reigns over the current application of charisma. Moreover, it should be apparent by now that those who have used the social approach have failed to concentrate on the psychological causes that produce the charismatic relationship. In this respect, the central questions that flow from Weber's discussion of charisma have been avoided: What causes the follower to develop a strong identification with the leader rather than his program? Once this identification is made, why does the follower lose his capacity to criticize the leader? And what factors will help to explain why the follower becomes completely submissive to the leader's will? These are questions that must be answered if charisma is to be explained, not just used for some other purpose. The answers must be sought in the mind of the follower, which will lead me, with some trepidation, into an assessment of personality. In fact, writing in the same period, Sigmund Freud advanced a psychological theory of leader-follower relations strikingly similar to Weber's treatment of charisma. Freud's pioneering achievement, *Group Psychology and the Analysis of the Ego*,[35] extends that part of the discussion Weber scarcely touched on—the psychological forces bearing on the formation of charismatic commitments. Freud clarifies and extends Weber's thoughts on the three major manifestations of charisma: identification with the leader, the loss of the follower's capacity to criticize, and his seemingly total submission to the whims of the leader.

Freud's discussion of leader-follower relations leads one to a somewhat different view of charisma than is popular today. The charismatic tie is seen as an outgrowth of a psychological exchange arising from tensions within the follower's personality. These tensions result from conflicts between the three agencies of the psychic apparatus (the id, ego, and superego), conflicts that tend to be aggravated by social changes that tax the capabilities of the ego. Identification with a leader, diminished capacity to criticize, and complete submission are related directly to the ego's attempt to find a solution to conflicts that produce anxiety, guilt, inferiority, insecurity, and/or ambivalence. The specific features of this perspective begin to unfold with Freud's analysis of the problem.

Intrapsychic Distance as a Cause of Charisma

In Freud's treatment of group psychology, identification with the leader results from conflicts between the follower's ego and superego that have not been satisfactorily resolved and that produce one of the varieties of ego discontent outlined in Chapter II. Why the follower identifies with the leader as a new model of behavior is explained by Freud in terms of tension arising from the intrapsychic distance between the follower's ego and ego-ideal (the goal system of the superego). Here, intrapsychic distance refers to the disparity between what the ego is capable of doing and what the ego-ideal demands from it in terms of performance.

What specific developments contribute to intrapsychic distance and how does the ego attempt to reduce the intensity of its suffering? From Freud's perspective, the superego develops out of the ego during the period of the oedipus complex. Its first function within the psychic apparatus is to repress the urge to possess the mother in the case of the son and to repress the hatred of the father as the competitor for the mother's affection. From this complex, the son develops ambivalent feelings toward the father incorporating the conflicting sentiments of love and hatred. The stronger the anxieties generated by this complex, according to Freud, the stronger and more dominant the superego must become in order to support the ego's attempt to control the instinctual drives originating in the id. This can result in a model of behavior and conscience that are rigid and far removed from the capabilities of the ego. For personalities that possess rigid superego structures of this kind, in which goals are set way beyond the capabilities of the ego, there is apt to be incessant anxiety, guilt, and self-criticism, a condition Freud associated with melancholia. He suggests that "the misery of the melancholic is the expression of a sharp conflict between the two agencies of his ego, a conflict in which the ideal, in an excess of sensitiveness, relentlessly exhibits its condemnation of the ego in delusions of inferiority and self-deprecation."[36] On the other hand, mania results when the goals of the ego-ideal are reached by the ego to its satisfaction. The ego and ego-ideal become fused together, says Freud, "so that the person in a mood of triumph and self-satisfaction, disturbed by no self-criticism, can enjoy the abolition of his inhibitions."[37]

Under conditions of extreme intrapsychic distance, the ego will attempt to find ways of reducing suffering, which requires the use of psychological defenses, such as identification (introjection), projection, reaction-formation, sublimation, repression, and so on.[38] Of these defenses against suffering, identification and projection are especially crucial factors bearing on the formation of the charismatic relationship.

Identification is the first defense against suffering, wherein the ego turns to an external object as a substitute ego-ideal in order to reduce intrapsychic distance and restore equilibrium to the personality. Freud has argued in this respect that the ego's identification with an external object is one way it resolves conflict, a condition especially prominent in love relationships. "It is obvious, in many forms of love-choice," he argues, "that the object serves as a substitute for some unattained ego ideal of our own. We love it on account of the perfections which we have striven to reach for our own ego, and which we should now like to procure in this roundabout way as a means of satisfying our narcissism."[39]

When an external object replaces the individual's ego-ideal, the superego ceases to perform one of its chief functions—criticism. Its capacity to criticize the object that has replaced the ego-ideal is impaired, sometimes to the point of extinction. The devotion of the ego to the object, which is the leader in a charismatic relationship, creates the condition noted by Freud where

the functions allotted to the ego ideal entirely cease to operate, the criticism exercised by that agency is silent; everything that the object does and asks for is right and blameless. Conscience has no application to anything that is done for the sake of the object; in the blindness of love remorselessness is carried to the pitch of crime. The whole situation can be completely summarized in a formula: *The object has been put in the place of the ego-ideal.*[40]

Here, the charismatic leader-follower relationship can be compared to the relationship noted by Freud between a hypnotist and his patient: "There is the same humble subjection, the same compliance, the same absence of criticism, toward the hypnotist as toward the loved object."[41]

The follower identifies with the leader in a way that is similar to a child's identification with its parents. For example, in the early development of a male child the father is idealized and comes to represent a model of behavior to be emulated. Just as the son's early emotional attachment to the father provides support for making the transition to a higher point of development, so too does the follower's identification and emotional attachment to the leader provide new opportunities for personal maturation.

Projection is also used by the ego to reduce psychic distance. First, the ego projects its conflict with the superego out into the external world, a defense that is facilitated by the clear presence of a scapegoat that can be identified as a threat. In the process of projecting the conflict outward, the ego splits its ambivalent feelings (which, in the son's case, developed from the conflicting sentiments of love and hatred for the father) in a way that leads to the resolution of intrapsychic conflict. The affectionate feeling for the father is transferred to the leader who is functioning as the substitute ego-ideal and the feelings of hatred are projected outward toward those who are the actual or fictitious enemies of the leader.[42] After the follower has split his ambivalence and secured the leader through identification, intrapsychic distance is reduced either because the new ideals of the leader are within reach of the follower's ego or because the new ego-ideal, in harmony with a changing conscience, dominates the ego so completely that the two agencies fuse. In either case, the follower's behavior is likely to show signs of mania, represented in reduced self-criticism and the abolition of inhibitions.[43] This is likely to be experienced as a general feeling of freedom and discovery, verbalized by the follower as "happiness" and "seeing the light."

The follower's strong identification with the leader as a new model of behavior creates the conditions that Weber associated with charisma. The follower's capacity to criticize the leader is impaired at the same time that he submits himself to the leader in an act of obedience. Substituting the leader for the follower's ego-ideal has the effect of transforming the attitudinal structure as well as behavior of the follower because his orientation to the environment is determined by a new set of goals that he derives from the leader's example and mission in life. This helps to explain Weber's claim that charisma results in a radical transformation of the follower's central system of attitudes as well as his orientation to social problems and social structures.[44]

The psychological perspective of charisma developed in the preceding pages is not without adherents, for George Devereux and Alexander Mitscherlich have offered similar interpretations in their separate psychoanalytic studies of charisma.[45] Beginning with Weber's view of charisma as a personal and transcendentally grounded type of authority, Devereux discusses the possible influence of stress and crisis in producing a charismatic relationship. He distinguishes stress, which is the result of objective social strains in the society, from crisis, which is the individual's subjective reaction to stress. This sense of personal crisis becomes acute when the individual's time-tested and traditional mechanisms for orienting to and acting to relieve stress fail to produce results. Personal disorientation develops under these conditions. This outcome is manifest in an intensification of fear leading to anxiety, which is the final and most intolerable mental state produced by the sense of inadequacy of one's own resources in the face of stress. Like Dostoyevsky, who emphasizes man's longing for security in the "Grand Inquisitor," or Erich Fromm, who has recognized man's desire to "escape from freedom," Devereux emphasizes the follower's low threshold for anxiety. Followers may be sufficiently strong to cope with fear, he argues, but not with intense anxiety. In fact, preoccupied with efforts to alleviate anxiety, they cease worrying about the stress that produced their anxiety in the first place.[46]

Unable to come to terms with these anxieties using their own resources, followers revert to infantile patterns of behavior, regressing to a state of submissiveness and demanding a leader who conforms to infantile ideas of adult behavior. Just as the child relates to the parent during the stage of delegated omnipotence, so the charismatic leader becomes a parental figure to be obeyed during periods of stress.[47] "It is indeed a dangerous fact," adds Mitscherlich, "that the great majority of people, including educated people, are easily induced to merge the ego and ego-ideal, that is, to fuse themselves with a leader with the greatest enthusiasm, whenever they find themselves in conflicts which at first seem to overtax their wits."[48] When the flow of nourishment from the state is interrupted, he continues, "aggressive irritation arises and seeks aimlessly for outlets; it is this mood that renders people susceptible to seduction by a demagogue."[49] Commitment to the charismatic leader thus becomes the follower's outlet for "aggressive unburdening." In the leader, the follower seems to discover a substitute father who will protect him: "Phenomena like Napoleon, Hitler, and Stalin show how difficult men find it to live without fathers," says Mitscherlich. "They cannot relinquish the protecting father of their childhood, they cling to a superfather who will regulate all their activities and also determine the 'meta'."[50]

The hypothesized relationship between the individual's loss of control over his immediate environment and his readiness to accept authority figures, pointed up by both Devereux and Mitscherlich, has been largely confirmed in James Davies' study, "Charisma in the 1952 Campaign."[51] An empirical analysis of electoral data bearing on the Stevenson-Eisenhower campaign, Davies' work attempts to test hypotheses that propose basic relationships between certain personality variables and the readiness to impute special gifts or power to a leader (Eisenhower). Through a content analysis of statements followers made about leadership, two groups were developed: those who attributed special qualities to the leader (the char-ismatics) and those who stressed the responsibility and independence of the leader but did not lavishly praise him (the non-charismatics). The general thesis was that followers "who react charismatically to leaders must do so because they differ from others in relatively basic needs and in ways of structuring the external world."[52] In harmony with the preceding psycho-logical interpretation of charisma, those who had been classified as char-ismatics showed a significant difference from non-charismatics in the fol-lowing ways: (1) The charismatics tended to have higher levels of intolerance for indecision and crisis; (2) they were also less well equipped to maintain ambiguous perceptions, preferring to make categoric judgments and devel-oping rather rigid categories of good and evil; and (3) they were more likely than non-charismatics to say that other people shared their opinions and acted as they did. Similar findings have been reported in other studies to demonstrate the psychological underpinnings of authoritarianism and dog-matism.[53]

Identity Diffusion as a Cause of Charisma

Intrapsychic distance is not the only conflict that causes the follower to substitute a leader for his ego-ideal, even though it is the common explana-tion offered. There is a second type of intrapsychic conflict that can produce the same manifestations of charisma outlined by Weber. It is conflict stem-ming from the incomplete development of the ego-ideal, which leaves the ego with an inadequate identity to guide its relations with the other psychic agencies and the external world. The specific features of an identity have been discussed by Carl Rogers in the following way. In his view, an "iden-tity" is

> an organized configuration of perceptions of the self which are admissable to awareness. It is composed of such elements as the perceptions of one's charac-teristics and abilities; the perceptions and concepts of the self in relation to others and to the environment; the value qualities which are perceived as associated with experience and objects; and the goals and ideals which are perceived as having positive or negative value.[54]

While the ego's identity is formed out of the ego-ideal in the developmental process of the personality, they are analytically distinct. Erik Erikson has pointed out the basic difference between them by referring to the ego identity as "a more or less actually attained but forever-to-be-revised sense of the reality of the self within social reality; while the imagery of the ego-ideal could be said to represent a set of to-be-strived-for but forever-not-quite-attainable ideal goals for the self."[55]

During the period when Freud lived and studied, intrapsychic tension was essentially due to the repression of instinctual drives. Today, argues Erikson, it is caused primarily by the incomplete formation of identity, which he calls "identity diffusion." Prolonged and rapid cultural change affecting patterns of socialization as well as the increasing complexities of modern life are two important factors producing this breakdown in the development of the personality.

Identity diffusion stems from factors external to the personality that inhibit the inculcation of the values and norms of society. For example, the development of the child's ego-ideal will tend to be impeded when parental authority is excessively weak, oppressive, or absent. Such situations reduce the opportunities for important identifications from which the child derives a conception of himself. During adolescence and young adulthood, the individual enters the stage of identity crisis when he asks himself: "What should I become, what are my capabilities, what is the essence of my relationship with my parents, and how do I view myself and how does this correspond to my perceptions of the way others view me?"[56] This is the period in the development of the personality when the individual must develop "some central perspective and direction, some working unity, out of the effective remnants of his anticipated adulthood."[57] If the ego-ideal of the adolescent has not been well developed, then the identity crisis is not likely to be resolved adequately.

Without a well-developed ego-ideal to guide the ego's behavior and an identity to structure its relationships with others, the ego experiences feelings of uneasiness and drift. This condition could be characterized as an "anomic" state, since the ego is confused about which values and norms should influence its decisions. Herbert McClosky and John Schaar have offered compelling evidence for the view that anxiety stemming from interferences with the learning process increases anomic feelings, a sense that the world and oneself are adrift, lacking the guidance of general rules and stable foundations. Those who feel anxious about themselves tend to project their own sense of confusion onto the society at large. "Their inner anxiety spills over onto the outer world," the authors conclude, "and they tend to project upon the external world the doubts and fears that dominate their own mental life. They see the society as uncertain, confused, lacking in clear standards and direction—in short, as anomic."[58]

Erikson refers to the period when the ego's identity is formed as a "psychosocial moratorium." During this stage of development the individual is relatively free from other commitments; he is free to form his own identity. Through his participation in society, the adolescent begins to differentiate himself from his parents, who have been the chief objects of his identification, and from his peers. If the child has successfully identified with his parents, then the ego-ideal will be well enough developed so that the ego will have a direction from which to begin the process of differentiation. However, when the ego-ideal is underdeveloped, the child will not resolve the identity crisis and the development of the personality consequently becomes fixed at that stage. Under these circumstances, identity diffusion is carried over into adulthood, leaving the ego weak in relation to the id, the conscience, and the external world.

The existence of severe identity diffusion makes the ego susceptible to a strong identification with a leader. As in the case of extreme intrapsychic distance, the follower substitutes the leader for his ego-ideal. In the situation elaborated by Freud, the leader replaces an ego-ideal that incorporated goals the follower's ego could not hope to achieve; whereas, under conditions of intense identity diffusion, the leader becomes a substitute for an underdeveloped ego-ideal. In the latter case, identification with the leader offers relief from the anxiety caused by the absence of firmly entrenched values and norms. By identifying with the leader, the follower unconsciously reestablishes the psychosocial moratorium in order to gain additional time to form an identity. The leader is idealized through the follower's imputation of special qualities and powers to him, which he had imputed to his parents at an earlier time. In addition, the follower returns to a state of submissiveness to authority that gives him the necessary freedom and security to discover who he is. In this sense, charisma, which includes identification, the imputation of special gifts, and submissiveness as important follower orientations to leadership, can and should be viewed as a relationship growing out of a follower's need to reestablish the psychosocial moratorium.

These causes of charisma—extreme intrapsychic distance and identity diffusion—show that the charismatic relationship can be beneficial to the follower. Through identification with and submission to the leader, the ego strength of the follower may be increased. By providing new goals that either reduce intrapsychic distance or create a positive identity, the leader enhances the follower's confidence and self-esteem. More confident of himself in his social relationships, the follower increases his level of activities, communications, and exchanges in social life. In turn, greater self-confidence and social contacts increase the ego's feeling of trust, especially as it sees the importance of specific norms in governing human relations, such as reciprocity, for example.

Braced by confidence and trust, the follower who was completely dependent on the leader for guidance can become more independent and autonomous. Having internalized the leader's ideals to the point where they have become differentiated from the person of the leader, the follower's ego comes under the control of the newly internalized ego-ideal. Under these conditions, the ego no longer needs to look to the leader for direction, since it has established itself as the coordinating agency of the psychic apparatus in harmony with the new ego-ideal. From this point of view, the charismatic relationship should be understood as a temporary regression to an earlier developmental stage for many followers. Relating to the leader on a charismatic basis provides the follower with a second chance to attain maturity, a chance to develop an ego sufficiently strong that it can successfully mediate the conflicts that arise between the id, the superego, and the external world. Therefore, the charismatic relationship, which has traditionally been seen in a negative light, has a positive side with respect to the development of the follower's personality.

Psychic Tension and the Formation of the Charismatic Commitment

Extreme intrapsychic distance and identity diffusion are causal factors that produce tension within the personality. Consequently, both fall within Stage I of the commitment process and thus should be considered necessary, but not sufficient, conditions for the formation of a charismatic commitment. It should be clear that intrapsychic tension arising from these two conflicts can be relieved in numerous ways. The individual under tension from extreme intrapsychic distance might revise his goals (perhaps through professional treatment) to more closely correspond to his capabilities. Or he might join an organization with an authoritarian structure in order to escape from decision-making, thus reducing pressure on the ego. On the other hand, the person suffering from extreme identity diffusion may solve his problems by excessive conformity, or through deviance and drugs.

Whether or not these two sources of tension will be reduced by a strong identification with and commitment to a leader depends to a great extent on the social situation. If we assume that the charismatic commitment is an active rather than passive relationship, then the other determinants of commitment must be considered. Persons experiencing extreme intrapsychic tension can identify with a leader who is geographically distant and yet fail to act in conformity to his initiatives. Identification of this type, without action, I shall call a passive charismatic relationship, but it is not a charismatic commitment until the identification is linked with action that conforms to the leader's initiatives. For it is by observing action that we decide whether a charismatic commitment exists and how strong it is.

Before extreme intrapsychic tension culminates in an enduring charismatic commitment, the person must be available for action. He must be relatively free to respond to the initiatives of the leader. In terms of my earlier remarks, he will be free to act (1) when he is between activities, (2) when his conscience does not directly prohibit conformity to the leader's initiatives, (3) when his resource capacity is great enough so that action can be taken above and beyond that necessary for survival, and (4) when his group affiliations are such that a commitment to the leader is not openly discouraged. Therefore, individuals who suffer from extreme intrapsychic tension might identify with a leader from afar (passive charisma), but the charismatic commitment (active charisma) will tend not to form when individuals are deeply invested in an activity, have doubts about the ethical consequences of some of the leader's initiatives, have no time or energy to act, or are restrained by their group affiliations. But even when availability is high, there must still be an opportunity to act, which leads us to a brief discussion of Stage III in the commitment process.

In the formation of a charismatic commitment, the opportunity for action is apt to be greater than strictly transactional relationships because the follower who identifies with a leader can transform his behavioral pattern without necessarily exchanging tangible goods with the leader. For example, the follower who experiences extreme intrapsychic tension and who is available for action can act when the leader initiates a new moral code that can be put immediately into practice, no matter how distant the leader and the opportunities for organizational activity. Such limited demands can be easily fulfilled, but when the leader requires more tangible transactions of the follower, the opportunity for action may still not be available, depending on the accessibility of the organization.

The psychological exchanges that occur between leader and follower at Stage IV of the commitment process reduce the follower's, and possibly the leader's, psychic suffering. For the follower, the consistent acceptance of the leader's initiatives stems from his strong identification with the leader as his ego-ideal, resulting in a loss of his critical capacity and a desire to submit himself to the authority of the leader. If this occurs, if the charismatic commitment is formed, we must assume that the relationship satisfies certain of the follower's psychological needs and is consequently gratifying. Under these conditions, the commitment will be maintained as long as the follower's intrapsychic conflicts persist and the leader is able to function as the follower's ego-ideal. In the case of identity diffusion, the charismatic commitment may actually strengthen the follower's ego to such a degree that independence from the leader is possible without causing a recurrence of extreme intrapsychic tension. When this happens, the strength of the charismatic commitment can be reduced or terminated entirely.

The Charismatic Leader and Social Change

So far in my discussion of the charismatic relationship, I have concentrated on the tensions within the follower's personality. But an equally significant consideration is the leader's personality disposition. Earlier, I attempted to demonstrate how the expressive relationship between leader and follower is symbiotic. As I tried to show in the analysis of Hitler and Goebbels, the psychological exchange that takes place may be as fundamental for the leader's personality as for the follower's. In this sense, the charismatic relationship can be a two-way exchange in which the leader comes to see himself as charismatic and lives from day to day on the deferential treatment he sees as rightfully his. Weber failed to consider this aspect of charisma largely because he was interested in viewing personal authority as it arose from the state of the follower's mind. And even when he discussed the demise of charisma in the face of rational-legal developments, there was no suggestion that the leader's personality would affect the ease with which the transition was made. However, both Devereux and Mitscherlich mention aspects of the charismatic leader's personality, following a rising tide of psychoanalytic studies of leadership.[59] Devereux notes the infantilism of the leader's behavior and his sense of dependence on subordinates and his general following. Some charismatic leaders may have been infantile and dependent long before they rose to eminence, he argues, while others become so after power has been bestowed upon them.[60] Mitscherlich emphasizes the charismatic leader's delusions of grandeur and personal power, which are manifestations of megalomania[61] (the fusion of the ego and ego-ideal). There is a hint that the causes that produce the charismatic relationship for the follower are the same for the leader who comes to believe that he is endowed with superhuman qualities, omitting the case wherein charisma arises from the enculturation process (as in traditional societies).

When a leader develops beliefs that he is infallible and indispensable to a social movement or nation, then the institutionalization of charismatic authority is inhibited or made impossible except by assassination, *coup d'état,* or counter-revolution. Hitler is the most striking example of a personality who could not have relinquished his personal authority except by involuntary means. One even suspects that for this personality type there is an inner gratification that comes with defeat, a sense of satisfaction for being punished for one's inability to control the evil side of the personality.[62]

David Apter's argument that, at a certain stage of political development, charisma becomes dysfunctional for further modernization[63] raises a number of important questions. Why are some charismatic leaders unable to routinize their personal authority? Why are some able to tolerate dissent while others appear anxious to crush all opposition? Why do some develop goals for their movements and nations that appear so unrealistic that they are self-defeating? In one study, Thomas Dow, Jr., has attempted to describe the problems of the conversion of charismatic leadership into rational-legal patterns in both Kenya and Ghana, but without first considering the personality dispositions of Kenyatta and Nkrumah as they affected transition. A hint that psychological factors were crucial is to be found in the radically different behavioral patterns of the two men. In Ghana, "political personalities—potential threats to Nkrumah's personal leadership—were nonexistent save as they were on the way to becoming non-persons." This oppression of opposition is explained by Dow, not in psychological terms, but as stemming from Nkrumah's "attempt to achieve 300 years of economic growth in 20 years."[64] But how can he explain the fact that such an unrealistic goal was formulated in the first place? In Kenya, on the other hand,

Kenyatta has provided rights of free association and criticism, granted some autonomy to the labor unions and press, and, most important, has allowed the development of a political opposition, suggesting a different psychological disposition entirely.

If we accept the view that charisma is an affective relation with strong psychological underpinnings, a position that I think Dow would not dispute,[65] then the study of the routinization of charisma might fruitfully consider the following. First, a careful analysis could be undertaken to determine the functions the charismatic relationship performs in maintaining balance within the leader's personality. Second, the analyst could consider the changes that are necessary or inevitable in the charismatic relationship for continued political development, and the possible consequences of those changes on the balance of forces within the leader's personality. And, third, consideration could then be given to the possible functional substitutes available to the leader for readjusting the internal balance of forces within his personality as the charismatic relationship is altered.

Weber's primary intention was to formulate a conception of authority that was personal and non-institutional. His analysis of charisma was intended to explain the basis of this type of rule as it emerged in periods of change. Yet, by reference to charismatic office and, more broadly, the routinization of charisma, he was alluding to a different aspect of personal authority. Regarding routinization, Weber has suggested:

> Charisma is a phenomenon typical of prophetic religious movements or of expansive political movements in their early stages. But as soon as the position of authority is well established, and above all as soon as control over large masses of people exists, it gives way to the forces of everyday routine.[66]

In the process of charismatic routinization the personal aura of the leader is transferred to office or status in an effort to achieve a greater degree of structural cohesiveness. Most frequently, charisma adheres to offices that are transcendental, such as are occupied by the Pope or bishops, and is attained through a process of succession that requires appointment by leader or tribunal. Also, succession to charismatic positions can become hereditary, typified by the caste system in India wherein deference is traditionally bestowed on special castes, or in many African tribes in which the charisma of office is reserved for those of select lineages.

Weber's allusion to the routinization of charisma seems strangely out of line with the dominant elements of his analysis. These elements, which emphasize the personal and non-institutional aspects of charisma, appear to be contradicted by his views concerning the institutionalized aspects of charismatic office. As one author asserts, "to speak of a permanently charismatic legitimacy is on the basis of Weber's own analysis to come to a contradiction of terms."[67] However, if we assume that Weber was consciously identifying two dimensions of charismatic authority—one non-institutional-ized and the other institutionalized—then the contradiction seems less significant, for both may produce personal authority, albeit by different routes. In essence, two types of charismatic authority emerge: Revolutionary charisma, wherein the follower's commitment is directly to the person of the leader, and institutionalized charisma, wherein the aura of the leader is bestowed on his ascension to office. If charisma becomes institutionalized, Robert Tucker argues, the charisma of the leader is passed on to a chosen successor whose function is to preserve the memory of the deceased. Through the routinization process, "the charisma of the founder of a religious move-ment survives, insofar as it survives at all, primarily in the cult of the founder, the revering of his memory by the followers who live after."[68] Yet, at times, charismatic offices may not emerge from the death of a charismatic leader at all, but from custom. For example, in the Ashanti tribe in Ghana the charisma of the chief is rooted in the customary belief that ancestors can communicate with the living through the tribal leader. This case would directly contradict Tucker's view that institutionalized charisma necessarily develops as a cult to revere a former charismatic figure.

Unlike its revolutionary counterpart, institutionalized charisma may actually be a conserving influence, as it is in the Ashanti tribe. This view Tucker fails to consider seriously, owing to the fact that he concentrated on the innovative features of charismatic authority.[69] Yet both the revolu-tionary and conservative dimensions of charisma are apparent in Weber's view that "the immediate effect of charisma is strongly revolutionary; indeed, often destructive, because it means new modes of orientation. But in case the process of routinization leads in the direction of traditionalism, its ultimate effect may be exactly the reverse."[70] Viewing non-institutionalized and institutionalized charisma as separate categories within a broader conception of charismatic authority has important analytic consequences. First of all, it requires a more careful refinement of the determinants of personal authority. Revolutionary charisma appears to be caused by extreme intrapsychic tension, while institutionalized charisma can emerge through an enculturation process that instills charismatic deference as a cognitive and affective element in "normal" personalities during "normal" times. It was in this context that I referred earlier to the charismatic leader as the "spokesman" for tradition. In considering the socialization process, the charismatic relationship is still viewed as a function of the follower's per-sonality, although it is understood in terms of custom and cultural rein-forcements. If charisma is culturally sanctioned and reinforced, it must be analyzed in somewhat different terms from revolutionary charisma, which is apparently more fluid and of shorter duration.

How these two aspects of personal authority are related is important for future studies of charismatic leadership. In this sense, it would be useful to examine the emergence of non-institutionalized charisma in environments in which its institutional counterpart is present and where it is insignificant. This would help us to determine: (1) the conditions under which revolutionary charisma is transformed into charismatic office and vice versa; (2) the conditions under which institutionalized charisma reinforces an already existing non-institutionalized charismatic relationship (a phenomenon seemingly operative in some African nations in which modernizing leaders have apparently received a residual benefit from traditional habits of charismatic deference to tribal chiefs); and (3) the conditions under which the institutionalized type inhibits the emergence of revolutionary charisma, for example, the strained relations between the Pope's institutionalized charisma and Mussolini's non-institutionalized base in Fascist Italy. Within a society plagued by structural strains, the counterbalance of institutionalized charisma can act as a conserving force. But if charisma is institutionalized as an office in rebel cults, such as in the Nation of Islam, we should expect the leader to draw upon his transcendental source of authority to make change, not prevent it.

I have said that the basis of charisma is the follower's belief in the God-like qualities of the leader, whether imputed to the leader or bestowed on him by office. In both these cases, Weber failed to explain the follower's tendency to identify a transcendental source of power from which the leader is thought to derive his special qualities and capabilities. The role of the transcendental in non-institutionalized charismatic relationships can be tentatively explained in terms of the earlier psychological interpretation of charisma. Seeking some way to either reduce the distance between his ego and ego-ideal or to find a positive identity, the follower legitimizes the leader's authority by clothing the leader in the sanctifying garments of a transcendental source of power. Seeing the leader as God's spokesman or as chosen by history to work out a plan of destiny gives the follower a rationalization for developing a strong identification with the leader. In this regard, submission and obedience to the leader can be placed in a moral context since it is necessary for working out a master plan that will produce the good life. From the psychological perspective, this sanctification of the leader provides a moral justification for gratifying instinctual drives when the goals and moral code of the leader make them socially acceptable behaviors, for example, Hitler making aggressive feelings and actions toward Jews socially respectable.

On the other hand, in the case of institutionalized charisma, a sufficiently compelling reinforcement of the follower's control mechanisms (especially repression) can occur when the leader's goals and moral code oppose the reign of the id. There are some types of charismatic office in which the conserving aspect of the transcendental source of power is clearly related to reinforcing controls that keep the personality of the follower in balance. Instead of God being the advocate of war, he is the advocate of peace through his emissary on earth.

Normally, the tendency is to suggest that a non-institutional type of charisma in its pure form is innovative because it unleashes the follower's id on the world. But, in fact, what appears to be non-institutionalized charisma on the surface can encompass both innovative and conservative tendencies. It may allow a freer reign of the id, but within certain moral limits. For example, in social movements in which the charismatic relationship exists for some followers, the sanctification of the leader can actually provide both possibilities for followers. Those who develop the charismatic tie may discover new avenues for the release of aggression, while at the same time they find a new basis for control. This is clearly the case in semi-religious movements, such as the Southern Christian Leadership Conference, wherein Martin Luther King, Jr., encouraged action against authority (giving freer reign to the follower's repressed hostility against whites), but who also emphasized the need for self-control. In this latter respect, his philosophy of nonviolence placed limitations on the aggressiveness that he had aroused in his following. Conversely, a leader who derives his personal authority from a charismatic office, such as Elijah Muhammad, might be innovative at the same time that he recommends caution. Thus, it should be clear that revolutionary charisma and the charisma of office are likely to incorporate both innovative and conservative tendencies, depending largely on the environments in which they exist and the times. The role of the social analyst is to determine how the innovative and conservative tendencies are distributed within a single case in which the charismatic commitment is identifiable.

In closing this section, it should also be pointed out that the transcendental referents acceptable to followers vary. Some followers are able to rationalize their commitment to the leader by reference to his relationship to God, others to history, and still others to race (or sanctification by nature). Within a single social movement, for example, followers can clothe their leader in essentially different sanctifying garments. One follower glorifies the leader as a direct descendent of God come to save the world from evil, while his atheistic companion praises the leader as the representative of a superior race.

Distinguishing Charismatic from Inspirational Leadership

One of my chief concerns in this chapter was to focus on the basic differences between charismatic and transactional bases of personal rule. Now, another distinction should be drawn between the charismatic and inspirational aspects of leadership. Given the narrower interpretation of charisma developed above, the reader might wonder what to call those leaders, such as John F. Kennedy and Martin Luther King, Jr., who appeared to generate enthusiastic support but seemed to perform the ego-ideal function for only a small group of fanatical types. In large measure, such leaders are inspirational, for their utopian themes and personal example provided meaning to action and purpose to suffering for many individuals who would be considered "normal" personalities. In terms of my analysis of expressive functions, these leaders performed the inspirational function effectively.

In common usage, the tendency has been to apply the "charismatic" label to those who are inspirational types. In fact, Dorothy Emmet has gone so far as to suggest that charisma is more applicable to leaders who provide inspiration than to those who possess a hypnotic hold over their followers.[71] My view is that all leaders with charismatic followings inspire, but not all inspirational leaders have extensive charismatic followings. In contradistinction to Emmet's position, I would prefer to maintain the core meaning given to charisma by Weber and to develop a separate category called "inspirational leadership."

The major point of distinction between charismatic and inspirational types is to be found in the source of the follower's disposition to accept the leader's initiatives. The follower who relates to a purely secular leader on a charismatic basis resolves intrapsychic tensions by identifying with the leader and forming a strong commitment to his person, revealed by the consistent and unquestioning obedience the follower gives to the leader's personal desires. This binding relationship is also apparent in the follower's incapacity to criticize the leader and in the tendency to impute God-given powers to him. On the other hand, the follower who relates to the leader on an inspirational basis suffers from a crisis of meaning. In the inspirational relationship, the follower perceives the leader to be enlightened and sensitive to the problems permeating the society. The leader is not perceived as a demigod and the follower consequently maintains his capacity to criticize the leader's behavior. Both leader and follower share a common set of impressions about what is wrong with society. Instead of the leader replacing the follower's ego-ideal, he represents very similar goals and beliefs that he articulates in a public fashion. Orrin Klapp describes the emergence of a "symbolic leader" in much the same terms: "A symbolic leader moves people through his image, the kind of man he seems to be, the style of life or attitude he symbolizes."[72]

Viewed as one of several determinants of personal authority, the concept of charisma can assume a precise role in the examination of leader-follower relations. Conceived as a psychological relationship, charisma should provide an analytic foundation for investigating strongly affective commitments to popular rebel leaders or leaders in general. In this sense, charisma may enlarge our understanding of the emotionally fanatical follower, but it has only marginal utility for assessing the motives of a larger number of followers who relate to the leader on a strictly inspirational or transactional basis. In the latter case, the emergence of personal rule can be better analyzed in terms of the concrete interests of followers and the leader's potential power to persuade and to punish. In the final analysis, the confusion surrounding the application of charisma in the social sciences is not rooted solely in the apparent ambiguities of its meaning, but also in our inadequate understanding of the diverse determinants of personal rule.

Notes

1. Hans Gerth and C. Wright Mills (eds.), *From Max Weber: Essays in Sociology* (New York: Oxford University Press, 1946), p. 249.

2. Max Weber, *The Theory of Social and Economic Organization* (New York: Free Press, 1946), p. 357.

3. Weber in Gerth and Mills (eds.), *op. cit.,* p. 246.

4. Weber, *op. cit.,* pp. 359–360.

5. Weber in Gerth and Mills (eds.), *op. cit.,* p. 246.

6. *Ibid.,* p. 53.

7. K. J. Ratnam, "Charisma and Political Leadership," *Political Studies,* 12 (October, 1964), p. 344.

8. David Apter, *Ghana In Transition* (New York: Atheneum, 1963), p 174

9. John T. Marcus, "Transcendentalism and Charisma," *Western Political Quarterly,* 14 (March, 1961), p. 237.

10. *Ibid.,* p. 238.

11. Carl Friedrich, "Political Leadership and the Problem of Charismatic Power," *Journal of Politics,* 23 (February, 1961), p. 19.

12. Richard Fagen, "Charismatic Authority and the Leadership of Fidel Castro," *Western Political Quarterly,* 18 (June, 1965), pp. 278–282.

13. Friedrich, *op. cit.,* p. 12.

14. Edward Shils, "The Concentration and Dispersion of Charisma," *World Politics,* 11 (October, 1958), p. 4.

15. Edward Shils, "Charisma, Order, and Status," *American Sociological Review,* 30 (April, 1965), p. 209.

16. *Ibid.,* p. 206.

17. For a good discussion of these relationships, cf. Richard Neustadt, *Presidential Power: The Politics of Leadership* (New York: John Wiley & Sons, 1960).

18. W. G. Runciman, "Charismatic Legitimacy and One-Party Rule in Ghana," *European Journal of Sociology,* 4 (1963), p. 154.

19. Irving Horowitz, "Party Charisma: Political Practices and Principles in the Third World Nations," *Indian Sociological Bulletin,* 3 (October, 1965), pp. 53–74.

20. Alex Simirenko, "Critique of Party Charisma," *Indian Sociological Bulletin,* 3 (October, 1965), pp. 75–78.

21. Ann Gifford adopts a similar position in her examination of Gandhi's charismatic appeal. His charisma was based in part on his success in crystalizing and providing the appropriate means for attaining independence, a pre-existing goal for Indians in general. Cf. "An Application of Weber's Concept of Charisma," *Berkeley Publications in Society and Institutions,* 1 (Spring, 1955), pp. 40–49. For an application of charisma to the *Bhoodan Gramdan* movement in India, cf. T. K. Oommen, "Charisma, Social Structure and Social Change," *The Comparative Study of Society and History,* 10 (October, 1967), pp. 85–89.

22. Ratnam, *op. cit.,* p. 345.

23. *Ibid.,* p. 354.

24. Now a part of Tanzania.

25. William Friedland, "For A Sociological Concept of Charisma," *Social Forces,* 43 (October, 1964), p. 23.

26. *Ibid.,* p. 25. A somewhat different point of view is offered by Ann Ruth Willner and Dorothy Willner to explain the development of deferential attitudes among followers. They argue that charisma emerges through the leader's ability to draw on and manipulate the body of myth in a given culture and the values associated with those myths. The charisma of the leader is tied to the feelings and thoughts of the public as it relates to its sacred figures, divine beings, or heroes. By associating with these sacred images, the charismatic leader elicits follower deference and devotion. Cf. "The Rise and Role of Charismatic Leaders," *Annals,* 358 (1965), pp. 77–88. A similar argument can be found in Orrin E. Klapp's *Symbolic Leaders* (Chicago: Aldine Press, 1964). However, Klapp does not equate symbolic aspects of leadership with charisma. This position seems preferable to that advanced by Willner and Willner, where one is never completely convinced that they are describing charismatic leadership, since many non-charismatic types may utilize symbols for building support.

27. Gunther Roth, "Personal Rulership, Patrimonialism, and Empire-Building in the New States," *World Politics,* 20 (January, 1968), p. 196.

28. *Ibid.,* p. 199.

29. *Ibid.,* p. 200.

30. Ratnam offers a similar criticism. *Op. cit.,* p. 345. For a more extensive critical analysis of charisma, cf. Harold Wolfe, "A Critical Analysis of Some Aspects of Charisma," *Sociological Review,* 16 (November, 1968), pp. 305–318.

31. Marcus, *op. cit.,* pp. 237–240.

32. Simirenko, *op. cit.,* p. 76.

33. Apter, *op. cit.,* p. 304.

34. Cf. Theodore Sorenson, *Decision-Making in the White House* (New York: Columbia University Press, 1963); and Neustadt, *op. cit.*

35. Sigmund Freud, *Group Psychology and the Analysis of the Ego* (New York: Bantam Books, 1960).

36. *Ibid.,* p. 82.

37. *Ibid.*

38. For a complete discussion of psychological defenses and their importance in assessing psychological disturbances, cf. Anna Freud, *The Ego and the Mechanisms of Defense* (London: Hogarth Press, 1937).

39. Freud, *op. cit.,* p. 56.

40. *Ibid.,* p. 57.

41. *Ibid.,* p. 56.

42. This point is made by George Devereux in his work, "Charismatic Leadership and Crisis," in Warner Muensterberger and Sidney Axelrod (eds.), *Psychoanalysis and the Social Sciences* (New York: International Universities Press, 1955), p. 153.

43. Freud, *op. cit.,* p. 79.

44. Weber, *The Theory of Social and Economic Organization, op. cit.,* p. 363.

45. Devereux, *op. cit.,* pp. 145–156 and Alexander Mitscherlich, "Changing Patterns of Authority: A Psychiatric Interpretation," in Lewis J. Edinger (ed.), *Political Leadership in Industrialized Societies* (New York: John Wiley & Sons, 1967), pp. 26–58.

46. Devereux, *ibid.,* p. 147.

47. *Ibid.,* pp. 149–150.

48. Mitscherlich, *op. cit.,* p. 52. Hadley Cantril has discussed this reaction in terms of suggestion. He argues that "a person is susceptible to suggestion when (1) he has no adequate mental context for the interpretation of a given stimulus or event or (2) when his mental context is so rigidly fixed that a stimulus is automatically judged by means of this context and without any examination of the stimulus itself. The first condition results from bewilderment; the second from the 'will to believe'." Cf. *The Psychology of Social Movements* (New York: John Wiley & Sons, 1963), p. 64.

49. *Ibid.,* p. 57. Leo Lowenthal and Norbert Guterman have reached a similar conclusion: "Taking advantage of all the weaknesses of the present social order, the agitator intensifies his listeners' sense of bewilderment and helplessness, terrifies them with the specter of innumerable dangerous enemies and reduces their already crumbling individualism to bundles of reactive responses. He drives them into a moral void in which their inner voice of conscience is replaced by an externalized conscience: the agitator himself. He becomes the indispensable guide in a confused world, the center around which the faithful can gather and find safety. He comforts the sufferers of malaise, takes over the responsibility of history and becomes the exterior replacement of their disintegrated individuality. They live through him." Cf. "Self-Portrait of the Fascist Agitator," in Alvin Gouldner (ed.), *Studies in Leadership* (New York: Harper & Brothers, 1950), p. 99.

50. Mitscherlich, *op. cit.,* p. 34.

51. James C. Davies, "Charisma in the 1952 Campaign," *American Political Science Review,* 48 (December, 1954), pp. 1083–1102.

52. *Ibid.,* p. 1089.

53. For example, cf. T. W. Adorno *et al., The Authoritarian Personality* (New York: Harper & Brothers, 1950); R. Christie and Marie Johoda (eds.), *Studies in the Scope and Method of "The Authoritarian Personality"* (Glencoe, Ill.: Free Press, 1954); and Milton Rokeach, *The Open and Closed Mind* (New York: Basic Books, 1960).

54. Carl Rogers, *Client-Centered Therapy* (Boston: Houghton Mifflin, 1951), p. 501.

55. Erik Erikson, "The Problems of Ego Identity," in Maurice Stein, Arthur Vadich, and David Manning White (eds.), *Identity and Anxiety* (New York: Free Press, 1962), p. 75.

56. Erik Erikson, *Identity, Youth, and Crisis* (New York: W. W. Norton, 1968), p. 314.

57. Erik Erikson, *Young Man Luther* (New York: W. W. Norton, 1958), p. 15.

58. Herbert McClosky and John Schaar, "Psychological Dimensions of Anomy," *American Sociological Review,* 30 (October, 1965), p. 29. The anomic state as characterized by McClosky and Schaar is very similar to identity diffusion. Factors such as feelings of inferiority, guilt, fear, and generalized feelings of suspicion and mistrust are associated with both theoretical concepts. For example, Erikson has

argued that incomplete identifications in the early stages of development, owing to lack of maternal support, produce the conditions in which the child's ego develops suspicious feelings about social relations and mistrustful attitudes toward others. The feeling of mistrust is also found to correlate positively with extreme feelings of anomy in the McClosky and Schaar study. They found that individuals with generalized feelings of suspicion and mistrust scored much higher on the anomy scale than those who trusted others. Only 6.3 per cent of those with a great deal of trust in people scored high on the anomy scale, as compared to 49.3 per cent of those manifesting very little trust in others. This seems to suggest that identity diffusion and anomy touch upon very similar psychological states.

59. An excellent example of this approach is E. Victor Wolfenstein, *The Revolutionary Personality* (Princeton: Princeton University Press, 1967).

60. Devereux, *op. cit.,* pp. 150–151.

61. Mitscherlich, *op. cit.,* p. 29.

62. This might help to explain the tendency for such types to set goals that are clearly unrealistic and self-defeating. In the same vein, Gandhi's policy of non-violence has been discussed by one author as a form of self-punishment for reducing guilt. Cf. Wolfenstein, *op. cit.,* p. 238.

63. Apter, *op. cit.,* p. 333.

64. Thomas Dow, Jr., "The Role of Charisma in Modern African Development," *Social Forces,* 46 (March, 1969), p. 337.

65. For example, Dow argues at one point in his analysis that "Weber may have overstressed the extent to which immediate objective success, that is, direct benefit to the followers, is necessary for sustained support. The African experience provides ample evidence of long periods in which the followers did not benefit, and yet devotion and faith in the leader were not diminished in like proportion. The explanation may be that the relationship between leader and follower is after all affective and not directly linked to objective evidences of success." *Ibid.,* ff. 7, p. 329.

66. Weber, *op. cit.,* p. 370.

67. Runciman, *op. cit.,* p. 151.

68. Robert C. Tucker, "The Theory of Charismatic Leadership," *Daedalus,* 97 (Summer, 1968), p. 754.

69. For a criticism of Tucker's position, cf. Stanley Stark, "Toward A Psychology of Charisma: The Innovation Viewpoint of Robert Tucker," *Psychological Reports,* 23 (1968), pp. 1163–1166.

70. Weber, *op. cit.,* p. 373.

71. Dorothy Emmet, *Function, Purpose and Powers* (New York: Macmillan, 1958), p. 242.

72. Klapp, *op. cit.,* p. 23.

7 □ THE SEARCH FOR IDENTITY THROUGH CHARISMA

□   One of the criticisms that can be advanced against the theory of charisma introduced in the last chapter is that, owing to its psychological character, it cannot easily be proven true or false. Indeed, this is not only a reasonable challenge of my theoretical account of charisma, it is also a direct attack on the utility of the concept of charisma itself. What constitutes a proof of the theory the reader must decide for himself, since an acceptable proof is determined by the consensus of many persons analyzing the same body of data. Therefore, you will have to decide for yourself whether the data offered in this chapter are sufficient proof of the theory. If it is judged not to be, then we will all be forced to ask ourselves whether we should not disregard the concept of charisma entirely. Thus, in either event, some good will come from my effort.

Since there are several sources of ego weakness that serve as stimuli for psychological exchanges, it must be assumed that there are also several sources of psychic conflict from which charismatic commitments might develop. These have been discussed briefly in terms of the charismatic leader as "comforter" (the provider of praise and security); as the "ideal" (a new model of behavior); and as the "spokesman" (the external representative of custom that regulates day-to-day routine). These three categories represent tendencies that are distributed in different proportion in different types of charismatic relations. In actual fact, all these sources of charisma are likely to influence the formation of the charismatic relationship, but in different degrees. Especially relevant to my immediate concern is the fact that the "comforter" role of the expressive leader reduces intrapsychic distance, while his capacity as the follower's "ideal" solves the problems of identity diffusion stemming from the incomplete development of the ego-ideal. In reality, intrapsychic distance and identity diffusion, which I have described as two separate sources of the charismatic bond, might be better seen as two facets of a single source. Therefore, while psychic distance appears to have been the major problem within the psychic structure of Goebbels, closer examination would probably show the presence of identity diffusion of some intensity. In looking at a single case, it is a matter of deciding which of these two problems—intrapsychic distance or identity diffusion—was the dominant cause of the formation of the charismatic commitment. The "comforter" aspects of the leader's expressive function have already been treated rather extensively in Chapter 2 where I discussed the psychological exchanges between Goebbels and Hitler, though their strong affective relationship was not directly tied to the formation of the charismatic commitment. In this chapter, primary attention will be placed on the charismatic leader as the follower's "ideal," especially as it pertains to the relationship between Malcolm X and Elijah Muhammad within the Black Muslim movement.

First, let us begin with a general hypothesis around which the remainder of the chapter will revolve. *Individuals suffering from extreme identity diffusion will be susceptible to the formation of a charismatic relationship when they are free to develop new commitments.* To test this hypothesis data will be drawn from *The Autobiography of Malcolm X,* a work that includes a rich body of data from all stages of Malcolm's life. Utilizing Erik Erikson's analytic approach, we shall see the extent to which Malcolm suffered from identity diffusion and how, when the other determinants of commitment were present, this mental crisis led him to develop a strong personal attachment to Mr. Muhammad, the primary leader of the Black Muslim movement. However, before I can make the connection between identity diffusion and the formation of the charismatic bond, it is necessary to trace quite thoroughly the development of identity diffusion in Malcolm's life. Thus, the hypothesis offered above will command our undivided attention only at a later point in the chapter.

A Method for Assessing the Extent of Identity Diffusion

In his various works,[1] Erikson has discussed the general factors that accompany extreme identity diffusion and has provided the corresponding specific indicators. With these indicators, he has given us a useful tool for collecting and organizing data from biographical and autobiographical sources.[2] Furthermore, his method can be utilized to test the hypothesized connection between extreme identity diffusion and charisma.

The factors and indicators that follow were developed by Erikson to correspond to the different stages in the development of the personality. Using his guidelines, we will be able to see in a specific case how extreme identity diffusion develops out of early socialization patterns and how it manifests itself in adult life.

Factor I: During infancy, mistrust predominates over trust.

Indicators: 1.   Evidence of a lack of continuous and consistent maternal support during infancy.
2.   Evidence of early traumatic experiences.
3.   Evidence of the infant's discontent and the presence of aggressive and hostile tendencies.

Factor II: During early childhood, shame and doubt predominate over feelings of autonomy.

Indicators: 1.   Evidence of a lack of consistent and coherent hierarchy of roles and rules provided by relationships within the family.
2.   Evidence of introversion rather than outgoing experimentation.

Factor III: During the play and early school age, guilt and inferiority predominate over industry.[3]

Indicators: 1.   Evidence of an inability to concentrate on any required or suggested task, or preoccupation with some self-defeating activity.
2.   Evidence of a feeling of being completely exposed and extremely self-conscious and ashamed.
3.   Evidence of little or no engagement with others, except with the most unlikely partners.
4.   Evidence of inferiority and guilt.
5.   Evidence of a lack of established models for identification.
6.   Evidence of doubt in one's own judgment and a resulting difficulty in decision-making. In severe cases, evidence of paranoic fears.

Factor IV: During adolescence, identity diffusion predominates over identity.

Indicators: 1.   Evidence of inferiority, lack of confidence, introversion, lack of mutuality, and a lack of solidarity or trust.
2.   Evidence of a lack of self-definition and extreme self-consciousness.
3.   Evidence of a fear of committing oneself to any path or direction, manifest in fears of social relations, such as close friendships.
4.   Evidence of skepticism whether the future holds any hope of positive change.
5.   Evidence of a readiness to repudiate, to ignore, or to

destroy those forces and people that appear dangerous.

Factor V: During young adulthood, isolation predominates over intimacy.

Indicators: 1. Evidence of little engagement with others.
                2. Evidence of an attempt to divide one's environment into two camps: good and evil.
                3. Evidence of an excessive contempt for one's background (religious, ethnic, or national origins).
                4. Evidence of a scornful hostility toward the roles offered as proper and desirable by one's own family or immediate community.

Factor VI: During adulthood, self-absorption predominates over generativity.

Indicators: 1. Evidence of extreme concern for the self and little concern for, or feeling of responsibility toward, one's peers or the next generation.

Although one factor may be associated with a single stage in Erikson's design, he cautions the reader to look for recurrences at advanced stages. For example, while mistrust is identified with infancy, it will predominate over trust in each of the succeeding stages of development. The same would be true for inferiority and aggressiveness against assumed enemies.

Factor I: Mistrust Predominates Over Trust During Infancy

There is considerable evidence in Malcolm's autobiography of a lack of continuous and consistent maternal support during infancy and early childhood, the first indicator of the development of mistrust. That Malcolm received inadequate affection and attention from his mother stemmed from several causes. First was the size of the family. One of eight children, Malcolm suffered from a situation in which his mother was unable to form close, prolonged, and enduring relations with any of her children, especially after the death of Malcolm's father, when she was forced to work outside the home.

But there was another condition that affected Malcolm's development exclusively—his mother's expressed dislike for him in relation to the other children. This reaction stemmed from the fact that his complexion and hair were much lighter than the other children's, a constant reminder of his mother's origin. For she was the offspring of a white man who had assaulted her mother, and she was so light, as a consequence, that she could easily pass as a white woman. Any reference to her father was always in terms of the shame she felt that he had been white. This shame apparently took the form of hostility against Malcolm, the lone manifestation of her white heritage. "Thinking about it now," Malcolm recalled, "I feel definitely that just as my father favored me for being lighter than the other children, my mother gave me more hell for the same reason. She was very light herself, but she favored the ones who were darker."[4] Because his father preferred him to the others, Malcolm escaped the beatings that were given the other children. So nearly all his whippings came from his mother, a condition unlikely to generate the close maternal ties out of which trustful attitudes form.

With respect to the second indicator of mistrust, Malcolm suffered, not one, but several traumatic experiences as a child. At a very early age members of the Ku Klux Klan set fire to his home, and he watched in fear and amazement as white firemen stood by doing nothing to extinguish the flames. A short time later, his father was murdered, his skull having been crushed by a blunt instrument and his body severed almost in two by the wheels of a streetcar. After his father's death, the strains of the Great Depression and the constant harassment of welfare agents caused his mother to lose her hold on reality and she began to deteriorate mentally. During this mental crisis, the children were left to fend for themselves, until their mother was declared legally insane and confined to a state mental hospital. The children thus became wards of the court. Assigned by the state to a foster home, Malcolm was separated from the last important source of affection, his brothers and sisters.

Of these experiences, the death of Malcolm's father was to have the most dramatic impact on the development of his personality. Owing to his mother's lack of affection, Malcolm grew much more closely attached to his father than did the other children. He was the only one of the children who was allowed to accompany his father to religious and political meetings, a privilege that reflected the close ties between himself and his father. His father was thus a positive object for identification and a source from which Malcolm could be sure to draw affection. This relationship grew even in the face of constant complaints from his mother about his father's eating habits and general character, an attempt by the mother, Erikson would say, to reduce the possibility that the father would become an important object for identification. How much these criticisms affected Malcolm is difficult to say, but one thing is sure: Malcolm idealized his father, as various references in his autobiography show. (In this sense, it should not be surprising that Elijah Muhammad, who became a strong object of identification in Malcolm's later life, would be similar to his father, both being religious leaders and black nationalists.) With the early death of Malcolm's father, the process of identification was interrupted and the model of behavior so essential for the development of an ego-ideal and ego identity was lost.

That mistrust dominated Malcolm's early development can also be seen in the expression of discontent and aggressiveness in his relationships with his mother and siblings.

> I learned early that crying out in protest could accomplish things. My older brothers and sisters had started to school when, sometimes, they would come in and ask for a buttered biscuit or something and my mother, impatiently, would tell them no. But I would cry out and make a fuss until I got what I wanted. I remember well how my mother asked me why I couldn't be a nice boy like Wilfred; but I would think to myself that Wilfred, for being so nice and quiet, often stayed hungry. So early in life, I had learned that if you want something, you had better make some noise.[5]

His hostility was also directed to his brother Philbert and fighting between them became a common occurrence in the family. Later, Malcolm would find other objects for his aggressiveness, for his schooling was marked by repeated fist fights with other boys.

Malcolm's early feeling of mistrust was generalized to most of his contacts, the lone exception being his brother Reginald. From an early age he developed very affectionate relations with this brother, another factor Erikson associates with identity diffusion.[6] Malcolm characterized his relation to Reginald by saying that he was the only person who he could really trust.

Factor II: Shame and Doubt Predominate Over Feelings of Autonomy During Early Childhood

Feelings of shame and doubt come to dominate the personality when a sense of helplessness emerges, growing out of an awareness that one has almost no control over his own life. This self-judgment originates from the child's observation that his own parents have little control over events, which leads him to lose faith in his own potential to control the forces around him and thereby reduces the feeling of autonomy that is the basis for a positive ego identity.

The child becomes aware of two areas in which parental control is important. First is the parents' ability to cope with forces outside the family. In this context alone, Malcolm had ample evidence that his parents were at the mercy of the surrounding white community. Experiences, such as the burning of his home by whites, the need to move frequently to escape retribution for his father's political activities, and the freedom that whites possessed to enter the home at will must have been proof enough that his parents could not autonomously control the outer world. Later, his father's death, the refusal to honor his father's insurance policy by a white insurance company, the constant interference of welfare agents in the affairs of the family would offer further testimony that his mother was at the mercy of the white community. Any sense of autonomy that might have existed was, in fact, ended with the death of his father.

A child's development is also affected by the parents' ability to control events within the family itself. If there is no consistent and coherent hierarchy of roles and rules, the child is likely to become confused about the appropriate objects of identification and the rules out of which those identifications begin to take shape. Among the children, there appears to have been considerable confusion about both roles and rules. Role confusion stemmed from the fact that, very much against the father's will, their mother repeatedly sought to play his role as the chief figure of authority. The fact that Malcolm's father was only able to get odd jobs and was not given responsibility for a religious congregation of his own must have added to the status conflicts between his parents. And after the death of his father, role confusion remained severe as the older children and his mother assumed the responsibility that the father had assumed previously.

The competitive relationship between the mother and father also increased the father's desire to exert his authority, leading to excessive and arbitrary punishments as the rules became so proliferated that the children could not remember them all. "The older ones he would beat almost savagely if they broke any of his rules—and he had so many rules it was hard to know them all."[7] Malcolm must have sensed his parents' inability to structure the roles and rules of the family, for at an early age he had already learned how to overcome the opposition of his parents and to avoid punishment for infraction of the rules. We have already seen how he would cry to get something from his parents that others in the family were forbidden to have. In a similar way, he avoided punishments from his mother by screaming excessively. Out of these early experiences validating an absence of parental control, Malcolm was already beginning to manifest a lack of autonomy both within the family and, most important, in the outside world. This diminished sense of autonomy and the accompanying feeling of shame and doubt would show up as symptoms of inferiority in the next stage of his personal development.

Factor III: Inferiority Predominates Over Industry During the Play and Early School Age

In the period immediately following his father's death, Malcolm contributed very little to the family while others assumed major responsibility. Describing the extensive contributions of Wilfred and Hilda, he concluded his assessment of the situation by saying that "Philbert and I didn't do anything."[8] Apparently, this was also true in his role as a student, since his poor record was probably the product of early refusals to follow the assignments of his teachers. By the time he had reached the first year of junior high school he was already widely known as a mischief-maker and finally he was expelled for putting a tack on one of his teacher's chairs. Instead of industriousness, Malcolm developed a carefree attitude toward those activities the society considered valuable. This attitude is seen in the early formation of delinquent patterns of behavior, especially stealing, and

of a more general aggressive tendency, both self-defeating in their consequence. "The more I began to stay away from home and visit people and
steal from stores," recalls Malcolm, "the more aggressive I became in my
inclinations. I never wanted to wait for anything."[9]

During his early school years and later, Malcolm felt exposed and
extremely self-conscious, a condition encouraged by a society hostile to
blacks. Several references in his autobiography suggest a dominant feeling
of being picked out and picked on. He felt self-conscious when the welfare
agents made him feel that he was not a person but a thing and when they
insisted on knowing why he was different from the other children. After
a neighbor discovered that his mother cooked dandelion greens for dinner,
the word got around until he was teased by other children for eating "fried
grass," and that made him feel ashamed. And when the family was forced
to go on relief during the Great Depression, he sensed that others knew
and condemned him for it. At school, he felt that the "on relief" finger was
suddenly pointed at him, an indication of a feeling of being exposed,
self-conscious, and ashamed. Later, these feelings influenced his social
relationships a great deal, as a member of his school basketball team and
at the dances that followed each game. "Whenever our team walked into
another school's gym for the dance, with me among them, I could feel the
freeze. It would start to ease as they saw that I didn't try to mix, but stuck
close to someone on our team, or kept to myself." The exposure that
Malcolm must have felt as a youth is conveyed in his own impression of
the way others perceived him, not as a person, but a mascot. Referring to
his own school dances, this sense of being something other than human is
communicated clearly. "Even at our own school, I could sense it almost as
a physical barrier, that despite all the beaming and smiling, the mascot
wasn't supposed to dance with any of the white girls."[10] We see in this case
how the racial attitudes of the white community intensified Malcolm's
feelings of mistrust and shame that had grown out of his family environment
but that also were caused by white racism.

During his early childhood and adolescence, limited and superficial
relationships with others were combined with an absence of meaningful
models for identification. Almost from the beginning, Malcolm tended to
operate alone, avoiding any real engagement with others. When he discusses
his early friendships there is a matter-of-factness about his description that
leads one to the view that his ties with others were not close; that he avoided
opening himself up to anyone. That he makes such a point of the fact that
he could talk openly with his brother Reginald indicates that he found it
hard to reach the point of intimacy with others where real friendships form.
This tendency toward introversion can be seen in his selection of social
contacts, since he preferred to travel with others who were also isolates and
avoided contacts with females, contacts that would have forced him to
communicate. His preference for isolation is also pointed up by the pattern

of his social life at school. For, although his junior high school was predominantly black, he hardly mixed at all with his schoolmates.[11] Even his adventures as a minor delinquent were apparently carried out in isolation, a tendency that would dominate his life until his last days in Harlem.

During this period of his life, Malcolm had no replacement for his father as a model of identification. Those "successful" blacks, such as the waiters at the country club or the bootblacks at the state capitol, who were the model for some were not for Malcolm. Like so many blacks at that time, he identified very strongly with an abstract model of the successful white man, an identification that would fail to give him an enduring identity. Later, when Malcolm realized the impossibility of reaching the goals incorporated into the model of the white man, he would replace it with a model of the well-to-do black—the successful hustler.

Factor IV: Identity Diffusion Predominates Over Identity During Adolescence

Adolescence is the crucial stage in the formation of an ego identity. It was during this stage that Malcolm strove hardest to discover who he was. But his search ultimately led to a deeper crisis in his personality as he recognized the futility of trying to be white. His presence at the Swerlin's home (the detention center on the way to reform school) provided him with the important ingredients that make the search for a positive identity possible—security, freedom, and affection. It is important to note that Mrs. Swerlin, especially, conveyed a feeling of warmth that had an unmistakably positive impact on Malcolm's life, since it was during this time that he began to excel and conform to the white man's rules. Strangely enough, the detention home created a psychosocial moratorium for Malcolm at a time when he entered the stage of identity crisis.

By the time he had reached adolescence, the problems of early childhood had accumulated so that the formation of a positive ego identity was difficult, even though his successes at school and the detention center show signs that he was trying to break out of the spiral of inferiority and mistrust. Numerous experiences would prove to him that American whites could not be trusted since they were an integral part of a society that fostered the belief that all blacks were basically inferior and must be forced into inferior positions.

There is evidence that, even at the peak of his success as an athlete and student leader, Malcolm continued to suffer from feelings of inferiority, lack of confidence, and mistrust, which were expressed through his unwillingness to form close ties with others and by his tendency toward introversion generally. It was during this period that he experienced the "freeze" at his school dances and made a special point of withdrawing from close contact with whites. But it was also a time when he was motivated to excel, partly because of his admiration of Mrs. Swerlin and partly because he was the first one from the detention center who had been allowed to enter public school. He wanted to prove to Mrs. Swerlin and himself that he could excel if he put his mind to it, and that he could conform to the rules of the white community.

Extreme conformity is symptomatic of identity diffusion. With a weakly established set of ideals and values, the ego is insufficiently strong to differentiate itself from others. Consequently, autonomy is improbable. Under these conditions, the individual escapes from his anxiety by conforming strictly to the norms of his social group.[12] During his junior high school experience, this lack of autonomy can be seen in Malcolm's acceptance of all invitations to join in school activities. Instead of choosing those activities that suited his interests, a sign of an autonomous ego, he entered activities without choosing, since all initiatives were accepted whether they were interesting to him or not. "It became hard for me to get through a school day without someone after me to join this or head up that—the debating society, the Junior High basketball team, or some other extracurricular activity. *I never turned them down.*"[13] (Emphasis added.) His conformity at the detention center and school, even in the face of abusive language and jokes from whites, was evidence that he had not yet found a positive ego identity. Later, his zoot suits, processed hair, and slang speech were evidence of his continuing attempt to find an identity through conformity.

During his adolescence, the image of the successful white was the only ideal that seemed worth emulating. However, this image was not internalized into Malcolm's personality, but was a temporary and external ideal that he could conform to, since he had been robbed by white society of an identification with his father that could have led to a strong, black ego identity. That he would try very hard to be white was a central aspect of his pattern of conformity in adolescence. "My grades were among the highest in the school. I was unique in my class, like a pink poodle. And I was proud; I'm not going to say I wasn't. In fact, by then, I didn't really have much feeling about being a Negro, because *I was trying so hard, in every way I could, to be white.*"[14] (Emphasis added.) This identification with a white ideal would not, however, help Malcolm through his identity crisis, but would contribute instead to more extreme identity diffusion.

Malcolm's attempt to become white is evidence of a lack of self-definition, which was coupled with extreme self-consciousness. Even though he tried, Malcolm could not escape the stigma of being black. For whites continually reinforced his feeling of self-consciousness, both at the detention center and at school. The Swerlins and other whites at the center constantly referred to blacks in terms of the Negro stereotype. "They would even talk about me, or about 'niggers,' as though I wasn't there, as if I wouldn't understand what the word meant. A hundred times a day, they used the word 'nigger.'"[15] And he remembered that one visitor often examined him as if he were a fine colt or pedigreed pup. At school, jokes were constantly made about blacks, with Malcolm being the primary target. During his first week of school, for instance, one of his teachers broke into song: "'Way down yonder in the cotton field, some folks say that a nigger won't steal.'" The same teacher laughed his way through the single paragraph about the place of blacks in American history, which, incidentally, emphasized the fact that they were "usually lazy and dumb and shiftless."[16] Considering this social milieu, it is little wonder that Malcolm was extremely self-conscious.

During the summer of 1940, Malcolm visited his sister Ella in Boston. It was the first time that he had seen and experienced a community of blacks. There, he began to change his attitudes toward whites and when he returned to school he felt restless in their company. He kept thinking about the way he felt at home in the Boston ghetto as a real part of a mass of his own kind. This uneasiness grew progressively more intense and was the beginning of a major change in his life.

But Malcolm still preserved a degree of hope that things would change; that he had a bright future. His excellent academic achievements and social successes fed that hope. Yet this positive attitude toward the future was short-lived and was followed by a feeling of pessimism about the future of any black man or woman in America. The end of his hopeful attitude came after a single experience. One day his English teacher asked him about his career plans. Never having considered the question carefully before, Malcolm said that he thought he would like to be a lawyer. He remembered the surprised reaction of his teacher and the half-smile on his face when he told him to be realistic. Law was not a "realistic goal for a nigger." Carpentry was much more what his teacher had in mind. For the first time, it seems, Malcolm understood his position: "It was a surprising thing that I had never thought of it that way before, but I realized that whatever I wasn't, I *was* smarter than nearly all of those white kids. But apparently I was still not intelligent enough, in their eyes, to become whatever I wanted to be. It was then that I began to change—inside."[17] This experience shattered what remained of Malcolm's hope in the future and what remained viable in the white ideal he had sought so hard to achieve.

It was in this stage of adolescence that Malcolm began to repudiate whites and to show his pent-up aggression, both indicators of identity diffusion. He withdrew from white people. Where he had tolerated the "nigger" label before, now he stopped and stared at any white person who used it. While he continued for some time to identify with whiteness, as is shown by his preference for straightened hair, his transformation in Boston and then New York reflected a substitution of external ego ideals. Instead of identifying with the ideal of the successful white man in a "normal" society, his ideal came to be the successful black hustler in the deviant subculture. The development of this negative identity is, according to Erikson, characteristic of individuals of minority status who suffer from identity diffusion. He suggests that the individual who is a part of an oppressed and exploited minority, which is aware of the dominant cultural ideals but is prevented from reaching them, is apt to combine the negative images developed by the dominant majority with the negative identity fostered by his own social group.[18]

Factor V: Isolation Predominates Over Intimacy During Young Adulthood

Malcolm passed through late adolescence into young adulthood in the black ghettos of Boston and New York, less troubled and harassed by white hatred and prejudice. But the identity problems that emerged from his earlier relationships with whites were pent up inside even as a self-confident hustler in Harlem. The negative identity that crystalized through those years was only partially a new solution to his intrapsychic conflicts. His rigid conformity to the negative model of the hustler was only a shift in emphasis from an earlier attempt in junior high school to alleviate anxiety by conforming rigidly to a white model of behavior. Malcolm describes his conformist tendencies—zoot suits, processed hair, "hip" language, and the use of liquor and drugs—as an attempt on his part to escape from his embarrassing past, or, one could say, from his feeling of shame, doubt, and inferiority.

In addition to the security he derived from excessive conformity, Malcolm found a new way to exclude from his consciousness the feelings of inferiority that the white community had stamped on his mind. His escape was through drugs, the path taken by numerous oppressed people in their attempt to tolerate their miserable condition, psychic and social. "I had gotten to the stage," he recalled, "where every day I used enough drugs— reefers, cocaine, or both—so that I felt above any worries, any strains. If any worries did manage to push their way through to the surface of my consciousness, I could float them back where they came from until tomorrow, and then until the next day."[19] Yet behind his mask of conformity and the cloud of drugs, his identity problems remained to haunt him, making their presence apparent in his desire to stay aloof and avoid real intimacy with others.

As Malcolm describes his life as a deviant in Harlem, one is left with the clear impression that his relationships with others were instrumental, rather than genuine and intimate. He used people for his own ends and mistrusted nearly everyone, the exceptions being Shorty and Sammy. Next to his brother Reginald, they were the only other persons Malcolm felt he could trust. Where, before, introversion and mistrust had grown as a social response to racial exclusion, in Harlem these feelings were nurtured by the social character of the hustling business. Survival as a hustler required that one know the basic rule: "that you never trusted anyone outside of your close-mouthed circle, and that you selected with time and care before you made any intimates even among these."[20] It would not be stretching the point to say that Malcolm's success as a hustler resulted from the fact that this rule had governed his life almost from the beginning of his social contacts. For a person experiencing extreme identity diffusion possesses the mental disposition that equips him for a successful life of hustling, which may explain Malcolm's statement that hustling came almost as second nature to him.

The instrumental character of Malcolm's social relationships is most clearly seen in his associations with Laura and Sophia. Warmth and affection were apparently conveyed between Malcolm and Laura in his first days in Boston, for he was apparently able to unfold a part of his inner life by identifying his aspiration to be a lawyer. Yet after Laura sacrificed herself socially at home in order to attend a dance with Malcolm, he jilted her for Sophia, a white woman. And Sophia became, not an object of an enduring friendship, but a means to higher status and recognition.

The use of others summarizes the life of hustling to a great extent, so it is little wonder that Malcolm utilized others and that they used him. The sense of solidarity that he would later develop with lower-class blacks was impossible when his hustling business required taking advantage of others if he was to survive. For example, it was a normal outgrowth of his trade that he would start his brother Reginald in a hustle that deceived Harlemites into believing that he was selling expensive, stolen goods for very low prices, when in fact he was peddling cheap, legitimate merchandise for twice its value.

There is little evidence that Malcolm attempted during his young adulthood to divide his environment into two camps: good and evil. However, his contempt for whites did surface from time to time, especially against those who attempted to mix with blacks on equal terms. His lack of respect for Sophia stemmed from this latent hostility toward whites,[21] which became dominant later in prison when he was freer to accept the Yakub myth. This myth is fundamental to the Black Muslim belief system because it imputes negative features to whiteness by tracing the development of the races from man's beginning. The myth specifies that God made the first man black and perfect. A mad scientist named Yakub, who was in rebellion against Allah, grafted out the blackness, and thereby the goodness, in man, creating a white, evil counterpart. This myth leads Black Muslims to the recognition that the white man is drained of Godliness and can legitimately be called a "white devil."

In Harlem, Malcolm was not yet ready to make this rigid distinction between the races in terms of good and evil, partly because conformity and drugs were sufficiently compelling defenses against anxiety, but also because he depended on whites for survival and status. Prison not only required that he alter his defenses, but it forced him to terminate a life-style in which he was dependent on whites. By freeing him from a commitment that required the suppression of hostility toward whites, prison life nurtured the beginning of a commitment that allowed this hostility full reign in thought and action. Then the division of the world into forces of good and evil was possible for Malcolm. This division is an attempt to find intimacy with those defined as "good" by excessive repudiation of those defined as "evil." According to Erikson, "weakness or excess in repudiation is an intrinsic aspect of the inability to gain intimacy because of an incomplete identity."[22]

Excessive contempt for one's background—religious, ethnic, or national origin—is another indicator of identity diffusion that is evident in Malcolm's early adult years. The assumption of a negative identity, which had atheistic and white standards attached to it, repudiated his early religious training with its strong moral teachings and Protestant ethic emphasis. And processing his hair in order to resemble the white man, which he tells us he did religiously, was a sign of contempt for his racial characteristics.

Running parallel to Malcolm's contempt for his background was his scornful attitude toward those roles offered by his family as "proper." Except for his attempt at conformity to "proper" roles in the detention center and at junior high school, his hostility toward the roles valued by his family had surfaced in childhood and early adolescence. His delinquent behavior and general hostility to the roles of "good" student and citizen are indicative of his early rejection of society's roles. This early tendency was carried over into young adulthood and then became accentuated as the embryo of his negative identity matured. Evidence of this development is seen in his first few weeks in Boston, when he rejected the roles that his sister considered proper ones. Ella encouraged him to work toward a legal degree, but Malcolm chose to shine shoes in the ghetto and decided to educate himself in the business of hustling. This was the first step he would take leading to an almost total rejection of the roles his family had told him were proper. As a successful hustler he became the antithesis of his parents' aspirations for him.

Factor VI: Self-Absorption Predominates Over Generativity During Adulthood

While Malcolm's hustling and prison days show evidence of concern for self as opposed to concern for others, his conversion to the Black Muslim movement produced a fundamental change in his attitude. Where before he had been basically self-interested and withdrawn, in the movement his efforts were toward uplifting his race through constant activity that denied the importance of self. This transformation of attitudes during adulthood, which Weber had associated with charisma, did, in fact, come after the formation of his commitment to Mr. Muhammad. Yet there were earlier signs in Harlem that some of the problems of identity diffusion were already being resolved.

Accepting a negative identity may help an individual solve the problems of identity diffusion, if indeed trustful relations and solidarity with others develop in the deviant subculture and the individual is able to achieve a sufficiently high status that the severity of shame, inferiority, and introversion is reduced. Instead of viewing the immersion into deviance as an escape from problems or an intensification of them, consider how deviant living may actually strengthen the ego. An analysis of Malcolm's experience as a hustler points up some of the positive features of deviance, for it was through this negative identity that he began to solve the problems he had been carrying with him from early childhood. In Harlem, his ego was strengthened, and a sense of racial pride and a feeling of solidarity with other blacks began to form, both changes that would contribute to the formation of an identity.

What are the experiences that led to these first steps toward the solution of his intrapsychic conflicts? However limited his intimate social ties may have been, Malcolm did find friendships outside his immediate family. His relations with Shorty and Sammy were apparently the first enduring and intimate ones in his life. The fact that he was able to build trust with someone besides Reginald was indeed a positive sign that he was reversing the earlier tendency to distrust everyone. These ties were only a small part of a larger discovery, however. More important was the feeling that he had found a place where he was accepted for what he was.

Acceptance cannot be underrated as a factor in Malcolm's development, for it nurtured the confidence that would later make him a talented organizer. From the beginning, the ghetto had a strong appeal for him. His comparison of the Hill and ghetto sections of Boston demonstrates why: "Not only was this part of Roxbury [the ghetto] much more exciting, but I felt more relaxed among Negroes who were being their natural selves and not putting on airs."[23] Once introduced into the heart of ghetto life, Malcolm recalled that he felt "great" because he was accepted. The increasing intimacy with others and this feeling of belonging should be contrasted with his earlier feelings of isolation and rejection, which sprang from a lack of maternal warmth and security in his family as well as the white society's policy of racial exclusion.

It is somewhat paradoxical that the jungle-like character of a hustling life would provide Malcolm with the warmth and security that had been denied to him from childhood. Remembering his Harlem experience, Malcolm captures this fact only in retrospect: "In one sense, we were huddled in there, bonded together in seeking security and warmth and comfort from each other, and we didn't know it."[24] And Malcolm felt this warmth and received this security in very specific ways: the lavish treatment given to old hustlers, like the pick-pocket Fewclothes, who were past their prime and survived because others cared; the sense of honesty that prostitutes conveyed and the genuine affection they exuded in their contacts with him; the trouble that others, especially Shorty, took to bail him out of trouble. These were all experiences that generated trust, enlarging the extent of certainty and predictability in his social relationships.

Status in the ghetto was possible for Malcolm. Upward mobility in deviance is contrasted with the impossibility of becoming a lawyer in white society with its reserved statuses. The status that had been denied to him in the larger society he could and did earn in the hustling life. His reputation was earned in different ways. His relationship with Sophia gave him considerable status, as I mentioned earlier. More important was his skill as a hustler, which earned him the respect of other big names in the business. Earlier, his reputation as a dancer contributed in no small measure to his sense of self-regard. Through this rise in status within the Harlem hierarchy, Malcolm's self-confidence gained some force over the gnawing feeling of inferiority and doubt that had marred his youth. This is nowhere clearer than in his return to Michigan for a visit, wearing zoot suit and conk, and dancing his most startling steps to dazzle the straight world. Unconcerned about the reactions of others, he left his former home town "shocked and rocked." This sense of inner strength should probably be seen in the context of the origin of racial pride.

Pride in his black heritage grew slowly in deviance. And it was nourished by the unmasking of the white man playing the double life. Malcolm was able to compare the virtues of white and black culture from the perspective of one who serviced the private face of the white public. As a "steerer" of white clients into the Harlem "fleshpots," he was given a vivid picture of a fundamental dualism in white culture in America: One thing is said for the sake of righteousness while its opposite is done for the sake of necessity. Thus, he steered "respectable" whites into the anonymity of Harlem where anything they could name or imagine, they could do or have done to them. Observing the white man off his guard gave Malcolm a more positive view of his own race. And later, as a Minister in the Nation of Islam, he would emphasize the virtues of being black by contrast to the hypocrisy and decadence of white culture. But his growing racial pride was also a result of experiences that led him to appreciate the virtues of black culture in its own right. His association with black musicians must have had a great impact on his development, judging from the fact that he was one of their biggest fans. Also, he became aware at a fairly early period in Harlem that black culture is more spontaneous and consequently freer than the white man's culture, which he saw to be built around façades and anchored in the fear of spontaneous living.

Given the positive features of Malcolm's life in deviance, it would not be exaggerating the point to say that the solution of his identity problems started in Harlem. Yet his final triumph over identity diffusion did not come even during his days in the Black Muslim movement, but rather when he was forced to leave the movement and become an autonomous leader in his own right. Consequently, his life as a hustler and as a mobilizer of converts for Mr. Muhammad should be viewed as a single period of development in which small increments of change led to gradual, but nonetheless basic, changes in personality. The major change in attitudes occurred in prison, when he discovered a new father who would take him through his time of trouble.

Stages in the Development of the Charismatic Commitment

Malcolm X's conversion in prison to the Black Muslim movement cannot be explained solely in terms of identity diffusion, although that was a major source of tension that prepared him for a charismatic commitment. The other three determinants of commitment have to be considered in order to understand how identity diffusion, which can lead a person into several different patterns of response, is channeled into the single pattern described as the charismatic bond. Having traced the development of a high level of intrapsychic tension in Malcolm's personality (Stage I), it is necessary to assess the extent of availability (Stage II), the opportunities for action (Stage III), and the potential for psychological and social rewards (Stage IV). While my discussion of Stage IV of the commitment process was centered on social rewards in an earlier chapter, it is clear that psychological rewards are also relevant during this stage. In the process of analyzing charismatic commitments especially, attention should be placed on the reduction of intrapsychic conflict in the follower's personality as he develops a strong identification with the leader, gives up his capacity to criticize, and becomes obedient to the leader's initiatives. At the same time that the psychological rewards of the charismatic bond are enumerated, we should be mindful of the transactional factors bearing on commitment formation, since the follower is apt to receive numerous tangible rewards that encourage and reinforce the charismatic tie.

Availability

Malcolm's imprisonment for burglary was probably one of the most significant events in his personal development, because it forced him to terminate a commitment to hustling and made him available for new options. And his imprisonment came at a time when his deviant behavior was escalating to more serious and risky criminal ventures. Thus, not only did detention free him from dependence on hustling and on whites, but it did so at a time when his commitment to the hustling business was under considerable strain. He was at the point in his career where the potential costs of deviance were outrunning the potential rewards, so much so that it would not be an exaggeration to say that he was hunting for a way out. Prison was the escape route, even though Malcolm himself was not conscious of it at the time. Yet being in a state of transition was only one of several factors that increased his availability for action in the Black Muslim movement.

Availability for a new commitment is also increased when the individual's conscience does not forbid involvement. In Malcolm's case, the moral teachings of his childhood not only allowed black nationalist activity, they encouraged it. The fact that his father had been a militant black nationalist as well as a minister undoubtedly influenced Malcolm's decision to follow Mr. Muhammad. For it was his father's activity as a follower of Marcus Garvey that left its greatest impression on him as a child. The images of his father depicting the rise of the black man in Africa must surely have prepared him to listen to Mr. Muhammad's teachings that one day the black man would rule the entire world.

His mother's eating habits might also be considered influential in Malcolm's conversion, since she had tried to socialize her children to believe that eating pork and rabbit were morally reprehensible. This was combined apparently with a general attitude toward work that conformed to the "Protestant ethic." Both these tendencies are to be found in the Black Muslim moral code. In part, Black Muslims must avoid long vacations, must attend meetings at least two nights each week, and must work the streets for new converts. They must accept the man as the dominant figure in the home, must sleep no longer than health requires, must not lie and steal, and must not dance, gamble, date, attend movies, or go to sporting events. Finally, they must not be sexually promiscuous (Muslim women may not be alone in a room with any man but their husbands), must not eat pork or corn bread, and must not overeat (an overweight Muslim may be fined).[25] This code is an effort to negate the general image of blacks as "docile but irresponsible, loyal but lazy, humble but given to lying and stealing—in short, carefree, happy-go-lucky, amoral children, albeit children with a powerful sexual drive and a lot of rhythm."[26]

These two factors—his father's black nationalist activities and his mother's moral teachings—increased Malcolm's availability for a commitment to Mr. Muhammad. Later, when that charismatic commitment was formed and then strengthened, he would reestablish the psychosocial moratorium. At that time he would return symbolically to his childhood in order to follow in his father's footsteps and listen to his mother's moral wisdom. The teachings of the leader would reestablish the teachings of his parents as a basis for developing his ego-ideal and his ego-identity.

Resource capacity is another factor to consider in assessing the extent of availability. For Malcolm, hustling in the ghetto had prepared him very well for the tasks of leadership within the Black Muslim movement. His own personal resources, such as knowledge of the ghetto environment, a sense for emerging opportunities, skill in rhetoric, and the like, were especially suited to the initial stages of the movement, when the chief order of business was to make new converts.

The final impinging factor that affects an individual's freedom to pursue a new activity is the posture or configuration of his group associations. When his reference groups oppose a new activity, the tendency is for the individual to be restrained. Conversely, a person will be freer to develop new activities when his group associations reinforce them. Prison separated Malcolm from groups within Harlem that would have frowned on black nationalist activities. More significantly, his detention put him back in touch with members of his family, most of whom, including Reginald, had already become followers of Mr. Muhammad. Thus, termination of ties with groups that would have opposed black nationalist activities was coupled with heavy reinforcements from his family encouraging him to join them in the movement. And their efforts to convert Malcolm were zealous. He began receiving letters every day from his brothers and sisters in Detroit who wrote about "the Messenger of Allah." Had his family not been Muslims or had they failed to contact him in prison, the chances are that Malcolm would not have become available for conversion and, instead of becoming a black nationalist leader, he would probably have returned to Harlem and to the cycle of deviance and detention.

Opportunity to Act

Little need be said about the opportunity that existed for action in Malcolm's case. From the beginning, he could act by altering his pattern of behavior to conform to the Black Muslim moral code. Abstaining from certain practices, like eating pork, smoking cigarettes, and taking drugs, could be readily combined with affirmations of faith through other actions, such as daily prayer to Allah and self-education. And as each of these opportunities were taken up by Malcolm, lower-level investments and sacrifices accumulated. Some of these new activities, especially praying, were not without suffering. "I had to force myself to bend my knees," Malcolm said of praying. "And waves of shame and embarrassment would force me back up."[27]

Since the opportunity for action accompanied efforts to convert him, Malcolm's last years in prison made it easier for him to solve the problems of identity diffusion. Transformation of character is one way to describe his experience. Another is to see it as a basic shift in his pattern of conformity. Previously, he had conformed to the white ideal and then to the model of the successful hustler. Now, in prison, he began conforming to the initiatives of Mr. Muhammad. Through the formation of a charismatic commitment, he could attempt to find a new way to control and solve his intrapsychic conflicts. The imputation of God-like qualities and powers to Mr. Muhammad helped Malcolm make the strong identification that would lead ultimately to a stronger ego and the formation of an authentic identity.

High Profit Potential

As I suggested in the preceding chapter, a charismatic commitment is best understood as the follower's consistent acceptance of a leader's initiatives, based on the belief that the leader is endowed with God-like powers and qualities. The development of consistent action on the part of the follower is apt to occur rapidly because the leader replaces his ego-ideal. And this transformation of goals within the superego is likely to be accompanied by new values and norms, combined in a new moral code. In this sense, spontaneous conversions to an ideology are likely to accompany the formation of charismatic commitments.

Furthermore, the development of a charismatic commitment is the follower's unconscious attempt to find a new way of minimizing or resolving his extreme intrapsychic conflicts. Extreme intrapsychic distance may be reduced through the formation of such a commitment. Or, if the follower's ego-ideal is underdeveloped and identity diffusion results, the leader's ideals and values are taken over by the follower as a means of reducing intrapsychic conflict and relieving the ego from incessant anxiety and guilt. Because he suffered from extreme identity diffusion, Malcolm X followed this second course.

The Formation of the Charismatic Commitment

Now it remains for me to show how and why extreme identity diffusion leads to the formation of the charismatic commitment. We know that a leader has assumed the functions of the follower's ego-ideal when the follower strongly identifies with and idealizes the leader. Imitating the leader is as symptomatic of identification as excessive praise is of idealization. Additionally, the follower loses his capacity to criticize the leader's behavior, which is connected with an apparent need to conform very strictly to the leader's initiatives and personal desires. We shall see that all these characteristics of the charismatic bond can be found in Malcolm's case.

The development of a charismatic commitment to Mr. Muhammad gave Malcolm another chance to form an identity. It reestablished the psychosocial moratorium, providing him with the security, freedom, objects of identification, ideals, and values that he had failed to secure at earlier stages of development. These were the psychological profits that Malcolm received through his commitment and they were vitally important for the further development of his personality. For, after Mr. Muhammad's ideals and values were internalized into his superego, Malcolm could secure his own identity and become genuinely autonomous for the first time in his life.

The Leader as a Substitute Ego-Ideal

Knowing the causes of identity diffusion within Malcolm's personality, it is easy to understand why he so readily embraced the ideals and values of Mr. Muhammad. For a person who has been psychologically and socially abused by society and believes that it is his own fault, rather than society's, will be susceptible to the words of a prophet who "sets things straight." Thus, when Reginald introduced Malcolm to the Yakub myth and the notion that "the white man is the devil," a void was filled in Malcolm's psychic life. He describes this revelation as having produced a "blinding light" and its impact was devastating. "I would sit in my room and stare," Malcolm recalled. "At the dining room table, I would hardly eat, only drink the water. I nearly starved." This is the period when the old ideals, first the white ideal and then that of the successful hustler, are reassessed in terms of the new ideals and values of the movement, which are implanted symbolically in its leader. "I was going through the hardest thing," related Malcolm, "also the greatest thing, for any human being to do; to accept that which is already within you, and around you."[28]

Especially for black convicts the idea that "the white man is the devil" rings true from experience. This fact Malcolm understood very well and by accepting this claim he found the solution to a riddle that had not previously entered his conciousness. In an "open" and "competitive" society, why were blacks as a group doing worse while whites were doing better? The explanation was to be found in the white man's devilish plan to keep the black man at the "bottom of the pile." Accepting this view of the white man presupposed that its opposite was true: The black man is good, if he will only recognize it and work to overcome the stigma of inferiority that prevents him from achieving perfection. The leader as the substitute ego-ideal comes to represent the perfect state that his followers must attempt to achieve through obedience to a code of conduct, to the new values and norms that redefine how men should relate to one another. By accepting the leader as the new model of behavior, or the new ideals in motion, and the code as the vehicle for attaining a state approximating that of the leader, the follower forsakes what he is for what he must become. Thus, Mr. Muhammad represented the perfect black man (the new ego-ideal) that Malcolm substituted for the earlier models of behavior that had guided his life. By following the code of conduct that the leader had handed down to all Muslims, he thought that he would find his salvation and, in the process, would become more like his leader. He would become more perfect. This substitution of ego-ideals, just as Weber said of charisma, created an almost total transformation or metamorphosis in Malcolm's pattern of life. "I still marvel at how swiftly my previous life's thinking pattern slid away from me," said Malcolm, "like snow off a roof. It is as though someone else I knew of had lived by hustling and crime. I would be startled to catch myself thinking in a remote way of my earlier self as another person."[29]

Idealization of and Identification with the Leader

Idealization of the leader in a charismatic relationship stems from the follower's need to see the leader as an embodiment of goodness possibly attainable in this life. As I said a moment ago, the leader represents the ideals the follower must strive to reach. It is this ego-ideal function of leadership that gives direction to a movement and, to the extent that a single person (as opposed to an office) is invested with these ideals, he will be the source of cohesiveness because followers will be united in their collective idealization of his person and in their collective emulation of his life-style through identification. When such a person achieves this place of prominence, he will become indispensable to a movement. That Mr. Muhammad attained such a position is clear in Malcolm's words:

> Anyone not a Muslim could not conceive what the possible loss of Mr. Muhammad would have meant among his followers. To us, the Nation of Islam was Mr. Muhammad. What bonded us into the best organization black Americans ever had was every Muslim's devout regard for Mr. Muhammad as black America's moral, mental, and spiritual reformer.

> Stated another way, we Muslims regarded ourselves as moral and mental and spiritual examples for other black Americans, because we followed the personal example of Mr. Muhammad.[30]

Because the leader is functioning as the follower's ego-ideal, there is a tendency to idealize him excessively. Special powers are imputed to him which set him off from the ordinary. For example, Malcolm makes numerous references to Mr. Muhammad's God-like qualities, but one statement especially captures the fullness of the idealization process:

> I went to bed every night ever more awed. If not Allah, who else could have put such wisdom into that little humble lamb of a man from the Georgia fourth grade and sawmills and cotton patches. . . .

> My adoration of Mr. Muhammad grew, in the sense of the Latin root word *adorare*. It means much more than our "adoration" or "adore." It means that my worship of him was so awesome that he was the first man whom I had ever feared—not fear such as of a man with a gun, but the fear such as one has of the power of the sun.[31]

By imputing these powers to a leader, the follower creates distance between the leader and himself. While the state of perfection achieved by the leader maintains its attraction as a goal to be striven for, the imputation of godliness makes the goal nearly impossible to reach. This tendency to set the leader apart by associating him with a transcendental power can be partially explained in terms of the normal function of the ego-ideal within the psychic apparatus. For the ego-ideal encompasses goals the ego is normally incapable of reaching in toto, this distance being one of the sources of aspiration and change within the ego. In the same way, the leader functioning as the follower's ego-ideal in a charismatic relationship is clothed in mystery and given the power of the Word. The resulting distance means that the follower may strive to become as perfect as the leader, but it forces him to recognize that he cannot be equally perfect, unless, of course, he too comes into possession of the Word. If the charismatic bond is strong, the follower will not dream of replacing the leader. As it weakens, the thought of taking the leader's place may pass through his mind. However, Malcolm seems not to have been tempted by his own successes to assume equality with Mr. Muhammad, knowing that he did not have the same relationship with Allah.

Loss of the Capacity To Criticize

Another indication that Malcolm had formed a charismatic relationship with Mr. Muhammad is that he would not tolerate criticisms of his leader and he himself lost his capacity to criticize. In fact, the need to preserve the unblemished image of Mr. Muhammad as a characterization of the perfect black man encouraged the use of a perceptual screening process that prevented disturbing information from entering Malcolm's consciousness, at least with sufficient clarity to shake his faith.

Malcolm himself took criticism from others very well, partly because it was normally the "white devil" that was its source and partly because he expected it as a normal reaction to his role as agitator. But when others criticized the "Messenger" it was a different story. "I would grow furious reading any harsh attack upon Mr. Muhammad. I didn't care what they said about me."[32] That Malcolm lost his capacity to criticize "the little lamb" is clear from numerous passages in his autobiography. And this phenomenon existed from the very beginning of his commitment. For instance, when Mr. Muhammad expelled Reginald from the movement because of charges of immoral conduct, Malcolm tried to defend his brother by writing a letter from prison and affirming the strong ties between them and appealing for charity. This appeal had no impact whatsoever on Mr. Muhammad, who simply returned a challenge, asking Malcolm why he had doubted the truth, unless it was because of his own personal weakness. That a strong charismatic relationship had formed in Malcolm's mind is evident in his total acceptance of Mr. Muhammad's decision on this matter, which completely transformed his relationship with Reginald, one of the few persons in his life whom he had trusted.

That stuck me [Malcolm said of Mr. Muhammad's challenge of his faith]. Reginald was not leading the disciplined life of a Muslim. And I knew that Elijah Muhammad was right, and my blood brother was wrong.

At that time, all of the doubt and confusion in my mind was removed. All of the influence that my brother had wielded over me was broken. From that day on . . . everything that my brother Reginald has done is wrong.[33]

Furthermore, Malcolm not only lost his ability to criticize, he also came to accept any word or initiative from Mr. Muhammad as uncontestable truth. Later, as a Minister of Islam, Malcolm would "sit, galvanized, hearing what I then accepted from Mr. Muhammad's mouth as being the true history of our religion, the true religion for the black man."[34] And, while Malcolm would not have thought to criticize his leader, he accepted criticisms of his own work from Mr. Muhammad regularly with the obedient attitude of one in a charismatic state of mind. "His patience and his wisdom in chastising me would always humble me from head to foot."[35]

Starting in 1955, Malcolm began to pick up clues that Mr. Muhammad had fathered several illegitimate children. Such immoral conduct was of course directly contrary to the Black Muslim moral code. More fundamentally, adultery ran against the current of expectations that a follower holds in a charismatic state of mind, that the leader represents perfection in every way. Indeed, the leader is expected to be as perfect as the follower's image of him. To preserve the idealized image of Mr. Muhammad the contradictory evidence was screened out by Malcolm. His "mind simply refused to accept anything so grotesque as adultery mentioned in the same breath with Mr. Muhammad's name." The feeling of trust in the leader that Malcolm had generated, after a life marked by incessant distrust, led him to deny his own senses and intelligence, as he says. "I don't think I could say anything which better testifies to my depth of faith in Mr. Muhammad than that I totally and absolutely rejected my intelligence."[36] He could not be convinced that "the little lamb" would betray his poor and trusting followers who sacrificed their meager change in order to support the movement.

In 1962, the rumors became so widespread that Malcolm could no longer push them out of his mind. And even when the rumors were confirmed, he would not condemn Mr. Muhammad, but instead sought an explanation for his conduct in the religious documents of the movement. It would be explained, he thought, through prophecy. "I desperately wanted to find some way—some kind of a bridge—over which I was certain the Nation of Islam could be saved from self-destruction."[37] For where followers relate to a leader on a charismatic basis, the shattering of the leader's idealized image destroys the centripetal force that binds his followers together. How drastically this fallen image of "the little lamb" affected Malcolm is reflected in his words:

> What began to break my faith was that, try as I might, I couldn't hide, I couldn't evade, that Mr. Muhammad, instead of facing what he had done before his followers, as a human weakness or as fulfillment of prophecy—which I sincerely believe that Muslims would have understood, or at least they would have accepted—Mr. Muhammad had, instead, been willing to hide, to cover up what he had done.

That was my major blow.

That was how I first began to realize that I had believed in Mr. Muhammad more than he believed in himself.[38]

This shattering of the leader's image was, for Malcolm, the beginning of a new stage of personal development. At this point, the son would begin to find his own way in the world without the guiding hand of the father.

Conformity and the Need for Approval

Excessive conformity is the final indicator of a charismatic commitment and this goes hand-in-hand with the need to be accepted by the leader in his role as "comforter." Both these tendencies are clearly marked in Malcolm's relationship with Mr. Muhammad, although the early years of their association is the period when conformity and the need for approval most clearly dominated Malcolm's mind. From the beginning of his tenure as a Minister of Islam, Malcolm conformed rigidly to the rituals and moral code of the movement. When he assumed the position of chief mobilizer, he took his instructions directly from Mr. Muhammad and constantly cleared his own ideas with him. The frequent meetings between the two, when Mr. Muhammad chastised Malcolm, was the forum from which he took instructions about how to make his own behavior conform to the wishes of the "Messenger." And in the beginning, when he wanted to emphasize the need for mobilizing new converts, he went to Mr. Muhammad first to seek approval for his initiative. How closely Malcolm sought to conform to the initiatives and wishes of his leader is manifest in the patience he demonstrated, even against his own instincts, when other blacks began to place the "hate" stamp on the movement. His reaction was to fight back, but the "Messenger" had decreed that blacks should not turn on other blacks because it would divide the race. Consequently, Malcolm held his ground, although he continually sought instructions on the matter, hoping to receive the go-ahead. Criticism of the movement from other parts of the black community did not abate, however, and after awhile it began to appear that the Black Muslims were afraid to fight back. Finally, Mr. Muhammad's patience wore out and he gave the go-ahead to Malcolm, who immediately began firing back. Even against his own instincts and judgment, he had been obedient to his leader's wishes. But it was typical that he would wait for that nod before acting.

Conformity can be partially understood as a result of the follower's need for love and approval. This appears to have been true in Malcolm's case, for he makes numerous references to the fact that conformity to and approval from Mr. Muhammad were more important to him than his own career as a leader. But rewards did come to Malcolm through the primary leader's approval, for the praise that he received from the leader's mouth and the affection he felt in their social exchanges provided strength to his ego.

Just as Goebbels was psychologically renewed in his periodic visits with Hitler, so too was Malcolm renewed during his meetings with Mr. Muhammad. "Mr. Muhammad—each time I'd go to see him in Chicago, or in Phoenix—would warm me with his expressions of his approval and confidence in me."[39] And at a rally, in 1963, Mr. Muhammad embraced Malcolm and told a mass audience that he had been his most faithful and hardworking minister, and that he would follow him until death. "He had never paid such a compliment to any Muslim," Malcolm says. "No praise from any other earthly person could have meant more to me."[40] Furthermore, there is a sense in which the relationship between the two men was symbiotic: Both needed approval and love, which were intangible goods exchanged in their frequent meetings. A sense of this psychological exchange is conveyed in Malcolm's words: "He was interested in my potential, I could tell from the things he would say. And I worshiped him."[41]

Growing Autonomy and Identity Formation

I have said that the formation of a charismatic commitment is an unconscious attempt to deal with extreme intrapsychic conflict. In the case of extreme identity diffusion, such a commitment counteracts the problems that originated in infancy and led to a failure to resolve the identity crisis. Identification and idealization of Mr. Muhammad, for example, gave Malcolm the goals and values that, as a child, he had failed to internalize through identification with his parents. Sharing these goals and values with the "Messenger" generated a feeling of trust in Malcolm's mind, because people who share a view of the world that leads to common perceptions and judgments are apt to develop trust in one another. Thus, the charismatic commitment counteracted the earlier tendency in Malcolm's life to mistrust everyone because it reproduced the strong expressive relationship of infancy that we associate with maternal love. In this respect, the "charismatic" leader should not be viewed as a substitute father figure, as Freud and others have seen him, but as a substitute mother-father figure, the mother function being most clearly representative of the "comforter" role of leadership.

The follower's intolerance of any criticism of the leader in a charismatic relationship also counteracts the problems of identity diffusion. Protecting the idealized image of the leader, as we see in Malcolm's experience, is a defense of the leader's idealized identity, which the follower emulates and internalizes. In the same way, children will defend the idealized images of their parents against the criticisms of their playmates. In both instances, criticism is an indirect challenge to the person defending the image, since it is by identifying with that image that the person develops a sense for who he is and what he wants to become. In a charismatic relationship, identification with the idealized image of the leader restores hope for improvement, a degree of certainty, confidence, and self-esteem within the follower's ego that counteracts the feelings of hopelessness, doubt, shame, and inferiority that mark his personality. The charismatic relationship transforms the follower, as Malcolm's words show so clearly:

> He was The Messenger of Allah. When I was a foul, vicious convict, so evil that other convicts had called me Satan, this man had rescued me. He was the man who had trained me, who had treated me as if I were his own flesh and blood. He was the man who had given me wings—to go places, to do things I otherwise never would have dreamed of. We walked, with me caught up in a whirlwind of emotions.[42]

Identification with the leader is a sign of an insufficiently developed identity within the follower's personality, while excessive conformity on the follower's part is an indication of an underdeveloped ego. Conformity to the leader's wishes lends support to the follower's ego at the same time that identification with the leader's idealized image gives him self-definition and direction. Thus, conformity adds a degree of security to the follower's psychic life such that an easier transition can be made from identity diffusion to autonomy, hopefully culminating in an ego-identity distinct from the leader's.

I have argued that a charismatic commitment, by helping to solve the problems just noted, can enhance the personal development of the follower (or the leader, for that matter). This statement is undoubtedly not universally true, but it can happen, as we have seen in the case of Malcolm X. For the problems of identity diffusion, which he had only begun to counteract as a hustler in Harlem, were largely overcome in the last years of his commitment to Mr. Muhammad. In contrast to his earlier tendency to mistrust people, he developed feelings of trust in blacks as well as in whites to some degree (even while he was in the movement). And his belief in the Black Muslim ideology, especially the Yakub myth, made him feel superior to whites, reversing the tendency in his youth and early adulthood to think of himself as inferior and whites as superior. This belief system gave him increasing ego strength in his relations with whites, as his testimony makes clear: "Mr. Muhammad has taught me that I never need fear any man's intellect who tries to defend or to justify the white man's criminal record against the non-white man—especially the white man and the black man in North America."[43]

These changes in his ego and ego-ideal produced increasingly strong feelings of independence. Autonomy was allowed, even encouraged, by Mr. Muhammad after ill health forced him to move to Arizona. Malcolm was given discretion on a number of vital issues, when previously any action whatsoever had to be cleared with the "Messenger." Just as parents must encourage their child to make his or her own choices in order to become autonomous, so, too, did Mr. Muhammad give Malcolm some of the freedom that he needed to differentiate himself from the idealized image of the leader that he had internalized. He told Malcolm to make the decisions for himself, and that his guideline in making those decisions should be what he thought was wise and in the best interests of the Nation of Islam. The evidence that Malcolm was indeed developing his own identity is found in the fact that he came to differ sharply with Mr. Muhammad on the question of direct action, something he would not even have considered in the earlier stages of his commitment.

The conflict that developed over this issue was the basis for Malcolm's expulsion from the movement in 1963. But the problems of identity diffusion were no longer as severe since the goals and values of Mr. Muhammad had been internalized by then and Malcolm was already manifesting the confidence that flows from an authentic identity. And his ability to stand without the leader who had guided him, after that leader had symbolically thrown him from the house to be on his own, was strengthened by the fact that other Muslims left the movement to become his followers. He was not entirely alone. This support must surely have increased his sense of self-assurance, so that his trip to North Africa to visit the source of the Islam religion was made with considerably greater personal strength than when he found and followed Mr. Muhammad. In Africa, his identity would come into full view. That his mother-father had expelled him from the house was another fortuitous event, as was his arrest in Harlem and his detention in prison, that turned out to be a turning point in his personal growth.

In the Black Muslim movement, Malcolm developed a sense of solidarity with others by participating in a collective ritual that inculcated deferential sentiments about the leader and by sharing with others a belief that neatly divided the world into good and evil camps (the Yakub myth). These patterns of behavior and belief are indicative of identity diffusion. Evidence that Malcolm had resolved the problems of identity diffusion can be seen, then, in the fact that he rejected both the charismatic tie and the Yakub myth after his expulsion and did not replace them with substitutes. His journey to Mecca introduced him to white men who were color-blind. And this experience challenged his previously entrenched beliefs: "The *color-blindness* of the Muslim world's religious society and the *color-blindness* of the Muslim world's human society: these two influences had each day been making a greater impact, and an increasing persuasion against my previous way of thinking."[44]

During his stay in the Muslim world he ate from the same plate, drank from the same glass, slept in the same bed, and prayed to the same God with other Muslims, whose eyes were blue, whose hair was blond, and whose skin was white. These same people would have been "blue-eyed devils" in the vocabulary that Malcolm had used earlier to describe whites in American society. But whites in Africa impressed him as being different "because their belief in one God had removed the 'white' from their *minds,* the 'white' from their *behavior,* and the 'white' from their *attitude.*"[45] This discovery led him to the conclusion "that the white man is *not* inherently evil, but America's racist society influences him to act evilly. The society has produced and nourishes a psychology which brings out the lowest, most base part of human beings."[46]

Accepting the view that the white man is not inherently evil destroyed the "validity" of the Yakub myth. This acceptance fundamentally changed the basis of Malcolm's solidarity with others, substituting radical humanism as a foundation of solidarity in place of racial hatred. This transformation of his basic attitudes is reflected in one of several letters from Mecca: "In the past, yes, I have made sweeping indictments of *all* white people. I never will be guilty of that again—as I know now that some white people *are* truly sincere, that some truly are capable of being brotherly toward a black man. The true Islam has shown me that a blanket indictment of all white people is as wrong as when whites make blanket indictments against blacks."[47]

Emerging from this change is a new man, one who trusts others more fully, who knows where he is going, who is proud; in short, one who knows who he is—a man who is free, honest, and humane. He had become a self-actualized man and no longer needed the white ideal of his youth, the ideal of the successful hustler of his early adulthood, or the idealized image of Mr. Muhammad that had given his life a direction in adulthood. In Africa, he faced up to the complexity and chaos of the world with an open mind and he would come to judge others in terms of his new identity. This is nowhere clearer than in his response to a white man who shouted to him from another car while he was waiting for a traffic signal to change: "'Malcolm X!' he called out—and when I looked, he stuck his hand out of his car, across at me, grinning, 'Do you mind shaking hands with a white man?' Imagine that! Just as the traffic light turned green, I told him, I don't mind shaking hands with human beings. Are you one?"[48]

The end of Malcolm's charismatic commitment to Mr. Muhammad followed the shattering of the Yakub myth and is further evidence that Malcolm had finally resolved his identity crisis. The appraisal of his relationship with Mr. Muhammad is beautiful testimony of the nature of the charismatic bond, as I have explained it, so I will quote his words at some length.

> In Mecca, too, I had played back for myself the twelve years I had spent with Elijah Muhammad as if it were a motion picture. I guess it would be impossible for anyone ever to realize fully how complete was my belief in Elijah Muhammad. I believed in him not only as a leader in the ordinary *human* sense, but also I believed in him as a *divine* leader. I believed he had no human

weaknesses or faults, and that, therefore, he could make no mistakes and that he could do no wrong. There on a Holy World hilltop, I realized how very dangerous it is for people to hold any human being in such esteem, especially to consider anyone some sort of "divinely guided" and "protected" person.[49]

Yet, if what I have said is correct, it was Malcolm's charismatic commitment to Mr. Muhammad that led him to a point in his personal growth where he could reject the leader as he did and stand alone with self-confidence. In the final analysis, charisma should be recognized as a source of personal development in addition to the already widespread belief that it is a source of social change. Malcolm's life affirms the validity of this point of view. Yet we may wonder how many Black Muslims are still dependent on their leader for guidance and how many have developed a strong ego-identity, but are restrained by the group and its deferential traditions from pursuing an independent course.

Notes

1. The basic outlines of his approach are to be found in his leading essay, "The Problem of Ego Identity" in Maurice Stein, Arthur Vidich, and David Manning White (eds.), *Identity and Anxiety* (Glencoe, Ill.: Free Press, 1960), pp. 37–87.

2. The virtues and vices of this approach have been discussed at length by Betty Glad, "The Role of Psychoanalytic Biography in Political Science," a paper delivered at the annual meeting of the American Political Science Association, 1968.

3. I have combined two of Erikson's stages here.

4. Malcolm X, *The Autobiography of Malcolm X* (New York: Grove Press, 1965), p. 7.

5. *Ibid.,* p. 8.

6. Erikson, *op. cit.,* p. 66.

7. Malcolm X, *op. cit.,* p. 4.

8. *Ibid.,* p. 11.

9. *Ibid.,* p. 15.

10. *Ibid.,* p. 30.

11. *Ibid.,* p. 20.

12. Heinz Hartmann, *Essays on Ego Psychology* (New York: International Universities Press, 1964), p. 52.

13. Malcolm X, *op. cit.,* p. 28.

14. *Ibid.,* p. 31.

15. *Ibid.,* p. 26.

16. *Ibid.,* p. 29.

17. *Ibid.,* p. 37.

18. Erik Erikson, *Identity, Youth, and Crisis* (New York: W. W. Norton, 1968), p. 303.

19. Malcolm X, *op. cit.,* p. 146.

20. *Ibid.,* p. 87.

21. *Ibid.,* p. 121.

22. Erikson, "The Problem of Ego Identity," *op. cit.,* p. 56.

23. Malcolm X, *op. cit.,* p. 43.

24. *Ibid.,* p. 90.

25. The elements of the code, which is not presented in total, are taken in part from C. Eric Lincoln, *The Black Muslims in America* (Boston: Beacon Press, 1961), pp. 80–81, and Malcolm X, *op. cit.,* p. 221.

26. Charles E. Silberman, *Crisis in Black and White* (New York: Vintage Books, 1964), p. 72. Silberman includes a 1963 *Newsweek* poll taken by Louis Harris that tends to confirm what he offers as elements of the Negro stereotype: 35 per cent of American whites believed that Negroes laugh a lot, 75 per cent that Negroes tend to be less ambitious than whites, 69 per cent that Negroes have looser morals than whites, 61 per cent that Negroes keep untidy homes, 50 per cent that Negroes have less native intelligence. In the South proportions were higher on every item.

27. Malcolm X, *op. cit.,* p. 70.

28. *Ibid.,* p. 164.

29. *Ibid.,* p. 170.

30. *Ibid.,* p. 288.

31. *Ibid.,* pp. 211–212.

32. *Ibid.,* p. 267.

33. *Ibid.,* p. 187.

34. *Ibid.,* p. 208.

35. *Ibid.,* p. 222.

36. *Ibid.,* p. 295.

37. *Ibid.,* p. 297.

38. *Ibid.,* p. 306.

39. *Ibid.,* p. 286.

40. *Ibid.,* p. 294.

41. *Ibid.,* p. 199.

42. *Ibid.,* p. 298.

43. *Ibid.,* p. 282.

44. *Ibid.,* pp. 338–339.

45. *Ibid.,* p. 340.

46. *Ibid.,* p. 371.

47. *Ibid.,* p. 362.

48. *Ibid.,* p. 363.

49. *Ibid.,* p. 365.

8 □ BEYOND THE HERO MYTH IN WEBER'S POLITICAL SOCIOLOGY

□ Those readers who are familiar with Weber's ideal types of authority should agree that his treatment of charismatic authority is the weakest link in his typology. It is quite apparent that his analysis of charisma lacks the depth and systematic exploration that he gave to both the traditional and rational-legal types of authority. Although he elevated charisma to an important place within his theory of social change, the concept was scarcely developed beyond the elementary point of definition. In fact, it is quite reasonable to argue that Weber failed to develop a theory of charisma, for he offered no hypotheses to account for the follower's submissive relationship to the so-called charismatic leader, which was the essential core of his definition of charisma. That he had no theory of charisma, but only a broad definition, is clear when one assesses the inconsistent and confusing way in which he, himself, applied the concept.[1] It is little wonder, then, that the concept of charisma has been so indiscriminately applied by both scholars and laymen.

That Weber paid so little attention to the charismatic relationship is surprising, for he attached great importance to charisma as the dynamic force behind historical development and institution-building. Within his theory of social change, charisma represented a large class of creative and innovative human impulses that periodically erupted in collective movements to challenge the conservative tendencies of traditional and rational-legal modes of social action and organization. With traditional forms of domination waning, Weber's principle worry was that the bureaucratic revolution would advance with finality on many fronts, seriously reducing the influence of the emotional currents of life that were necessary for revitalizing culture and social structures. Because of its nature, he feared that bureaucracy would extinguish a good part of what was human in human history. The specific nature of bureaucracy develops the more perfectly, he argued, when bureaucratic life is dehumanized, or "the more completely it succeeds in eliminating from official business love, hatred, and all purely personal, irrational, and emotional elements which escape calculation."[2]

Opposed on principle to these dehumanizing and conformistic trends, Weber resurrected charisma from religious studies in order to emphasize conceptually that part of social life that remains forever beyond the reach of bureaucratic domination. Charisma and bureaucracy were then juxtaposed in this thinking as opposing social forces. Bureaucratic domination represented that part of society that was bound by intellectually analyzable rules, while charismatic domination he considered specifically irrational in the sense that it is foreign to all rules.[3] In contrast to the restrictive and conformistic attributes of bureaucratic life, charisma became the analytic category wherein Weber placed the irrational impulses that free individuals to oppose the social order. It is in this sense that S. N. Eisenstadt speaks of charisma as the nucleus of Weber's analysis of individual freedom and creativity.[4]

Educated in the liberal European tradition, Weber was worried that the increasing strength of bureaucracy would stifle freedom and consequently reduce the creative alternatives of action. "As he was not willing to see bureaucrats as harbingers of freedom," we are told, "Weber felt that the field of responsible freedom was shrinking. He saw himself, in this connection, as an old-fashioned liberal, unafraid of being on the defensive or of swimming against the stream."[5] In principle, Weber was not opposed to bureaucracy, for he realized the great need for bureaucratic organization to cope with the problems of an increasingly complex and overpopulated world. Rather, his concern was that action would lose its artistic qualities, that its innovative character would be submerged in rules and orders to such a great extent that societies would lose their cultural vitality. To achieve a better balance of bureaucratic and charismatic forms of social action was possibly the most important goal of modern society, from Weber's perspective. Yet, in terms of his view of history, he would probably have labeled this goal utopian.

Although cast in a somewhat different light, the conflict that Weber saw between charisma and bureaucracy was basically a replica of the classic dichotomy between freedom and autocracy. The tension between charisma and bureaucracy was the dynamic feature of a loosely structured dialectic framework, which allowed Weber to outline a conception of historical development and to assess the nature and direction of change in situations contemporary to his own time. As an element of his dialectics, charisma was thus a vital part of Weber's view of history and of social development. Therefore, although he had no theory of charisma per se, Weber did use the concept as an analytic unit within a broader theory of social change.

Weber gave special significance to the charismatic leader within his dialectic framework as the repository of the creative impulses that check the march of bureaucratization. In his view, "charismatic leader" was almost synonymous with "creative personality," which he contrasted with the temperament of the technical personality manufactured by the bureaucratic machine. These two personality types became antagonists in a constant struggle for social supremacy, as Mommsen's interpretation suggests:

> The creative personality, whose attitude is directed by metaphysical values and which is therefore "free" of the conditions of the environment, is in continual conflict with the "technician" and the "organization man" (*Ordnungsmensch*) whose acts are exclusively determined by existing conditions and the chances of success, and for whom the supreme law is adaptation and obedience to the powers that be.[6]

In the Nietzschean tradition, the charismatic leader was elevated to a commanding position over the masses, making the leader both the spark that ignites collective opposition to the social and moral order and the creator of new forms of social existence. The attachment of God-like qualities to the charismatic leader was in harmony with Weber's general tendency to think that religious beliefs were some of the most powerful transforming influences on secular social forms. Unless they were fused to religious sentiments, material interests by themselves could not establish new lines of historical development. Connecting the religious and leadership sectors of social action, Weber came to believe "that religious convictions, in the final instance, the religious charisma of individual saints and prophets, are the principal driving force of social change—though not of every social movement."[7]

Devotion to a utopian vision sets the charismatic leader off from the rest of society and sets him on a collision course with the forces defending the status quo. For such a leader to shape the social order required not only the power to shake society's foundations to prepare it for change, but also a strong enough character to reconstruct the moral order in accordance with an ethic of ultimate ends and an ethic of responsibility. Consider Weber's words:

> It is immensely moving when a *mature* man—no matter whether old or young in years—is aware of a responsibility for the consequence of his conduct and really feels such responsibility with heart and soul. He then acts by following an ethic of responsibility and somewhere he reaches the point where he says: "Here I stand; I can do no other." That is something genuinely human and moving. And every one of us who is not spiritually dead must realize the possibility of finding himself at some time in that position. In so far as this is true, an ethic of ultimate ends and an ethic of responsibility are not absolute contrasts but rather supplements, which only in unison constitute a genuine man—a man who *can* have the "calling for politics."[8]

From this perspective, the charismatic leader must be more than a utopian visionary; he must be a moralist as well. Thus, unlike Nietzsche, who allowed the "superman" to tyrannize his flock, Weber assumed that the charismatic leader would act in a responsible fashion and would consequently guide his followers with the gentle hand of love, rather than whipping them into submission.

Much as a utopian social theory that transcends our perceptions of reality in order to create a society through art,[9] the vision of the charismatic leader allows him to transcend his own sense of limits in order to create a new society through action. To achieve this state of transcendence requires not merely a powerful vision, but also a sense of mission, or, in Weber's words, a "steadfastness of heart":

> Certainly all historical experience confirms the truth—that man would not have attained the possible unless time and again he had reached out for the impossible. But to do that a man must be a leader, and not only a leader but a hero as well, in a very sober sense of the word. And even those who are neither leaders nor heroes must arm themselves with that steadfastness of heart which can brave even the crumbling of all hopes. This is necessary right now, or else men will not be able to attain even that which is possible today. Only he has the calling for politics who is sure that he shall not crumble when the world from his point of view is too stupid or too base for what he wants to offer. Only he who in the face of all this can say "In spite of all!" has a calling for politics.[10]

A utopian vision that may be impossible to reach gives meaning to action because it provides the leader with a purpose beyond the utilitarian dictates of his own selfish interest. Both the leader's vision and his steadfastness of heart thus become a part of his calling as a political artist, one who is guided by a vision and motivated by passion, but who remains forever bound by ethical considerations. Weber's consuming interest in charisma as a feature of a broader theory of social change can therefore be understood as an attempt to preserve, at least in theory, enough freedom of action for creating new forms of social life, but stopping considerably short of license, so that one could truly speak of leadership as an art form.

Like so many great thinkers, Weber had extraordinary insights into history and social change that won him disciples and a special place in sociology and political science. Yet, unlike many in the social theory tradition, he encouraged others to criticize and expand his work. For example, in his essay "science as a vocation" he invites his audience to exceed his own accomplishments when he says that every scientific achievement asks to be surpassed and to be outdated. "We cannot work without hoping that others will advance further than we have."[11] In the preceding two chapters I have developed a theory of charisma to fill one void in Weber's work. Now, in this closing chapter, I would like to go further and suggest that there are a number of problems in both Weber's theory of social change and in his typology of authority that stem from his acceptance of a hero myth. By laying my own work on leadership and mass mobilization alongside Weber's ideas, I hope to sharpen the thrust of my own general findings in the further hope that some of Weber's statements about charisma, leadership, and social change will be surpassed or at least revised. To try to advance further than Weber in these areas does not diminish his greatness as a thinker; on the contrary, it is the highest compliment, for his were the guiding insights from which I started.

The Hero Myth and Weber's Glorification of the Charismatic Leader

Stories about heroic leaders are plentiful in human history. Together, these stories, many of them biblical and religious in nature, have become chapters of a more general story, or hero myth, which depicts great leaders as saviors of their age and the star performers in the drama of social change. To sustain the belief that great leaders are indispensable to the success of collective movements, superhuman qualities are imputed to them by observers, if not by their followers. By this device, there is some assurance that someone is in a commanding position as we try to make sense of the fragmented images that are called up in our minds by allusions to such notions as "revolution" or "social change." In essence, then, the use of the hero myth is one way that order is imposed on the chaos of collective movements.

A myth grows and spreads because it has the appearance of truth. As is true for utopian thinking, a myth takes a tendency in the real world and transforms it into a universal regularity. For instance, the tendency for leaders to shape the character of collective movements is transformed in mythic thinking into something akin to charismatic domination in which the leader alone plays a commanding role in social change processes. It is the partial truth of the hero myth—that leaders do indeed shape the character and direction of social change—that sustains it even against the evidence of facts or the gentle prodding of our own better judgment.

While skepticism is the normal response to uncertain conclusions in science, the very opposite is true for a myth. Because a myth provides some order in the face of complexity, it is usually embraced fully. In this process, the critical impulse gives way to that part of us that demands certainty. When the hero myth has been internalized to the point where it is considered as fact, then when a collective movement is observed the mythic story will unfold since it is through the myth that the movement becomes coherent. For those who participate in this hero myth, every collective movement (especially one of revolutionary proportions) will include a leader who possesses the powers of prophecy and the magical personality traits that their mythic expectations demand. Allusions to the dominance of the hero will be regarded as self-evident and in no further need of elaboration. The assumption is that those who hear the story accept the hero myth as fact, and thus will nod their heads in agreement while preparing themselves for the next point.

There are several indications that Weber's thinking about social change was greatly influenced by the hero myth. Certainly, the great powers he imputed to the charismatic leader in the process of social change point to this conclusion. Moreover, there is a strong impression that when Weber alluded to charisma he assumed that his ideas were self-evident. Eisenstadt has also recognized this tendency:

> What is it in the charismatic that appeals to people, that makes them willing to follow a charismatic leader, to accept his call to give up some of their resources—wealth, time, energy, or existing social bonds and commitments—for the implementation of his vision? And when are people most willing to follow his appeal?
>
> In Weber's own writings this problem is not explicitly dealt with. *For the most part, he takes for granted the nature of the charismatic.*[12] (Emphasis added.)

An illustration of this point is found in Weber's work. After a very brief discussion of charismatic authority as it relates to the corporate group, he concluded with the curt statement: "The above is scarcely in need of further discussion."[13] Of course what he said was not only in need of further discussion, but it was desperately lacking in theoretical development. Yet, guided by the hero myth, these abbreviated thoughts were all that he considered necessary. Furthermore, the claim that Weber's thinking was influenced by the hero myth may help to explain why he treated charisma with such brevity in his vast works even though the concept was so critical a part of his theory of social change, and why he failed to develop a theory of charisma that identified the causal factors bearing on the creation of the charismatic bond.

Problems in Weber's Conception of Social Change

How much the hero myth affected Weber's ideas about social change we can surmise in part from the dramatic role he assigned the charismatic leader as change agent. Of course, within the broader boundaries of his thinking, Weber considered what Aristotle called the "motor cause" of change to be the dialectic struggle between charisma (representing the irrational side of social life) and bureaucracy (representing the rational side). However, since Weber assumed that charisma resides in the leader, the motor cause of change became, in effect, the charismatic leader. He regarded the charismatic leader as the critical force of social movement, capable of dislodging individuals from the social fabric by the sheer power of his will and thus freeing them from the shackle of rules to oppose the old order.

What makes the charismatic leader a powerful agent of change is his ability to convert others, who, in their mutual obligations to him, constitute what Weber called a "corporate group." Through the collective adherence to the leader's will and mission, a sense of community emerges among those, who, previously, could not have been united purely in terms of material interests. Oriented to the charismatic leader as the nucleus of the revolutionary community, these followers become highly integrated through an emotional bond to the leader whose strength constitutes the real threat to the rational or traditional bulwarks of society. Thus, the corporate group is the power base from which the charismatic leader challenges the social order. Yet adherence to the will and mission of the charismatic leader not only revolutionizes society, it also revolutionizes the convert's soul. As Weber said, the collective belief in heroes and revelation "revolutionizes men from the inside out . . . and seeks to shape things and situations in accordance with its revolutionary will."[14]

One of the problems in Weber's conception of social change is that he took the existence of charisma for granted. The presence of charisma was taken as the starting point in his thinking about change, rather than as an effect whose causes needed to be identified and analyzed.[15] Thus, his tendency was to assess the historical processes leading from charismatic movements to increasing bureaucratization, omitting from consideration the historical conditions and social processes that give rise to charismatic movements.[16] This procedure left Weber with a skeletal theory of social change, since it neglected to touch upon the crucial problem of how and why followers develop commitments within revolutionary movements. Thus, he failed to realize that there could be more than one type of commitment.

Furthermore, except for his brief admission that the rise of charismatic leaders is associated with periods of societal crisis, Weber had almost nothing to say about the influence of structural strains on personal inclinations to join revolutionary movements. Had he focused his attention on the conditions that produce revolutions, he would have recognized the theoretical importance of structural strains both as they affect personal tensions and as they free individuals to begin new commitments. What we see in the case studies in Chapter V is that the rebel leader's success in mobilizing converts was not simply a function of his will or mission, as Weber would lead us to believe, but stemmed from the configurations and insoluble conflicts of political systems and the purposeful choices of ruling leaders, both factors intensifying structural strain.

Had Weber attempted to isolate the psychological factors that produce charismatic commitments, he would have recognized that charisma is not the primary motor cause of change. Strains resident in social structure are much more critical mechanisms bearing on the formation of revolutionary commitments, for these strains are the basis for the development of commitments derived from material interest as well as those created to deal with extreme psychological disturbances. In earlier chapters, I tried to show how charismatic bonds are psychologically induced, yet also how extreme intrapsychic distance and identity diffusion can in some cases be traced to structural strains, such as inadequately operating socialization structures, inadequate opportunities for upward mobility, and the existence of social control problems that make the preservation of privacy impossible. Arthur Koestler summarizes this appropriately when he says: "It is true that the case-history of most revolutionaries and reformers reveals a neurotic conflict with family and society. But this only proves, to paraphrase Marx, that a moribund society creates its own morbid gravediggers."[17]

By deductively granting charisma an exclusive role within his dialectic view of social change, Weber also failed to take sufficient account of the rational and traditional aspects of the commitment process. What is surprising about this omission is that it was basically at odds with his conception of ideal types, for he presses the point home that each of his three ideal types of authority are likely to be present in all situations and at all times, although in different degrees.[18] When he discussed traditional societies, for example, he was careful to take into account all three types of authority, yet references to collective movements were almost exclusively couched in terms of charisma. This inclination to discuss charisma when referring to the political forces of creativity and innovation was of course very much in keeping with Weber's mythic expectations. But this led him to a position that basically contradicted his view that ideas, or values, make a major difference in guiding the direction of historical development.

Weber's attack on Marx's historical determinism was based on his view that ideas have social power and that individuals are capable of shaping the direction of history. His "liberal heritage and urge prevented him from taking a determinist position. He felt that freedom consists not in realizing alleged historical necessities but rather in making deliberate choices between open alternatives."[19] Yet his dialectic view of change diminished the importance of ideas and choice. By claiming that the conflict between charisma and bureaucracy was the primary motor cause of change, he undermined the notion that the critical elements in historical development are ideas, which, assuming the character of an ideology, identify the sources of structural strains and suggest ways of acting to relieve them.

Weber regarded charisma as an innovative force, whose vitality was easily destroyed through routinization. But charisma is not innately innovative: It is innovative only when it serves an innovative idea. On the contrary, when charisma serves a conservative idea, as it does to some extent within the Nation of Islam, it will hold certain innovative and creative tendencies in check. The same argument applies to the rational-legal and traditional forms of domination: Whether they assume an innovative character or not depends on the nature of the ideas that are being propagated by those engaged in action. This perspective should force us to reexamine Weber's contention that rational and traditional modes of social action and organization do not lend themselves very readily to innovative change.

My analysis of transactional relations suggests that rational social action is not only a more powerful force in revolutionary movements than Weber assumed, but all indications point to the conclusion that transactional relationships are a far more significant factor than charisma in accounting for the development of revolutionary commitments. In this respect, we might better spend our time discussing revolution, not as a struggle between the irrational forces of charisma and the rational aspects of bureaucracy, but rather as a conflict between powerful ideas, or ideologies, which are propagated and defended by different organizations attempting to win the loyalty of the masses.

By connecting charisma to irrationality, then collective movements to charisma, Weber derived the logical deduction that collective movements are irrational. In this process, the possibility that both rational and traditional modes of social action could assume a strong revolutionary character was almost entirely excluded from consideration. Thus, Weber scarcely mentioned the possibility that bureaucratic regimes could be overthrown by bureaucratically dominated revolutionary organizations in the name of new ideas. He was certainly aware that revolutionary leaders would spawn bureaucratic structures, yet he did not develop that insight beyond the length of a few words: "When those subject to bureaucratic control seek to escape the influence of the existing bureaucratic apparatus, this is normally possible only by creating an organization of their own which is equally subject to the process of bureaucratization." And given the nature of bureaucratic domination, he had little faith that revolution would reverse the tide of bureaucratic expansion: "Even in the case of revolution by force or of occupation by an enemy, the bureaucratic machinery will normally continue to function just as it has for the previous government."[20]

Because Weber assumed that charisma was the primary source of innovation, his feeling that charisma was diminishing in importance as a result of increasing bureaucratization could only make him pessimistic about the prospects for modern society. I think this pessimistic view is not necessarily warranted, however. For if we start from the vantage point that it is the conflict of ideas that is the crucial motor cause behind historical development, then diminishing charisma in the world should not be so alarming. For bureaucracy can be innovative and creative if it serves innovative and creative ideas. Certainly, both the Bolshevik and Nazi revolutions had well-developed bureaucratic structures that served revolutionary ends. It was not charisma that made the major difference in these two revolutions, as Weber might have expected, but rather the power of the revolutionary idea (ideology) and the bureaucratic and political effectiveness of the respective revolutionary organizations.

Weber's allusion to the freedom-inducing qualities of charisma is another problem within his conception of social change. He uncritically assumes that those who are a part of the collective aspects of charismatic domination are freed for action. Apparently, he thought this was true for leader and follower alike, although he sees the follower giving up much of his newly found freedom by forming new obligations to the charismatic leader.[21] Yet, as this study has shown, it is not primarily charisma that dislodges the follower from the social fabric. Rather, the freedom to choose and to act arises from dislocations in social structure or from events. As my theory of commitment tries to make clear, availability for action grows out of situations in which the individual is forced to terminate a commitment to one form of activity, thus releasing him to start new activities. For example, unemployment and military disengagement freed individuals for revolutionary activity within the Bolshevik and Nazi revolutions, just as prison paradoxically freed Malcolm X to begin forming a commitment within the Black Muslim movement. It was not charisma that set Malcolm free, unless we are speaking of psychological freedom experienced as mania; rather, he was freed from the restraining factors of ghetto life and became available for action because of prison detention. Freed by detention, he was able to follow Mr. Muhammad.

The main limitation Weber places on the charismatic leader is success: If he fails to work miracles or reach the movement's goals, the charismatic leader is apt to lose his charisma in the eyes of his following. However, looking back on my case studies, the limitations on the leader's action must be expanded far beyond this point. Rebel leaders are not nearly as free to act as Weber's mythic thinking led him to suppose; in fact they are bound by follower expectations, organizational norms, resource limitations, counter-strategies, and the like. They cannot will a revolution, but they must patiently organize their forces and study the situation so as to arrive at a correct diagnosis of its revolutionary potential. "They must feel out the growing insurrection in good season," Leon Trotsky writes, "and supplement it with a conspiracy."[22] The objective must be "not to hurry forward too far, but also not to stay behind."[23] In this respect, the rebel leader who wants to maintain his authority within the corporate group may have to follow as often as he leads. While I must admit that the rebel leader is freer than the bureaucrat to engage in creative action, this study points out many more forces restraining the rebel leader than Weber would have admitted.

Operating in terms of the hero myth, Weber overly exaggerated the role of the charismatic leader as the locus of creativity. In contrast to his view, this study points up other considerations that have to be taken into account in assessing the different modes of creative action within collective movements. As I pointed out in the opening chapters, leadership in general is a creative status and can be initiated by individuals who might normally be defined as followers. As the coordinating structure of social systems, leadership can innovate by developing creative strategies of action without possessing charisma. Lenin's leadership is an excellent example of the creative nature of an instrumental style, as is Hitler's flair for organization and planning. Also, creative action can be initiated by ruling leaders who attempt to reduce structural strains by affecting the law or by changing the priorities of the general goal system.

In contrast to Weber's view that the charismatic leader is the primary source of creativity in collective movements, I have tried to show how leaders share functions, thus sharing in the creative work of coordinating the direction of social movement. (Indeed, there are as many creative modes of action as there are functions of leadership.) In each of the four movements studied, more than one primary leader was engaged in creative action and followers added great vitality to the process of change by initiating action themselves. Take the Nazi revolution, for example. There we saw how Hitler's failure to bureaucratize the whole party apparatus worked ultimately to his benefit, for unfettered by bureaucratic domination local leaders and so-called followers were able to create political forms of action out of day-to-day problems. This is not to suggest that the bureaucratization of the party led in the direction of political stagnation, for, on the contrary, it provided a chain of command and numerous horizontal points of entry that helped to achieve Hitler's revolutionary goals.

Even the coercive features of leadership can have creative consequences. Because Weber was primarily concerned with legitimate leadership, he failed to take into account the innovative undercurrents that flow from the follower's fear of the leader or the leader's use of social control mechanisms to arouse support within the movement.[24] As Malcolm X's case illustrates, even charisma has a coercive dimension, for his awe of Mr. Muhammad was partially a consequence of the fear aroused in his mind as he contemplated the Messenger's divine and superhuman powers. The transactional uses of control, on the other hand, were apparent in the Nazi revolution, wherein Hitler utilized his roving ambassadors, state inspectors, and secret police to initiate changes within the movement or to ensure conformity to plans already formulated and enacted.

Treating the creative features of leadership in the most general terms, Weber excluded from his analysis of change the creative aspects of the mobilization process. Certainly, creating a collective movement is a test of a leader's imagination as well as the viability of his vision for society. How leaders encourage individuals through the initial stages of commitment to strong dedication is clearly an art. In fact, the bond that the leader is able to create with a single follower may become the example for a new state. In this respect, one can argue that leaders prepare themselves for statecraft through experimentation and practice within collective movements. For example, Hitler's experience in developing the Nazi party paved the way for the construction of the Nazi totalitarian state. Here, we see the nature of the follower's commitment and the forms of organization as the initial sketches that ultimately become the rudiments of the leader's major work of art—the state. Art can also be seen in the leader's effort to amalgamate different types of followers into a single line of organizational effort, something that Weber mentions only in passing: "Loyalty may be hypocritically simulated by individuals or by whole groups on purely opportunistic grounds, or carried out in practice for reasons of material self-interest. Or people may submit from individual weakness and helplessness because there is no acceptable alternative."[25]

Using the concept of commitment to understand the dynamic forms of creativity within collective movements, one begins to see the struggle between ruling and rebel leaders for the loyalty of the masses not simply as a conflict between competing ideologies, but also as a conflict between two forms of art. Here, opposing leadership structures and organizations compete to secure control over political life. Ruling leaders attempt to reinforce commitments to the regime through creative action, while rebel leaders work creativity to unlock individuals from the social fabric while offering them the opportunity to join in a life of "political crime."

Problems in Weber's Typology of Authority

Given Weber's dialectic view of social change, it is understandable that he chose to give charismatic authority equal status alongside the traditional and rational-legal types of rule.[26] Indeed, how much the hero myth dominated his analysis of authority can be discerned from the fact that he chose to discuss other forms of personal leadership, such as patrimonialism and sultanism, within the context of traditional authority. Totally committed to charisma in spirit, he could not see that patrimonial authority, sultanism, and charismatic authority were actually subtypes of a less exclusive type of authority, which I chose to call *personal authority*. I think Weber was wrong in assuming that charismatic authority was synonymous with personal rulership, for, while charismatic relationships can exist within systems of personal authority, the evidence of this study shows that there is more than one source of legitimation for personal rule. Therefore, it is time to revise Weber's typology of authority by relegating charismatic authority to a subtype status within a broader conception of personal rule.

Personal authority is distinguished from traditional and rational-legal bases of rule by the greater role of leadership in decision-making processes. Within a system of personal authority, decision-making power is concentrated in the hands of leadership, and may be exercised arbitrarily over a public that expects personal rulers to transcend customs, constitutions, and their own decrees. Thus, the follower's relationship to the state is through loyalty to the ruler, rather than through obedience to custom or law. It is precisely in this sense that Weber speaks of patrimonial authority and sultanism:

> Where authority is primarily oriented to tradition but in its exercise makes the claim of full personal powers, it will be called "patrimonial" authority. Where patrimonial authority lays primary stress on the sphere of arbitrary will free of traditional limitations, it will be called "Sultanism."[27]

Decision-making power within a system of personal authority does not have to reside exclusively in a single leader, as Weber suggests in his analysis of charismatic domination. It can either be shared among leaders, as it was between Lenin and Trotsky within the Bolshevik revolution, or it can be more fully concentrated in a single leader, as it was within the Nazi movement, where Hitler deliberately isolated important secondary leaders from one another in order to prevent the formation of competing power blocs. How power is distributed within systems of personal authority is an important focus for future research, but it is not the critical issue here.

Since Weber did not examine authority relationships fully in terms of leader-follower interactions, he failed to recognize that, in addition to his ideal types of authority, there are also three bases of commitment and numerous sources of trust from which those commitments form. Several lines of thinking have been developed in this study that, if united in schematic form (see figure), suggest a broader and more complex conception of authority than that advanced by Weber. The figure shows that there are basically three layers of analysis that one must undertake when assessing the specific character of a system of personal authority. Starting at the lowest level, the sources of trust must first be identified and then analyzed as they bear on the formation of the three bases of commitment. The strength of each type of commitment should be considered next, as the second level of analysis. Finally, how the three bases of commitment are distributed within a system of personal authority should be determined. Although this schematic view can be used to assess the character of all three types of authority—traditional, rational-legal, and personal—I will briefly discuss only personal authority here.

The right of leadership to rule arbitrarily in the name of a public, found in medieval European kingdoms, modern dictatorships, and collective movements, can reside in any or all three of the sources of legitimacy that I have identified as the transactional, inspirational, and charismatic bases of commitment. A system of personal rule may derive its legitimacy from the manipulation of rewards as well as punishments, from the manipulation of myths and symbols that give meaning to action and suffering, and from

The Social and Psychological Foundations of Personal Authority

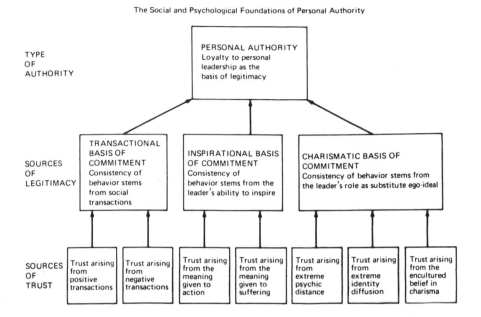

the presence of leaders who are able to provide security, a new identity, or cultural reinforcements for those whose psychological dispositions or socialization require that they obey orders.

Trust is the attitudinal disposition from which the follower grants the leader rights and powers.[28] Social transactions between leader and follower can generate trustful feelings in the follower's mind that lead him to develop a strong transactional commitment. The meaning that a leader gives to action and suffering as the representative of a collective spirit can also be a source of trust that culminates in strong inspirational ties with the leader. Or a follower who identifies with a leader as his ego-ideal may develop a childlike trust in the leader as a prelude to the formation of an enduring charismatic commitment.[29] Each of these sources of trust represents the more specific relational basis of legitimacy. While all three sources of legitimacy may be present as the foundation stones of a system of personal authority, there may be instances in which one source of legitimacy is dominant, leaving its special mark on the structure of leadership.

The general character of a system of personal authority should reflect its dominant source of legitimacy, if indeed one dominates. If the transactional source of legitimation prevails, for example, the structure of personal rule may develop the character of boss rule if negative transactional relationships are emphasized. Personal authority in the Soviet Union under Joseph Stalin's rule would be illustrative of this type. For even though Stalin longed to be called by the affectionate and respectful term "Starik" (meaning

"The Old Man"), his negative transactional orientation to his subordinates earned him the title "Khozyain," which meant "The Boss."[30] When the source of legitimacy stems primarily from the inspirational role of leadership, the character of a system of personal authority is likely to revolve around the sacrifices of leaders and followers. Representative of this form would be the Indian independence movement in which both Gandhi and his followers derived meaning from their denial of physical comforts and violence. Indeed, Gandhi's philosophy of nonviolence was based on the idea that suffering through passive resistance had meaning beyond the act of resistance. Finally, as Weber correctly argued, when a system of personal authority includes a large charismatic following, leadership is apt to be endowed with God-like qualities, a phenomenon to be seen in the structure of personal rule within the Nation of Islam.

While it is possible to explain the general character of a system of personal authority by identifying its dominant source of legitimacy, all three sources of legitimation should be present in different degrees. Instead of identifying only one source, as has been the tendency in using charismatic authority, we should look for all three sources of legitimacy when analyzing systems of personal rule. As a consequence, we might avoid the traditional problem that Weber's analysis has created, of having to attribute charismatic qualities and powers to a leader within a system of personal authority even if none appeared objectively to be present—as, for example, the tendency to regard leaders like Lenin and Stalin as charismatic leaders.

Notes

1. The following sample of uses that Weber found for charisma illustrate my point: "'charismatic' justice," "holder of charisma," "charismatic ruler," "charismatic domination," "charismatic war lords," "charismatic qualifications," "charismatic states," "charismatic community," "charismatic qualities," "magical charisma," "sacred charisma," "charismatic search," "religious charisma," "charisma of 'ability,'" "charisma of illumination," "charisma of the mind or of taste," "charisma of magical powers of sorcery," "charismatically correct life conduct," "charismatic virtues," "orthodox charisma of virtues," "to awaken charisma," "a magical-charismatic meaning," "charismatic interpretation," "charismatic inspiration," "charismatic 'revolutionary,'" "charismatic missionaries," "charismatic discipleship."

2. Max Weber in Hans Gerth and C. Wright Mills (eds.), *From Max Weber: Essays in Sociology* (New York: Oxford University Press, 1946), pp. 215-216.

3. Max Weber, *The Theory of Social and Economic Organization* (New York: Free Press, p. 361. In the introductory essay to this volume, Talcott Parsons notes the two ways in which Weber applied the term "irrational": ". . . Ultimate values tend to be treated as an absolutely 'irrational' force. In a closely connected sense affect is also treated as irrational. Weber again and again, in these methodological remarks, refers to it in these terms." Cf. p. 16.

4. S. N. Eisenstadt (ed.), *Max Weber: On Charisma and Institution Building* (Chicago: University of Chicago Press, 1968), p. xviii.

5. Gerth and Mills (eds.), *op. cit.,* p. 70.

6. Wolfgang Mommsen, "Max Weber's Political Sociology and his Philosophy of World History," *International Social Science Journal,* 17 (1965), p. 29.

7. *Ibid.,* p. 31.

8. Weber in Gerth and Mills (eds.), *op. cit.,* p. 127.

9. For a brief analysis of the nature of utopian social theory, cf. my essay "Reflections on Political Philosophy," in James V. Downton, Jr., and David K. Hart (eds.), *Perspectives on Political Philosophy: Thucydides Through Machiavelli,* Vol. I (New York: Holt, Rinehart and Winston, 1971), pp. 1–16.

10. Weber in Gerth and Mills (eds.), *op. cit.,* p. 128.

11. Weber in Gerth and Mills (eds.), *op. cit.,* p. 138.

12. Eisenstadt, *op. cit.,* p. xxii.

13. Weber, *The Theory of Social and Economic Organization, op. cit.,* p. 362.

14. Weber quoted in Mommsen, *op. cit.,* p. 33.

15. Claude Ake makes a similar criticism of Weber from the perspective of one interested in political integration: "Strictly speaking, charisma implies integration. The concept of charisma describes a situation in which different people have identified with a particular leader and developed a 'communistic relationship' through their common involvement in his mission. If charisma implies integration, the theory of charismatic legitimation offers a deductive, not an enlightening, explanation of integration. The theory seeks to explain how solidarity may be forged; but it does so by means of a concept which assumes the existence of solidarity. It is mainly because of the absence of a leader or an institution capable of commanding the loyalty of the citizenry that the problem of integrating the new state arises in the first place. To the extent that the theory of charismatic legitimation assumes the existence of a symbol of national identity—the charismatic leader—it is a circular explanation of integration." Cf. "Charismatic Legitimation and Political Integration," *Comparative Studies in Society and History,* 9 (October, 1966), p. 12.

16. Peter M. Blau, "Critical Remarks on Weber's Theory of Authority," *American Political Science Review,* 57 (June, 1963), p. 309.

17. Arthur Koestler in Richard Grossman (ed.), *The God That Failed* (New York: Bantam Books, 1949), p. 12.

18. For a discussion of the analytic use of ideal types, cf., Reinhard Bendix, "Max Weber's Sociology Today," *International Social Science Journal,* 17 (1965), pp. 14–15 and Ben Nefzger, "The Ideal Type: Some Conceptions and Misconceptions," *Sociological Quarterly,* 6 (Spring, 1965), pp. 166–174.

19. Gerth and Mills (eds.), *op. cit.,* p. 70.

20. Weber, *The Theory of Social and Economic Organization, op. cit.,* p. 338.

21. Weber in Gerth and Mills (eds.), *op. cit.,* p. 254.

22. Leon Trotsky, *The Russian Revolution* (Garden City, N.Y.: Doubleday, 1959), p. 309.

23. Leon Trotsky, *Lenin* (New York: Capricorn Books, 1962), p. 74.

24. Others have criticized Weber for omitting coercive forms of rule from his typology of authority. Cf., for example, Karl Loewenstein, *Max Weber's Political Ideas in the Perspective of Our Time* (Northampton: The University of Massachusetts Press, 1966), p. 90 and Blau, *op. cit.,* p. 306.

25. Weber, *The Theory of Social and Economic Organization, op. cit.,* p. 326.

26. Blau, *op. cit.,* p. 309.

27. Weber, *The Theory of Social and Economic Organization, op. cit.,* p. 347.

28. It is fairly clear that Weber failed to grasp the importance of trust as the fountainhead of legitimacy, thus of authority.

29. It is important to understand that personal rulers may be great inspirational figures without having a large charismatic following. And we should realize that all followers who develop a charismatic commitment will be inspired by their leader, if nothing else by the leader's life as an example of a meaningful existence. That Weber failed to recognize the analytic distinction between the charismatic and inspirational bases of commitment lay partially in his choices of examples when discussing the forms of charismatic domination. By taking cases mainly from religious movements, where charisma was clearly present, he quite naturally discovered inspirational relationships between leader and followers. Operating from a mythic view of the charismatic leader, it was easy for him to subsume the inspirational source of legitimacy within his diffusely structured conception of charismatic authority. Had he chosen cases of a secular nature, he would have found inspirational relationships between leaders and followers that could not have been classified as charismatic, even by stretching the imagination.

30. Bertram D. Wolfe, *Three Who Made A Revolution* (New York: Delta Books, 1964), p. 154.

□ REFERENCES

Books (Annotated)

ABEL, THEODORE, *Why Hitler Came Into Power.* New York: Prentice-Hall, 1938. An examination of the social bases of Hitler's conquest of power derived from extensive autobiographical accounts of Nazi party members.

ADORNO, T. W. *et al., The Authoritarian Personality.* New York: Harper, 1950. A study of right-wing extremism based on psychoanalytic theory.

ALMOND, GABRIEL *et al., The Appeals of Communism.* Princeton: Princeton University Press, 1954. An empirical study of the structure and mobilization processes of the Communist party.

ALMOND, GABRIEL and JAMES COLEMAN, *The Politics of Developing Areas.* Princeton: Princeton University Press, 1960. A structural-functional analysis of political development in the new states with a good introductory chapter outlining the approach.

ALMOND, GABRIEL and SIDNEY VERBA, *The Civic Culture.* Princeton: Princeton University Press, 1963. A cross-national survey of citizen attitudes toward their governments in Great Britain, Germany, Mexico, Italy, and the United States.

ALMOND, GABRIEL and G. BINGHAM POWELL, *Comparative Politics: A Developmental Approach.* Boston: Little, Brown, 1966. An analysis of political development that greatly expands the process features of the structural-functional model.

APTER, DAVID, *Ghana in Transition.* New York: Atheneum, 1963. A structural-functional analysis of political development in Ghana.

ARENDT, HANNAH, *Origins of Totalitarism.* New York: Harcourt Brace Jovanovich, 1951. The leading work on the structure and process of Nazi totalitarianism, with sections dealing with antisemitism, imperialism, and totalitarian rule.

BARNARD, CHESTER, *The Functions of the Executive.* Cambridge, Mass.: Harvard University Press, 1962. A study of executive functions within a theory of formal organization.

BASS, BERNARD M., *Leadership, Psychology and Organizational Behavior.* New York: Harper & Row, 1960. A theoretical work that focuses on the situational aspects of leader-follower relations.

BELL, WENDELL, RICHARD HILL, and CHARLES WRIGHT, *Public Leadership,* San Francisco: Chandler Press, 1961. A survey of the literature dealing with leadership.

BLAU, PETER M., *Exchange and Power in Social Life.* New York: John Wiley & Sons, 1964. A theoretical application of exchange theory that focuses on such problems as integration, power, change, legitimation, and values.

BULLOCK, ALLAN, *Hitler: A Study in Tyranny.* New York: Bantam Books, 1958. A historical study of Hitler's life from birth to death and the events that led him to total power and total destruction.

BUSIA, K. A., *The Position of the Chief in the Modern Political System of Ashanti.* London: Oxford University Press, 1958. Structural and operational aspects of the Ashanti political system are explored in this work, with special emphasis on sharing leadership functions.

CAMPBELL, ANGUS et al., *The American Voter.* New York: John Wiley & Sons, 1960. One in a series of survey research reports on presidential elections.

CANTRIL, HADLEY, *The Psychology of Social Movements.* New York: John Wiley & Sons, 1963. An analysis of social movements, from lynchings to revolution, in terms of compensation for losses in self-esteem.

CARLYLE, THOMAS, *Heroes, Hero-Worship and the Heroic in History.* Boston: Heath, 1913. A romantic conception of leadership pointing up the critical role of the leader as the creator of history.

CARMICHAEL, JOEL, *A Short History of the Russian Revolution.* New York: Basic Books, 1964. A historical account of events from February to October, 1917, as they shaped the development of the two pseudo-governments and the eventual Bolshevik victory.

CARR, E. H., *The Bolshevik Revolution, 1917–1923,* Vol. I. Baltimore: Penguin Books, 1966. A historical study of the roots of Bolshevism and the two revolutions of 1917, including the Bolshevik attempt to create a viable state through the process of federation.

CHAMBERLAIN, WILLIAM H., *The Russian Revolution 1917–1921,* Vol. I. New York: Macmillan, 1952. A historical treatment of the 1905 rebellion, the 1917 revolutions, and the problems the Bolsheviks faced during the consolidation of power.

CHRISTIE, RICHARD and MARIE JOHODA (eds.), *Studies in the Scope and Method of "The Authoritarian Personality."* Glencoe, Ill.: Free Press, 1954. A critique and further exploration of the concept of authoritarianism by six distinguished scholars.

COHEN, ELIE, *Human Behavior in the Concentration Camp.* New York: Grosset & Dunlap, 1965. An account of the behavioral adaptations to scarcity and insecurity within a German concentration camp where Cohen was detained.

CROSSMAN, RICHARD (ed.), *The God That Failed.* New York: Bantam Books, 1952. A collection of essays written by former Communists about how they became members of the party, became disillusioned with it, and finally left the movement.

CURRY, R. L. and L. I. WADE, *A Theory of Political Exchange: Economic Reasoning in Political Analysis.* Englewood Cliffs: Prentice-Hall, 1968. An exchange analysis of political linkages, decision-making, and political action.

CURTISS, JOHN SHELTON, *The Russian Revolutions.* New York: D. Van Nostrand,

1957. A compact history of the revolutions of 1917 accompanied by a number of readings that complement the historical text.

DAHL, ROBERT A., *Who Governs?* New Haven: Yale University Press, 1961. A community power study of New Haven that examines the distribution of power around four major social issues.

DAHL, ROBERT A., *Modern Political Analysis*. Englewood Cliffs: Prentice-Hall, 1963. A short textbook with a comparative perspective of power, political behavior, and political conflict.

DAVIES, JAMES C., *Human Nature in Politics*. New York: John Wiley & Sons, 1963. A social-psychological examination of political behavior taking off from Maslow's hierarchy of needs and tension theory.

DEUTSCHER, ISAAC, *The Prophet Armed*. London: Oxford University Press, 1954. A biography of Trotsky covering his early life through his rise to power.

DOWNS, ANTHONY, *An Economic Theory of Democracy*. New York: Harper & Row, 1957. An attempt to explain the structures and processes of democracy in terms of the model of rationality explicit in exchange theory.

EASTON, DAVID, *A Systems Analysis of Political Life*. New York: John Wiley & Sons, 1965. An elaboration of Easton's earlier work dealing with input-output processes, this book covers such aspects of political life as system response patterns, the bases of public support, and system maintenance processes.

EDINGER, LEWIS J. (ed.), *Political Leadership in Industrialized Societies*. New York: John Wiley & Sons, 1967. An anthology of distinguished essays covering such aspects of leadership as authority, style, personal charisma, and recruitment.

EISENSTADT, S. N. (ed.), *Max Weber: On Charisma and Institution Building*. Chicago: University of Chicago Press, 1968. A complete collection of Weber's work on charisma, with an excellent introductory essay outlining the main features of Weber's position.

EMMET, DOROTHY, *Function, Purpose and Powers*. New York: Macmillan, 1958. A philosophical analysis of functionalism and purposeful behavior, with a chapter devoted to "charismatic power."

ERIKSON, ERIK, *Young Man Luther*. New York: W. W. Norton, 1958. A psychological interpretation of Martin Luther's life and ideas, cast in terms of the role of youth in the creation of history.

ERIKSON, ERIK, *Childhood and Society*. New York: W. W. Norton, 1963. An analysis of the developmental stages of childhood and their bearing on the formation of personal identity.

ERIKSON, ERIK, *Identity, Youth, and Crisis*. New York: W. W. Norton, 1968. A revision of some of Erikson's earlier work on identity crisis in the life cycle and in history.

ESSIEN-UDOM, E. U., *Black Nationalism*. New York: Dell, 1962. Probably the most definitive treatment of the black nationalist tradition and the growth, structure, and strategies of the Nation of Islam.

FAGEN, RICHARD, *Politics and Communication*. Boston: Little, Brown, 1966. An examination of the structure, use, performance, and changes in political communication processes.

FESTINGER, LEON, HENRY RIECKEN, and STANLEY SCHACHTER, *When Prophecy Fails*. New York: Harper, 1956. A participant-observer study of an "end of the world" movement that emerged in the 1950's.

FISCHER, LOUIS, *The Life of Lenin.* New York: Harper & Row, 1964. Noted for its comprehensiveness and depth, this work is considered one of the leading biographies of Lenin.

FRANKL, VIKTOR E., *Man's Search for Meaning: An Introduction to Logotherapy.* New York: Washington Square Press, 1959. An account of the concentration camp experience and the development of the central features of logotherapy, a new form of psychotherapy.

FREUD, ANNA, *The Ego and the Mechanisms of Defense.* London: Hogarth Press, 1937. An extension of Sigmund Freud's analysis of psychological defenses.

FREUD, SIGMUND, *Group Psychology and the Analysis of the Ego.* New York: Bantam Books, 1960. Freud's major work on the psychology of leader-follower relationships.

FREUD, SIGMUND, *The Ego and the Id.* New York: W. W. Norton, 1961. Freud expands his thinking on the structure and interrelationship of the ego and id in this last major work of his life.

FREUD, SIGMUND, *Civilization and Its Discontents.* New York: W. W. Norton, 1961. Freud's major sociological work dealing with the role society plays in the repression of human instincts.

GERTH, HANS and C. WRIGHT MILLS (eds.), *From Max Weber: Essays in Sociology.* New York: Oxford University Press, 1946. A collection of Weber's writings in the area of politics, religion, and culture.

GAMSON, WILLIAM, *Power and Discontent.* Homewood, Ill.: Dorsey Press, 1968. An examination of the interplay between influence and social control in the process of social change, emphasizing the importance of political trust as it affects the means of influence and control.

GOEBBELS, PAUL JOSEPH, *The Early Goebbels Diaries: 1925-1926,* Helmut Heiber (ed.). New York: Praeger, 1962. These early diaries cover much of Goebbels' introspective discussions of his intrapsychic conflicts.

GOEBBELS, PAUL JOSEPH, *The Goebbels Diaries, 1942-1943,* Louis P. Lochner (ed.). Garden City, New York: Doubleday, 1948. In these later diaries, Goebbels is preoccupied with the problems of the war and with the internal crises of the Nazi state.

GOFFMAN, ERVING, *The Presentation of Self in Everyday Life.* Garden City, New York: Doubleday, 1959. A dramaturgic analysis of face-to-face interactions in everyday life with special attention given to front and back stages and team performances.

GOFFMAN, ERVING, *Encounters.* Indianapolis: Bobbs-Merril, 1961. This work combines two essays covering fun in games and role distance.

GREENSTEIN, FRED I., *The American Party System and the American People.* Englewood Cliffs: Prentice-Hall, 1963. An overview of the structure and process of the American political party system.

HARTMANN, HEINZ, *Essays on Ego Psychology.* New York: International Universities Press, 1964. A collection of essays from Hartmann's earlier years dealing with psychoanalytic theory, psychoanalysis, and ego psychology.

HILL, J. E. CHRISTOPHER, *Lenin and the Russian Revolution.* London: English Universities Press, 1947. A historical account of Lenin's life before, during, and after the Russian revolutions of 1917.

HOFFER, ERIC, *The True Believer.* New York: Mentor Books, 1951. An examination of the mass character of revolution and the fanatical nature of revolutionary actors.

HOFFER, ERIC, *The Ordeal of Change.* New York: Harper Colophon Books, 1963. A collection of thoughts dealing with the social dynamics of change.

HOLLANDER, E. P., *Leaders, Groups, and Influence.* New York: Oxford University Press, 1964. An examination of leadership in terms of a larger influence process.

HOMANS, GEORGE C., *The Human Group.* New York: Harcourt Brace Jovanovich, 1950. An application of exchange theory in the analysis of several specific cases.

HOMANS, GEORGE C., *Social Behavior: Its Elementary Forms.* New York: Harcourt Brace Jovanovich, 1961. An exchange analysis of influence, conformity, competition, esteem, and interactions.

HORROCKS, JOHN E., *The Psychology of Adolescence: Behavior and Development.* Boston: Houghton Mifflin, 1951. An interpretive work that draws on many scientific sources to explain the developmental configuration of adolescence.

JOHNSON, CHALMERS, *Revolutionary Change.* Boston: Little, Brown, 1966. A structural-functional analysis of revolutionary change.

KAPLAN, ABRAHAM, *The Conduct of Inquiry: Methodology for Behavior Science.* San Francisco: Chandler Press, 1964. An analysis of methods and the attendant problems of theory construction, measurement, experimentation, and the like.

KATZ, DANIEL and PAUL F. LAZARSFELD, *Personal Influence.* New York: Free Press, 1955. One of the leading analyses of the social basis of opinion leadership.

KLAPP, ORRIN E., *Symbolic Leaders.* Chicago: Aldine Press, 1964. A study of leadership that emphasizes the symbolic character of leaders who are able to accurately reflect the disposition of their followings.

KORNHAUSER, WILLIAM, *The Politics of Mass Society.* Glencoe, Ill.: Free Press, 1959. A study of the sources and social composition of mass movements that points to the decay of secondary groups as a critical determinant of successful mass mobilization.

KRISLOV, SAMUEL, *The Supreme Court in the Political Process.* New York: Macmillan, 1965. An examination of the Supreme Court's relationship to other political institutions and the impact of those relationships on the operations of the court.

KUHN, ALFRED, *The Study of Society: A Unified Approach.* Homewood, Ill.: Dorsey Press, 1963. A comprehensive analysis of the structure of society with excellent discussions of communications, decision-making, transactions, and organizations.

KUHN, THOMAS, *The Structure of Scientific Revolutions.* Chicago: University of Chicago Press, 1962. An examination of scientific revolutions as paradigmatic changes.

LANE, ROBERT, *Political Ideology.* New York: Free Press, 1962. A study of the ideological perspectives of blue collar workers based on limited but intensive interviews.

LEMERT, EDWIN M., *Human Deviance, Social Problems, and Social Control.* Englewood Cliffs: Prentice-Hall, 1967. An exploration of secondary deviation and the stigmatization process.

LENIN, N., *What Is To Be Done?* New York: International Publishers, 1929. Lenin's major work on organizational strategy for revolution.

LEVY, MARION J., JR., *The Structure of Society*. Princeton: Princeton University Press, 1952. A structural-functional analysis of society taking off from the theory of social action and strongly emphasizing the relationship between structures.

LINCOLN, C. ERIC, *The Black Muslims in America*. Boston: Beacon Press, 1961. A study of the Black Muslims within the broader historical context of black nationalism.

LOEWENSTEIN, KARL, *Max Weber's Political Ideas in the Perspective of Our Time*. Northampton: The University of Massachusetts Press, 1966. An examination of Weber's political thinking in the context of his practical concern with the reconstruction of the German state.

LOMAX, LOUIS, *The Negro Revolt*. New York: Signet Books, 1962. An early analysis of the black revolution as it emerged in the civil rights movement of the 1950's.

LOMAX, LOUIS, *When the Word Is Given*. New York: Signet Books, 1963. A study of the historical development of the Black Muslim movement, emphasizing the dynamic roles of Elijah Muhammad and Malcolm X.

MACHIAVELLI, NICCOLO, *The Prince*. New York: Modern Library, 1950. The classic study of leadership and power in the conquest of the state.

MANVELL, ROGER and HEINRICH FRAENKEL, *Doctor Goebbels: His Life and Death*. London: Westhouse, 1947. A biographical account of Goebbels' life.

MARTINDALE, DON (ed.), *Functionalism in the Social Sciences*. Philadelphia: American Academy of Political and Social Science, 1965. A collection of essays tracing the role of functionalism as it emerged in the various social sciences.

MEEHAN, EUGENE J., *Contemporary Political Thought: A Critical Study*. Homewood, Ill.: Dorsey Press, 1967. An analysis of functionalism, psychological explanations, and formalism as types of explanation in political science.

MERTON, ROBERT, *Social Theory and Social Structure*. Glencoe, Ill.: Free Press, 1957. A leading structural-functional analysis of society that offers insights into such concepts as anomie, bureaucracy, reference groups, and influence.

MITCHELL, WILLIAM C., *The American Polity*. New York: Free Press, 1962. A structural-functional analysis of the structure and process of American government.

MOOREHEAD, ALAN, *The Russian Revolution*. New York: D. Van Nostrand, 1957. A historical account of the events surrounding the 1905 rebellion and the two revolutions of 1917.

NEUMANN, FRANZ, *Behemoth: The Structure and Practice of National Socialism, 1933–1944*. New York: Harper & Row, 1966. A complete analysis of the political and economic structures of the Nazi state with two chapters devoted to charisma and charismatic leadership.

NEUSTADT, RICHARD, *Presidential Power*. New York: John Wiley & Sons, 1962. One of the leading studies of presidential power, emphasizing the persuasive aspects of the President's influence.

ORLOW, DIETRICH, *The History of the Nazi Party: 1919–1933*. Pittsburgh: University of Pittsburgh Press, 1969. A historical account of the development of the Nazi party with special emphasis on Hitler's role as chief organizer and strategist.

PARSONS, TALCOTT, *The Social System*. New York: Free Press, 1951. A study of the components of social action with a lengthy examination of the basic elements of the structural-functional model.

PARSONS, TALCOTT, *Structure and Process in Modern Societies.* Glencoe, Ill.: Free Press, 1960. Organizational theory, economic development, and political structures and processes are discussed within a broad conception of social change.

PASLEY, VIRGINIA, *21 Stayed.* New York: Farrar, Straus & Cudahy, 1955. A demographic analysis of the background of the 21 men who stayed to live in China after the Korean War.

PETRULLO, LUIGI and BERNARD BASS (eds.), *Leadership and Interpersonal Behavior.* New York: Holt, Rinehart and Winston, 1961. A collection of essays dealing with leadership and interpersonal behavior in the context of psychological theory, small groups, and large organizations.

RADCLIFFE-BROWN, A. R., *Structure and Function in Primitive Society.* Glencoe, Ill.: Free Press, 1965. A functionalist interpretation of kinship, religion, and law in primitive society.

RATTRAY, ROBERT S., *Ashanti Law and the Constitution.* London: Oxford University Press, 1929. An analysis of the development of the legal, political, and judicial institutions in the Ashanti tribal system.

ROGERS, CARL, *Client-Centered Therapy.* Boston: Houghton Mifflin, 1951. A study of the theory and use of nondirective therapy.

ROGERS, EVERETT, *Diffusion of Innovations.* New York: Free Press, 1962. A theoretical account of the adoption of innovations with a careful appraisal of the literature in the field.

ROKEACH, MILTON, *The Open and Closed Mind.* New York: Basic Books, 1960. An attempt to link dogmatism to the structure of the thinking process.

ROSSITER, CLINTON, *The American Presidency.* New York: New American Library, 1956. An analysis of the presidency as a political institution, with an especially good discussion of the President's many political roles.

SANFORD, FILLMORE, *Authoritarianism and Leadership.* Philadelphia: Stephenson-Brothers, 1950. An empirical study of the follower's orientation to leadership in terms of authoritarian psychological disposition, with the treatment of such additional dimensions as ideology, leadership selection, and the acceptance of responsibility.

SCHOENBAUM, DAVID, *Hitler's Social Revolution.* Garden City, N.Y.: Doubleday, 1966. A statistically rich study of the Nazi conquest of power with an excellent analysis of the ideological character of the movement.

SELEKMAN, BENJAMIN M., *Labor Relations and Human Relations.* New York: McGraw-Hill, 1947. A discussion of the development of collective bargaining, the problems of administering an agreement, and the critical role of leadership in the bargaining process.

SELZNICK, PHILIP, *Leadership in Administration.* Evanston, Ill.: Row, Peterson, 1957. A theoretical treatment of leadership and organization revolving around the view that leadership is a coordinating and creative structure.

SEMMLER, RUDOLF, *Goebbels: The Man Next to Hitler.* London: Westhouse, 1947. A diary account of Goebbels' private and public life as Minister of Propaganda by his Chief Press Officer.

SHERIF, CAROLYN and MUZAFER SHERIF, *Groups in Harmony and Tension.* New York: Harper & Row, 1953. An empirical study of intergroup relations with special emphasis on the development of prejudice and social distance.

SILBERMAN, CHARLES E., *Crisis in Black and White.* New York: Vintage Books, 1964. A provocative study of the "Negro problem" that offers a number of constructive solutions.

SIMON, HERBERT A., *Administrative Behavior.* New York: Macmillan, 1961. A leading study of organizational theory emphasizing decision-making factors, authority, communication, and commitment.

SMELSER, NEIL, *Theory of Collective Behavior.* New York: Free Press, 1963. Using the social action perspective, Smelser develops a sequential theory of collective behavior with specific references to panics, riots, crazes, reform movements, and revolutions.

SMELSER, NEIL J. and WILLIAM T. SMELSER (eds.), *Personality and Social Systems.* New York: John Wiley & Sons, 1963. An anthology integrating important essays from sociology and psychology.

SORENSON, THEODORE, *Decision-Making in the White House.* New York: Columbia University Press, 1963. A study of the sources of influence involved in presidential decision-making.

SUKHANOV, N. N., *The Russian Revolution,* 1917, Volumes I and II. New York: Harper, 1962. An objective, diary account of the day-to-day events of the Russian revolution.

TOCQUEVILLE, ALEXIS DE, *The Old Regime and the French Revolution.* Garden City, New York: Doubleday, 1955. A leading work on the French revolution.

TROTSKY, LEON, *The Russian Revolution.* Garden City, New York: Doubleday, 1959. A good abridged version of Trotsky's massive history of the Russian revolution.

TROTSKY, LEON, *Lenin.* New York: Capricorn Books, 1962. A short, affectionate account of Lenin's life by one who knew him well.

TRUMAN, DAVID, *The Governmental Process.* New York: Alfred A. Knopf, 1951. An early formulation of the group basis of governmental decision-making.

TURNER, RALPH and LEWIS KILLIAN, *Collective Behavior.* Englewood Cliffs: Prentice-Hall, 1957. An original contribution to the theory of collective behavior, combined with excellent case studies.

ULAM, ADAM B., *The Bolsheviks.* New York: Macmillan, 1965. A history of the events and persons that shaped the character of Bolshevism from 1900 to 1924, with special emphasis on Lenin's life and role.

WALLACE, ANTHONY, *Culture and Personality.* New York: Random House, 1961. An anthropological account of revolution as cultural revitalization.

WEBER, MAX, *The Theory of Social and Economic Organization.* New York: Free Press, 1946. This volume includes Weber's thinking on basic concepts of sociology, the rationality of economic exchange and organization, types of authority, and social stratification.

WHEATON, ELIOT B., *Prelude to Calamity: The Nazi Revolution, 1933–35.* Garden City, New York: Doubleday, 1968. A historical study focusing on Hitler's life, the Weimar period, the development of the Nazi movement, and the consolidation of Nazi power.

WHEELER-BENNETT, JOHN W., *The Nemesis of Power: The German Army in Politics 1918–1945.* London: Macmillan, 1964. A study of the collapse of the German army after 1918, its political awakening and political intrigues during the Weimar period, and its ultimate destruction under Nazi rule.

WHYTE, WILLIAM F., *Street Corner Society.* Chicago: University of Chicago Press,

1955. A participant-observer study of a street-corner gang, emphasizing the exchange aspects of leader-follower relations.

WOLFE, BERTRAM D., *Three Who Made a Revolution.* New Delta Book, 1964. Biographical accounts of Lenin, Trotsky, and Stalin are interwoven within a rich historical treatment of the Russian revolution and the consolidation of Bolshevik rule.

WOLFENSTEIN, E. VICTOR, *The Revolutionary Personality.* Princeton: Princeton University Press, 1967. A psychoanalytic analysis of Lenin, Trotsky, and Gandhi as revolutionary types.

X, MALCOLM, *The Autobiography of Malcolm X.* New York: Grove Press, 1964. An account of Malcolm X's life that offers considerable insight into the commitment process and the role of identity diffusion in the formation of charismatic commitments.

YOUNG, ORAN, *Systems of Political Science.* Englewood Cliffs: Prentice-Hall, 1968. A short textbook outlining the approaches in political science that revolve around the notion of "system," such as general systems theory, structural-functionalism, cybernetics, distributive analyses, and group theory.

Articles

ABRAMSON, E. *et al.,* "Social Power and Commitment: A Theoretical Statement," *American Sociological Review,* 23 (February, 1958), pp. 15–22.

AKE, CLAUDE, "Charismatic Legitimation and Political Leadership." *Comparative Studies in Society and History,* 9 (October, 1966), pp. 1–13.

AMANN, PETER, "Revolution: A Redefinition," *Political Science Quarterly,* 77 (1962), pp. 36–53.

ARONSON, ELLIOT, "The Effect of Effort on the Attractiveness of Rewarded and Unrewarded Stimuli," *Journal of Abnormal and Social Psychology,* 63 (September, 1961), pp. 375–380.

ASCH, S. E., "Effects of Group Pressure Upon Modification and Distortion of Judgments," in Harold Guetskow, (ed.), *Groups, Leadership and Men.* Pittsburgh: Carnegie Press, 1951, pp. 177–190.

BARKER, ROGER G., BEATRICE A. WRIGHT, and MOLLIE R. GONICK. "Adjustment to Physical Handicap and Illness," *Social Science Council, Bulletin 55* (1946), pp. 32–44.

BECKER, HOWARD S., "Notes on the Concept of Commitment," *American Journal of Sociology,* 66 (July, 1960), pp. 32–40.

BECKER, HOWARD S., "The Implications of Research on Occupational Careers for a Model of Household Decision-Making," in Nelson Foote (ed.), *Household Decision-Making: Consumer Behavior.* New York: New York University Press, 1961.

BENDIX, REINHARD, "Max Weber's Sociology Today," *International Social Science Journal,* 17 (1965), pp. 9–22.

BETTELHEIM, BRUNO, "Individual and Mass Behavior in Extreme Situations." *Journal of Abnormal and Social Psychology,* 38 (1943), pp. 417–452.

BITTNER, EGON, "Radicalism and the Organization of Radical Movements," *American Sociological Review,* 28 (December, 1963), pp. 928–940.

BLAU, PETER M., "Critical Remarks on Weber's Theory of Authority," *American Political Science Review,* 57 (June, 1963), pp. 305–316.

BLAU, PETER M., "Justice in Social Exchange," *Sociological Inquiry,* 34 (Spring, 1964), pp. 193–206.

BLUMSTEIN, PHILIP and EUGENE A. WEINSTEIN, "The Redress of Distributive Injustice," *American Journal of Sociology,* 74 (January, 1969) pp. 408–418.

BORGATTA, E., L. COTTRESS, JR., and L. WILKER, "Initial Expectations, Group Climate, and the Assessments of Leaders and Members." *American Psychologist,* 5 (1950), p. 311 (abstract).

BREHM, JACK W., "Increasing Cognitive Dissonance by a *Fait Accompli.*" *Journal of Abnormal and Social Psychology,* 58 (May, 1959), pp. 379–382.

BURKE, W. WARNER, "Leadership Behavior as a Function of the Leader, the Followers and the Situation," *Journal of Personality,* 33 (1965), pp. 60–81.

CARLSON, EARL R., "Attitude Change Through Modification of Attitude Structure," *Journal of Abnormal and Social Psychology,* 52 (1956), pp. 256–261.

COLEMAN, JAMES S., "Collective Decisions," *Sociological Inquiry,* 34 (Spring, 1964), pp. 166–181.

COLES, ROBERT, "Social Struggle and Weariness," *Psychiatry,* 27 (November, 1964), pp. 305–315.

DAHL, ROBERT A., "The Concept of Power," *Behavioral Scientist,* 2 (1957) pp. 201–215.

DAHL, ROBERT A., "Decision-Making in a Democracy: The Role of the Supreme Court as a National Policy-Maker," *Journal of Public Law,* 6 (1957), pp. 279–295.

DAVID, KENNETH H. and STEPHAN BOCHNER, "Immediate Vs. Delayed Reward Among Arnhemland Aborigines," *Journal of Social Psychology,* 73 (December, 1967), pp. 157–159.

DAVIES, JAMES C., "Charisma in the 1952 Campaign." *American Political Science Review,* 48 (December, 1954), pp. 1083–1102.

DE FLEUR, MELVIN and FRANK WESTIE, "Verbal Attitudes and Overt Acts: An Experiment on the Salience of Attitudes," *American Sociological Review,* 23 (December, 1958), pp. 667–673.

DEVEREUX, GEORGE, "Charismatic Leadership and Crisis," in Warner Muensterberger and Sidney Axelrod (eds.), *Psychoanalysis and the Social Sciences.* New York: International Universities Press, 1955, pp. 145–156.

DEVEREUX, GEORGE, "Two Types of Modal Personality Models," in Neil J. Smelser and William T. Smelser (eds.), *Personality and Social Systems.* New York: John Wiley and Sons, 1963, pp. 22–32.

DOW, THOMAS, JR., "The Role of Charisma in Modern African Development," *Social Forces,* 46 (March, 1969), pp. 328–338.

ELKIN, FREDERICH, GERALD HALPERN, and ANTHONY COOPER, "Leadership in a Student Mob," *Canadian Journal of Psychology,* 16 (September, 1962), pp. 199–201.

ERIKSON, ERIK, "The Problems of Ego Identity," in Maurice Stein, Arthur Vadich, and David Manning White (eds.), *Identity and Anxiety.* New York: Free Press, 1962, pp. 37–87.

ETZIONI, AMITAI, "Dual Leadership in Complex Organizations," *American Sociological Review,* 30 (October, 1965), pp. 688–698.

FAGEN, RICHARD, "Charismatic Authority and the Leadership of Fidel Castro," *Western Political Quarterly,* 18 (June, 1965), pp. 278–282.

FESTINGER, LEON and JAMES M. CARLSMITH, "Cognitive Consequences of Forced Compliance," *Journal of Abnormal and Social Psychology,* 58 (March, 1959), pp. 203–210.

FLANIGAN, WILLIAM and EDWIN FOGELMAN, "Functionalism in Political Science," in Don Martindale (ed.), *Functionalism in the Social Sciences.* Philadelphia: American Academy of Political and Social Science, 1965, pp. 111–126.

FRENCH, JOHN R. P., JR., and BERTHAM RAVEN, "The Bases of Social Power," in Darwin Cartwright (ed.), *Studies in Social Power.* Ann Arbor: Research Center for Group Dynamics, 1959, pp. 150–162.

FRIEDLAND, WILLIAM, "For A Sociological Concept of Charisma." *Social Forces,* 43 (October, 1964), pp. 18–26.

FRIEDRICH, CARL, "Political Leadership and the Problem of Charismatic Power," *Journal of Politics,* 23 (February, 1961), pp. 3–24.

GERTH, HANS, "The Nazi Party: Its Leadership and Composition." *American Journal of Sociology,* 45 (January, 1940), pp. 517–541.

GIFFORD, ANN, "An Application of Weber's Concept of Charisma," *Berkeley Publications in Society and Institutions,* 1 (Spring, 1955), pp. 40–49.

GOLDMAN, RALPH, "A Transactional Theory of Political Integration and Arms Control," *American Political Science Review,* 63 (September, 1969), pp. 719–733.

GORDON, LEONARD V. and FRANCES M. MEDLAND, "Leadership Aspects and Leadership Ability," *Psychological Reports,* 17 (1965), pp. 388–390.

GOULDNER, ALVIN W., "The Norm of Reciprocity: A Preliminary Statement," *American Sociological Review,* 25 (April, 1960), pp. 161–178.

GREGOR, JAMES A., "Political Science and the Uses of Functional Analysis," *American Political Science Review,* LXII (June, 1968), pp. 427–431.

GUSFIELD, JOSEPH R., "Functional Areas of Leadership in Social Movements," *Sociological Quarterly,* 7 (Spring, 1966), pp. 137–156.

HAMBLIN, ROBERT L., "Leadership and Crisis," *Sociometry,* 21 (December, 1958), pp. 322–335.

HEISE, GEORGE A. and GEORGE A. MILLER, "Problem Solving by Small Groups Using Various Communication Nets," *Journal of Abnormal and Social Psychology,* 46 (1951), pp. 327–335.

HEMPHILL, JOHN K. *et al.,* "A Proposed Theory of Leadership in Small Groups," *Second Preliminary Report.* Columbus, Ohio: Ohio State University, 1954.

HOLT, ROBERT T., "A Proposed Structural-Functional Framework for Political Science," in Don Martindale (ed.), *Functionalism in the Social Sciences.* Philadelphia: American Academy of Political and Social Science, 1965, pp. 84–110.

HOMANS, GEORGE, "Social Behavior as Exchange." *American Journal of Sociology,* 62 (May, 1958), pp. 597–606.

HOROWITZ, IRVING, "Party Charisma: Political Parties and Principles in the Third World Nations," *Indian Sociological Bulletin,* 3 (October, 1965), pp. 53–74.

HOUSE, R. J. and A. C. FILLEY, "Leadership Style, Hierarchical Influence and the Satisfaction of Subordinate Role Expectations." *Proceedings of the 76th Annual Convention of the American Psychological Association,* 3 (1968), pp. 557–558.

JAFFEE, CABOT and RICHARD FURR, "Numbers of Reinforcements, Conditioned Leadership and Expectancy of Reward," *Journal of Social Psychology,* 76 (October, 1968), pp. 49–53.

JENNINGS, M. KENT, MILTON C. CUMMINGS, JR., and FRANKLIN P. KILPATRICK, "Trusted Leaders: Perceptions of Appointed Federal Officials," *Public Opinion Quarterly,* 30 (Fall, 1966), pp. 368-384.

KANTER, ROSABETH MOSS, "Commitment and Social Organization: A Study of Commitment Mechanisms in Utopian Communities," *American Sociological Review,* 33 (August, 1968), pp. 499-517.

KIPNIST, D. and C. WAGNER, "Character Structure and Response to Leadership Power," *Journal of Experimental Research in Personality,* 2 (1967), pp. 16-29.

KORTON, DAVID, "Situational Determinants of Leadership Structure," *Journal of Conflict Resolution,* 6 (September, 1962), pp. 222-235.

KRUPP, SHERMAN, "Equilibrium Theory in Economics and in Functional Analysis as Types of Explanation," in Don Martindale, (ed.), *Functionalism in the Social Sciences.* Philadelphia: American Academy of Political and Social Science, 1965, pp. 65-83.

LERNER, DANIEL, "The Nazi Elite," in Harold D. Lasswell and Daniel Lerner (eds.), *World Revolutionary Elites.* Cambridge, Mass.: M.I.T. Press, 1965, pp. 194-318.

LEWIN, KURT, "Group Decision and Social Change," in Guy E. Swanson, Theodore Newcomb, and Eugene L. Harley (eds.), *Readings in Social Psychology.* New York: Henry Holt, 1952, pp. 197-211.

LOFLAND, JOHN and RODNEY STARK, "Becoming a World-Saver: A Theory of Conversion to a Deviant Perspective," *American Sociological Review,* 30 (December 1965), pp. 862-875.

LONG, NORTON, "The Political Act as an Act of Will," *American Journal of Sociology,* 69 (July, 1963), pp. 1-6.

LOWENTHAL, LEO and NORBERT GUTERMAN, "Self-Portrait of the Fascist Agitator," in Alvin Gouldner (ed.), *Studies in Leadership.* New York: Harper and Brothers, 1950, pp. 80-99.

MARCUS, JOHN T., "Transcendentalism and Charisma," *Western Political Quarterly* 14 (March, 1961), pp. 236-241.

MAYER, THOMAS F., "The Position and Progress of Black America: Some Pertinent Statistics," in Howard Gadlin and Bertram E. Garskof (eds.), *The Uptight Society,* Belmont, Calif.: Brooks/Cole, 1970, pp. 102-116.

McCLOSKY, HERBERT, PAUL J. HOFFMAN, and ROSEMARY O'HARA, "Issue Conflict and Consensus Among Party Leaders and Followers," *American Political Science Review,* 54 (June, 1960), pp. 406-427.

MITSCHERLICH, ALEXANDER, "Changing Patterns of Authority: A Psychiatric Interpretation," in Lewis J. Edinger (ed.), *Political Leadership in Industrialized Societies.* New York: John Wiley and Sons, 1967, pp. 26-58.

MOMMSEN, WOLFGANG, "Max Weber's Political Sociology and his Philosophy of World History," *International Social Science Journal,* 17 (1965), pp. 23-45.

MORGAN, WILLIAM R. and JACK SAWYER, "Bargaining, Expectations and the Preference for Equality Over Equity," *Journal of Personality and Social Psychology,* 6 (June, 1967), pp. 139-149.

MULDER, MAUK and AD STEDMERDING, "Threat, Attraction to Group and the Need for Strong Leadership," *Human Relations,* 16 (November, 1963), pp. 317-334.

MYERS, ROBERT, "Anti-Communist Action: A Case Study," in Ralph Turner and Lewis Killian (eds.), *Collective Behavior.* Englewood Cliffs: Prentice-Hall, 1957, pp. 113-116.

NEFZGER, BEN, "The Ideal Type: Some Conceptions and Misconceptions," *Sociological Quarterly,* 6 (Spring, 1965), pp. 166–174.

NEWCOMB, THEODORE M., "An Approach to the Study of Communicative Acts," *Psychological Review,* 60 (November, 1953), pp. 393–404.

NINANE, PAUL and FRED E. FIEDLER, "Member Reactions to Success and Failure of Task Groups," *Human Relations,* 23 (February, 1970), pp. 3–13.

O'LESSKER, KARL, "Who Voted for Hitler? A New Look at the Class Basis of Nazism," *American Journal of Sociology,* 74 (July, 1968), pp. 63–69.

OOMEN, T. K., "Charisma, Social Structure and Social Change," *The Comparative Study of Society and History,* 10 (October, 1967), pp. 85–89.

PUTNEY, SNELL and GLADYS PUTNEY, "Radical Innovation and Prestige," *American Sociological Review,* 27 (August, 1962), pp. 548–551.

RATNAM, K. J., "Charisma and Political Leadership," *Political Studies,* 12 (October, 1964), pp. 341–354.

RIEZLER, KURT, "On The Psychology of Modern Revolution," *Social Research,* 10 (September, 1943), pp. 320–336.

ROBY, THORNTON B., "The Executive Function in Small Groups," in Luigi Petrullo and Bernard Bass (eds.), *Leadership and Interpersonal Behavior.* New York: Holt, Rinehart and Winston, 1961, pp. 118–136.

ROTH, GUNTHER, "Personal Rulership, Patrimonialism, and Empire-Building in the New States," *World Politics,* 20 (January, 1968), pp. 194–206.

RUNCIMAN, W. G., "Charismatic Legitimacy and One-Party Rule in Ghana," *European Journal of Sociology,* 4 (1963), pp. 148–165.

SCHEIN, EDGAR *et al.,* "Distinguishing Characteristics of Collaborators and Resisters Among American Prisoners of War," *Journal of Abnormal and Social Psychology,* 55 (September, 1957), pp. 197–201.

SCHMITT, DAVID R. and GERALD MARWELL, "Reward and Punishments as Techniques for the Achievement of Cooperation Under Inequity," *Human Relations,* 23 (February, 1970), pp. 37–45.

SCHRAG, CLARENCE, "Leadership Among Prison Inmates," *American Sociological Review,* 19 (February, 1954), pp. 37–42.

SHIBUTANI, TAMOTSU, "Reference Groups as Perspectives," *American Journal of Sociology,* 60 (May, 1955), pp. 562–564.

SHILS, EDWARD and MORRIS JANOWITZ, "Cohesion and Disintegration in the Wehrmacht in World War II" *Public Opinion Quarterly,* 12 (1948), pp. 280–315.

SHILS, EDWARD, "The Concentration and Dispersion of Charisma," *World Politics,* 11 (October, 1958), pp. 1–19.

SHILS, EDWARD, "Charisma, Order and Status," *American Sociological Review,* 30 (April, 1965), pp. 199–213.

SIMIRENKO, ALEX, "Critique of Party Charisma," *Indian Sociologial Bulletin,* 3 (October, 1965), pp. 75–78.

STARK, STANLEY, "Toward A Psychology of Charisma: The Innovation Viewpoint of Robert Tucker," *Psychological Reports,* 23 (1968), pp. 1163–1166.

STILLMAN, RICHARD II, "Negroes in the Armed Forces," *Phylon,* 30 (Summer, 1969), pp. 139–159.

THEODORSON, GEORGE A., "Elements in the Progressive Development of Small Groups," *Social Forces,* 31 (1953), pp. 311–320.

THORNTON, ROBERT, "Terror as a Weapon of Political Agitation," in Harry Eckstein (ed.), *Internal War.* New York: Free Press, 1964, pp. 71–99.

TUCKER, ROBERT C., "The Theory of Charismatic Leadership," *Daedalus,* 97 (Summer, 1968), pp. 731–755.

VANDER ZANDEN, JAMES W., "The Non-Violent Resistance Movement Against Segregation," *American Journal of Sociology,* 68 (March, 1963), pp. 544–549.

WALZER, MICHAEL, "Puritanism as a Revolutionary Ideology," *History and Theory,* 3 (1963), pp. 59–90.

WILLNER, RUTH and DOROTHY WILLNER, "The Rise and Role of Charismatic Leaders," *Annals,* 358 (1965), pp. 77–88.

WISPE, LAUREN G. and KENNETH E. LLOYD, "Some Situational and Psychological Determinants of the Desire for Structured Interpersonal Relations," *Journal of Abnormal and Social Psychology,* 51 (July, 1955), pp. 57–60.

WOLFE, HAROLD, "A Critical Analysis of Some Aspects of Charisma," *Sociological Review,* 16 (November, 1968), pp. 305–318.

YARROW, MARIAN RADKE, JOHN D. CAMPBELL, and LEON J. YARROW, "Interpersonal Change: Process and Theory," *Journal of Social Issues,* 14 (1958), pp. 60–63.

INDEX